CALLED TO SERVE

CALLED TO SERVE

A Handbook on Student Veterans and Higher Education

Florence A. Hamrick,
Corey B. Rumann,
and Associates

JOSSEY-BASS
A Wiley Imprint
www.josseybass.com

Published by Jossey-Bass
A Wiley Imprint
One Montgomery Street, Suite 1200, San Francisco, CA 94104-4594—www.josseybass.com

Jossey-Bass books and products are available through most bookstores. To contact Jossey-Bass directly call our Customer Care Department within the U.S. at 800-956-7739, outside the U.S. at 317-572-3986, or fax 317-572-4002.

Wiley publishes in a variety of print and electronic formats and by print-on-demand. Some material included with standard print versions of this book may not be included in e-books or in print-on-demand. If this book refers to media such as a CD or DVD that is not included in the version you purchased, you may download this material at http://booksupport.wiley.com. For more information about Wiley products, visit www.wiley.com.

Library of Congress Cataloging-in-Publication Data

Hamrick, Florence A. (Florence Aileen)
  Called to serve : a handbook on student veterans and higher education / Florence A. Hamrick, Corey B. Rumann.
     p. cm.
   ISBN 978-1-118-17676-4 (hardback)
 ISBN 978-1-118-22718-3 (pdf)–ISBN 978-1-118-24014-4 (epub)–ISBN 978-1-118-26481-2 (mobi)
  1. Veterans–Education (Higher)–United States–Handbooks, manuals, etc. I. Rumann, Corey B. II. Title.
   UB357.H36 2012
   362.860973–dc23

                                                                          2012027906

Printed in the United States of America
FIRST EDITION
HB Printing   10 9 8 7 6 5 4 3 2 1

THE JOSSEY-BASS HIGHER AND
ADULT EDUCATION SERIES

CONTENTS

PREFACE: SETTING THE CONTEXT

Florence A. Hamrick and Corey B. Rumann

Military veterans enrolling or reenrolling at colleges and universities is not in itself a new phenomenon. However, existing literature about student veterans from previous eras provides at best only partial insights into the current generation of returning veterans as well as the institutional implications of their presence. The broadened access to higher education and rapid growth of colleges and universities associated with the post–World War II influx of veterans and the student activism and dissent characterizing the Vietnam era and postwar era inform current understandings of enrolling veterans and the appropriate institutional responses to their presence. However, this represents a mixed legacy. For example, although the Vietnam era may understandably be regarded by many as noteworthy in higher education history for its robust free speech and political activism, that era is also noteworthy for the regrettable treatment experienced by many returning service members and veterans who subsequently enrolled in college. This handbook draws upon prior and current research to inform institutional efforts to meet the needs of contemporary veterans and service members.

Due to the recent conflicts in the Middle East and the military operations elsewhere that increasingly rely on National Guard and Reserve members to augment the active duty military ranks, the numbers of veterans and service members enrolling in higher education have grown rapidly (Sander, 2012). In addition, educational benefits packages for military veterans and service members (for example, Guard and Reserve benefits, Reserve Officers' Training Corps, GI Bill) have become one of the few remaining federal sources of grant funds (irrespective of need) for students pursuing higher education.

With respect to current enrolled service members and veterans, times have changed. For example, service members may experience multiple deployments and returns plus the corresponding withdrawals and reenrollments in college. In addition, higher education costs for students have risen, military educational benefit programs have evolved to include higher levels of benefits, and incentives such as the Yellow Ribbon program have been created. A final complicating circumstance in serving veterans and service members is the generational likelihood that the numbers of current senior administrators and faculty members with recent military experience or experience serving student veterans are few. On the one hand, the campus resources that shared institutional memory can provide may be scant.

On the other hand, significant changes in higher education and in military service and benefits since the Vietnam era suggest that harkening back to past practices or policies may not be sufficient or appropriate to facilitate the enrollment and success of new generations of veterans and service members. The purpose of this handbook is to highlight research, programmatic efforts, and recommendations for serving student veterans that will assist college and university administrators, faculty members, and student affairs professionals in helping contemporary student veterans and service members succeed. This book is intended to be a primary source of updated information and practical resources for meeting the needs of current student veterans.

Academic administrators (for example, provosts, deans, department chairs), faculty members, and student affairs administrators at all levels (such as vice presidents for student affairs, deans of students, and directors of counseling, academic advising, enrollment management, and orientation program offices) will find the information in this book relevant to creating policies or improving services for student veterans. Others who work directly with veterans and service members—including individual faculty members, residence directors, student activities advisers, judicial officers, and transfer student advisers—would benefit from the information and recommendations in this handbook. This handbook principally focuses on college and university settings rather than postsecondary education as a whole, which would include postsecondary certificates or vocational training programs, although readers may find some of the handbook information to be applicable in those settings.

On some campuses, efforts to serve student veterans and service members may be evolving from group discussions—whether by appointed committees or grassroots collectives—of interested and committed individuals. Some of these ad hoc or informal groups seek to garner institutional attention and support, whereas others may be formally charged with designing and recommending an appropriate array of services for which institutional resources have already been reserved. On a large and growing number of campuses, services and programs for veterans are already offered, ranging from designation of an individual contact person to serve essentially as ombudsperson to establishment of a separate office—at times, with its own dedicated facilities—to offer comprehensive services and program contacts for enrolled veterans and service members.

Regardless of the levels and types of services currently offered by a college or university, this handbook will prove useful for enhancing and strengthening these efforts. Particularly in light of resource constraints affecting most colleges and universities, many chapter authors outline strategies for identifying and coordinating the efforts of existing campus-based services and programs with community-based or government-sponsored veterans' programs, services, and affiliated groups. Although the potential savings that may result from these collaborations are attractive, appropriate levels of collaborations with groups such as community veterans' organizations, Veterans Administration staff, and military bases or units can also be key factors in assisting and providing support to returning service members and veterans engaged in negotiating personal and academic transitions.

Higher education scholars—especially (but not only) those who study student subpopulations, demographic trends, policy development and analysis, and student or adult development—will find the handbook chapters useful in introducing or reinforcing many critical issues. These issues include conceptualizing the breadth and heterogeneity among veterans and service members, and the complex, multidimensional needs, experiences, and assets that veterans and service members bring with them to college and university campuses.

This handbook brings together the work of leading scholarly and professional experts with knowledge of higher education and military contexts; service members' and veterans' experiences and circumstances; college and university programs for veterans and service members; relevant social, political, and financial contexts surrounding contemporary veterans and service members; and higher education assessment and evaluation models and strategies.

In Chapter One, Dexter Alexander and John R. Thelin trace and analyze multiple features of the long-intertwined history of higher education and the military in the United States. Using the first Morrill Act as their starting point, they discuss key historical aspects, such as educating military officers at civilian colleges and universities, military-sponsored research and development programs, and the evolution of federal benefits programs—particularly educational benefits—for military veterans. They also discuss the profound changes to higher education and society stemming from the first GI Bill. Sally Caspers and Robert Ackerman describe successive GI Bill programs, key provisions, and associated influences on veterans' higher education attendance and educational decision making in Chapter Two. They also outline the range of contemporary educational funding sources available to veterans and service members that fund—and in many cases, enable—pursuit of higher education.

In Chapter Three, which is focused on individual transitions, Wade G. Livingston and Mark C. Bauman describe the progression of multiple, ongoing transitions—including the "deployment cycle"—that characterize military service particularly for, but not limited to, National Guard and Reserve members. College enrollments and withdrawals are part of these successive transitions that must be negotiated successfully, and the authors discuss theoretical understandings and practical strategies that colleges and universities can implement to support transitioning veterans and service members.

Danielle DeSawal provides overview and demographic characteristics of enrolled veterans and service members in Chapter Four, with particular attention to the types of student engagement reported by these students. Levels and types of student engagement have been associated with persistence, learning, and the ultimate goal of degree completion, but there is currently little systematic research on the possible unique patterns and types of engagements that foster success for veterans and service members.

Veterans and service members are an astonishingly diverse group of individuals, and if campus services are to meet the needs of all enrolled veterans and service members, services must reflect and honor this diversity. In Chapter Five, Susan V. Iverson and Rachel Anderson discuss how understandings and expressions of multiple, simultaneous identities related to gender, race, ethnicity, and sexual orientation usefully complicate generalized and possibly stereotypical images and assumptions about military service members. Otherwise, for example, women's military service and the challenges to social and institutionalized gender assumptions that they embody and experience can go unrecognized despite the increasing numbers of women entering the armed forces.

A great deal of media coverage has focused on how contemporary service members are more likely than those in earlier wars to sustain service-related injuries that prove to be nonfatal yet nonetheless have profound implications for their lives and educational success. Amanda Kraus and Nicholas A. Rattray address the experiences, needs, and identity negotiations of veterans with service-related physical, emotional, and learning disabilities as well as the importance of focused counseling and support services. Frameworks and assumptions, along with misperceptions and stereotypes of veterans with disabilities, are presented and discussed in Chapter Six.

In Chapter Seven, John D. Mikelson and Kevin P. Saunders examine the importance of institutional infrastructures and policies related to enrollment, transfer, and degree completion. Over the course of their educational and military careers, service members can earn educational and training credits. The authors discuss the need for judicious evaluation of service members' and veterans' prior credits and experiences for transfer potential, as well as the importance of providing expert advising that ensures timely degree completion and career readiness.

As they describe options and strategies for organizing and staffing services for veterans and service members in Chapter Eight, Stephen G. Abel, Robert J. Bright, and R. M. Cooper stress the importance of creating and implementing models for service delivery that are appropriate to individual campuses. Although the creation of a comprehensive veterans services office is strongly advocated by the authors, initial assessment work on individual campuses will help determine particular needs of enrolled veterans and service members as well as the levels and types of institutional and community resources that can be dedicated to these efforts.

In Chapter Nine, Sarah Minnis, Stephanie Bondi, and Corey B. Rumann discuss how groups of faculty and staff members who frequently, but not always, have previous or current military affiliations have established a variety of focused learning or living-learning environments for enrolled veterans and service members that provide enriched opportunities for support, mentoring, and challenge. The authors describe some of these programs and examine their contributions to the educational experiences and success for participating students.

According to Brian Hawthorne, Mark C. Bauman, and Leah Ewing Ross, one unique and growing opportunity for enrolled veterans and service members is membership in campus-sponsored student veterans organizations, as described in Chapter Ten. Whether the organizations are locally chartered or affiliated with national student veterans' groups, these campus organizations can provide valuable opportunities for accessing and providing peer support; engaging in campuswide, state-level, or national advocacy efforts; providing campus leadership; and actively serving the community.

Once decisions are reached on a campus to explore or strengthen services for enrolled veterans and service members, leadership from senior administrators is necessary to make these efforts a top institutional priority. In Chapter Eleven, Tom Jackson Jr., Charles J. Fey, and Leah Ewing Ross identify senior college and university administrators as leaders who are best positioned to drive these efforts forward. Institutional leaders can allocate monetary resources and staff time, ensure that strategic planning reflects the priority of serving veterans and service members, and initiate communication channels—and perhaps partnerships—with government officials, community resource administrators, and other campus leaders and potential benefactors.

The ultimate aim of creating a campus that is "veteran-friendly" goes beyond establishing service offices or programs and instead seeks to transform the larger campus climate into one that is welcoming and attentive to the needs of enrolled service members, veterans, and family members. With reference to a formal advocacy model, in Chapter Twelve Jan Arminio and Tomoko Kudo Grabosky illustrate best practices in initiating broadbased networks and efforts that offer support to students and family members. They also identify strategies for navigating potential barriers and constraints to creating such supportive networks and relationships.

In recognition of the increased calls for accountability in higher education and demonstrations of responsible stewardship of resources, chapter authors also discuss assessment and evaluation frameworks and models relevant to the topic at hand. These strategies encompass conducting initial and ongoing needs assessments as well as designing formative and summative program evaluations. These strategies, plus concrete suggestions for collecting or obtaining relevant data, will help campuses focus on efforts tailored to students' needs on the particular campus and ensure that continuing efforts to serve veterans and service members are systematically reviewed and improved.

Chapter authors have also created lists of resources that are relevant to the chapter's topic. In addition to the reference sources that have informed the content of each chapter, these resource lists are intended to assist readers who seek additional information about relevant topics and issues. The web sites, reports, organizations, networks, government agencies, not-for-profit groups, and other offices and programs will assist administrators and faculty with broadening their expertise and making informational contacts that will be helpful in their efforts to establish or improve services for veterans and service members.

To maintain focus on student veterans and service members and the campus professionals with whom they work, the handbook also incorporates brief personal stories that invite readers to pause and consider the experiences and perspectives of individuals "on the ground." Although the collection of vignettes assuredly does not capture the entire range of individuals' experiences, the stories provide small glimpses into their successes and supports as well as frustrations and barriers that must be overcome.

Campus-based counseling and clinical professionals can access a rich and growing set of resources on diagnosing and treating physiological and psychological conditions such as TBI and PTSD that can affect contemporary veterans and service members. Although these topics are addressed briefly in some chapters, and within Chapter Six in particular, the topics are not covered in great depth. Readers are advised to consult specialized sources for more information.

As colleges and universities are "called to serve" growing numbers of veterans and military service members, this handbook is a key resource to ensure high-quality programs and outreach that maximize students' opportunities for success.

Reference

Sander, L. (2012, March 11). Out of uniform: At half a million and counting, veterans cash in on Post-9/11 GI Bill. *Chronicle of Higher Education*. Retrieved from http://chronicle.com/article/Out-of-Uniform/131112/

ABOUT THE EDITORS

Florence A. Hamrick is professor and director of the college student affairs program at Rutgers University. Her research agenda emphasizes higher education equity, access, and success—particularly among members of traditionally underrepresented or nondominant populations. She is author or editor of two books; over seventy articles, chapters, and invited publications; and over one hundred scholarly or professional presentations, invited lectures, and conference addresses. Hamrick is active in scholarly and professional organizations, and she is currently a Senior Scholar of ACPA—College Student Educators International and a Faculty Fellow of the National Association of Student Personnel Administrators (NASPA).

Corey B. Rumann is assistant professor of practice in the department of educational administration at the University of Nebraska–Lincoln. Rumann has studied and written extensively about the transition experiences of student veterans in higher education. He has presented his research findings at numerous regional and national conferences and has been invited to speak at meetings and symposia focusing on student veterans' experiences at colleges and universities. Rumann received his bachelor's in psychology and master's in counselor education from the University of Wyoming, and his doctorate in educational leadership from Iowa State University.

ABOUT THE CONTRIBUTORS

Stephen G. Abel was appointed the Rutgers University director for the office of Veteran and Military Programs and Services in 2010. He is responsible for the development and coordination of a comprehensive program of support services for student veterans at all three campuses of the university. He serves as the principal advocate for student veterans; ensures the quality of policies, programs, activities, and services designed to enhance their educational experiences; and also serves as the university's liaison with outside agencies and offices whose work affects the lives of student veterans. Prior, Abel was the New Jersey deputy commissioner for veterans affairs. In this capacity, Abel was responsible for administering all of New Jersey's veterans programs. Abel's 27-year military career with the U.S. Army took him across the country and around the world from Fort Riley, Kansas, to Korea, Hawaii, and back home again to the United States. He has a bachelor's in education from Indiana University of Pennsylvania and a master's in national security strategy from the National Defense University/National War College in Washington, DC.

Robert Ackerman is professor emeritus of higher education and vice president emeritus of student services at the University of Nevada, Las Vegas. He coedited *Creating a Veteran-Friendly Campus: Strategies for Transition and Success* (Jossey-Bass, 2009) and published research on the transitions combat veterans make when they become college students. He served in the U.S. Navy and is a member of the board of directors of Student Veterans of America.

Dexter Alexander is an adjunct lecturer in the School of Public Affairs at Morehead State University where he teaches "Ideology and Policy Development in Appalachia." Alexander is emeritus faculty and retired dean of institutional effectiveness and research at Somerset Community College (Kentucky). Formerly, he was a banker and a soldier.

Rachel Anderson is the director of the Center for Adult and Veteran Services at Kent State University. She has worked with adult students and veterans for over twenty years at public and private colleges and universities. She is currently a doctoral candidate in cultural foundations of education at Kent State.

Jan Arminio is professor and director of the Higher Education Program at George Mason University. Previously, she served as chair in the Department of Counseling and College Student Personnel at Shippensburg University. She received her doctorate in College Student Personnel Program at the University of Maryland, College Park. From 2004 to 2008, Dr. Arminio served as president of the Council for the Advancement of Standards in Higher Education (CAS). She also was appointed to and later chaired the Faculty Fellows of the National Association of Student Personnel Administrators and the Senior Scholars of the American College Personnel Association. Dr. Arminio's scholarship focuses on multicultural issues, qualitative research, assessment, and campus programs and leadership. Her most recent book is *Why Aren't We There Yet: Taking Personal Responsibility for Creating an Inclusive Campus.* She is the 2011 recipient of the Robert H. Shaffer award for excellence in graduate teaching.

Mark C. Bauman worked at Bloomsburg University for 16 years in a variety of student affairs positions before accepting his current role as assistant professor of counseling and college student affairs. In addition to researching and writing about student veterans, Bauman advises the Bloomsburg University student veterans organization, which was formed in 2009. Since 2003, he has served in the U.S. Coast Guard Reserve. Bauman earned his doctorate in higher education administration from Pennsylvania State University.

Stephanie Bondi is a lecturer at the University of Nebraska–Lincoln. She has studied student development and social justice in higher education for over 10 years. Bondi received her bachelor's in accounting from Butler University, master's in higher education and student affairs from Indiana University, and her doctorate in educational leadership from Iowa State University.

Robert J. Bright is a U.S. Navy Veteran of more than 10 years, having spent much of that time as an intelligence specialist with various units including the Naval Special Warfare Community. As a KPMG and Goldman Sachs alumnus, Bright has more than seven years of experience in corporate America and on Wall Street following his military service. Bright is currently the assistant director for the office of Veteran and Military Programs and Services at Rutgers University.

Sally Caspers is the Rebel Veteran Education and Transition Support (VETS) program coordinator at the University of Nevada, Las Vegas (UNLV). A five-year U.S. Air Force veteran and intelligence officer, she now serves proudly as a military spouse. She has a bachelor's degree in Russian/area studies from American University and a master's in higher education leadership from UNLV. Caspers' educational and research interests include the ways in which higher education can better serve and support today's student veterans and military families.

R. M. Cooper is assistant professor and doctoral program director for the School of Education at Drake University. Cooper's research interests include the impact of the campus environment on students' well-being; underrepresented populations in science, technology, engineering, and mathematics (STEM); and research methodologies.

Danielle DeSewal is the master's program coordinator and clinical assistant professor for higher education and student affairs at Indiana University. Prior to joining the faculty, DeSewal worked on a federally funded grant investigating Latino/a college students' collegiate experiences and served as the educational program coordinator for the Association of College Unions International (ACUI). She teaches courses in higher education administration, student development, professional development in student affairs, student organization advising, and leadership development. DeSewal holds her bachelor's in consumer and family studies education from Colorado State University, her master's in higher education administration from the University of Arkansas, Fayetteville, and her doctorate from Indiana University.

Charles J. Fey is the vice president for student engagement and success at The University of Akron. He has held board positions with ACPA—College Student Educators International, the National Association for Student Personnel Administrators (NASPA), and the Association of Public and Lang-Grant Universities (APLU, formerly NASULGC). Fey was the founding president of the Massachusetts College Personnel Association and was president of the Texas Association of College and University Personnel Association. He has received numerous national awards, including the ACPA Esther Lloyd Jones award. Fey earned his bachelor's in liberal arts and his master's in education from The Pennsylvania State University, and holds a doctorate in higher education administration from Texas A&M University. Fey's prior positions include vice president for student affairs at University of Maryland, Baltimore County, dean of students at the University of Texas at El Paso, vice president and dean of student life at Our Lady of the Lake University (Texas), dean of students at St. Mary's University (Texas), associate dean of student affairs at Keene State College, director of housing/resident life at Catholic University of America, and associate dean of students at Newbury College.

Tomoko Kudo Grabosky is associate professor/psychological counselor at Shippensburg University. As a counselor who practices from the multicultural counseling perspective, Grabosky strongly believes in the importance of counselors taking on roles as advocates, especially when working with marginalized groups of students whose problems are magnified by the function of their environments. Grabosky is a strong advocate for developing a veteran-supportive campus and works closely with student veterans as well as families and significant others of military service members.

Brian Hawthorne has served in the U.S. Army Reserves since 2003, with two tours in Iraq. He currently serves as a jumpmaster and civil affairs team sergeant out of College Park, Maryland. Hawthorne has been deeply involved in veterans advocacy, becoming the first Legislative Director and now Board Member for Student Veterans of America. He cofounded the GW Veterans Organization at The George Washington University, where he earned his bachelor's in 2010. At graduation, he was presented with the George Washington Award, the university's highest honor, for his work helping veterans. Hawthorne completed his master's at GW in 2012. He has testified before Congressional Committees regarding GI Bill Benefits and the transition from the military to civilian life. Hawthorne was recognized with the President's Lifetime Volunteer Achievement Award in 2010 for his volunteer work.

Susan V. Iverson is associate professor of higher education administration and student personnel at Kent State University, where she is also an affiliated faculty member with the women's studies and LGBT studies programs. Iverson earned her doctorate in higher educational leadership, with a concentration in women's studies, from the University of Maine, where she also served as an instructor in higher educational leadership and women's studies. Prior to becoming a faculty member, Iverson worked in student affairs administration for more than ten years. Iverson's scholarly interests include women and equity, multicultural competence, civic engagement, critical pedagogy, and the use of feminist poststructural research.

Tom Jackson Jr. has served as vice president for student affairs and adjunct professor in the college of education at the University of Louisville since 2007. Previous positions include assistant director of residence life at St. Mary's University (Texas); area coordinator at the University of Southern California; academic development specialist in residence life at Cal Poly-San Luis Obispo; director of the student activities center at the University of Texas at El Paso; dean of students at McMurry University (Texas); and vice president for student affairs at Texas A&M University-Kingsville. He earned his doctorate in educational management from the University of La Verne in California, master's in counseling from Shippensburg University, bachelor's in business from Southwest Minnesota State University, and associate's from Highline Community College in his native home of Seattle. Jackson is an instrument-rated private pilot and has served in the U.S. Coast Guard Reserve, Army National Guard, and Texas State Guard. He currently serves as an officer in the Indiana Guard Reserve.

Amanda Kraus received her doctorate from the University of Arizona (UA) in higher education. Kraus currently works at UA's Disability Resource Center and is also adjunct faculty in the Center for the Study of Higher Education at the UA. Her research interests include student development, disability identity, and disability dynamics in the student veteran community. Kraus has presented her research at numerous regional and national conferences and symposia.

Wade G. Livingston is assistant professor of higher education/student affairs at Clemson University in Clemson, South Carolina. His primary research agenda is founded on the student veteran experience in college, and he has published refereed articles and facilitated national conference presentations on this topic. Dr. Livingston's other research interests include law and policy in higher education, the student-institution relationship, the history of higher education, and intercollegiate athletics. He also enjoys following U.S. foreign policy developments and studying military history. Dr. Livingston can be reached at livings@clemson.edu or (864) 656-1446.

John D. Mikelson returned to school after retiring in 2004 from a 25-year career with the Army, Sergeant First Class, Iowa Army National Guard (Active Guard and Reserve) to earn a bachelor's in history and a master's in education policy and leadership studies from the University of Iowa. He now works in the University of Iowa's Veterans Center. He is a cofounder of the Student Veterans of America, chair of the National Association of Student Personnel Administrators (NASPA) Veteran Knowledge Community, and vice chair of the Iowa Advisory Council on Military Education. Mikelson has presented at numerous national conferences on the integration and transition of student veterans from reintegration to graduation and beyond.

Sarah Minnis is the manager of the campus services program for Wounded Warrior Project. Her experience working with diverse populations, including veterans, in student affairs and employee development has given her the opportunity to provide advising to institutions of higher learning and wounded warriors in higher education on a variety of academic and life concerns. Her experiences helping veterans have given her the passion to serve student veterans and help their institutions build holistic service programs to meet their unique needs on campus. She has a bachelor's degree in psychology from Central Washington University and a master's degree in education and student affairs from Western Kentucky University. Minnis is currently pursuing a doctorate in human resource development with specific research interests in veterans' career development.

Nicholas A. Rattray earned his doctorate in sociocultural anthropology at the University of Arizona, and currently conducts qualitative research with student veterans through the Disabled Veterans Reintegration and Education Project. Funded by a Fulbright grant from the Institute of International Education, his dissertation draws on ethnographic fieldwork among Ecuadorians with physical and visual disabilities to investigate the cultural meanings of disability, spatial exclusion, and social identity in the Andes. He is a graduate of University of California-Berkeley and holds a master's degree in urban planning from Rutgers University.

Leah Ewing Ross is a freelance writer, editor, and consultant based in Davis, California. Previously she worked for MGT of America, Inc. and the National Association of Student Personnel Administrators (NASPA). Ross also served as managing editor of the *Journal of College Student Development* and held campus positions at Randolph-Macon Woman's College (now Randolph College), Vanderbilt University, Agnes Scott College, and Tallahassee Community College. She is a graduate of Mount Holyoke College, Florida State University, and Iowa State University.

Kevin P. Saunders is the director of Institutional Research and Assessment at Drake University. He is currently participating in the Teagle Assessment Scholars Program through the Center of Inquiry at Wabash

College. Previously he served as the coordinator of continuous academic program improvement and chaired the learning communities assessment committee at Iowa State University. Saunders received his bachelor's in psychology and sociology and master's in higher education from Drake University, and his doctorate in educational leadership from Iowa State University.

John R. Thelin is university research professor of the history of higher education and public policy at the University of Kentucky. He is author of *A History of American Higher Education* (2nd edition, 2011). In 2011 he received the Research Achievement Award from the Association for the Study of Higher Education (ASHE). Thelin is an alumnus of Brown University and received his master's and doctorate from the University of California-Berkeley.

CALLED TO SERVE

CHAPTER ONE

THE MILITARY AND HIGHER EDUCATION IN THE UNITED STATES

Dexter Alexander and John R. Thelin

This chapter traces the principal evolving relationships between the U.S. military and U.S. higher education, beginning with the Morrill Act of 1862. The impact of military-sponsored research and development on U.S. higher education is discussed, with particular attention to the World War II and post–World War II eras. The chapter also explores the impact of consecutive GI Bill programs on individuals and society, as well as the influence of student veterans on colleges and universities and on higher education as a social institution.

The First Morrill Act and Military Training

Government land grants for U.S. higher education did not begin with the first Morrill Act; however, the 1862 Morrill Act provided impetus to agricultural and technical education. The "M" in the "A&M" colleges founded with funds derived from 1862 Morrill Land-Grant Act land and warrant sales provided needed education in mechanics, mining, and military education, while the "A" provided the opportunity for scientific instruction in agriculture.

Higher education in the United States, including provision for military education, was a beneficiary as a *secondary* consideration in major national legislation involving the sale and settlement plans for large expanses of western lands as part of the Morrill Land-Grant Act of 1862 (Key, 1996). The U.S. government devised a sophisticated formula for a partnership with each state in the sale of lands, with proceeds designated for each state to teach "agriculture and the mechanic arts ... in order to promote the liberal and professional education of the industrial classes" (Williams, 1991, p. 12). Although this was a significant event for higher education, the foremost concern of the first Morrill Land-Grant was orderly sale and settlement of land. The educational provisions were incorporated in deference to Senator Justin Morrill's long and persuasive advocacy. A further irony of the landmark legislation was that it had been stalled in Congress and by two presidents between 1850 and 1861, in large part due to strong objections by senators and congressmen from states in the South. The secession of these states from the Union negated the congressional voting power of this Southern bloc and thus allowed the Land-Grant Act finally to gain Congressional approval. At the same time, this turn of events in combination with the outbreak of the Civil War meant that the educational provisions were obscured by the national war effort and hence were essentially dormant until the end of the war in 1865.

When Justin Morrill introduced his bill in the House of Representatives on December 16, 1861, Ulysses S. Grant had not yet won the battles at Forts Henry and Donelson. George McClellan was still building his grand army (a showpiece organization he was reluctant to test in battle). By the time President Lincoln signed the Morrill Act into law on July 2, 1862, the massive Shiloh battle was recent history and the newly appointed commander of the Army of Northern Virginia, Robert E. Lee, had pushed George McClellan away from Richmond, Virginia. From Washington's perspective, the war news was not good (Eddy, 1957).

Due in part to the superior military skill of generals and officers in the Confederate army, defeats suffered by Union forces in 1861 and 1862 led to post hoc speculation that perhaps one aim of the Morrill Act was to offset the defection of numerous West Point graduates to leadership roles in the Confederate States of America military service. This has dubious historical plausibility because it suggests that there was a long-planned move by active duty officers in the U.S. Army to change allegiance. The tenets of the proposed land-grant legislation had been in place for years prior to the outbreak of war in 1861. Furthermore, the situation was not merely one in which all U.S. officers with roots and family in Southern states declared for states' rights. Equally important to note was the reverse, such as rising

U.S. officer General George H. Thomas of Virginia, who sacrificed his land holdings, family, and state heritage with a thoughtful, deliberate decision to remain willfully and loyally an active duty commissioned officer in the Union army. Besides, since the early nineteenth century, privately owned military academies had been a staple of the educational landscape in all regions of the young United States, separate from the federally chartered academies at West Point and Annapolis. In sum, there is little evidence to suggest that Senator Morrill or anyone else regarded the military education provisions of the Land-Grant Act as a means to counteract what would be a future loss of military talent to a yet nonexistent Confederate States of America.

Although the notion of agricultural and mechanical education might have been new at that time, the idea of endowing enterprises with public lands was not. Congress had made federal land grants to improve the land, to compensate soldiers, to encourage frontier settlement, and to support education. By 1862, Congress had given land grants to fund construction canals, highways, and railroads. Revolutionary War soldiers had received land grants in compensation for their service to the nation. Congress made section and township grants for common schools and state universities (Edmond, 1978). By 1857, governments at all levels had distributed more than six million acres for educational institutions (Williams, 1991). Furthermore, the first Morrill Land-Grant Act was not the largest distribution of land Congress had made. In an 1873 address to the National Education Association, future Penn State University president George Atherton noted that since 1859, Congress had given railroads 186 million acres compared with 17.4 million acres distributed for colleges and universities under the 1862 Morrill Act (Williams, 1991).

The "proportional or quantity grant" established by the 1862 Morrill Land-Grant Act was a new type not used in previous U.S. public land distributions. The states were to receive land grants based on the size of their congressional delegations, and the more populous states received proportionately more land. Each state received 30,000 acres in land or land scrip for each member of Congress from that state. States without public land available for grants were given transferable certificates, called land scrip, for public land in other states. Each state was then to sell the land or land scrip and use the proceeds to endow an agricultural and mechanical college. No state in rebellion against the central government could receive a land grant (Williams, 1991). This provision changed in 1890 with the passage of the second Morrill Act in which each state previously excluded from the legislation received funding plus the option to maintain racially segregated land-grant institutions on the condition that the state establish a historically White and a historically Black land-grant college. This meant that a southern stretch of 15 states, ranging from Delaware to Oklahoma, gained inclusion in the network of state land-grant institutions (Thelin, 2004).

Although the federal government distributed 17,430,000 acres of land under the 1862 Morrill Land-Grant Act, most of that land was in the states west of the Mississippi River. Of the states east of the Mississippi, only Illinois, Michigan, and Wisconsin had any public land remaining in 1862. Congress authorized land scrip, or "land procurement certificates," for distribution to states without public lands. These states could not hold titles to land in other states, but individuals who bought the land scrip could purchase federal land wherever it was available. Generally, a state's governor appointed a commission to advertise and receive bids for the sale of land scrip, and the purchasers were usually "private citizens or land companies that dealt in large blocks of scrip" (Williams, 1991, p. 46). Each state had to accept its grant within two years and establish its college within five years, so states were under pressure to sell their land and land scrip quickly (Williams, 1991).

Congress effectively depressed the value of the 1862 Morrill Act land grants by passing the 1862 Homestead Act, which transferred approximately 234 million acres of public land to private ownership—at 160 acres per individual homesteader—free of charge (Edmond, 1978). Consequently, the total sales of 1862 Morrill Act land and land scrip raised only $7,545,405 (approximately $164,844,463 in 2010 dollars), slightly less than 35 percent of what was expected. In total, the 17,430,000 acres of Morrill Act land grants raised an average of 43 cents per acre (approximately $9.40 per acre in 2010 dollars) (Williams, 1991). However, a surplus of land was not the only thing that drove down the state A&M colleges' total endowments. Negligence, speculation, and corruption contributed to the poor return on Congress's gift to higher education.

The landmark legislation did not lead to immediate success in enrolling or educating students. For example, 1890 enrollments at most of the land-grant colleges in the Midwest were 1,000 to 2,000 students at most, often lower than those of "small" liberal arts colleges in the Northeast (Axtell, 1971). Nor did the explicit curricular provisions such as agriculture and military education gain widespread favor among undergraduates. Mandatory military training required of all male students at land-grant colleges was universal, but not universally appreciated.

In his 1934 memoir, James Thurber, a humorist who wrote for *The New Yorker*, described his military training experience as a freshman at Ohio State University during World War I:

> Ohio State was a land-grant university and therefore two years of military drill was compulsory. We drilled with old Springfield rifles and studied the tactics of the Civil War even though the World War was going on at the time. At eleven o'clock each morning thousands of freshmen and sophomores used to deploy over the campus, moodily creeping up on the old chemistry building. It was good training for the kind of warfare that was waged at Shiloh but it had no connection with what was going on in Europe. Some people used to think that there was German money behind it, but they didn't dare say so or they would have been thrown in jail as German spies. It was a period of muddy thought and marked, I believe, the decline of higher education in the Middle West. (Thurber, 1934/1958, pp. 439–440)

Thurber, of course, was not necessarily the typical student of his era. Despite the snags and problems he observed, the required military training persisted as an enduring feature of state land-grant education well into the mid-twentieth century. Thurber made an invaluable point about a problem in any campus-based program of professional training: without state-of-the-art instruction and equipment, future leaders (whether army officers or engineers) would not be optimally prepared for new demands of decision making. Discarded Springfield rifles had no place in the education of officers in the armed services of the twentieth century.

Post-Morrill Act Military-Related Activity at Colleges and Universities

The range of collaborations between the military and institutions of higher education have included ROTC programs and sponsored research and development. In addition, military service and sacrifice have been memorialized in various ways on university campuses.

Reserve Officers' Training Corps

The U.S. Government initially established a Reserve Officers' Training Corps (ROTC) in 1916 to provide Reserve Army commissions to male students who completed prescribed courses of military study at universities and colleges, including, but not limited to, 1862 Morrill Land-Grant Act institutions (U.S. Army Cadet Command, n.d.). The U.S. Navy created a Naval Reserve Officers' Training Corps (NROTC) in 1926 that offered male university and college students opportunities to obtain Reserve commissions in the Navy or, beginning in 1932, the U.S. Marine Corps (NROTC, 2011a). The Army Air Service created Air ROTC units at seven universities beginning in 1920, which lasted until 1932, when funding problems forced the programs to be abolished (U.S. Air Force ROTC [AFROTC], 2011b). The AFROTC was created after the U.S. Air Force was established from the U.S. Army Air Force in 1946 (AFROTC, 2011b). The U.S. Coast Guard does not offer ROTC (U.S. Coast Guard, n.d.).

In fiscal year 2009, ROTC programs provided 30 percent of the newly commissioned active duty officers in the U.S. Army, Navy, Marine Corps, and Air Force combined (U.S. Department of Defense, 2010). The development of ROTC programs is a good example of a mutually satisfactory "great American compromise." ROTC programs' reliance on established colleges and universities to educate students for commissioned officer status has satisfied the demand for a military leadership closely associated with civil society; this is distinguished from the approach in nations with closed military oligarchies and, all the while, provides reasonable assurance for national defense that remains fluid and not crystallized.

World War I. The United States' entry into World War I in April 1917, and the institution of the military draft in May 1917, accelerated a decline in male higher education enrollment that began before the United States declared war against Germany. Decreased enrollment in colleges and universities created fear in the academy of institutional closings (Levine, 1987). In response to the concerns that the higher education establishment conveyed to President Woodrow Wilson and the Congress, the federal government created a series of War Department training units on campuses throughout the United States. Initiated in May 1918, the Student Army Training Corps (SATC) established training units at 525 universities and colleges, which were "full-time army training facilities ... [that enlisted] more than 140,000 male students" into the U.S. Army on October 1, 1918 in "simultaneous ceremonies at 525 colleges" (Levine, 1987, pp. 27–28.) The November 11, 1918 Armistice ended this brief experiment of partnership between the colleges and the military before its military efficacy could be tested in combat (Levine, 1987).

World War II. U.S. universities and colleges were mobilized to assist the war effort during World War II. Buildings and grounds became War and Navy Department facilities for technical training of soldiers, sailors, and airmen. Dormitories, lecture halls, laboratories, gymnasia, dining halls, and athletic fields provided the necessary space, structures, and equipment for these new programs and nontraditional students. The U.S. Army and the U.S. Army Air Corps trained service members on college and university campuses through the Army Air Corps Air Crew Training Program, the Army Specialized Training Program, and the Army Specialized Training Reserve Program. Partnerships between the U.S. Navy and higher education included temporary wartime programs, such as the V-5 (Aviation Cadet Pilot Training Program), V-7 (Naval Reserve Midshipmen's School), and V-12 (Navy College Training Program). The V-12 program included 131 U.S. colleges and universities, and from April 1943 to June 1946, producing more than 60,000 Navy and Marine Corps officers (Cardozier, 1993).

Monuments and Memorials

In her book *This Republic of Suffering*, historian Drew Gilpin Faust (2008) quoted a Confederate enlisted soldier from Texas on the subject of monuments and memorials to combatants killed in action during the Civil War: "The officers get the honor ... you get nothing. They get a monument, you get a hole in the ground and no coffin" (p. 80). In the post–Civil War era, universities and colleges in the North and the South often named buildings after prominent Civil War officers. For example, the University of Kentucky's (UK) Buell Armory is named for Union General Don Carlos Buell (University of Kentucky, n.d.). Furthermore, some institutions were named for favored sons, such as Washington and Lee University, which honors George Washington and Robert E. Lee (Washington and Lee University, n.d.). Yet the common soldier's contribution to the Civil War remained unmarked in higher education, with the exception of a few monuments, such as Harvard University's Soldiers Field, which was dedicated in 1890 to memorialize six friends of the land's donor, Civil War veteran Henry Lee Higginson (Hannon, 2005).

Prior to World War I, the historic colleges of the Northeast tended to dominate the national rankings and media coverage of intercollegiate football. After World War I, however, there was a discernible geographic and demographic shift westward in support of local teams by spectators, donors, students, and college officials. The emergent large state universities of the Midwest, especially members of the Big Ten Conference, seized the opportunity to combine honoring veterans with the construction of new, large sports facilities.

At the University of Illinois, for example, patriotic rhetoric was fused with state pride and historic memory. A fundraising booklet published for the new campus stadium cautioned readers and prospective donors, "Lest we forget those Illini who died in the war" (University of Illinois Athletic Association, 1921, p. 25). Among the thousands of Illini students and alumni who were World War I veterans, special attention was bestowed on the 183 who died in military service. The fundraising brochure emphasized that "the spirit that sent them into action, the spirit which brought 183 of them forever out of our vision and understanding, is still with us. It is a living thing, and the Stadium will exist to keep that living thing before the eyes of future generations, of the hundreds of future generations who will walk through its archways, sit in its seats and move strenuously on its fields" (University of Illinois Athletic Association, 1921, p. 25). During the 1920s, there were variations on this theme and related initiatives at several state universities, especially as college sports and national service became indelibly linked with state boosterism for public higher education (Thelin, 2004).

The large number of campus facilities named to honor World War I veterans and alumni was due in part to timing and opportunity. State universities, especially those in the Midwest, were growing and were predisposed to construct new buildings and stadia. Most of these universities were located in rural areas and had abundant land that provided inexpensive sites for large memorials. After World War II, colleges and universities continued the tradition of honoring veterans through memorials, but often these were supplements and upgrades to the incumbent memorial buildings constructed in the 1920s. Yet there are relatively few memorials on college campuses for veterans of the Korean War, perhaps due in part to its official status as a "police action" and its proximity to World War II. In the case of the Vietnam War, the lack of support for the war, especially in higher education communities, fostered an atmosphere of contention or opposition that dispelled any patriotic monuments comparable to those created after World Wars I and II. Indeed, national service of any sort tended to be trumped by philanthropy as a new generation of campus buildings immortalized major donors rather than soldiers and statesmen.

Military-Sponsored Research and Development

Starting in the early nineteenth century, U.S. colleges and universities demonstrated—and hosted—a substantial and historically enduring overlap of military education with the professional education of skilled, trained engineers. Military instruction, including that offered at colleges and universities, incorporated mathematics, such as trigonometry and algebra, for application to surveying, cartography, and artillery, and eventually to engineering (Cipolla, 1969). Additionally, the United States found in its military ranks a readily available source of dedicated expertise to design and build bridges, canals, forts, dams, and other parts of a growing infrastructure that would help realize the creation of what was called "The American System" (Baxter, 1995). The demand for technically skilled engineers in that era represented a national need for a "public good" that could best be provided by a substantial national and public entity such as the military, rather than by a fragmented and uneven private enterprise.

Engineering as part of campus-based military education for future officers also was fortuitous and mutually beneficial for sustaining the military as a viable profession in the U.S. economy because it provided cadets with employable professional skills during extended periods when there were no wars or military campaigns; it also provided retired or furloughed military officers civilian occupations. Hence, as one reads the diaries and journal entries of military cadets and commissioned officers, it is not unusual to find as much coverage devoted to accounts of engineering projects and problems as to drill, war games, and battle strategies (Forman, 1952/1958).

The Morrill Land-Grant Acts of 1862 and 1890 formalized and increased this custom of bringing utility to higher education curricula. The acronym of "A&M" often included cadets as civil engineers since the "M" referred both to military and mechanics, with mechanics as a synonym for engineering. These courses of instruction drew from a deep strand within U.S. culture known for innovation and experimentation in design and construction. Achievements and advancements in areas such as bridge construction and ship building gained U.S. engineers the respect and envy of Europeans for cutting-edge work in what is now called "applied science" (Calhoun, 1973).

Warfare—or, rather, the quest for sophisticated and advanced tools for warfare—demonstrated in the early twentieth century the close ties between the national military effort and research, science, and institutions of higher education. James B. Conant, a prodigious young Harvard chemist who would later become the institution's president, provided the high-level laboratory research that led to the refinement of "mustard gas" as a highly effective weapon for U.S. forces in trench warfare during World War I (Hershberg, 1995). Another initiative brought to fruition in the combination of U.S. ingenuity, campus-based scholars, and military applications during World War I was the development of, and reliance on, large-scale testing and placement for cadets and recruits (Levine, 1987). Such assessments allowed organizations, whether large universities or military induction centers, to systematically gather information and make prompt, informed decisions about prospective matches between students or recruits and advanced training and placement opportunities. Educational psychology combined with the nascent field of statistics to epitomize another productive liaison between college campuses and the military to address "national needs" of the era.

James B. Conant expanded the military-industrial-educational compact when he was president of Harvard from 1933 to 1953, especially during World War II (Harvard University, n.d.). Notable scientists and university officials such as Vannevar Bush placed campus-based research and development programs in service of the war effort. Foremost was the legendary Manhattan Project in which a team of academic physicists, chemists, and engineers used secret laboratory spaces, including the abandoned football stadium at the University of Chicago, to collaborate with the U.S. Army and the U.S. Department of Defense to develop the hydrogen bomb (Geiger, 1993). In addition to such obvious alliances in terms of weaponry, U.S. campuses and faculty expertise were valuable sources of language instruction and cultural studies that helped equip military personnel with the backgrounds and skills necessary to function effectively in such relatively unknown areas as Asia, the Pacific Theatre, and Eastern Europe (Thelin, 2004).

One legacy of this World War II military-academic alliance was the creation and Congressional funding of enduring peacetime support for academic research and development. It was in part a sign of thanks for a job well done during the immediate wartime projects (Geiger, 1993; Thelin, 2004). This development also signaled that Congress and the U.S. public recognized that scholarly expertise had potential to solve domestic, peacetime problems in a wide range of areas of national interest (Geiger, 1993). Key contemporary legacies are the National Science Foundation (NSF) and the National Institutes of Health (NIH), along with myriad projects funded by the U.S. Department of Defense (Kerr, 1963; Rosenzweig, 1982).

The appeal and tenacity of the strategy of having the military provide project funding for research and development conducted on college and university campuses continued through several decades after the end of World War II (Kerr, 1963). For example, the established plan of applied science research provided by faculty in departments of chemistry, physics, biology, and engineering eventually was supplemented to include funding for political scientists, geographers, economists, and other disciplines to bring their expertise to bear on counter-insurgency research during the Vietnam War of the 1960s and early 1970s. In sum, the collaboration between the military and higher education had been both consolidated and expanded in the latter half of the twentieth century, especially at such high-powered centers of scientific research as Stanford University, Massachusetts Institute of Technology, and other universities, both private and public, whose abilities to attract sponsored research grants from federal agencies led them to be known as "Federal Grant" universities (Kerr 1963; Lowen, 1997).

Ironically, in the late 1960s and early 1970s, the alliances between military-sponsored research and development and official university institutes and centers led to a paradox of prosperity, and a heavy price for success. The consensus and relatively united missions of military and academe were fractured as part of the intense and growing antiwar sentiment at U.S. colleges and universities. During the late 1960s, local and national press coverage of campus demonstrations and unrest gave primary attention to such events as the burning of ROTC buildings. Less conspicuous, but nonetheless crucial, were the real and symbolic acts of defiance and destruction in which students (including some who were themselves veterans of the Vietnam War) bombed and burned research laboratories and offices that were identified as representations of the inordinate influence and presence of U.S. military policy on the funding and direction of campus-based research. Most publicized were bombings of research sites at the University of Wisconsin and the University of California, Berkeley (Rorabaugh, 1990).

These incidents were symptomatic of a widespread, albeit contentious, statement to reject and rebel against what Dwight D. Eisenhower had critically called the "military-industrial complex" in his 1961 farewell presidential address. These volatile episodes left university officials, legislators, and the U.S. public with mixed messages and images. Foremost, they showed the diversity of opinions and activities housed within a complex multiversity. For example, student antiwar demonstrations took place in Sproul Plaza at Berkeley at the very time the Livermore Laboratories hosted counterinsurgency research projects elsewhere on the same campus. Military veterans as students no longer represented a united front; their participation and ascription to war-related student activities ran the gamut from loyal support to vocal condemnation of existent national policies and campaigns, including the mandatory selective service and military draft. One consequence of these tensions was concern by federal agencies that perhaps in the future, federally sponsored research and development projects might seek locations or sites other than university campuses to assure hospitable, supportive work environments (Rorabaugh, 1990). Thirty years later, in stark contrast to the Vietnam era, the range of campus events and activities dealing with U.S. warfare in Iraq and Afghanistan showed relatively few signs of strong polemics on one side or another. The best estimate is that the military-academic-industrial alliance for research and development has been maintained and restored.

GI Bill Programs

The 1944 GI Bill laid a key foundation for providing educational and financial benefits to qualifying veterans and service members. The original GI Bill also led to record enrollments and campus expansions during the postwar years.

Pre–World War II. Before the United States' involvement in World War II (1941–1945), the federal government compensated its citizen-soldiers for military service during the nation's major conflicts. Revolutionary War (1775–1783) veterans were given land for service. The new nation awarded pensions to disabled soldiers and to soldiers' widows and orphans. The federal government also provided pensions for service to veterans of the War of 1812 (1812–1815), the Mexican War (1846–1848), and the Spanish-American War (1898). After the Civil War (1861–1865), the federal government provided pensions to Union military veterans (U.S. Department of Veterans Affairs, 2008, 2011); the former Confederate states provided pensions to their veterans (Green, 2006).

Following World War I (1917–1918), the federal government approved a bonus for veterans (World War Adjusted Compensation Act of 1924), in the form of certificates that could not be redeemed until 1945. An economy in depression led to a veterans march on Washington, DC in 1932. The "Bonus Army" marchers failed to gain early payment of their World War I compensation certificates, and were forced from the city by troops commanded by Army Chief of Staff General Douglas MacArthur (U.S. Department of Veterans Affairs, 2008). In January 1936, Congress overrode a presidential veto and passed legislation that replaced the bonus certificates with bonds that still bore a 1945 maturity date, but that World War I veterans could redeem earlier (Bonus Bill Becomes Law, 1936).

World War II. The memory of the "Bonus Army" march was on the minds of federal legislative and executive branch members as planning for post–World War II began in 1944. Some economists forecasted a return to the economic depression that had engulfed the nation before its industries turned to war material production. The productive employment of millions of young soldiers, sailors, and airmen after the war was a major concern of economic and social observers. Among the benefits offered by the Serviceman's Readjustment Act of 1944 (legislation popularly known as "The GI Bill") were payments to veterans to attend post-secondary institutions after their military service; the subsequent delay in their return to the workforce would reduce the labor surplus economists expected in the postwar period (Greenberg, 1997).

The convergence of two distant groups in this postwar venture was demonstrated by the nation's oldest academic institution—Harvard University—which took the initiative to encourage and attract the nation's newest student constituency—war veterans—who had no prior socialization to the college experience. Harvard initiated a vigorous advertisement and recruitment program among overseas servicemen before World War II ended. In projecting an official image to GIs, the university sought to stimulate interest in Harvard among those who were talented yet unfamiliar with college life. The 1945 *Official Register of Harvard University* included a small, brief brochure with photographs of campus life designed for bulk delivery and fast reading. Emblazoned on a cream-colored glossy cover in crimson letters was the title, *What About Harvard?* The university's strategy was to make "college life" attractive to older, mature, and capable men who, prior to the war, might not have considered attending any college, let alone prestigious, historic Harvard. The preface by President James B. Conant emphasized the university's cardinal aim of flexibility and individual consideration of the background, experience, and promise of each veteran who applied for admission.

Although the war had not yet been won, Harvard's deans and special counselor for veterans were preparing to supply the latest information about opportunities for higher education. Along with predictable formal guidelines, the brochure set out to dispel the popular stereotype of Harvard as a college for "rich boys." At the same time, Harvard officials did not seek mass applications and took care to emphasize that admission standards had been made more elastic, but had not been relaxed. The public relations effort gave deliberate attention to the ways in which the university was attempting to reduce "red tape" that might work against "men who have been fighting instead of studying." Finally, the brochure encouraged applications from those who were "of serious purpose" and "who meant business ... This does not mean that intellectual brilliance is required for admission—or for success after admission. Character, experience, promise, all-around performance are vital . . . Harvard recognizes that the veteran of this war will expect something else from education than the ordinary peace-time student. Clearly the man who has been making life and death decisions at sea, in the air, and on the ground has other ideas than the man who comes direct from high school. The University is bending every energy to meet the needs of these men'' (Harvard University, 1945, p. 4).

Some observers, including the nationally popular weekly magazine *Saturday Evening Post*, forecasted that most veterans would ignore the opportunity offered by the GI Bill to attend college. In an issue dated just days after the Japanese Empire accepted an unconditional surrender in September 1945, the *Saturday Evening Post* ran an article informing readers that veterans were rejecting the chance to go to college to return to their prewar jobs, or destinies, on farms and in factories. However, choosing to pursue different careers path than their fathers, veterans streamed into college and university registrar offices (Olson, 1974). By August 1946, a year after Japan's surrender and the *Saturday Evening Post* article, one million veterans of the U.S. war effort had enrolled in post-secondary education paid for by the GI Bill (Kiester, 1994).

It was no accident that the Harvard recruitment brochure referred to veterans and prospective students as ''men.'' Harvard College was gender exclusive, as were many of the university's graduate and professional schools. Elsewhere, however, women veterans used the GI Bill to enroll in a variety of institutions and degree programs (Barnum, 2007). The flood of veterans brought both a rising tide of tuition money, but also the need for more student housing, classrooms, learning facilities, and professors. College infrastructure evolved to meet the new needs, but in the short term, campus administrators created temporary solutions for the enviable problems caused by the growth in student enrollment. Military Quonset huts and surplus military barracks were pressed into use for housing and classrooms. Veterans brought their families to college, a rarity on quieter prewar campuses (Greenberg, 1997; Olson, 1974). Living accommodations for veterans' spouses and children were often provided by universities and colleges when the housing demand grew beyond what the private sectors surrounding campuses could supply. Campuses built play areas and equipment; eventually elementary schools were built in or near many of the veterans' villages that grew on many U.S. campuses in the postwar years (Kiester, 1994).

The influx of veterans changed the physical appearance of college campuses and affected campuses' social cultures. Stories of college life during the interwar period of 1919 to 1940 described an easy mood of coed parties, dancing, drinking, and occasional attendance in classes taught by absent-minded professors. Magazine articles, college-based novels, and the movies portrayed lively campuses that included ritual hazing, such as new students wearing the freshman beanie, and fixed in the popular culture university and college life as a youthful, prank-filled interlude between high (or prep) school graduation and the serious business of life, assuming father's bank presidency or marrying the college football hero, followed by mornings of bond coupon–clipping and afternoons spent on the country club golf course or in the clubhouse (Greenberg, 1997; Mettler, 2005). The postwar students who enrolled under the GI Bill—veterans of battles in Africa, Europe, Asia, and the Pacific Rim—resisted wearing freshmen beanies or swallowing goldfish, and many college traditions established during the interwar period fell to the wayside. Veterans were building futures for themselves, their spouses, and their children, and had no time for the life of "Joe College" (Kiester, 1994).

The editor of *Esquire* magazine recalled veteran and famous novelist Sloan Wilson's memorable short story, *School Days*, published in the March 1946 issue of *The New Yorker*:

> The author of *The Man in the Grey Flannel Suit* here turns his attention to those old-young men of Cassino, North Africa, Okinawa, who went back to school. They were for the most part, disoriented, too quickly and too destructively come of age, the possessors of skills in the arts of war, men who had looked on a living nightmare before fully growing out of the dreams of childhood. Returned as students to the academic world, their adjustment was—in a sense—backwards, to adolescence. Sloan Wilson, who served in the Navy during World War II and now teaches at the University of Buffalo, tells in this story about these men and about those years immediately after the war when they returned to our campuses. (Spectorsky, 1958, p. 160)

Sloan Wilson's short story effectively presented that each conventional step in undergraduate life was the source of conflict or confusion because U.S. campuses had not had sufficient time to adjust myriad details, such as registration forms, parental consent affidavits, and other recordkeeping to the realities, ages, and often the married status of GIs.

Whereas veteran and novelist Wilson was relatively sanguine about the incongruities he described, another veteran turned writer, Sylvan Karchmer (1949), left readers with no doubt about the conflicts and adjustment difficulties veterans faced on campus—not only in navigating institutional regulations, but also in their dealings with fellow veterans whose shared war experiences did not translate into harmonious, shared experiences at college. Karchmer depicted the awkwardness of three veterans who had known each other and fought alongside one another in North Africa. Yet at the university, the protagonist is a graduate student and teaching assistant in English, whereas his comrades are, respectively, a student in physics and a bewildered freshman struggling with a basic composition course. What becomes evident is that the maturity and decisive actions that characterized them in military service did not carry over into civilian life, especially in academia. Despite their mutual experiences and good intentions, each was of limited help to the others in the alien world of postwar college life.

The complex legacy of post–World War II veterans as presented by their fictional memoirs, along with more official records, was that the 1944 GI Bill transformed more than U.S. university and college infrastructures and campus cultures; it created a generation of men and women who were the United States' most educated and eventually its most financially successful (Hart, 1983). A society that many expected would slip back into the prewar economic depression educated those called to serve beyond their wildest dreams, and brought them from farm fields and factory assembly lines into professions that continued the economic prosperity of the World War II years into the second half of the twentieth century. Many of the new college students and graduates were the first of their families to pursue higher education. These men and women spent their youth in the depression years and their young adulthoods in combat in foreign surroundings, and passed the desire for an improved standard of living earned through college educations on to their children. The following chapter traces some of the major post–World War II evolutions of the GI Bill as well as other veterans' benefits programs.

Conclusion

The Morrill Land-Grant Act of 1862 introduced a formal tie between civilian higher education institutions and the military. The 1862 Act's creation of A&M colleges made instruction in military tactics part of higher education curricula. The establishment of the Reserve Officer Training Corps just prior to the United States' entry into World War I, and the implementation of the short-lived Student Army Training Corps in 1918 further formalized the ties between higher education and the U.S. military establishment. The provision of education benefits to World War II veterans in 1944 created an enrollment boom in U.S. universities and colleges. This expansion of higher education created the solid middle-class social status of well-educated citizens who otherwise would have had few alternatives to returning to their prewar farm and factory employment. During and following World War II, higher education and the military also forged close ties in research and development. The partnership between research universities and the military continued through the second half of the twentieth century and into the twenty-first century. The alliance between higher education, the military, and industry forged in World War II continues advances in science and technology that create both military and civilian applications.

References

Axtell, J. (1971). The death of the liberal arts college? *History of Education Quarterly*, *11*(4), 339–354.

Barnum, N. (2007). *Leaving home: Patriarchy, nursing education and the nurse veterans use of the GI Bill.* (Doctoral dissertation). University of Kentucky, Lexington.

Baxter, M. G. (1995). *Henry Clay and the American system.* Lexington: University Press of Kentucky.

Bonus bill becomes law: Repassed in Senate, 76–19: Payment will be speeded. (1936, January 28). *New York Times*, pp. A1–A2.

Calhoun, D. (1973). *The intelligence of a people.* Princeton, NJ: Princeton University Press.

Cardozier, V. R. (1993). *Colleges and universities in World War II.* Westport, CT: Praeger.

Cipolla, C. (1969). *Literacy and development in the west.* Baltimore, MD: Penguin Books.

Eddy, E. D. (1957). *Colleges for our land and time: The land-grant idea in American education.* New York: Harper.

Edmond, J. B. (1978). *The magnificent charter: The origin and role of the Morrill land-grant colleges and universities.* Hicksville, NY: Exposition Press.

Faust, D. G. (2008). *This republic of suffering: Death and the American Civil War.* New York: Knopf.

Forman, S. (1952/1958). Cadets. In A. C. Spectorsky (Ed.), *The college years* (pp. 58–68). New York: Hawthorn.

Geiger, R. (1993). *Research and relevant knowledge: American research universities since World War II.* New York: Oxford University Press.

Green, E. C. (2006). Protecting confederate soldiers and mothers: Pensions, gender, and the welfare state in the U.S. south, a case study from Florida. *Journal of Social History*, *39*(4), 1079–1104.

Greenberg, M. (1997). *The GI Bill: The law that changed America.* New York: Lickle.

Hannon, H. (2005, June 9). Soldiers field: The story of a monument, the man who built it, and the men it honors. *Harvard Gazette*. Retrieved from http://news.harvard.edu/gazette/2005/06.09/07-monument.html

Hart, J. (1983). *When the going was good: American life in the fifties.* New York: Better Books.

Harvard University. (n.d.). *James Bryant Conant* [web site]. Retrieved from http://www.harvard.edu/history/presidents/conant

Harvard University. (1945, March 27). *Official register of Harvard University.* Cambridge, MA: Author.

Hershberg, J. G. (1995). *James B. Conant: Harvard to Hiroshima and the making of the nuclear age.* Palo Alto, CA: Stanford University Press.

Karchmer, S. (1949, Winter). Hail brother and farewell. *Epoch.* Ithaca, NY: Cornell University Department of English.

Kerr, C. (1963). The realities of the federal grant university. In C. Kerr (Ed.), *The uses of the university* (pp. 46–84). Cambridge, MA: Harvard University Press.

Key, S. (1996). Economics or education: The establishment of American land-grant universities. *Journal of Higher Education, 67*(2), 196–220.

Kiester, E., Jr, (1994). The G.I. Bill may be the best deal ever made by Uncle Sam. *Smithsonian, 25*(8), 128.

Levine, D. O. (1987). *The American college and the culture of aspiration, 1915–1940.* Ithaca, NY: Cornell University Press.

Lowen, R. S. (1997). *Creating the Cold War university: The transformation of Stanford.* Berkeley: University of California Press.

Mettler, S. (2005). *Soldiers to citizens: The G.I. Bill and the making of the greatest generation.* New York: Oxford University Press.

Naval Reserve Officers Training Corps. (2011a). *History* [web site]. Retrieved from http://www.nrotc.navy.mil/history.aspx

Olson, K. W. (1974). *The G.I. Bill, the veterans and the colleges.* Lexington: University Press of Kentucky.

Rorabaugh, W. J. (1990) *Berkeley at war: The sixties.* New York: Oxford University Press.

Rosenzweig, R. M. (1982). *The research universities and their patrons.* Berkeley: University of California Press.

Spectorsky, A. C. (Ed.). (1958). *The college years.* New York: Hawthorn Books.

Thelin, J. R. (2004). *A history of American higher education.* Baltimore, MD: Johns Hopkins University Press.

Thurber, J. (1934/1958). University days. In A. C. Spectorsky (Ed.), *The college years* (pp. 436–441). New York: Hawthorn Books.

United States Air Force ROTC. (2011b). *History* [web site]. Retrieved from http://afrotc.com/learn-about/history/

United States Army Cadet Command. (n.d.). *History of Army ROTC* [web site]. Retrieved from http://www.rotc.usaac.army.mil/history.html

United States Coast Guard. (n.d.). *Officer FAQS* [web site]. Retrieved from http://www.gocoastguard.com/find-your-career/officer-opportunities/officer-faqs

United States Department of Defense, Office of the Under Secretary of Defense, Personnel and Readiness. (2010). *Population representation in the military services: Fiscal year 2009.* Retrieved from http://prhome.defense.gov/MPP/ACCESSION%20POLICY/PopRep2009/index.html

United States Department of Veterans Affairs. (2008). *VA history in brief.* Washington, DC: Author. Retrieved from http://www.va.gov/opa/publications/archives/docs/history_in_brief.pdf

United States Department of Veterans Affairs. (2011). *America's wars fact sheet.* Washington, DC: Author. Retrieved from http://www.va.gov/opa/publications/fact sheets/fs_americas_wars.pdf

University of Illinois Athletic Association. (1921). *The Story of the stadium.* Retrieved from http://ia600300.us.archive.org/7/items/storyofstadium00univ/storyof stadium00univ.pdf

University of Kentucky. (n.d.). *Barker Hall and Buell Armory* [web site]. Retrieved from http://sweb.uky.edu/StudentOrgs/SDC/markers/BarkerBuell2.html

Washington and Lee University. (n.d.). *About W&L* [web site]. Retrieved from http://www.wlu.edu/x52548.xml

Williams, R. L. (1991). *The origins of federal support for higher education: George W. Atherton and the land-grant college movement.* University Park: Pennsylvania State University Press.

CHAPTER TWO

CONTEMPORARY POLITICAL AND LEGISLATIVE FRAMEWORKS FOR SERVING VETERANS AND SERVICE MEMBERS

Sally Caspers and Robert Ackerman

United States veterans have been provided postservice educational benefits regularly since World War II. Today, as the all-volunteer military continues to evolve, the educational benefits of the current GI Bill also function as a recruitment initiative—a motivator that attracts potential students to military service as a means to a better life. Research suggests that young adults join the military in response to various motivations, but important among those is to receive the educational benefits attached to having served (Ackerman, DiRamio, & Mitchell, 2009; DiRamio & Jarvis, 2011; Rumann & Hamrick, 2009). That being the case, it is important that college administrators at all levels be familiar with the evolution, context, purposes, and details of the many programs under which student veterans access their earned educational benefits. These programs have become very complex over time, and frequent updates have an impact on funding for current and future students.

Student veterans who joined the military to earn educational benefits may become frustrated as they attempt to navigate the bureaucracy that administers those benefits. Campus representatives who are committed to assisting student veterans should be sufficiently familiar with the range of benefit programs to engage students in meaningful, helpful, and accurate conversations about veterans' and service members' educational benefits. The purpose of this chapter is to provide basic information about various programs and introduce the nomenclature associated with specific programs, since familiarity with that language can help individuals avoid misunderstandings and confusion.

Legacy GI Bill Programs

To the uninitiated, the name "GI Bill" harkens images of fresh-from-the-war military service members enrolling in college and enjoying free rides (full scholarships) to achieve their college degrees. In reality, the GI Bill is a shorthand call sign for a wide range of U.S. Department of Veterans Affairs (VA) education funding programs available to U.S. military veterans based on a complex algorithm of length and type of service. Since its origin as the Servicemen's Readjustment Act of 1944, the GI Bill has evolved to serve each successive generation of veterans. As the United States involves itself in various military engagements worldwide, the obligation to the education of service men and women has been met with varying degrees of political scrutiny, goodwill, and public support. To understand today's GI Bill and student veteran education, one must first understand the evolution of the original GI Bill, which is introduced in Chapter One and elaborated in this chapter with respect to student-level circumstances and impacts.

When the GI Bill was first enacted, higher education was largely a privilege reserved for the wealthy (Hunt, 2006). Initial contemporary predictions forecasted that, at most, one million World War II veterans would take advantage of the new benefits. In fact, over two million veterans, both men and women, pursued higher education using GI Bill benefits (Bellafaire, 2006). The Women in Military Service for America Memorial Foundation noted that "women veterans...were even more interested than their male counterparts in obtaining a college degree; more than 19.5 percent of 332,178 eligible women veterans elected to attend college after the war as compared to 15 percent of 15 million eligible male veterans" (Bellafaire, 2006, para. 2).

The initial GI Bill was instrumental in that it not only changed the lives of an entire generation of veterans, it also changed the landscape of higher education. The structure of the GI Bill and its payment arrangements drove the choices that veterans made regarding institutions and degree plans, and those same structures also influenced the ways institutions of higher learning supported those students. At a minimum, institutions wishing to recruit veterans employed staff, usually in financial aid or registrar's offices, to handle the certification of student veteran enrollment, thereby bridging the benefit from the VA to the students and institutions. Even now, campuses with no other specialized support or programs for veterans are likely to have at least one staff member dedicated to certification of veterans' and service members' enrollment statuses.

The original post–World War II GI Bill "covered full tuition, fees and book costs, in addition to a living stipend at most public and private colleges for a period of up to 48 months depending on the veteran's length of service. It also only required a 90-day enlistment with an honorable discharge" (McBain, 2008, p. 4). Although history has ultimately been kind to the authors of the original GI Bill, it is important to note that the GI Bill was not passed unanimously or without conflict. The bill contained several provisions to support veterans, including education benefits, home loan guarantees, and unemployment payments, and certain parts of the legislation were quite controversial (U.S. Department of Veterans Affairs, 2009). In the end, veterans using the original GI Bill received the most comprehensive and complete support of any GI Bill recipients to date. The generous benefits "allowed veterans to receive a college or other vocational education and cross class lines in the process" (McBain, 2008, p. 3) while also laying a foundation for the U.S. economic boom of the 1950s. Because of the industrial nature of the U.S. economy in the mid-twentieth century, it was possible for veterans to pursue vocational training and establish strong middle-class statuses for their families.

The GI Bill also opened educational doors for women veterans:

> Overall, the educational level of women in the U.S. declined during these years, making the women veterans who chose to go to college under the G.I. Bill a very privileged group. The G.I. Bill had a positive impact on the lives of thousands of women veterans; and they, just like men, used their educational benefits to pursue professional careers that would otherwise have been unavailable to many of them given their family finances. Regardless of whether or not these women eventually opted to get married and have families, their G.I. Bill educations expanded their horizons, and often those of their families as well. (Bellafaire, 2006, para. 5)

The World War II–era GI Bill served veterans and the U.S. economy as intended and changed higher education irrevocably. However, the educational benefit in particular was politically controversial. Eligibility requirements and related educational benefit levels for veterans of succeeding wars evolved in the contexts of contemporary political climates.

Most college administrators interested in serving student veterans realize that the GI Bill was established to serve the World War II generation and that it was revamped in 1984 and renamed the "Montgomery GI Bill." However, the GI Bill underwent two additional evolutions during that period, and each had an important impact on the way GI Bill funds were paid and used. The amount of funding available to veterans, and to whom those funds were paid, drove veterans' enrollment choices (Radford, 2009).

Though the GI Bill has been in effect since 1944, data collected by the VA about the students it has served and their training and educational choices have varied with each iteration of the bill. Consequently, researchers lack a complete data set from which to make comparative assessments regarding student choices among institutions or programs of study. What is certain is that the VA, via the GI Bill, enabled the greatest investment in occupational training of any federal program (Arnstein, 1981). Between World War II and the Vietnam Conflict, student choices regarding programs of study showed preferences for academic degrees (either associate's or bachelor's degrees); however, veterans using VA education benefits enrolled in two-year institutions and vocational programs at higher rates than in other undergraduate college programs: "The total VA investment in education, as of September 1980, was $55 billion. Of this, almost half was devoted to *occupational* [emphasis in original] education below the baccalaureate level" (Arnstein, 1981, p. 3).

The Vietnam-era GI Bill (originally known as the Post-Korean GI Bill) went into effect in 1966. Veterans had ten years from the date of discharge to use the benefits because eligibility for this phase of the GI Bill expired in 1976. Usage trends peaked in 1975, after which point data that tracked the progress of Vietnam-era veterans through college were no longer collected. However, the usage data from that time period are illustrative: Vietnam veterans tended to favor occupational and vocational education, and sought that education at community colleges. This marked a shift in veterans' education priorities, but we cannot be sure whether this shift was driven by a change in the funding levels and payment methods or by student veterans' career choices (Arnstein, 1981). Additionally, Vietnam-era veterans—including those enrolled at colleges and universities—were themselves targets of protest (DeBenedetti, 1990), leading many to resist self-identifying as military veterans (Summerlot, Green, & Parker, 2009).

In accordance with the provisions of the original GI Bill (for World War II veterans), two separate subsidy payments were made to enrolled veterans: one for tuition costs and one for living expenses. Of significance was the regulation that tuition funds could not be used for living expenses and vice versa. The tuition part of the benefit was generous, but the cost-of-living benefit was less so. Thus, in order to use the benefit to the fullest extent, World War II–era veterans enrolled in four-year colleges and universities and lived simply or obtained part-time employment to supplement the cost-of-living stipend.

When the GI Bill was updated for Korean War–era veterans in 1952, the benefits were reduced from those provided by the original GI Bill, and an additional change was made that fundamentally shifted the way veterans chose to use their educational benefits. Following allegations of fraud on the part of colleges and other institutions receiving VA monies, the funds allotted for Korean War veterans' educations were lumped into single monthly payments made directly to the students, forcing veterans to make choices as to whether to defray their living expenses with the funds or use them to pay tuition (Arnstein, 1981). "The consequences of this shift to a combined payment were massive. Under the GI Bill thousands of trainees shifted to low-tuition or no-tuition schools [as did their nonveteran peers]" (Arnstein, 1981, p. 13). The combined, smaller GI Bill payment to veterans constituted an unintended incentive for veterans to attend two-year and vocational training programs rather than four-year baccalaureate programs. The benefit program was changed in 1966, during the Vietnam era, and "an explicit new objective was to provide educational incentives to make military service more attractive" (Arnstein, 1981, p. 6).

An additional 1966 provision allowed military members to use the GI Bill before they left active duty. Because active duty members were receiving salaries, it was less likely that they would need to work part-time while attending college. In these cases, the entire benefit could be used toward the cost of tuition. Vietnam veterans intending to use the benefit as the sole means of funding their educations and living expenses were less likely to choose to attend the more expensive institutions, an option more feasible for their active duty contemporaries who were still receiving military pay.

With the changes to the legislation in the 1984 update, known as the Montgomery GI Bill, one monthly stipend was paid directly to the student. As with the Korean- and Vietnam-era benefits, the lump sum payment indirectly encouraged veterans to pursue lower-cost education options so that they could also use some of the funds to offset living expenses. As of the 2007–08 academic year (before the Post-9/11 GI Bill went into effect), the Montgomery GI Bill (referred to by the VA as Chapter 30) covered "approximately 73 percent of the cost of tuition, fees, room and board at a public four-year college, and cover[ed] much less of the cost at a private nonprofit four-year college: 31 percent when using the 2007–2008 College Board estimate average cost of $32,307" (McBain, 2008, p. 4). For veterans, the costs of higher education are frequently part of family budgets that must cover other expenses; there is strong incentive to keep education costs low and to retain portions of the stipends for living expenses and family support. Thus, the trend toward enrolling in vocational and two-year training and education programs continued under the Montgomery GI Bill, in spite of a growing national trend toward an information-driven, high-tech economy that demands four-year degrees.

The Post-9/11 GI Bill and Other Contemporary Veteran Education Benefits

As service members transition from active duty to the civilian world, they are often given an overload of information via a military-taught transition course (U.S. Department of Defense, 2011) that may or may not have been fully understood and internalized. By the time veterans become students, it is quite possible that any useful information has faded from memory or become outdated because of changes to the GI Bill. Although it is the responsibility of individual veterans to know which benefits will best serve their needs, higher education administrators—especially those who will serve student veterans—should have a working knowledge of the options for veterans, or at least be able to make knowledgeable referrals to appropriate resources. The perception that with the advent of the Post-9/11 GI Bill, veterans' education benefits are now standardized across all generations may be the greatest fallacy among higher education professionals who are only tangentially familiar with veterans' issues. Additionally, the Montgomery GI Bill is still in effect, as are several separate programs for Guard and Reserve forces members. These multiple programs are complex to administer and often difficult for student veterans to fully understand, making it vital for practitioners who assist these students to be well informed and current.

The Post-9/11 GI Bill

In June 2008, Congress passed a new GI Bill designed to fill some of the gaps in education benefits that existed in the Montgomery GI Bill. This was the most comprehensive change to the GI Bill since World War II, and once again refocused VA education benefits on supporting students in the completion of four-year degrees (McBain, 2009). Although the contemporary higher education climate appears to be increasingly sensitive to the needs of student veterans, and changes to the GI Bill are occurring in generally favorable political environments, the current education benefits offer a blend of old benefit structures. Payments are higher and more comprehensive—similar to the World War II–era bill—and the types of education and training to which the benefits may be applied are diverse. All GI Bills prior to the Post-9/11 Bill supported the pursuit of vocational, apprentice, or on-the-job training opportunities as well as college or university degree programs. The first version of the Post-9/11 GI Bill offered more generous funding, but limited the range of educational programs to which that funding can be applied. That limitation was corrected with revisions to the bill in 2011.

The Post-9/11 GI Bill, referred to as Chapter 33 by the VA, is certainly the most financially generous education benefits package since the World War II program and will likely have a significant impact on contemporary veterans. This GI Bill once again divides monies into separate payments that address specific student expenses. The new benefit pays tuition and fees in full at the in-state tuition rate at a public institution or up to $17,500 per year at a private institution; provides a monthly housing allowance during the term of enrollment, the amount of which is based on the zip code of the institution attended; and offers an annual $1,000 stipend for books (U.S. Department of Veterans Affairs, 2010b).

To be eligible for the Post-9/11 GI Bill, veterans must have served at least 90 days of aggregate active duty days after September 10, 2011. At the time of this writing, prorated eligibility begins at 40 percent for those with 90 days of active duty service, and full eligibility is achieved after three years of aggregated active duty service. The bill offers 36 total months of benefits and does not cost anything for the service member to join, as opposed to the Montgomery GI Bill, for which service members contributed $1,200 in order to use the benefit later (U.S. Department of Veterans Affairs, 2010b).

In all cases prior to the current GI Bill, benefits were reserved strictly for the use of the veteran him or herself. Veterans' dependents were left out of the federal benefits programs (U.S. Department of Veterans Affairs, 2010b), although some state-funded veterans benefits programs made provisions for surviving spouses or children of the service members who were killed in action or severely disabled, such as the Alabama GI Dependents Scholarship Program (2011) administered by the Alabama Department of Veterans Affairs. Under Post-9/11 GI Bill rules, active duty members may transfer any portion of their benefit (up to 100 percent) to any of their dependents; that is, the allotment may be split among children, for example, or the full benefit can be reserved for one dependent only, such as a spouse or single child (U.S. Department of Defense, 2009). This involvement of dependents in the VA education benefits process is important as it changes the way higher education institutions can support student veterans and their families. The VA application and disbursement processes remain the same, but the needs of a military spouse or child are likely to be quite different from those of service members and veterans. A military spouse using an active duty member's benefit while the member is deployed, for example, may require additional financial, social, or academic support. Indeed, this change in who may access VA education benefits means that those who wish to serve veterans on campus now must start thinking of veterans within the context of their eligible family members as well.

As an additional incentive for institutions of higher learning to support student veterans, included in the Post-9/11 GI Bill is a public-private partnership opportunity called the Yellow Ribbon program. The Yellow Ribbon program requires participating institutions to make additional funds available to student veterans that equal 50 percent of outstanding tuition after initial GI Bill payments are made; the VA then matches the contributions and issues payment directly to the institutions (U.S. Department of Veterans Affairs, 2011a). In other words, the institutions offer students scholarships and the VA matches the amount up to the full cost of tuition and fees. This program is most often in use at private colleges or universities and public colleges and universities that enroll out-of-state student veterans.

The Post-9/11 GI Bill went into effect on August 1, 2009. Its debut was rocky in that it was hampered by poor information-technology systems, an overwhelming number of program applicants, and short lead time for preparation. The legislation instituted a completely new way of certifying, processing, and paying veterans' education benefits, and the automated system to process payments could not be finalized until the VA had successfully and accurately interpreted the legislation. By late summer 2009, new regulations for the Post-9/11 GI Bill were still being finalized; all of the payments—nearly a quarter of a million—had to be processed manually (McBain, 2009). This led to a backlog of payments, resulting in late fees charged to students and situations in which students did not have enough money available for cost-of-living expenses; anecdotal evidence indicates that some student veterans abandoned their educational pursuits in frustration.

Among the issues accompanying the rollout of the Post-9/11 GI Bill was that college campuses were unprepared to handle the increased work-load that certifying this more complex benefit entailed. The certification of enrollment and processing of payments—which were often made late by the VA—were much more laborious than previous GI Bill benefits because student enrollment had to be certified per class, rather than simple enroll-ment verifications (Campbell, 2009). In fact, the Post-9/11 GI Bill is the only program still being used by student veterans that makes payments directly to their institutions. The prior standard for other GI Bill programs had been that students were responsible for their tuition bills, regardless of whether the VA made their payments. The Post-9/11 GI Bill specifies that students receive payments for housing and books, and institutions receive separate payments for tuition and fees. However, problems arise when VA payments are made after institutions' deadlines. These challenges in the new VA payment process were not anticipated—especially not to the extent that they were realized, such as delays of up to 20 weeks—and campuses were left scrambling to enact policies to accommodate the new financial realities of student veterans utilizing Post-9/11 GI Bill benefits (McBain, 2009). Over time, the VA has streamlined its processes so that certifications and payments clear within a matter of weeks rather than months, and students now experience much smoother processes.

Although the landscape of veterans' education benefits programs has changed with the Post-9/11 GI Bill, colleges and universities still enroll students who use Montgomery GI Bill benefits as well as other veterans' education benefits programs. It is a common misconception that all users of legacy benefits have been transitioned to the new Post-9/11 GI Bill; in fact, some users of the Montgomery GI Bill are not eligible for the Post-9/11 GI Bill, and some others who are eligible for both GI Bills choose to use Montgomery benefits rather than Post-9/11 benefits. Veterans may only receive assistance from one of these VA educational programs at a time, and a change is irrevocable, so the choices veterans make are important; in some cases, the Montgomery GI Bill is still a better choice (Radford, 2009).

If it is not already apparent that VA education benefits programs are an ever-changing landscape, some provisions of the Post-9/11 GI Bill changed in August and October 2011 in response to the experiences of the program's initial users, and it is likely that additional changes will follow. First, effective October 1, 2011, the Post-9/11 GI Bill may be used for non–college degree programs. This change expands educational options for all 9/11 era veterans as the bill's rules previously left out those veterans who did not pursue college degrees. Second, adjustments to the bill remove the previous state cap on tuition and fees and instead mandate payment of all in-state tuition and fees. This means that no out-of-state fees may be paid, but that in-state tuition and fees for graduate education, for example, are paid in full. For example, a student charged in-state tuition will be completely covered by the Post-9/11 GI Bill, but a student charged out-of-state fees is responsible for the amount of tuition exceeding the in-state rate. Finally, these changes eliminated "break pay," a continuation of housing benefits through the traditional winter break month. Students must plan their personal budgets to accommodate this drop in income.

Post-9/11 GI Bill benefits are now available to a wider cross-section of student veterans, but some continuing users will find that their benefits have shrunk for their particular eligibility situations. For example, out-of-state students, including veterans, generally pay higher tuition and fees to attend public colleges and universities; under the original Post-9/11 GI Bill, the out-of-state premium was covered in part. Because of the new, stricter no out-of-state fees rule, student veterans enrolling at out-of-state institutions are responsible for the entire tuition and fee differential. Those costs can be considerable depending on state policies and institutional tuition structures.

The Post-9/11 GI Bill is often discussed in terms of watershed change, much like its predecessor, the World War II–era GI Bill. In fiscal year 2009, the first partial year of the program, Post-9/11 GI Bill users numbered 34,393 but jumped to 365,640 for fiscal year 2010 (U.S. Department of Veterans Affairs, 2010a). Post-9/11 GI Bill enrollments were only 70,000 short of matching all other current VA education benefit program recipients combined. The Post-9/11 GI Bill is more generous than its most immediate predecessors, and veterans' and service members' enrollments are expected to continue to increase (Radford, 2009). Fiscal year 2010 postsecondary enrollment rates generated $5.1 billion in benefit payments on behalf of student veterans (U.S. Department of Veterans Affairs, 2010a) and tuition and fees were approximately half the total amount, making student veterans big business for higher education. "During fiscal year 2010, approximately 37 percent of all beneficiaries pursued degrees while attending junior colleges (2 year schools), 49.7 percent used their VA education benefit attending undergraduate college, 9.6 percent were in graduate school and 3.7 percent used their VA education benefit in vocational or technical training programs" (U.S. Department of Veterans Affairs, 2010a, p. 39).

More changes to the Post-9/11 GI Bill are likely in the future. Although all students, including veterans, are ideally their own best advocates and take time to educate themselves about their options, they often turn to trusted on-campus advisors or financial aid counselors for guidance. In these cases, perhaps the best way higher education professionals can support student veterans is to be generally knowledgeable and conversant about benefit programs and know where and how to make appropriate referrals to further assist students. A little knowledge has the potential to be dangerous, especially since program provisions continually change, but professionals interested in serving students can make efforts to stay up-to-date and also rely on expert referrals. As a start, a list of informational and referral web sites is provided at the end of this chapter.

Other VA Education Benefit Programs

As referenced earlier in this chapter, the GI Bill is part of the larger federal VA education benefits system, and its parts are identified as chapters. This section presents information on some of the lesser-known, yet important chapters. Key VA education benefit chapters are:

- Chapter 30: Montgomery GI Bill
- Chapter 31: Vocational Rehabilitation Program
- Chapter 33: Post-9/11 GI Bill
- Chapter 35: Survivors and Dependents Assistance (DEA)
- Chapter 1606: Montgomery GI Bill Reserves
- Chapter 1607: Reserve Educational Assistance Program (REAP)

Chapters 35, 1606, and 1607 provide monthly stipend payments, similar in structure to Chapter 30. Chapter 31 partners students with VA education officers to identify personalized education plans based on the students' vocational goals; the resulting education plans are then paid in full by VA educational benefits, and cost-of-living stipends are provided as well (U.S. Department of Veterans Affairs, 2010b).

Use of each chapter of VA education benefits requires that school certifying officials verify student enrollment. Institutional verification procedures may vary, but typically students provide enrollment information and documentation from the VA that they are eligible for the programs they intend to use. Depending on the size of the institution and the number of student veterans enrolled, this process can be quick and painless or slow and challenging. Often campuses have only one certifying official, and when veteran enrollments grow, the increased workload may make timely responses and claims processing unmanageable. For those programs that make direct payments to students, such as the Montgomery GI Bill, the process is simpler for institutions because students are responsible for paying tuition. Yet challenges arise when the VA does not pay students accurately or on time and the students lack the funds to pay tuition and related education expenses on time to avoid late fees or involuntary enrollment withdrawal. Although it is not the optimal solution, in many cases these students are treated in the same manner as other students with funding challenges—they are offered payment plans and student loans, which factor as much into their funding situations as VA education benefits (McBain, 2009). Institutions that have been lauded as the most "veteran-friendly" have processes that exempt veterans from paying overdue tuition until VA monies are received. A review of institutional policies, student advocacy, and general familiarity with the challenges student veterans face in this regard can help minimize disruptions.

VA education benefits are used as recruiting tools by the U.S. Armed Forces; this was one of the stated purposes for the Montgomery GI Bill (Spaulding, 2000). However, future students can develop unrealistic expectations regarding their eligibility for certain programs. For example, Guard members may be told by recruiters or ill-informed peers that they will be eligible for Post-9/11 GI Bill benefits, but eligibility is contingent on the number of days deployed on active duty orders; training and nonactivated days do not ordinarily count toward eligibility. Consequently, Guard or Reserve members may enroll in higher education believing they have adequate benefits to finance their educations. School certifying officials may bear the brunt of students' frustrations in this area even as they attempt to assist students with exploration of other options. In the case of payment issues arising from VA mistakes or processing schedules, student veterans' frustrations are more properly directed to the VA itself. The challenge for school certifying officials is to help students determine their eligibility up front and accurately while placing responsibility with the students for their interactions with VA staff.

As of fiscal year 2010, data about use of veterans' educational benefits demonstrated that Post-9/11 GI Bill benefits were more attractive to individuals who would otherwise qualify for Montgomery GI Bill or Reserve Education Assistance Program benefits: between fiscal years 2009 and 2010, Montgomery GI Bill beneficiaries decreased 31 percent and Reserve Education Assistance Program beneficiaries decreased 36 percent (U.S. Department of Veterans Affairs, 2010a). VA education benefits are not easy programs to understand. Student veterans must do what is necessary to identify the programs for which they are eligible. However, their decisions are only as good as the resources they find and comprehend; higher education professionals can assist them by providing accurate, reliable, easily accessible information (such as on web sites for student veterans) and guide them in the direction of VA benefits offices and resources.

Other Sources of Student Veteran Education Funding

If one major myth about education funding for veterans is that all veterans receive the same GI Bill benefits, another is that the GI Bill is the only type of educational funding available to veterans and active duty service members. In fact, additional programs exist for active duty members, Guard and Reserve members, future veterans, current veterans ineligible for GI Bill benefits, and veterans who elect to save their VA benefits for use later.

Some active duty and reserve component members may access tuition assistance programs that resemble corporate-sponsored education assistance programs for employees. In exchange for an extended service commitment, or sometimes simply by virtue of signing an initial contract, service members may be eligible for U.S. Department of Defense funding for educational purposes. These programs are frequently administered at military bases or command education centers and are usually processed through campus cashier or bursars' offices. Each branch of the armed forces has its own rules, including guidelines that differ based on pay levels within the branch, but institutional bursar staff members often know the types of tuition assistance used in the local area, especially because participating students are likely to be stationed at nearby military installations. Tuition assistance programs usually cover a portion of students' tuition and fees, meaning that students likely have some out-of-pocket costs each semester.

Like other students, service members and veterans may be eligible for federal financial aid and other forms of financial aid, and they may use those funds for any remaining expenses not covered by VA or U.S. Department of Defense educational assistance programs (U.S. Department of Veterans Affairs, 2011b). Therefore, early in the admissions process, student veterans and service members should be encouraged to complete the Free Application for Federal Student Aid (FAFSA) and apply for institutional funding and other scholarship opportunities. Currently, GI Bill payments are not treated as income in federal financial aid calculations, meaning that student veterans may be eligible to receive more financial assistance than they realize (U.S. Department of Veterans Affairs, 2011b). Lack of awareness about eligibility for financial aid beyond veteran and service member benefits extends to higher education professionals as well; for example, campus admissions representatives may fail to encourage students to apply for other forms of aid because they know the students have GI Bill benefits and do not realize the full scope of their eligibility.

Many states offer tuition assistance to members of National Guard units as enlistment incentives. Because National Guard units are funded by state budgets rather than federal budgets, tuition assistance may differ depending on the location. However, this benefit is usually processed through the same campus office that handles active duty tuition assistance programs. Additional National Guard enlistment incentives may include in-state tuition rates since members are essentially state government employees.

As one learns about approaches and resources to support student veterans, it is important to remember that campus Reserve Officers Training Corps (ROTC) programs are available to undergraduates who have never served in the military as well as prior enlisted veterans. However, only undergraduate degree holders are eligible for the commissioned officer corps of each branch of the military. Accordingly, high school graduates or GED holders who enlist are ordinarily not eligible for the officer corps until they complete four-year degrees. Under some circumstances, it is possible for enlisted members of the military to separate from active duty and pursue undergraduate degrees while completing ROTC obligations that lead to commissions. Enlisted service members may also be allowed to stay on active duty while pursuing their degrees full-time and completing ROTC requirements. Still other programs are tailored for Guard members to complete their enlistment obligations through participation in ROTC (U.S. Army, 2011). These programs may be viable options for students, and representatives of the ROTC units are able to provide specific details regarding opportunities. ROTC programs and incentives change often and are based on the current needs of that branch of service, so it is advisable for campus administrators to stay abreast of changes and updates in order to make appropriate referrals.

VA benefits and additional programs, some of which were described above, may be combined in some situations for enhanced benefits. For example, active duty members using tuition assistance who are eligible for Post-9/11 GI Bill benefits may use tuition assistance funds to cover the majority of their tuition bills and use the current "Top Up" program of the GI Bill to meet the rest of their tuition costs. In these cases, students use small proportions of their GI Bill benefits under this arrangement and can access the remaining balances after separating from active duty (U.S. Department of Veterans Affairs, 2010a).

One of the most important ways in which higher education administrators and faculty members can develop their understanding of VA education benefits is to foster relationships with their campuses' school certifying officials. These individuals are the best resources for gaining information about the benefits for which individual students may be eligible. Fortunately, much of the information students need to make informed decisions or to keep up-to-date with changes in policy is also available on the Internet, which allows faculty and staff to access the resources needed to educate themselves and to point students in the right direction. Much of the information, policies, and guidelines change frequently, and it is worthwhile to bookmark key web sites, subscribe to reliable listservs, and engage in relevant social media outlets in order to remain updated. A number of applicable web sites are listed at the end of this chapter.

Relationships with school certifying officials are merely the beginning of supporting student veterans on campus. By empowering more campus staff with up-to-date information and resources regarding the GI Bill and other programs, student veterans will be able to navigate the college experience more successfully. In partnership with other support efforts, VA educational benefits provide strong foundations from which student veterans may explore educational opportunities. Throughout the history of the GI Bill, campuses have attempted this type of holistic support to varying degrees of success, but always with the GI Bill as a driver of change and a foundation from which to expand. Student veteran support services that are in addition to the VA educational funding and are provided for by institutions of higher learning tend to expand when GI Bill benefits expand, and retract when benefits retract; thus, an understanding of the trends in GI Bill support, and staying abreast of changes, benefits higher education professionals who have interest in sustaining and improving those supplemental veteran services programs.

Conclusion

Although attitudes toward and support for the current wars in the Middle East in which the U.S. military has been engaged for the past decade will likely continue to change, as a nation there remains strong support for members of the military. Campus leaders, including those in student affairs units, have developed programs in efforts to assist student veterans with their transitions to and success in college. Fundamental to the success of those efforts is a commitment on the part of program administrators who appreciate the importance of the GI Bill's educational benefits for students. By volunteering to serve their country, student veterans are able to access a complex set of educational benefits. An important way for campus administrators to assist student veterans and service members to achieve their educational goals is to provide the information and contacts those students need so that they can obtain the benefits gained through their service.

While the nation, through the VA, attempts to serve those who have served all of us, colleges and universities have unique opportunities to help shape the educations and future livelihoods of millions of current and future veterans. Depending on the era and the social forces that shaped each time period, the VA and higher education have taken advantage of those opportunities to varying degrees. One widely held but dangerous belief is that providing funding for education is enough to ensure that student veterans will be successful. Indeed, relieving student veterans' financial worries is a remarkable and necessary statement of support, but educational funding is just a part of providing support for student veterans. GI Bill funding may make it possible for individual veterans to become college students, and more important, college graduates.

Resources

American Council on Education Military Programs
http://www.acenet.edu (use Programs and Services drop-down menu to select Military Programs)

This site provides policy and research documents related to serving veterans and military members in higher education. Transfer credit equivalency tables for military training are also included, and are considered the standard in this area.

Facebook
http://www.facebook.com/

Facebook pages are maintained by various groups and on a variety of topics, including Student Veterans of America, Iraq and Afghanistan Veterans of America, American Women Veterans, and the Post-9/11 GI Bill. Visit the U.S. Department of Veterans Affairs page for up-to-date information and to track current conversations on important topics for student veterans and service members.

NASPA Veterans Knowledge Community

http://www.naspa.org/kc/veterans/

This site provides information and resources from the greater student affairs community tailored to supporting student veterans on campus.

National Resource Directory

https://www.nationalresourcedirectory.gov/

This site provides holistic resources to support veterans on campus and in the community.

Twitter

http://twitter.com/

Follow @studentvets, @iava, @DeptVetAffairs, @USWomenVeterans for as-it-happens information and to keep in touch with the work veterans are doing on their own behalf.

U.S. Department of Veterans Affairs GI Bill Website

http://gibill.va.gov

This site offers a comprehensive overview of each of the GI Bill chapters as well as information on who is eligible and how to apply for benefits. Tools are available for comparing benefits and contact information for experts is provided. This is *the* resource for answers to questions regarding the GI Bill.

U.S. Department of Veterans Affairs "VAntage Point" Blog

http://www.blogs.va.gov/VAntage/

Written by VA staffers, this site offers updates, trends, and FAQs for matters related to veterans benefits. This site is not solely focused on education benefits; it is also a useful source of information about supporting the "whole" student veteran through VA resources.

References

Ackerman, R., DiRamio, D., & Mitchell, R. L. (2009). Transitions: Combat veterans as college students. In R. Ackerman & D. DiRamio (Eds.), *Creating a veteran-friendly campus: Strategies for transition and success.* New Directions for Student Services, 126, pp. 5–14. San Francisco: Jossey-Bass.

Alabama Department of Veterans Affairs. (2011). *Alabama GI dependents scholarship program* [web site]. Retrieved from http://www.va.state.al.us/laws.htm#GIBILL

Arnstein, G. (1981). *The vocational education study: Report on veterans education.* Washington, DC: National Institute of Education.

Bellafaire, J. (2006). *History highlight—Women veterans and the WWII GI Bill of Rights* [web site]. Retrieved from http://www.womensmemorial.org/H&C/History/historyhl.html

Campbell, P. (2009, October 15). *Written testimony on the status of implementing the Post-9/11 GI Bill: Hearing before the Committee on Veterans' Affairs, Subcommittee on Economic Opportunity, House of Representatives*. Retrieved from http://democrats.veterans.house.gov/hearings/Testimony_Print.aspx?newsid=485&Name=_Patrick__Campbell

DeBenedetti, C. (1990). *An American ordeal: The antiwar movement of the Vietnam War.* Syracuse, NY: Syracuse University Press.

DiRamio, D., & Jarvis, K. (2011). Veterans in higher education: When Johnny and Jane come marching to campus. *ASHE Higher Education Report, 37*(3). San Francisco: Jossey-Bass.

Hunt, J. B., Jr. (2006). Educational leadership for the 21st century. In. J. B. Hunt Jr., & T. J. Tierney (Eds.), *American higher education: How does it measure up for the 21st century?* (pp. 1–6). San Jose, CA: National Center for Public Policy and Higher Education. Retrieved from http://www.highereducation.org/reports/hunt_tierney/Hunt_Tierney.pdf

McBain, L. (2008). *When Johnny [or Janelle] comes marching home: National, state and institutional efforts in support of veterans' education.* Washington, DC: American Association of State Colleges and Universities.

McBain, L. (2009, November). *Implementing the Post-9/11 GI Bill: Lessons learned and emerging issues.* Washington, DC: American Association of State Colleges and Universities. Retrieved from http://www.congressweb.com/aascu/docfiles/pmnov09.pdf

Radford, A. W. (2009, July). *Military service members and veterans in higher education: What the new GI Bill may mean for postsecondary institutions.* Washington, DC: American Council on Education.

Rumann, C. B., & Hamrick, F. A. (2009). Supporting student veterans in transition. In R. Ackerman & D. DiRamio (Eds.), *Creating a veteran-friendly campus: Strategies for transition and success.* New Directions for Student Services, 126, pp. 25–34. San Francisco: Jossey-Bass.

Spaulding, D. J. (2000). The four major GI Bills: A historical study of shifting national purposes and the accompanying changes in economic value to veterans. (Doctoral dissertation). University of North Texas, Denton. Retrieved from http://digital.library.unt.edu/ark:/67531/metadc2692/m1/1/high_res_d/dissertation.pdf

Summerlot, J., Green, S.-M., & Parker, D. (2009). Student veterans organizations. In R. Ackerman & D. DiRamio (Eds.), *Creating a veteran-friendly campus: Strategies for transition and success.* New Directions for Student Services, 126, pp. 71–79. San Francisco: Jossey-Bass.

United States Army. (2011). *Army ROTC: Ways to attend* [web site]. Retrieved from http://www.goarmy.com/rotc/ways-to-attend.html

United States Department of Defense. (2009). *Post-9/11 GI Bill transferability fact sheet.* Washington, DC: Author. Retrieved from http://www.defense.gov/home/features/2009/0409_gibill/

United States Department of Defense. (2011). *Turbo Tap* [web site]. Retrieved from http://www.turbotap.org

United States Department of Veterans Affairs. (2009, November). *Born of contro-versy: The GI Bill of rights* [web site]. Retrieved from http://gibill.va.gov/benefits/history_timeline/index.html

United States Department of Veterans Affairs. (2010a). *Annual benefits report: FY 2010*. Washington, DC: Author. Retrieved from http://www.vba.va.gov/REPORTS/abr/2010_abr.pdf

United States Department of Veterans Affairs. (2010b). *Benefit comparison chart*. Washington, DC: Author. Retrieved from http://gibill.va.gov/documents/Benefit_Comparison_Charts.pdf

United States Department of Veterans Affairs. (2011a). *Benefits of the Yellow Ribbon program* [web site]. Retrieved from http://gibill.va.gov/benefits/post_911_gibill/yellow_ribbon_program.html

United States Department of Veterans Affairs. (2011b). *FAFSA and VA education benefits*. Washington, DC: Author. Retrieved from http://www.gibill.va.gov/documents/presentations/fafsa_and_va_education_benefits.pdf

VIGNETTE

Joshua Lang

Student, Shippensburg University

As I prepared to transition from my military service to college, I was very fearful of what to expect. What would life be like on the outside? How would I relate to other students as I began college? I had recently returned from a deployment from Afghanistan and faced many struggles. I felt as though I was still over there and I often snapped at people who did not share my views.

When I began college in January 2009, I had no friends to rely on and had no clue about what I needed to do to receive my GI Bill benefits. Finally, during orientation I was directed to the right office and was able to figure out everything I needed to do in order to receive my educational benefits. Although the institution's certifying official was able to inform me about all my benefits, she did not make me aware of all the other educational opportunities I was eligible for at the university.

I asked about scholarships, but she told me there were none available. It wasn't until later that I found out about other benefits and services I could apply for. I moved into my dorm room not knowing my roommate, who was 18, and found it very difficult to relate to him. But at the same time I was exposed to a whole new perspective on life.

I remember how excited I was the day before I would officially start college. After all of the hardships, I was finally getting the opportunity to fulfill my destiny. I woke up at 5:30 a.m., just as I did in the military, to prepare for the first day. I dressed in slacks and a buttoned shirt—prepared and ready to go. As I walked in to the college it was nothing like what I had expected. The stares I received (or felt) from other students gave me an empty feeling in my stomach. I counted the minutes until class was over and sat close to the door so I could leave as soon as class was dismissed.

It took me months to truly find myself as an individual, or to even open up and speak to my peers. I spent several months being a loner, not taking part in any other activities. One day I received an e-mail from Student Veterans of America (SVA) asking me if my school was affiliated with them, which we were not. I didn't realize until later, but at that moment my life and the lives of future veterans at my school would be changed forever.

I eventually started an SVA chapter at my school, which allowed me to meet other veterans who shared the same interests. Through this chapter our school now provides more efficient services that have made the transition a smoother process for student veterans. My dedication to veterans would lead me through the ranks of SVA and allow me to be a voice for student veterans in my state and around the nation.

Overall, I would say that transition for me was very difficult. Having no one to relate to often made going to classes a daunting experience. But through meeting other veterans who shared the same common bond, I have been able to enjoy my overall college experience. I am very delighted that my school now has an SVA chapter, which has ultimately made the college experience for student veterans more rewarding.

CHAPTER THREE

ACTIVATIONS, DEPLOYMENTS, AND RETURNS

Wade G. Livingston and Mark C. Bauman

During the Cold War, the U.S. government instituted defense policies that enabled Guard and Reserve personnel to heavily augment the United States' large standing army (Fautua, 1997); the end of conscription in 1973 (Selective Service System, 2003) and the changing nature of the GI Bill—a shift from a reward for service to a recruitment incentive—further solidified this Guard and Reserve augmentation. The United States military's current level of reliance on National Guard and Reserve troops has not been seen since the World War II (Doubler & Listman, 2007) and Korean War eras (Carter & Glastris, 2005). According to a U.S. Department of Defense (2012) news release dated April 4, 2012: "The total number currently on active duty from the Army National Guard and Army Reserve is 52,095; Navy Reserve, 4,668; Air National Guard and Air Force Reserve, 9,895; Marine Corps Reserve, 4,651, and the Coast Guard Reserve, 800" (para. 2). These numbers fluctuate with each round of deployments, activations, and deactivations. The college experience for National Guard and Reserve student service members is often characterized by constant transition. This state of flux is largely a result of the United States' most recent foreign interventions; the standing military has decreased in size and has utilized various methods to field the requisite level of personnel in theaters of operation (O'Hanlon, 2004). These methods include the activation and deployment of National Guard and Reserve personnel and the implementation of a mobilization scheme characterized by lengthy troop rotations and multiple deployments (O'Hanlon, 2004). The long-term nature of current foreign interventions and the smaller size of the U.S. armed forces mean that many service members who are also enrolled students at colleges and universities have been, or are likely to be, deployed more than once to a combat theater. Even one deployment can present transitional challenges, but multiple deployments create situations in which student service members must face additional rounds of transitions that may affect them personally, socially, and academically.

This chapter describes the military deployment process and the nature of the transition for student veterans before, during, and following a deployment. The transition into the college environment is highlighted, and implications and recommendations for student service members and higher education representatives and institutions are presented.

Military Processes and Student Service Members in Transition

Transitions navigated by National Guard and Reserve student service members begin with the enlistment decisions made by these individuals frequently, but not only, in response to national events, including foreign policy decisions and actions that involve mobilization of the armed forces. Consequently, service members who are students—referred to in this chapter as *student service members*—do not simply experience isolated or bounded transitions limited to, for example, withdrawing or reenrolling in college. Before they enter the activation or demobilization pipeline, student service members have already transitioned from initial enlistment to basic training; following basic training, many continue with more specialized, job-specific training.

All five branches of the armed forces provide a variety of initial intake, basic training, and specialized training sequences. Throughout this sequence of initial intake and military training, National Guard and Reserve personnel may also be enrolled in college. For example, a newly enlisted Air National Guard member could complete basic training the summer immediately before she enters college. This same student service member may then complete her first year of college and begin her specialized, job-specific training the following summer. In between these two summers, not only must the Airman—this term is used regardless of a person's sex or gender identity—successfully navigate the new college experience, she must also attend "drill" once per month at her assigned unit. For most branches, drill involves two to three days per month of training, education, field experience, or other activities designed to promote military preparedness and fluency with one's military "job." As this brief example demonstrates, transition is thus ongoing, even before the student service member enters the mobilization pipeline.

The constant transitions mean that student service members must not only navigate short or long, interconnected, and multifaceted transitions, but must also occupy two sometimes conflicting identities, those of *student* and *service member*. Once activated, and to be fully effective in their newly immersed military roles, student service members must shift their mindsets and principal identities away from that of college student. As they experience the next transition of deployment, they must cope with leaving family and friends while entertaining thoughts of the dangers of their forthcoming missions. Once their mobilization is complete, the subsequent transition they face is *demobilization* and return to civilian life. For increasing numbers of veterans and service members, this is followed by the transition of enrolling or reenrolling in college, where they further adjust to civilian life by refocusing as students. Though the length of any one deployment may vary, most range between 12 and 24 months; therefore, rather than a transition occurring in isolation, student service members essentially seek to negotiate an extended period of prolonged, often intense and complex transitions. Although there are commonalities in the experiences and challenges associated with the phases noted here, the transition experiences themselves may differ markedly among individual service members and veterans.

Student service members represent all five branches of the armed forces and a variety of affiliation statuses as military personnel or veterans, and also include officers and enlisted members at all ranks (see Appendix). Some student service members are active duty personnel who are returning to campus after recent deployments in the Middle East and elsewhere. Others are National Guard and Reserve personnel who may be activated to full-time military status at any time. This wide variety of personnel also suggests a wide variety of transitions. Former active duty student service members may have severed ties with the military upon completion of their enlistment contracts and enrolled in college using their GI Bill benefits. Other student service members who serve in National Guard and Reserve capacities may have experienced multiple cycles of activations, deployments, and returns. And still other student service members may be in the infancy of their military commitments, perhaps completing basic training and now waiting for the forthcoming summer and more specialized training. The aforementioned examples underscore that the type and number of transitions—as well as how the cycle(s) and associated transitions are experienced—will differ from individual to individual. The common thread, however, is that all student service members experience transitions and, as a result, will face some level of challenge as they navigate between the roles and identities of *student* and *service member*.

The Deployment Cycle

Before discussing activation, deployment, and return in depth, we provide an overview of the deployment cycle, a phrase that captures the overarching process that many National Guard and reserve student service personnel experience. As noted in the *Military Deployment Guide* (U.S. Department of Defense, 2011), the military defines certain terms (*deployment* and *activation*, for example) that do not convey the totality of the deployment cycle. This discussion of the deployment cycle as a whole sets the context for subsequent sections in which student service members' transitions are discussed in greater detail.

The deployment cycle applies to three subpopulations of military service members: active duty, National Guard/Reserve, and Individual Augmentee (service members who are activated individually). Active duty personnel are those service members who serve in the military full-time; it is their primary occupation. National Guard and Reserve personnel are service members who can be activated and federally mobilized to full-time military status. Individual Augmentees are personnel (including active duty, National Guard, and Reserve) who are transferred from a supporting command to a command authority (operational unit) by power of the secretary of defense and the president of the United States (Gortney, 2011). In essence, the cycles are very similar, with minor exceptions of, for example, National Guard/Reserve deployments and Individual Augmentee deployments. For National Guard, Reserve, and Individual Augmentee personnel, a demobilization phase is enacted where units and individuals transition to non–active duty status. For Individual Augmentee deployments, individual personnel may be deployed with little or no warning, thus shortening the overall deployment timeframe (this is discussed later in more detail) (U.S. Department of Defense, 2011).

Although there are some subtle differences regarding the three subpopulations mentioned above, the typical deployment cycle has four phases: *predeployment, deployment, postdeployment*, and *reintegration* (U.S. Department of Defense, 2011).

Predeployment. The goal of the *predeployment* phase is unit readiness. During this time, units engage in ongoing training, readiness activities, and medical evaluations. For personnel in the National Guard or Reserve, including those who are enrolled college students, the predeployment phase can last for years, especially during peacetime. It is only toward the end of this phase, when the "service member or unit is alerted for possible deployment" (U.S. Department of Defense, 2011, p. 5) that changes in that individual's regular life might occur. Although these changes can vary, once a unit receives orders to mobilize, personnel will attend required briefings and engage in specific, theater-oriented training and preparation activities. During this phase, the individual is generally at his or her home unit, though some relocation may occur (U.S. Department of Defense, 2011). For the bulk of this phase—especially in the early portions—enrolled student service members are generally advised not to withdraw from college. Once a unit is alerted, and certainly once a unit receives orders, decisions to withdraw, and specifically when to withdraw, can be made.

Prior to leaving their home bases, service members engage in a variety of often required activities intended to prepare them and their families for deployment. Service members ensure that their legal affairs are in order by creating and filing wills and other documentation. They update passports and ensure that emergency record data and family care plans are in place. Service members put their finances in order and designate where their pay will be delivered. National Guard and Reserve personnel complete the proper paperwork to ensure that their regular full-time civilian employment positions will be available upon their return. Finally, families engage in readiness activities, examples of which include learning about medical benefits for the family members who remain at home, readying the family finances, and developing an emergency contact plan (U.S. Department of Defense, 2011).

Deployment. Briefly, the *deployment* phase entails the physical movement of the unit to the area of operation. The area of operation can either be stateside or overseas (U.S. Department of Defense, 2011). This specific phase is discussed later in this chapter.

Postdeployment. The *postdeployment* phase occurs when the unit returns to its demobilization station; contingent upon individuals' normally assigned units, this station could be an entirely separate facility in a different part of the country (U.S. Department of Defense, 2011). During this phase, service members revisit many of the activities noted in the *predeployment* phase. They review their legal, administrative, and financial affairs and ensure that they are in order; additionally, they undergo medical and counseling evaluations. This is the period in which service members can assess their educational goals and begin to review their education benefits (U.S. Department of Defense, 2011).

Reintegration. *Reintegration* refers to the attempted return to normality. The U.S. Department of Defense (2011) noted that this is a difficult period for service members and their families. During this phase, service members are encouraged to be patient with relationships and roles that have changed. Moreover, service members are encouraged to pay special attention to signs of combat stress, posttraumatic stress disorder, relationship violence, and other issues that may arise (U.S. Department of Defense, 2011). Though there are services available—particularly through the VA—many student service members will negotiate this phase utilizing their own coping skills and the informal availability of friends, family, and other members of their units. The college or university, through its programs and outreach, can also offer support and assistance to enrolled veterans and service members at this time.

Understanding the four phases of the deployment cycle denoted by the U.S. Department of Defense (2011) is important for higher education professionals who assist student service members. As this cycle suggests, transitions abound and the cycle is tumultuous for service members and their families. The following sections focus on student service members' transitions through *activation*, *deployment*, and *return* more specifically, and discuss their navigation of corresponding roles and identities in greater detail.

Activation

Though individual student service members have unique transition scenarios, activation is a common transition that many National Guard and Reserve personnel must navigate. In military parlance, *activation* means "an order to active duty" to engage in "full-time duty in the active military service of the United States" (Gortney, 2011, p. 2). According to the U.S. Department of Defense Instructions (McGinn, 2010), military activation has four general components: (1) units receive an alert notification that foretells mobilization; (2) orders to active duty are disseminated; (3) reservists report for active duty; (4) reservists execute their orders and begin the mission. Additionally, the Department of Defense noted that Individual Ready Reservists (IRR) should have at least 30 days' notice to execute mobilization and activation orders (McGinn, 2010). The IRR includes those members who have fulfilled their base contracts, normally of four to six years, during which time they have completed monthly drills along with two to three weeks of required annual training. Members may then elect to transition to the IRR, during which time they are to maintain their basic readiness should they be needed. Though it may vary by contract, a typical IRR period is two years.

The implications of the U.S. Department of Defense Instructions should not be lost on higher education administrators and student support personnel: student service members could receive activation orders at any point during an academic term and, within 30 days, must be prepared to execute those orders. Furthermore, personnel who are classified as Individual Augmentees may have even smaller activation windows (U.S. Department of Defense, 2011). Complicating this quick turnaround time is that rumors of activation often precede the official notification from the military chain of command. Service members may feel pressured to make important life decisions in advance of official notification, as they fear that time spent waiting for official notification can actually worsen their situations and leave them with smaller windows of time to take action (Bauman, 2009). Thus, it is important for college administrators, staff, and faculty to realize that (a) student service members have to make quick, life-altering decisions, (b) these decisions are high-pressure events and are sometimes made with incomplete information, and (c) the military's activation timetable rarely matches neatly with the academic calendar and other institutional time markers.

The quick, life-altering decisions that must be made concern both educational issues and life circumstances. For example, a student service member who, upon hearing rumors of activation, has to determine if, or when, to drop classes. Coinciding with the class decision, the same student service member must decide whether to sign a lease or look to sublet the apartment. The interrelated myriad decisions concerning school and life both mirror and accentuate the delicate identity balance of *student* and *service member*. As Bauman (2009) explained, student service members, prior to either hearing rumors of activation or receiving activation orders, could more readily switch between the *student* and *service member* identities because college life and military life were neatly parceled: student service members were either in the classroom or fulfilling a once-a-month drilling obligation. Thus, while student service members transitioned between identities, the difficulty of the transitions was mitigated because the college and military experiences remained largely separate, and because the military obligations did not consume much time on a regular basis.

Student service members may be able to compartmentalize their college and military lives prior to activation but, once activated, college and military lives begin to collide. Bauman (2009) described the transition during this anticipatory period with the common military slang expression, "hurry up and wait." The activation period leading up to deployment can last months and, during that time, student service members begin to perceive the collision of two very different cultures. As the activation period commences, college and military cultural differences become increasingly palpable and student service members find it increasingly difficult to transition between *student* and *service member* due, in large part, to the military, which quickly immerses the individual. Thus, in the activation phase, the primary transition facing student service members is discernment of their *student service member* identities.

The activation phase is characterized by uncertainty, rumor, and identity confusion. As the next section explains, these same characteristics are very much a part of the deployment transition, too, albeit in a different manner. Bauman's analogy (2009) of "hurry up and wait" again applies to the deployment phase, as student service members are mobilized and begin to physically deploy to their posts.

Deployment

Following activation, the next transition student service members face is deployment. *Deployment*, as defined by the U.S. Department of Defense Instructions, is "the relocation of forces and material to desired operational areas" (McGinn, 2010, p. 105). Deployment does not imply an immediate transfer of the student service member into the theater of operation to which she or he may eventually be sent. Rather, the "relocation" of forces means that military personnel are mobilized stateside and begin the buildup for deployment. The result is that while student service members may have physically left their campuses, joined their units, and relocated to a mobilization point, they have not yet actually been sent to the locations of their missions.

The buildup to deployment brings with it many related transitions. By this point, student service members have left college life and family behind, and they begin focusing on their missions. However, they are still stateside and are faced with everyday reminders of their civilian and student lives. The experience is characterized by limbo, impatience, and again, "hurry up and wait." It is at this point, however, that student service members' navigation of *student* and *service member* identities fundamentally shift; the constant training and preparation (and desire to see this training put into practice) to undertake a specific mission forces them to actualize their military identities.

Bauman (2009) explained that the shift to *service member* identity occurs because of the depth and duration of deployment as a military experience; during deployment, student service members are fully immersed, perhaps for the first time, in protracted military activity. The depth and length of deployment demands that student service members focus solely on their identities as military service members. This is not to say that student service members forget about their lives outside of the military; on the contrary, many external pressures abound and accompany student service members through their deployments. However, the predominant focus of deployment is preparing for missions as military units.

Preparing for the mission as a unit implies that camaraderie is established among military personnel, intensifying the experience of the service member identity (Bauman, 2009). The connection with fellow military personnel creates a unique and powerful bond that also reinforces student service members' military identities. Bahraini et al. (2008) noted that service members overwhelmingly emphasized "a sense of connection with other military personnel" (p. 219). Wong, Kolditz, Millen, and Potter (2003) found that service members' most frequent description regarding combat motivation was "fighting for my buddies" (p. 9), and posited that the essence of this statement was "social cohesion—the emotional bonds between soldiers" (p. 10).

The military social cohesion and immersive deployment experience reinforce the intensity of the military identity for student service members. Ultimately, the deployment experience is highly impactful, to the point that student service members' military identities and the bonds formed with other service members remain when they demobilize and return to their campuses. As the next section explains, student service members who subsequently either enroll or reenroll in college draw upon the military experience of deployment, which can simultaneously be an aid and a hindrance in their returns to college.

Return

Before student service members return to college, they must demobilize as military personnel. The U.S. Department of Defense Instructions defined *demobilization* as the transition "to a peacetime configuration while maintaining national security'' (McGinn, 2010, p. 103). The notion of "peacetime configuration" may seem oxymoronic to student service members considering the United States' commitment to the War on Terror. The question of whether they actually transition into "peacetime" is particularly pertinent for National Guard and Reserve personnel who have come to play significant roles in the Iraq and Afghanistan conflicts because the active duty military is engaged in other missions throughout the world (O'Hanlon, 2004).

Because of the nature of U.S. foreign policy and the immersive experience of deployment, student service members retain military mindsets as they return to campus. Although studying may have replaced military activities as their primary efforts, student service members may still identify more as *service members* than as *students*, which can lead to role and identity conflict and confusion (Bauman, 2009). Rumann and Hamrick (2010) explained that student service members experienced incongruities between their military and academic lives, enacted aspects of their service member roles during college, and expressed lingering stress and anxiety stemming from their deployments.

Role and identity confusion intensify as student service members demobilize and prepare to return to campus. Once back on campus, they face a new series of transitions that must be navigated. Academically, student service members must either start afresh or pick up where they left off; in either scenario there are challenges. Livingston (2009) reported that student service members complained of forgetting academic concepts during their deployments. Additionally, some student service members noted that degree programs had changed, and they had to adjust to new curricula and sometimes new sets of degree requirements (Livingston, 2009).

Accompanying the academic challenges are social challenges. Returning student service members have developed deep bonds with other military personnel during their deployments, and the longing for military kinship endures when they return to campus (Bauman, 2009). Livingston (2009) found that student service members selectively disclosed their military identities to other service members and utilized fellow student service members as social and support conduits. This kinship was important because the social networks that student service members had prior to deployment did not exist in the same ways when they returned; friends had graduated and student service members' mindsets did not always mesh with those of their nonmilitary student peers (Livingston, 2009).

The lingering military mindset (Bauman, 2009; Livingston, 2009; Livingston, Havice, Cawthon, & Fleming, 2011; Rumann & Hamrick, 2010) could be both an asset and a hindrance to student service members' navigation of reenrollment. For example, returning student service members regarded themselves as more mature than their student peers (Livingston, 2009; Livingston and colleagues, 2011; Rumann & Hamrick, 2010). Their increased maturity was an asset in that it helped student service members prioritize their schoolwork and focus on the academic experience. However, increased maturity could also be a social hindrance, as student service members expressed difficulty relating to nonmilitary student peers and understanding their mindsets. Similarly, returning student service members emphasized autonomy and "can-do" attitudes because of their military experiences (Livingston, 2009). Autonomy and "can-do" attitudes can be assets as student service members demonstrated academic commitment, perseverance, and resilience. However, these characteristics can be hindrances when student service members put a great deal of pressure on themselves as individuals to persist without tapping into many of the institutional support structures available to them.

Student service members' military experiences, mindsets, and identities markedly affect their transitions when returning to campus. Indeed, student service members' navigation of their *student* and *service member* identities is the central transition theme throughout activation, deployment, and return. Although individual student service members may experience unique transitions because of their own circumstances, the common thread is identity navigation; understanding this concept allows higher education administrators, staff, and faculty to view the transition as a long, interconnected, inherently complex negotiation of roles, processes, and cultures. The next section describes the nature of this transition and details a number of specific experiences that student service members reconcile within their student and service member lives.

The Nature of the Transition

The previous sections concerning activation, deployment, and return touched broadly on the situations that student service members face when they are called to serve, are deployed to theaters of operation, and return to college. However, in order to understand more fully the scope and effect of these transitions, it is important to contextualize the transitions in two key ways. First and foremost, the transitions from activation through deployment to return should be regarded as ongoing, inherently complicated transitions rather than as series of disconnected transitions and events. Second, the transitions should be viewed as containing elements at both the personal and environmental levels, as student service members simultaneously navigate multiple identity roles and institutional policies, procedures, and cultures. Ultimately, these two points, the ongoing transitions and the bureaucratic and personal nature of the transitions, better capture the student service member experience and explain why student service members exhibit military culture in the college environment. This section presents the bureaucratic and personal nature of the complex transitions in greater detail. In addition, we provide a thematic overview of research findings concerning student service members' transitions and comment on Goodman, Schlossberg, and Anderson's theory of adult transitions (2006), which is the theoretical lens that many researchers have used to conceptualize the student service member experience in college.

The Dual Nature of the Transition: Environmental and Personal

The student service member experience in college is characterized by a simultaneous navigation of bureaucratic and personal transitions that are interconnected and highly impactful.

Environmental Transitions. Environmental transitions are those in which student service members must negotiate both military and educational systems and processes. These transitions begin prior to activation and deployment for many student service members who serve in National Guard and Reserve roles. National Guard and Reserve personnel accept obligations for regular drill, service, and training, and must prioritize these obligations even as they are enrolled as full-time students. For example, final examination schedules—especially those that extend into the weekend—may conflict with drill or training requirements; student service members may need to request from instructors alternate final exam dates and times (Livingston, 2009).

Preactivation environmental transitions require a great deal of coordination and communication among multiple constituents. Timely coordination and communication becomes extremely important when student service members are activated and receive deployment orders. They must then begin to work with their institutions on several levels to withdraw from school. If they live in campus housing, student service members must initiate contact with the housing or residence life office to arrange prorated fee refunds and appropriate checkout processes from their campus residences. They must work with representatives in undergraduate studies or the graduate school, and sometimes with each of their instructors, to withdraw from classes without penalty. Finally, they need to collaborate with the campus Veterans Affairs certifying official to clarify their periods of eligibility to receive educational benefits. According to the U.S. Department of Veterans Affairs (Veterans Affairs or VA) (2011), student service member benefits are extended by the duration of the deployment and an additional four-month period.

Ongoing, high levels of communication between student service members and their institutions are also critical as student service members begin to demobilize and plan their returns to campus. For example, some student service members informally navigate the anticipated environmental transitions toward the end of their deployments, such as beginning the readmissions process while still overseas, or communicating with professors, academic advisors, and Veterans Affairs certifying officials in attempts to gather as much information as possible prior to reenrollment (Livingston, 2009).

There is a great deal of pressure on student service members during this time. Many want to resume their educational pursuits at the earliest possible date; however, demobilization and return schedules are not necessarily congruent with institutional calendars and deadlines. This misalignment can result in even lengthier separations from college work. For example, Livingston (2009) found that during demobilization, some student service members initiated readmission paperwork, enrolled for classes, and worked with their schools' certifying officials to reactivate their benefits, only to find that their returns to campus would be delayed by unforeseen military bureaucratic processes and timetable changes. These unanticipated changes cause many student service members to have high degrees of anxiety and force them to scramble to successfully reenroll. A range of individual efforts undertaken by student service members must all be successful for them to reenroll in college quickly, including requesting late starts with the various course instructors, working with academic advisors to alter class schedules if instructors do not permit delayed starts, negotiating late move-in dates with university housing if they reside in campus facilities, attempting to secure off-campus housing in what could be already saturated housing markets, and finally, reasserting their intents to reenroll with Veterans Affairs certifying officials.

The high level of anxiety that stems from environmental transitions does not dissipate when student service members return to campus. Upon their reenrollment, student service members must obtain and continue to show proof of their service and their matriculation in order to receive educational benefits; this entails (as noted earlier) constant communication with the military, the U.S. Department of Veterans Affairs, and the campus Veterans Affairs certifying officials. Student service members may also present military transcripts detailing coursework and training that they completed during their service; some institutions readily accept certain military offerings while other institutions have procedures in place through which student service members can "test out" of courses. Either circumstance entails navigation of yet another bureaucratic process in order to receive academic credit for the earned military credits.

Student service members who have been wounded physically or psychologically must find appropriate care and ensure that their Veterans Affairs health care benefits can be applied to cover treatment costs. However, if campus health care facilities and programs for enrolled students are inadequate or do not accept student service members' health care benefits, student service members must travel to Veterans Affairs care facilities and undertake additional navigation processes of coordinating health care appointments with their academic schedules. In addition, for returning National Guard and Reserve personnel, the return to campus is accompanied by resuming their work with academic advisors and instructors to ensure that they can fulfill their drill and academic requirements.

Whether prior to activation or upon their return to campus, the sheer amount of environmental flux alone means that student service members' transitions are time-intensive, can be highly complicated, and often very stressful. In many ways, however, student service members are only in control of portions of these transitions. Each time a contact is made, each time a request for late enrollment is submitted, or a reactivation of benefits is initiated, faculty and staff within the college or university must also do their parts. If student service members' needs are tabled, forgotten, or otherwise delayed due to slow or no action, those individuals risk further delay in their returns to college. Moreover, these environmental transitions are only half of the equation; student service members must also navigate simultaneous personal transitions.

Personal Transitions. Personal transitions require student service members to navigate their identities and their relationships with others. Similar to environmental transitions, the navigation of personal transitions begins prior to activation and deployment; student service members start to negotiate their *student* and *service member* identities when they first enlist. By merely joining the armed forces, student service members adopt military identities for themselves. And these new identities can, at times, compete with other salient identities—in particular, college student identities. At times, they align, as in the case of college students organizing to form student-military organizations. But at other times they diverge, as when drill or annual training requirements mandate student service members' attendance.

Apart from the competition between identities, adopting new military identities inspires other personal transitions. Student service members begin to make new friends who are service members. They contemplate how their military service will affect their personal lives, and they begin to understand the gravity of their military commitment, an impact that becomes more apparent when student service members are activated and deployed. As they prepare to deploy, student service members have to start saying their good-byes to family members and friends. The bureaucratic process of withdrawing from school is accompanied by a type of social withdrawal through which student service members begin to detach from college friends, other students in their majors, and organizations of which they are members. This social withdrawal can include lingering feelings of sadness and anxiety that carry into deployment.

During deployment, student service members, like all military personnel, cope with feelings of homesickness and fear (U.S. Department of Defense, 2011). They develop even closer bonds with their comrades-in-arms and experience grief and loss when close friends are injured or die in combat (Hoge, 2010). Student service members may maintain communication with family members and nonmilitary friends, but these relationships may seem surreal or alien to them during their deployments (U.S. Department of Defense, 2011). In effect, student service members exist on very different identity planes during this time, and their *service member* identities clearly predominate.

The two planes of personal identity and existence are brought into conflict when student service members demobilize and return to campus. During the demobilization process, student service members begin to leave intense friendships and the now-familiar highly structured, hierarchical military culture behind. When they return to campus and attempt to reconnect with family members and college friends, they often find that those connections and relationships are difficult to manage and reengage (Bauman, 2009). Deployed student service members perform specific roles within focused missions and rigid environments, and find it difficult upon their return to rekindle a variety of roles and relationships within the much more amorphous and loosely structured environments of civilian life and college. They have to manage multiple roles, such as those of spouse, parent, family member, friend, and student in the absence of structure and orders.

Student service members experience bureaucratic and personal pressures, hardships, and transitions prior to activation and throughout deployment, demobilization, and the return to campus. When compared with the bureaucratic transitions, the personal transitions of student service members may not be as visible to higher education administrators, staff, and faculty—especially those who are not directly or personally involved with student service members. The next section further contextualizes student service members' transitions using findings from current research directly related to this population. Furthermore, the section highlights specific transition themes found in current research and offers analysis and critiques of the theoretical concepts used to generate these themes and findings.

Research Findings: Thematic Overview

Beginning in 2008 with DiRamio, Ackerman, and Mitchell's study of combat service members returning to the classroom, much of the current literature has highlighted student service members' transitions using various components of Goodman, Schlossberg, and Anderson's theory of adult transition (2006). DiRamio and colleagues (2008) used Schlossberg, Lynch, and Chickering's Moving In, Moving Through, Moving Out (1989) model of adult transition as a theoretical lens to describe service members' transitions from the military to college. The researchers explained how student service members moved into the military by joining, being called up, and serving overseas; how they moved through the military by seeing or engaging in combat, experiencing memorable events, and expressing desire to earn college credit; how they moved out of the military with the aid of transition programs, academic preparation, and the return home; and how they then moved into college by blending in, connecting with peers, working with the campus VA office, and several other actions. DiRamio and colleagues (2008) determined that a holistic process centered on identification, orientation, and mentoring of enrolled student service members was needed to assist individuals in navigating transitions.

Following the work of DiRamio and colleagues (2008), several doctoral dissertations used components of Goodman and colleagues' theory (2006) to further the body of research on student service members' transitions.

Livingston (2009) utilized four broad coping categories—"situation," "self," "supports," and "strategies," commonly referred to as the *4 S's*— as a lens to understand how student service members navigated and coped with academic and social transitions following reenrollment. In general, Livingston found that student service members wanted to be back in school; had a strong sense of self, maturity, and autonomy; relied more on informal social support structures consisting of fellow service members than on institutional support services; and that, typically, navigation of and coping with reenrollment was an isolated, individual experience. Rumann (2010) also used the *4 S's* and Schlossberg's theory of transition (Goodman et al., 2006) as a lens to understand how service members coped with and experienced reenrollment in the community college setting. Rumann explained that service members exhibited increased maturity and altered worldviews, and that a primary transition was renegotiating identities between student and service member. Bauman (2009) created a three-phased model that reflected the mobilization process and the subsequent challenges experienced by student service members.

Recent research concerning student service members' transitions has yielded several themes. For the purposes of this chapter, the following themes are explored in more detail: (a) student service members' navigation of dual identities; (b) student service members' articulation of military and academic cultural differences; and (c) the ways in which student service members cope with the transitions from activation to return.

Navigating Identity: Student or Service Member? Several researchers found that student service members' military experiences are inevitably parts of their identities (Bauman, 2009; DiRamio et al., 2008; Livingston, 2009; Livingston et al., 2011; Rumann, 2010; Rumann & Hamrick, 2010). DiRamio and colleagues (2008) and Livingston (2009) discussed various aspects of student service members' desires to blend in when returning to college. This discussion was advanced by Bauman (2009), Rumann (2010), and Rumann and Hamrick (2010), which created a clearer picture of student service members' conceptions of self.

DiRamio and colleagues (2008) noted that student service members articulated desires to blend in and be college students. Similarly, Livingston (2009) found that service members very selectively disclosed their military experiences to others because they wanted to be known as college students rather than as student service members. The implication of these findings is important: for some student service members, leaving behind the military experience and self-identifying as college students is an important step in the transition process. DiRamio and colleagues (2008) and Livingston (2009) found that service members accomplished blending in through various methods, such as not talking about their military experiences, not speaking out in class, and adopting civilian dress. However, Livingston (2009) found that some service members attempted to blend in, yet still displayed their military affiliations. The displays were often subtle in the form of unit T-shirts or military-issued backpacks, and these cues allowed current or former service members to identify one another while frequently escaping the notice of nonmilitary students.

The subtle display of military affiliation by the very student service members who were trying to blend in can imply that their military identities remain important. The importance of the interaction of military identity and student identity was more thoroughly examined by Bauman (2009) and Rumann and Hamrick (2010). Their examinations highlighted a coexistence of student and military identities and explained how these identities interacted. Bauman (2009) explained how student service members' *service member* identities became increasingly predominant once student service members were activated, and especially when they were immersed into military culture during deployment. Rumann and Hamrick (2010) explained how identity renegotiation was difficult for some returning student service members as they searched for a middle ground of identity in which to engage and interact.

Academic Versus Military Culture. Closely related to student service members' navigation of identity are the cultural differences between the military and higher education; as a result, the transition is "less structured, more individualized, may take a little longer, and can be frustrating" (Student Veterans of America, 2011a). The transition back and forth from the loosely structured environment of a college campus to the rigidly structured military environment can be difficult for many service members (Livingston, 2009; Rumann & Hamrick, 2010). Many student service members characterized college culture as loose, independent, and self-directed, whereas the military was characterized by its rigidity, structure, formality, conformity, and uniformity (Livingston, 2009). It is difficult for student service members to transition from environments in which they were told what to do, when to do it, and how to do it to environments in which the command structure has been replaced by much more indistinct organizational infrastructures. Similarly, it is quite a challenge when student service members are activated and must quickly negotiate time-sensitive service obligations while still in school.

Another important aspect of military and academic cultural differences is the variance between unit and individual mentality. The military's formal grouping of units and training conveys that military personnel are more focused on unit and mission than they are on individual experiences; the college environment is quite the opposite. During activation and deployment, student service members must realize that their individuality is not valued in the same way it was in college; conversely, when returning, student service members have to understand that the unit structure will not be in place to aid them in their transitions.

Coping with Transition. Because the formal military unit is not in place on college campuses, student service members utilize other sources of support when navigating reenrollment. Often, they create their own units in the form of campus-based student service member organizations or informal groups of student service member peers with whom they associate. A consistent theme in the research is that student service members utilize other service members to help them navigate transitions. Moreover, their military mentalities can be a coping mechanism; in the military, student service members learn the importance of perseverance and individual will, two factors that motivate them to achieve their educational goals (Livingston, 2009).

Although perseverance and individual determination can be assets, they can also be detriments. Livingston (2009) found that student service members' lingering military mentalities could also be counterproductive to the successful navigation of reenrollment. For example, student service members can sometimes be both proud and stubborn; they may attempt to suffer through transitions in isolation because they are taught in the military to quietly endure and figure things out for themselves. Additionally, student service members may have difficulty making new connections with nonmilitary peers that could be beneficial to them both socially and academically.

Schlossberg's Theory as a Lens. Recent literature regarding student service members' transitions has drawn overwhelmingly from Goodman and colleagues' theory of adult transition (2006). More specifically, researchers have used the *4 S's* to interpret how student service members cope with transition. The use of this theoretical perspective is helpful, but it is also necessary to briefly acknowledge potential limitations of this theory.

Goodman and colleagues' theory of adult transition (2006) is appropriate in that it encourages researchers to consider the altered roles, relationships, and assumptions that student service members experience as they transition through activation, deployment, and reenrollment. Additionally, the *4 S's* offer context as to how student service members cope with change. From this standpoint, Goodman and colleagues' theory is pertinent because it (a) highlights the continual and complex nature of navigating transitions, (b) illustrates common coping strategies adults use to mitigate challenges associated with transitions, and (c) explains the phenomenon of student service member transition through a lens that is applicable to any adult transition. In short, this theoretical perspective offers an easily understood and highly relatable theory through which campus constituents can begin to understand student service members' transitions and challenges.

Aspects of Goodman and colleagues' theory (2006) may, at the same time, contain certain limitations. For example, because the theory is applicable to adult populations in general, it may lack the specificity needed to encompass the unique nature of the student service member experience. The paramount transition in student service members' experiences is navigation of identity, so a companion theoretical focus on identity development or constructions would be important to include in order to understand the nature of these transitions more fully. Thus, Goodman and colleagues' theory of adult transitions and its emphasis on altered roles, relationships, and assumptions provide good starting points for understanding transitions in general, but researchers should also examine student service members' identity development as a precursor or a companion focus in understanding their transitions.

Whether looking at student service members' identities, their perceptions of military and academic cultural differences, or their coping strategies, it is important to remember that contemporary military personnel policies have resulted in more service members' experiencing deployment and reenrollment alone or in small groups. In these situations, natural or sizable support networks may not be in place to aid individuals in their transitions. Further complicating this challenge, most higher education administrators, staff, and faculty members do not have military backgrounds or experiences. Clear communication and coordination is needed among military and higher education constituents who may otherwise have little in common when it comes to military culture, experiences, and identity. This lesson is reasserted in the next section regarding implications for student service members and institutions.

Implications for Student Service Members and Institutions

Student service members and higher education representatives have responsibilities to ensure students' successful navigation of the military-educational transition. This section provides practical observations and recommendations that both constituent groups can apply as they attempt to mitigate the challenges of the student service member transition. In addition, the authors highlight some recommended practices that are designed to assist service members in transition.

Implications for Student Service Members

Whether enrolling for the first time or reenrolling after deployments, student service members transitioning from the military into college can take steps that will help them successfully navigate their collegiate experiences. First and foremost, developing understandings of institutional policies and guidelines related to matriculation and withdrawal and identifying institutional resource persons will allow service members to more readily navigate their institutions and ensure their continued good standings with respect to enrollment, health benefits, housing, and degree progress.

Student service members should seek one another out for support and practical assistance. The rationale for this activity is simple: student service members are the real experts on their transitions, and through their own experiences, they may have useful knowledge to help each other navigate deployments and reenrollments. Moreover, if student veterans connect with one another, they can become a more visible population on campus and can better advocate for shared needs and priorities.

Although student service members can learn the bureaucracy and connect with each other on campus, they need to evaluate whether or not they are ready to attend college prior to enrolling (or reenrolling). Perhaps more than anything else, this self-assessment of readiness is vital to student service members' abilities to successfully navigate these transitions. They need to have conversations with fellow veterans who have attended college to garner their insight; they need to discuss college enrollment or reenrollment with their family members and evaluate their levels of support at home; and, finally, they need to meet with institutional administrators and agents to gauge their comfort and "fit" with the institutions.

Implications for Institutions

In addition to acknowledging the growing presence of service members on campus and reaching out to them, institutional administrators should establish clear lines of communication to assist student service members with matriculation as they navigate institutional bureaucracy, both before enrollment begins and during their tenures on campus.

Prior to enrollment, institutions should clearly communicate to prospective student service members all of the policies and procedures related to this duality. For example, included in this material should be information about policies related to enrollment and withdrawal due to military obligations, refunds in response to mobilization, academic course make-ups for service personnel who depart mid-semester, and individual class absences for drill or other nondeployment military obligations. However, institutions' efforts should clearly transcend the administrative realm. Colleges and universities should consider identifying and training faculty and staff who are committed to fully assisting these student service members; those individuals should then be actively promoted to the campus service members, thus establishing clear and accessible networks of support for these students. Further, institutions should clearly identify the services that are available to service members and educate key personnel about the needs and challenges of student service members. Communication should not cease during student service members' deployments. Rather, institutions should initiate and maintain communication with student service members during their deployments and prior to their returns to campus; this will assure service members that they are valued by their institutions and that their institutions are dedicated to their success as students. Furthermore, ongoing communication may help student service members retain senses of their *student* identities during the separation, and equip them to reengage as students upon their return.

Recommended Practices for Assisting Student Service Members in Transition

As this chapter has shown, student service members' transitions are complicated and would be better facilitated by greater knowledge, communication, and cooperation among the multiple constituencies involved in these students' experiences. The following list of recommended practices provides examples of collaborative institutional approaches that can assist student service members' navigations of transitions related to activation, deployment, and return. The examples are derived from the authors' own research on student service members and veterans as well as their work with student service members. Many of these recommended practices are also discussed in *Creating a Veteran Friendly Campus: A Guide for College and University Administrators* (Student Veterans of America, 2011b).

Identify and Track Student Service Members

Institutions should create systems for identifying, counting, and tracking student service members who withdraw and reenroll. Doing so will provide more complete pictures of the size and scope of this population and enable institutions to make more informed decisions about additional service offerings related to withdrawal, reenrollment, and other needs and experiences unique to student service members. Establishing these systems should be joint efforts between admissions offices and VA certifying officials, as these offices have initial, and perhaps regular, contact with prospective and enrolled service members. Although student service members often attempt to blend in and may resist self-identifying to peers, this administrative practice will maximize the likelihood that enrolled service members can be identified and reports can be generated about relative trends and individuals' progress.

Formulate Dedicated Service Member Orientation Sessions

Because the needs and experiences of student service members differ in fundamental ways from those of their nonmilitary student peers, it can be beneficial to design and offer designated orientation sessions for enrolling service members. These sessions should focus on building awareness of supports and infrastructure, and introduce service members to critical resource persons on campus as well as currently enrolled student service members, thus providing an organic means for new students to initiate friendships and connections. It is useful to have financial aid representatives, VA certifying officials, Reserve Officers Training Corps (ROTC) detachment commanders, service member faculty and staff members, and current student service members in attendance. For campuses with notable military heritages, overviews or tours of military monuments, traditions, and celebrations are appropriate.

Create Student Service Member "University Seminar" Course Section(s)

Combat to College: A Transition Guide for Veterans (Student Veterans of America, 2011a) noted that student service members should ease into classes, take courses that tap into a variety of their skills, get to know key constituents on campus, and begin to break down barriers between themselves and other students. Especially if colleges or universities offer first-year seminar experiences for newly enrolling students, designating one or more sections for student service members would allow them to gather and examine topics of special interest and relevance for service members. University seminar courses could serve as excellent follow-up programs to student service member orientation programs by affording student service members opportunities to continue to identify important institutional contacts. Seminar content can be tailored to emphasize the identification and building of support networks, and seminars can allow student service members to make social connections and help one another navigate institutional bureaucracies.

Establish Military Safe Zones

Van Dusen (2011) noted education as a critical component for institutions interested in creating veteran-friendly campuses. Accordingly, he suggested the formulation of "Green Zones," veteran-friendly spaces where student service members can connect with staff members who are designated as "allies" and have been educated on student service members' needs. Taken more broadly, institutions can enact programs similar to this through which personnel can increase their knowledge about student service members and serve as additional support resources. This practice helps connect student service members to key bureaucratic offices, and moreover, provides additional social connections on campus. Further, as student service members constantly transition from one culture to the next, these Green Zones can be readily identified as stable and consistent outlets for guidance and assistance delivered by committed members of the campus community. After a two year stop-out from college, a student service member's friends may have graduated and moved on, but personnel identified as Green Zones have remained connected through the deployment and will be there through the return and reintegration process.

Create Pre- and Postdeployment Checklists

Checklists are one key feature of military culture that student service members readily understand. The creation of easy-to-follow, step-by-step checklists that explain withdrawal procedures and time frames as well as enrollment and reenrollment requirements (with relevant contact persons and offices noted for each checklist item) can help smooth the bureaucratic processes student service members must navigate at crucial junctures of their college careers. Because of their direct experiences with these processes, student service members themselves would be excellent sources of information in the creation of such checklists.

Maintain Connections During Deployment

A final practice that institutions can enact is keeping open communication lines with student service members during their deployments. Student service members may have Internet access at certain points of their deployments, and institutions can reach out to deployed service members with campus news and updates as well as information pertinent to return and reenrollment. As one of Livingston's (2009) respondents noted, e-mail contact with an academic advisor during his deployment to the Middle East was a welcome reminder of home and allowed the student service member to prepare for reenrollment in advance of his return.

Conclusion

Although the transitions experienced by student service members are multiple, complex, and protracted, one central theme in these transitions is the navigation of two primary identities: *service member* and *student*. It is vital that higher education staff, faculty, and administrators understand that student service members are challenged to balance these identities in addition to navigating both personal and bureaucratic transitions and processes. Together, institutions and student service members are responsible for ensuring successful transitions out of college and the subsequent reenrollments. Communication and clarity are vital components. Institutions should clearly communicate processes and procedures (and be prepared to make warranted exceptions to these processes in unusual circumstances), and student service members should learn, actively engage, and communicate with key administrative personnel. Moreover, student service members themselves—as experts regarding transition processes—should seek out and assist each other.

Institutions can implement recommended practices to enable smoother transitions for student service members. Although some of these recommendations may require resources in the form of time and personnel, others do not require extra funding. Finally, all institutional constituents—student service members included—should understand that successful transitions require partnership, collaboration, and communication. Ongoing education and awareness of student service members' needs and challenges is equally important. If all stakeholders make commitments to educate and learn from each other, the challenges student service members face during their college transitions can be mitigated.

Resources

Student Veterans of America, *Combat to College: A Guide for the Transitioning Student Veteran*
   http://www.studentveterans.org/resourcelibrary/documents/ Combat_to_College_Guide.pdf

Student Veterans of America, *Creating a Veteran Friendly Campus: A Guide for College and University Administrators*
   http://www.studentveterans.org/resourcelibrary/documents/ CreatingaVeteranFriendlyCampus_AGuideforCollegeandUniversity Administrators.pdf

Student Veterans of America, *How to Start an SVA Chapter*
   http://www.studentveterans.org/resourcelibrary/documents/ HowtoStartanSVAChapter.pdf

U.S. Department of Defense, *Dictionary of Military and Associated Terms*
   http://www.dtic.mil/doctrine/new_pubs/jp1_02.pdf

U.S Department of Defense, *Military Deployment Guide*
   http://www.militaryhomefront.dod.mil/12038/Project%20 Documents/MilitaryHOMEFRONT/Service%20Providers/ Deployment/2011_DeploymentGuide.pdf

U.S Department of Defense, *U.S. Military Rank Tables*
   Enlisted: http://www.defense.gov/about/insignias/enlisted.aspx
   Officers: http://www.defense.gov/about/insignias/officers.aspx

References

Bahraini, N., Brenner, L. A., Betthauser, L. M., Cornette, M. M., Gutierrez, P. M., & Staves, P. M. (2008). A qualitative study of potential suicide risk factors in returning combat veterans. *Journal of Mental Health Counseling, 30*, 211–225.

Bauman, M. (2009). *Called to serve: The military mobilization of undergraduates.* (Doctoral dissertation). The Pennsylvania State University, State College. Available from ProQuest Digital Dissertations. (AAT 3380873)

Carter, P., & Glastris, P. (2005). All-volunteer recruitment is not supplying enough troops. In V. Wagner (Ed.), *Military draft* (pp. 42–52). Detroit: Thomsen Gale.

DiRamio, D., Ackerman, R., & Mitchell, R. L. (2008). From combat to campus: Voices of student-veterans. *NASPA Journal, 45*(1), 73–102.

Doubler, M. D., & Listman, J. W. (2007). *The National Guard: An illustrated history of America's citizen-soldiers* (2nd ed.). Washington, DC: Potomac.

Fautua, D. T. (1997). The "long pull" army: NSC 68, the Korean War, and the creation of the Cold War U.S. Army. *The Journal of Military History, 61*(1), 93–120.

Goodman, J., Schlossberg, N. K., & Anderson, M. L. (2006). *Counseling adults in transition: Linking practice with theory.* New York: Springer.

Gortney, W. E. (2011, May 15). *Department of Defense dictionary of military and associated terms (joint publication 1–02).* Washington, DC: United States Department of Defense. Retrieved from http://www.dtic.mil/doctrine/new_pubs/jp1_02.pdf

Hoge, C. W. (2010). *Once a warrior, always a warrior: Navigating the transition from combat to home.* Guilford, CT: Globe Pequot.

Livingston, W. G. (2009). *Discovering the academic and social transitions of re-enrolling student veterans at one institution: A grounded theory.* (Doctoral dissertation). Clemson University, Clemson, South Carolina. Available from ProQuest Digital Dissertations. (AAT 3355150)

Livingston, W. G., Havice, P. A., Cawthon, T. W., & Fleming, D. S. (2011). Coming home: Student veterans' articulation of college re-enrollment. *Journal of Student Affairs Research and Practice, 48*(3), 315–331.

McGinn, G. H. (2010, February 4). *Department of Defense instruction number 1235.12.* Washington, DC: United States Department of Defense. Retrieved from http://ra .defense.gov/documents/rtm/123512p.pdf

O'Hanlon, M. (2004). The need to increase the size of the deployable army. *Parameters: U.S. Army War College, 34*(3), 4–17.

Rumann, C. B. (2010). *Student veterans returning to a community college: Understanding their transitions.* (Doctoral dissertation). Iowa State University, Ames. Available from ProQuest Digital Dissertations. (AAT 3403830)

Rumann, C. B., & Hamrick, F. A. (2010). Student veterans in transition: Re-enrolling after war zone deployments. *Journal of Higher Education, 81*(4), 431–458.

Schlossberg, N. K., Lynch, A. Q., & Chickering, A. W. (1989). *Improving higher education environments for adults: Responsive programs and services from entry to departure.* San Francisco: Jossey-Bass.

Selective Service System. (2003). *Induction statistics.* Palatine, IL: Author.

Student Veterans of America. (2011a). *Combat to college: A guide for the transitioning student veteran.* Washington, DC: Author. Retrieved from http://www.studentveterans .org/resourcelibrary/documents/CombattoCollege_AGuidefortheTransitioning StudentVeteran.pdf

Student Veterans of America. (2011b). *Creating a veteran friendly campus: A guide for college and university administrators.* Washington, DC: Author. Retrieved from http:// www.studentveterans.org/resourcelibrary/documents/CreatingaVeteranFriendly Campus_AGuideforCollegeandUniversityAdministrators.pdf

United States Department of Defense. (2011). *Military deployment guide*. Washington, DC: Author. Retrieved from http://www.militaryhomefront.dod.mil/12038/Project %20Documents/MilitaryHOMEFRONT/Service%20Providers/Deployment/2011_ DeploymentGuide.pdf

United States Department of Defense. (2012, April 4). *National Guard (in Federal Status) and Reserve Activated as of April 03, 2012*. Washington, DC: Office of the Assistant Secretary of Defense (Public Affairs). Retrieved from http://www.defense .gov/releases/release.aspx?releaseid=15159

United States Department of Veterans Affairs. (2011). *Answers* [web site]. Retrieved from https://gibill.custhelp.com/app/answers/detail/a_id/271/kw/suspended/ related/1

Van Dusen, R. L. (2011). *A quantitative study on student veterans' intent to persist*. (Doctoral dissertation). Texas Tech University, Lubbock.

Wong, L., Kolditz, T. A., Millen, R. A., & Potter, T. M. (2003). *Why they fight: Combat motivation in the Iraq war*. Carlisle, PA: United States Army War College Strategic Studies Institute. Retrieved from http://www.strategicstudiesinstitute .army.mil/pdffiles/pub179.pdf

VIGNETTE

Nina Duong

Graduate Student, Rutgers University

During my senior year of high school, I enlisted in the Texas Army National Guard. My intention was to acquire a college education without accumulating any debt, and joining the military provided this financial support. I signed up for eight years total, and departed for basic training the summer after my graduation. In fall 2005, I began my studies at the University of North Texas (UNT). Although I was a service member, I identified more with my role as a student leader, and my role in the National Guard seemed like a contractual part-time job.

When I was a resident assistant during my sophomore and junior years, I found it difficult to leave one weekend a month to attend military drills. The drill dates conflicted with residence life trainings, football games, and major university events. However, through all those moments, my professors and my hall directors were understanding, supportive, and flexible. For example, at the beginning of my junior year, my National Guard unit was called to assist with Hurricane Dean relief efforts. I missed my first week of school, and was unable to welcome my first-year residents in their transitions to UNT. Without question, my supervisors and hall staff worked together to take care of my residents while I was away. Because of the multitude of weekend events that I missed those years, I often felt like an inconvenience to my staff. However, at no point did anyone question my excessive absences or the potential effects they had on my role as a resident assistant.

In the first semester of my junior year, my unit informed me that we would be deploying to Iraq. Mobilization training began that upcoming summer; I took two years off from school, and returned for my senior year in January 2010. Because most of my previous colleagues graduated in 2009, I came back to UNT with few close social ties. The UNT Housing Department hired me back as a housing ambassador, which made my transition back to college easier. This office position was different from the resident assistant job because it consisted mostly of administrative and customer service–related work. Although I loved being a resident assistant, when I returned to school, I was more interested in a "nine to five" job because it allowed me to have a routine schedule. That semester, I focused on my academics and was not actively involved on campus. It was not until the following, and last, semester that I began to feel connected to the university in the same manner I had prior to deployment.

It was interesting to see how much a university can change in two years. When I returned, a new football stadium was under construction and there were different faces all over campus. A few new offices were established as well, including the UNT Veterans Center in the student union. Honestly, beyond the occasional visit to the VA representative in the Registrar's office, I rarely utilized the other support services. This was probably because I had attended the institution previously and was familiar with the campus environment. However, I can see how beneficial—and even necessary—these programs are to veterans who are new to the higher education experience. My personal success in college is attributed to my support system throughout my four years at UNT: the housing department, my supervisors, mentors, and friends.

CHAPTER FOUR

CONTEMPORARY STUDENT VETERANS AND SERVICE MEMBERS

Enrollment Patterns and Student Engagement

Danielle M. DeSawal

Military service members and veterans are part of growing student populations on many college campuses; in 2008, they represented about 4 percent of all undergraduates in the United States (Radford & Wun, 2009). Military and veteran undergraduate and graduate student populations are expected to grow primarily as a result of the Post-9/11 GI Bill, which provides the most attractive set of educational benefits the government has offered this student population (Steele, Salcedo, & Coley, 2010). The increase in the numbers of enrolled veterans and service members on U.S. campuses requires higher education administrators to examine how institutions can best serve these students, and recent studies can provide valuable insights for educators. For example, in 2010, the National Survey of Student Engagement (NSSE) surveyed over 11,000 self-identified current and former members of the U.S. military who were enrolled in U.S. institutions.

A recent focus on this population within the research indicates that social and academic factors influence how veterans and service members view their collegiate experiences. For example, they may feel academically unprepared for college (Ackerman, DiRamio, & Mitchell, 2009; DiRamio, Ackerman, & Mitchell, 2008). This student-level perception is challenged by findings that veterans and service members have strong study habits (Cate, Gerber, & Holmes, 2010); the time they spend studying is equivalent to the time spent by their civilian counterparts (National Survey of Student Engagement [NSSE], 2010).

As a group, veterans and service members appear to be entering college with the skills and dedication necessary to succeed, even though their initial experiences can be complicated by numerous transitional challenges. Those challenges include meeting academic expectations, establishing balances between academic and life responsibilities, relating to nonveteran students, and coping with service-related mental and physical disabilities (Steele et al., 2010). Veterans and service members are also more likely than their peers to work off-campus, engage in fewer out-of-class activities, and care for dependents (NSSE, 2010). Creating campus conditions that foster success, as well as creating appropriate support services and structures, requires knowledge of these students as a group, their transitions into student roles, and factors related to their academic and career success. This chapter provides insight into the inputs that veterans and service members bring to campus, how the campus and military cultures influence the engagement of these students, and explores how institutions can create conditions for military students to achieve the desired learning outcomes associated with higher education.

Assessing the Campus Environment for Veterans and Service Members

Assessing the impact of college on the population of enrolled service members and veterans requires campus administrators to recognize how these students' expectations and experiences interact with campus cultures. Astin (1970a, 1970b, 1991) developed the input-environment-outcome (I-E-O) model of assessment to examine college impact. This model connects learning outcomes (O) to two factors: inputs (I), such as demographic characteristics, family backgrounds, and previous social and academic experiences, and environment (E), such as campus cultures, including programs and services. In terms of the input phase, veterans and service members are, on average, entering college with the discipline, focus, and drive necessary to complete academic programs (Steele et al., 2010), although they are also likely to be working full-time and to have families (NSSE, 2010). This student population also enters the campus environment having had experiences that may be difficult for nonmilitary student and campus administrators to understand. Astin's model (1970a, 1970b, 1991) recognizes that inputs influence how students will choose to interact with the higher education environment. Although student veterans and service members may share a range of inputs associated with their military experiences, campus environments can be tailored to maximize the desired educational outcomes.

Colleges and universities, as well as higher education associations and collective bodies, recognize that student veterans and service members are a growing student population. One principal challenge is to build on this recognition by further understanding how veteran and service member characteristics, cocurricular and academic engagement patterns, and the military cultures into which these students have been socialized can combine to have an impact on their successes in civilian-oriented campus cultures. Research focused on campus environments indicates that when compared to nonveteran students, student veterans are less engaged with faculty and perceive that their campus environments are less supportive (Moltz, 2010). This lack of engagement with faculty could potentially affect veterans' personal and social learning outcomes. In order to foster student veterans' and service members' campus engagement, administrators need to recognize the lenses through which student veterans and service members view the campus environments.

Although student veterans and service members are just as likely to report satisfaction with their collegiate experiences as nonveterans, this student population appears to be less academically engaged (NSSE, 2010). Reflective learning and higher-order thinking are areas in which veterans and service members reported lower levels of engagement than nonveterans (NSSE, 2010). Integrating reflective learning into the collegiate environment has been recommended as a best practice by numerous reports that address desired common educational goals in U.S. higher education (Baxter Magolda & King, 2004). Without examining how to incorporate reflective learning into student veterans' and service members' college experiences, these students are at risk of leaving college without achieving the desired outcomes related to cognitive growth that are at the core of the academic mission. Astin's model (1970a, 1970b, 1991) refers to outcomes as the end results, or the characteristics, behaviors, and knowledge gained during the college experience. Those end results are dependent on the levels and types of interaction that enrolled veterans and service members have within multifaceted institutional environments.

Characteristics of Student Veterans and Service Members

One strategy—albeit partial—for beginning to understand the student veteran population is to review characteristics associated with nontraditional college students. The National Center for Education Statistics (NCES) recognizes that no single definition captures nontraditional students. However, variables that are often linked to nontraditional student status include age, point at which they enter higher education, financial status, employment, and enrollment status (Choy, 2002). Although student veterans and service members as a group reflect a number of these characteristics, the population can be more clearly defined with reference to demographics of the population *and* characteristics that are connected to their military experiences.

On average, student veterans and service members are likely to be male, white, over the age of 24, and married (Radford, 2009). Almost 85 percent of veterans surveyed for one study identified as white, 11.2 percent as African American or black, 5.1 percent as Hispanic, and 2.2 percent as multiple races (Westat, 2010). Although men remain the vast majority of veterans and service members, women represent an increasing proportion of the total student veteran population (U.S. Department of Veterans Affairs, 2007). It is critical to understand diversity within this student population, as colleges and universities seek to better serve student veterans and service members, and other chapters within this handbook address broad aspects of diversity and identity among service members and veterans.

Terms Related to the Student Population

College campuses enroll a variety of students affiliated with the armed forces. As a result, it is critical to understand terms that are used to reference students who are or have been affiliated with the armed forces. For example, the general term *veteran* refers to individuals who are former members of the military (Radford, 2009). The term *combat veteran* is frequently used to characterize veterans who were on active duty while in combat operations during periods of war. *Military undergraduate* references undergraduate students who are: (a) veterans, or (b) currently on active duty, or (c) members of the reserve component or the National Guard (Radford, 2009). *Military graduate students* are also a growing population on campuses and account for about 10 percent of all veterans who used military education benefits in 2010 (Donahue, 2011).

Given the above definitions, individuals may identify with multiple terms. For example, in 2007–08, approximately 1 percent of students identified as military undergraduates (Radford, 2009; Radford & Wun, 2009). Among that population, approximately 75 percent also identified as veterans, 16 percent were military service members on active duty, and 9 percent were military service members in the reserves (Radford, 2009; Radford & Wun, 2009). These terms provide a context for campus administrators to understand how members of this multifaceted student population identify themselves in relation to their prior or current military service.

More than any other time in recent history, campus personnel should anticipate working with students prior to activations or deployments, during active duty periods, and after students return home. This entire range of contexts and circumstances is crucial to consider as colleges and universities seek to offer or expand campus-based services to create optimal conditions in which veterans and service members can succeed.

Socialization and Military Culture

Veterans and service members reference their military training as preparation for how they approach the collegiate environment (Steele et al., 2010). Specifically, "the focus, discipline and drive to overcome obstacles, to improvise as needed, and to succeed in an academic setting" (Steele et al., 2010, p. 35) are cited as skills that help to create smoother transitions. This training is a reflection of the military culture that is part of this student population's environment. Campus administrators need to be cognizant of the transitions that student veterans and service members face when moving from the military culture to the campus culture and acknowledge the fact that these students are experiencing both cultures simultaneously.

Campus cultures guide the behavior of individuals and groups based on elements such as institutional histories, missions, physical settings, norms, traditions, communication, language, values, practices, beliefs, and assumptions (Kuh & Whitt, 1997). Socialization processes provide a context for how new members of the community should behave within the environment. An important element of socialization to undergraduate college life occurs through "interaction in normative contexts with other members of the college community" (Weidman, 1984, p. 449). Understanding the military culture of armed service organizations provides insight about the lenses through which enrolled veterans and service members may view and interpret higher education environments.

A number of aspects of military organizations distinguish them from typical civilian organizations (Lang, as cited in Soeters, Winslow, & Weibull, 2006). The first aspect is *character of life in uniform*, which refers to the levels of control that organizations have over individuals' personal lives. Military culture provides a controlled environment in which norms are identified, controlled, and enforced by the organization. These norms and expectations clearly communicate how individuals are to spend both their personal and work time as members of the organization. The second aspect of military organizations is *hierarchy*, which refers primarily to organizational structures and how authority functions within those structures. Soeters and colleagues (2006) pointed out that military organizations are more coercive, incorporate greater power distances within vertical structures, and foster strong social orders grounded in vertical structure and associated classifications and regulations. The final aspect is *discipline*, which is closely connected to *hierarchy* (Soeters et al., 2006). Discipline within the military culture refers to the extent to which the members' behaviors are controlled by organizational rules and regulations. This aspect of the culture contains overt as well as subtle or even hidden cues about acceptable behaviors. A clear distinction exists between those who belong to a group and those who are outside the group (Soeters et al., 2006). The appeal of distance education and for-profit institutions for veterans could be connected to the perception that these environments provide more structured, clear paths to degree completion, and these paths are characterized by, for example, the relative ease with which military credits can be transferred and the flexibility offered to meet adult learners' preferences and schedules (Steele et al., 2010). These types of educational environments entail relatively low levels of socialization and integration into institutional cultures that prescribe different ways of being or behaving.

Contemporary college learning outcomes focus on cognitive maturity, integrated identity, and mature relationships (Baxter Magolda & King, 2004). These learning outcomes may be seen as part of higher education's avowed or tacit culture. Although it is expected that students within collegiate environments will work toward these goals, the outcomes may not be directly communicated as expectations. Research indicates that veterans are less likely than nonveterans to talk with faculty members or participate in out-of-class activities (NSSE, 2010), which may make sense given the difference in cultures. For example, in military cultures, expectations, rules, and procedures are clearly outlined in formal documentation and communicated by authority figures. In many cases, what is right and what is wrong are clear within the culture. Within higher education cultures and environments, faculty may provide outlines of expectations for assignments but typically expect that students will make meaning of the material themselves. As a result, within academic learning environments, clear right and wrong answers often do not exist. Rather, the focus is on reflective learning to assess and communicate what the material under discussion means in the context of an academic discipline, a professional setting, or other relevant context.

NSSE (2010) found that undergraduate combat veterans in particular were, on average, less academically engaged in complex learning approaches and that they perceived lower levels of campus support than nonveterans. In recognition that military students may be struggling with how to make meaning of their experiences—in essence, socialization—within military and campus cultures, college and university administrators should consider creating points of contact or organizational offices for these students that provide hierarchical structures and basic scaffolding to assist students with this socialization process. Creating contextual environments that focus on the experiences of the students are first steps toward the creation of optimal conditions for student learning.

College Choice

Radford (2009) found that military undergraduates were most likely to select their institutions based on location, followed by programs or coursework offered, and cost. With the addition of convenience and support systems, these aspects are consistent with what veterans and college officials indicate as significant factors in college choice (Sewall, 2010). In many ways, college choice for veterans and service members tends to be based on how the institutional environment fits into the other aspects of their lives. NSSE (2010) also found that veterans and service members were more likely to attend public institutions and enroll in distance education.

In 2007–08, veterans and service members enrolled in for-profit institutions at three times the rate of traditional, nonveteran undergraduate students (Radford, 2009). The University of Phoenix enrolled more than 10,000 veterans in 2009–10, the most of any other higher education institution in the United States, primarily due to the convenience of the online environment (Sewall, 2010). However, enrollment of veterans and service members at for-profit institutions is statistically equivalent to that of nontraditional, nonveteran students (Radford, 2009). The learning environments offered by for-profit institutions may well be attractive to both these student populations, which, as discussed earlier, share some important characteristics.

In general, the rapid enrollment growth among for-profit institutions occurred primarily as a result of the online education options made available by these institutions (Deming, Goldin, & Katz, 2011). The flexibility offered through online education provides easy access to academic courses and makes for-profit institutions appealing choices. Comparatively, NSSE (2010) found that veterans and service members were less likely than their nonveterans counterparts to attend baccalaureate arts and sciences colleges or research-intensive doctoral-granting universities. Furthermore, "only a handful" of the 256,391 veterans enrolled in U.S. colleges and universities in fall 2010 attended Ivy League schools (Govil, 2011, para. 2). In 2011, approximately 232 veterans were enrolled in 31 of the most highly selective colleges in the country (Sloane, 2011).

An educational environment with Web-based courses also offers veterans and service members a possible reprieve from younger civilian students who may ask inappropriate questions related to their military experiences (Steele et al., 2010), such as "Did you kill anyone when you were deployed?" Relating to nonmilitary students is frequently cited as a transitional challenge for this student population (DiRamio et al., 2008; Radford, 2009; Steele et al., 2010). Veterans who struggle with relating to nonmilitary students and avoid those interactions as a result (Steele et al., 2010) may be less likely to advance their own growth in mature relationships or establishing integrated identities.

Campus administrators must be cognizant of the need to create learning opportunities on campus for all students that focus on creating respectful dialogue between groups. Nonmilitary undergraduate students who enter college without contextual understandings of cultures and how to relate to others can be compounded by curiosity about military culture that finds expression in awkward, inappropriate questions like the preceding. Creating conditions that allow for dialogue between military and nonmilitary groups, and, most important, within the student veteran and service member population, are critical for establishing supportive campus climates for student veterans and service members.

Many veterans and service members also seek campus environments in which their previous training and experiences are valued. Often that translates into opportunities to transfer military training and experiences into academic credit; the acceptance of military transfer credits varies by institution (American Council on Education [ACE], 2011). ACE convenes faculty representatives to assess military courses to determine whether the learning outcomes are equivalent to learning outcomes associated with college-level coursework. The University of Phoenix (n.d.) highlights on its web site that "credits earned through specific military training and national testing programs can help you complete your undergraduate degree even sooner" (para. 1). These types of messages convey to veterans and service members that the institutions offer learning environments that recognize military experiences and training as academically relevant, and as a result, are potentially perceived as more supportive and appealing than institutions that do not offer similar benefits.

The majority of veterans use federal programs, such as the GI Bill, to provide the financial support necessary to attend college (Sewall, 2010). That funding is only available to veterans for specific amounts of time, which motivates many students to complete their academic requirements before their educational benefits expire (see Chapter Two of this handbook for a more detailed discussion of funding programs). Attending college with the pressure to complete academic requirements within specified time frames may decrease the likelihood that student veterans and service members will engage in out-of-class activities. This pressure may also contribute to the strong desire among these students to establish sources of contact on campus in advance of their enrollments and request more detailed information about successfully navigating campus environments (ACE, 2010).

Making meaning of the transition from military classrooms to the academy's traditional classrooms is also a common concern for student veterans and service members. The academic rigors of higher education combined with teaching approaches designed to promote reflection and higher-order thinking may create cultural dissonance for student veterans. Steele and colleagues (2010) shared a comment from a student who articulated how the expectations of traditional college environments vary based on the class, the requirements, or both: "Getting here, the standard is so high. That was where I really struggled. I thought I was really strong in some areas, but when I came here I found it was like comparing apples to oranges . . . [in the military] the expectations are clear; it is very structured, but here, every professor does something different" (p. 37). It can be difficult for students to make meaning of those variations as they transition from military cultures where the expectations were clearly defined to higher education environments in which the goal may be to engage in reflective processes that ultimately yield more questions than answers.

When the challenge presented in an environment is not adequately offset by the support available, students begin to disengage. NSSE (2010) found that enrolled veterans and service members were less academically engaged than their nonveteran peers. Student veterans and service members who transition from cultures in which structure, social order, and discipline are highly valued to environments where independent thought and freedom to challenge authority are core tenets can experience difficulties in their attempts to relate to campus communities, and vice versa. Veterans and service members are entering college with experiences that set them apart from nonveteran students on campus (Steele et al., 2010). The military training and experiences they have gained, both academically and socially, are delivered in ways that create and reinforce clear rules and expectations. Weidman (1984) recognized that socialization plays a role in how students transition to college. However, for veterans, this socialization process needs to include recognition that the campus community understands students' previous ways of being. Veterans and service members enter college having been socialized by their training and experiences in the military. College and university representatives should recognize that the transition from the structure of a military environment to a higher education institution may create a dissonance for veterans and service members that is not immediately reconciled.

Creating Conditions for Success

O'Herrin (2011) outlined a number of practices that institutions have implemented to foster the conditions necessary for the success of veterans and service members, including:

- Identification of specific sources of contact within campus offices.
- Creation of campus working groups that span departments.
- Collaborative initiatives with community organizations to provide comprehensive services.
- Development of orientation programs to ensure that veterans and service members receive thorough introductions to the institution.
- Establishment of student veteran groups.
- Targeted education efforts for faculty and staff that address specific issues affecting this population.
- Creation of veteran-specific resource centers, spaces on campus, and learning communities.
- Streamlining of disability services and veteran services.

These practices stress that contemporary student veterans and service members seek orientation to the collegiate environment that complements the military cultures they have experienced, campus climates that respect their backgrounds, community members who understand how to interact respectfully and engage in thoughtful dialogue, and programs and services that allow student veterans and service members to connect with one another.

Student veterans and service members themselves recognize the challenges of transitioning to college campuses. In 2010, ACE hosted an online dialogue called the *Veteran Success Jam*. Participants included higher education faculty, staff, professional association representatives, and student veterans. Generated from that dialogue were key insights into structures with potential to create conditions to foster the success of veterans and service members. Ideas resulting from the dialogue included the creation of a handbook for the campus community to provide insight into military cultures and highlight common transitional issues for veterans and service members. The creation of an index of military- or veteran-friendly campuses was also proposed. Additionally, veterans who participated in the dialogue favored establishment of single points of contact at colleges and universities to assist with their navigation of campus environments, as these resources would reduce confusion and minimize time spent searching for relevant information.

Many of these recommendations highlight the need to understand military culture within higher education contexts. Campus administrators need to meet these students where they are developmentally in relation to their transitions to college. Environments that recognize that these students are looking for elements of social order, discipline, and structure can use that framework to create conditions for students to explore and transition to educational outcomes that focus on reflective learning and higher-order thinking.

Conclusion

Recognizing that veterans and service members may be contending with how to integrate their military and student cultures and identities could help explain the comparatively lower levels of traditional campus engagements related to learning that were reported by NSSE (2010). Campus administrators should explore how their campus cultures offer opportunities for engagement, and perhaps also explore creating alternate, tailored opportunities for veterans and service members to engage. Astin's I-E-O model (1970a, 1970b, 1991) provides a logic for studying the effects of college in light of the various influences that impact students. This model could be particularly relevant in seeking to further understand how military cultures and combat duties are affecting students' college experiences.

Campus environments are malleable, providing opportunities to design and implement programs and services that recognize how these students' interactions on campus affect their abilities to achieve desired sets of learning outcomes. However, campus administrators must be aware that making changes and improvements to campus environments takes time (Kuh, 2000). Veterans enter college with clear time constraints accompanying their educational benefits. The military cultures and related socializations that are salient to veteran and military students' identities provide them with lenses that can shed light on how they approach their academic careers; those lenses are focused on drive and determination to complete their tasks—the attainment of college degrees.

Creating conditions on campus for veterans and service members to succeed requires that college administrators and faculty members understand how to create better outcomes for this student population by creating environmental or cultural bridges to help students make meaning of their previous and current ways of being in light of the expectations of college life. This chapter has highlighted a number of inputs that may challenge current campus environments and assumptions, including military cultures and socializations, restrictions on completion times based on benefits, understanding the value of previous training and education within the military, and greater focus on home, work, and family.

Higher education administrators should work to create symbols and messages within their campus cultures that indicate to veterans and service members that they are respected, appreciated, and welcomed. These environmental messages are critically related to how this student population will be socialized into campus communities. Tinto (1975) described his theory of social integration into college as interactions that were focused on informal peer groups, out-of-class activities, and interactions with faculty and administrators. Enrolled veterans and service members have repeatedly identified hesitations to engage with nonveterans on campus due to the frequency of inappropriate questions—or expectations that inappropriate questions will be asked or stereotyped assumptions about them will be made. Providing programs and services that are visible to the campus community (such as brochures at orientation and information posted on campus web sites) could send messages to this population that the campus is learning to be more supportive.

A number of institutions have begun to establish courses for veterans and service members to ease the transition to campus. These courses offer opportunities to discuss the cultural differences between military and academic environments. Lane Community College and Park University, for example, established series of courses to help students understand how their previous ways of being in the military and the skills they garnered can be translated to academic contexts (ACE, n.d.). As a result, these programs provide contexts for situating learning grounded in veterans' and service members' experiences. Park University has reported that students who participated in the program were retained at the institution and that the students also perceived their transitions from military to college environments to be more fluid (ACE, n.d.).

Examining institutional type has revealed that veterans and service members are attracted to and enroll in distance education programs. Recognition that the online environment provides students the flexibility to manage other aspects of their lives while enrolled in courses provides the opportunity for campus administrators to explore how to use technology to connect with this student population. California State Polytechnic University, Pomona created an optional online orientation program specifically for student veterans (ACE, n.d.). The orientation program, although similar to the general orientation program, offers specific modules that address issues pertinent to student veterans, including information about how to utilize GI Bill benefits. Delivery of programs through mechanisms that are attractive to this student population and are tailored to meet their specific needs allows veterans to create relationships that are based on shared authority and expertise.

Establishment of cocurricular activities that are salient to how this student population identifies provides the opportunity to support veterans and service members as they begin to understand how their identities are central to knowledge construction. At Colorado State University, campus administrators started SALUTE National Honors Society for veterans (ACE, n.d.). The program recognizes academic achievement and engagement and provides opportunities for veterans and service members to engage in cocurricular activities on campus that promote educational outcomes aligned with more traditional ideas of campus involvement; it also allows students to create meaningful relationships with each other and provides a "home" within the campus community.

As discussed earlier, military culture places high values on order and hierarchy. As student veterans and service members navigate college environments, they draw on their previous ways of being and understanding. It is important to identify campus administrators and staff who can offer support to this student population, with the ultimate goal of hiring designated point persons or coordinators who work with student veterans and service members. The challenge that is associated with navigating new environments can be supported by creating relationships in which knowledge about the environment is actively and socially constructed. Making meaning of how student veterans and service members reconcile their previous ways of being with their new environments is complex; the provision of venues for dialogue about those complexities can lead to optimal learning outcomes consistent with reflective learning and higher-order thinking.

References

Ackerman, R., DiRamio, D., & Mitchell, R. L. (2009). Transitions: Combat veterans as college students. In R. Ackerman, & D. DiRamio (Eds.), *Creating a veteran-friendly campus: Strategies for transition and success*. New Directions for Student Services, 126, pp. 5–14. San Francisco: Jossey-Bass.

American Council on Education. (n.d.). *Promising practices in veterans' education: Outcomes and recommendations from the Success for Veterans Award Grants*. Washington, DC: Author. Retrieved from http://www.acenet.edu/AM/Template.cfm?Section= serving&TEMPLATE=/CM/ContentDisplay.cfm&CONTENTID=42786

American Council on Education. (2010). *Veteran success jam*. Washington, DC: Author. Retrieved from http://www.acenet.edu/AM/Template.cfm?Section=Home& TEMPLATE=/CM/ContentDisplay.cfm&CONTENTID=37400

American Council on Education. (2011). *A transfer guide: Understanding your military transcript and ACE credit recommendations*. Washington, DC: Author. Retrieved from http://www.acenet.edu/Content/NavigationMenu/ProgramsServices/Military Programs/TransferGuide_Updated2011.pdf

Astin, A. W. (1970a). College influence: A comprehensive view. *Contemporary Psychology, 15*(9), 543–546.

Astin, A. W. (1970b). The methodology of research on college impact. *Sociology of Education, 43*, 223–254.

Astin, A. W. (1991). *Assessment for excellence: The philosophy and practice of assessment and evaluation in higher education*. New York: McMillan.

Baxter Magolda, M., & King, P. M. (2004). *Learning partnerships: Theory and models of practice to educate for self-authorship*. Sterling, VA: Stylus.

Cate, C. A., Gerber, M., & Holmes, D. L. (2010). *A new generation of student veterans: A pilot study*. Santa Barbara: University of California, Santa Barbara Institute for Social, Behavioral, and Economic Research. Retrieved from http://www.uweb.ucsb.edu/ ~chriscate/PilotReport09.pdf

Choy, S. (2002). *Nontraditional undergraduates: Findings from "The Condition of Education, 2002."* Washington, DC: United States Department of Education National Center for Education Statistics. Retrieved from http://eric.ed.gov/PDFS/ED471077.pdf

Deming, D. J., Goldin, C. & Katz, L. F. (2011). *The for-profit postsecondary school sector: Nimble critters or agile predators?* (Preliminary draft). Retrieved from http://www.frb atlanta.org/documents/news/conferences/11employment_education_demming .pdf

DiRamio, D., Ackerman, R., & Mitchell, R. L. (2008). From combat to campus: Voices of student-veterans. *NASPA Journal, 45*(1), 73–102.

Donahue, H. (2011, June 7). Veterans take advantage of GI Bill benefits for grad school. GIBill.com. Retrieved from http://www.gibill.com/news/gibill-grad-school-355.html

Govil, H. (2011, January 31). Veterans at the elites. *The Stanford Review.* Retrieved from http://stanfordreview.org/article/veterans-at-the-elites/

Kuh, G. D. (2000). Understanding campus environments. In M. J. Barr, & M. K. Desler (Eds.), *The handbook of student affairs administration* (2nd ed., pp. 50–72). San Francisco: Jossey-Bass.

Kuh, G. D., & Whitt, E. J. (1997). The invisible tapestry: Culture in American colleges and universities. In E. J. Whitt (Ed.), *College student affairs administration* (2nd ed.). ASHE Reader Series. Boston: Pearson.

Moltz, D. (2010, November 4). Veterans, less engaged but satisfied. *Inside Higher Ed.* Retrieved from http://www.insidehighered.com/news/2010/11/04/nsse

National Survey of Student Engagement. (2010). *Major differences: Examining student engagement by field of study.* Bloomington: Indiana University Center for Postsecondary Education. Retrieved from http://nsse.iub.edu/NSSE_2010_Results/pdf/NSSE_2010_AnnualResults.pdf#page=18

O'Herrin, E. (2011). Enhancing veteran success in higher education. *Peer Review, 13*(1). Retrieved from http://www.aacu.org/peerreview/pr-wi11/prwi11_oherrin.cfm

Radford, A. W. (2009). *Military service members and veterans in higher education: What the new GI Bill may mean for postsecondary institutions.* Washington DC: American Council on Education.

Radford, A. W., & Wun, J. (2009). *Issue tables: A Profile of military servicemembers and veterans enrolled in postsecondary education in 2007–08.* Washington, DC: United States Department of Education National Center for Education Statistics.

Sewall, M. (2010, June 13). Veterans use new GI Bill largely at for-profit and 2-year colleges. *Chronicle of Higher Education.* Retrieved from http://chronicle.com/article/Veterans-Use-Benefits-of-Ne/65914/

Sloane, W. (2011, November 11). Veterans Day 2011. *Inside Higher Ed.* Retrieved from http://www.insidehighered.com/views/2011/11/11/essay-annual-count-veterans-elite-college-campuses

Soeters, J. L., Winslow, D. J., & Weibull, A. (2006). Military culture. In G. Caforio (Ed.), *Handbook of the sociology of the military* (pp. 237–254). New York: Kluwer.

Steele, J. L., Salcedo, N., & Coley, J. (2010). *Service members in school: Military veterans' experiences using the Post-9/11 GI Bill and pursuing postsecondary education.* Washington, DC: American Council on Education. Retrieved from http://www.acenet.edu/AM/Template.cfm?Section=Programs_and_Services&TEMPLATE=/CM/HTML Display.cfm&CONTENTID=38956

Tinto, V. (1975). Dropout from higher education: A theoretical synthesis of recent research. *Review of Educational Research, 45*, 89–125.

United States Department of Veterans Affairs. (2007). *Women veterans: Past, present, and future*. Washington DC: Author.

University of Phoenix. (n.d.). *Military experience* [web site]. Retrieved from http://www .phoenix.edu/admissions/transfer_information/military_experience.html

Weidman, J. C. (1984). Impacts of campus experiences and parental socialization on undergraduates' career choices. *Research in Higher Education, 20*(4), 445–476.

Westat. (2010). *National survey of veterans, active duty service members, demobilized National Guard and Reserve members, family members, and surviving spouses*. Rockville, MD: Author. Retrieved from http://www.va.gov/vetdata/docs/SurveysAndStudies/NVS SurveyFinalWeightedReport.pdf

VIGNETTE

Sally Caspers

Rebel Veteran Education and Transition Support Program,
University of Nevada, Las Vegas

In spring 2009, the University of Nevada, Las Vegas (UNLV) applied for the ACE/Wal-Mart Veteran Services grant like so many other universities across the country. UNLV had experienced a significant rise in our veteran population on campus after the advent of the Post-9/11 GI Bill, and we knew that supporting these students was going to entail more than just money for their tuition. We were ultimately not one of the grant awardees, but the process of writing the proposal identified many actions that the campus could take with little or no drain on existing resources. At the time, I was a graduate assistant working on nontraditional student issues and scholarships, so a simple shift of priorities allowed me to spend some time considering how we could support the student veteran population.

By July 2009, we had formed a campuswide committee that met on a monthly basis to identify and address student veteran and military family needs and issues. We were not attempting to reinvent the wheel—just streamline the processes that student veterans and military families were using the most. At the same time, my work shifted to serving as the point person for incoming student veterans and for those already on campus.

As I worked with more student veterans, it became clear that an important part—perhaps the most important part—of their successful transitions was simply having a safe place to talk and ask questions. Providing that resource—an empathetic ear and some clarity on existing processes—was an exceedingly simple thing to do. A direct phone line to my desk, a web site full of information, and time to answer questions became the most priceless resources for student veterans at UNLV.

In combining the efforts of the UNLV Veteran and Military Family Services committee in shaping campus policies with my own efforts to serve as a single point of reference for student veterans, we have begun to build a foundation of support for the student veteran and military family community here that reaches beyond any one office or program. That foundation enabled the opening of the Office of Veteran Services in August 2011. That office houses the Rebel VETS program, the school certifying official (SCO), and the student veterans organization (SVO). Through the Rebel VETS program, UNLV is able to offer support to veterans that goes beyond the GI Bill. Although the organization of the office is yet to be integrated—Rebel VETS is funded by educational outreach, and the SCO reports to financial aid—shared space means that the effort is seamless to veterans. Commemorative events on 9/11, Veterans Day, and at commencement help to acknowledge and welcome all veterans on campus, including those who are faculty, staff, and students. A new student information system will enable us to more easily identify veterans on campus, and new champions for the cause have emerged from many departments and units. For example, members of the UNLV grounds team, many of whom are veterans, donated hours of labor and materials to the effort of placing the veteran memorial statue purchased by the SVO; without their efforts, the related costs would have set the project back by months. Spring 2012 saw the launch of SERV training for faculty and staff in an effort to bridge the gap between those on campus who have served and those who have not.

When I explain the work I do to others, I often argue that the problems we are addressing are not artifacts of either the military culture or the higher education culture, but that they are essentially problems of language. Both cultures have sets of rules, many of which are the same (such as ranks and hierarchies, codes of conduct, and bureaucratic procedures), that merely must be communicated in language that both sides can understand. I have been continually encouraged that both sides are ready and willing to learn about one another; I take it as my responsibility to facilitate those conversations and serve as an interpreter when necessary.

In the end, supporting student veterans is a long-term undertaking that will require significant effort long after all the troops come home. Our efforts today, if they are well supported, thoughtful, and integrated into campus culture, can lay a foundation for successful educational experiences for veterans in the future.

CHAPTER FIVE

THE COMPLEXITY OF VETERAN IDENTITY

Understanding the Role of Gender, Race and Sexuality

Susan V. Iverson and Rachel Anderson

Much has been written about the growing numbers of post-9/11 veterans attending college. Yet, this body of scholarship has given little attention to the demographic diversity of veterans. Thus, as scholars and practitioners call for campuses to become veteran-friendly, we are left to wonder, *which veterans?*

This chapter provides an overview of the status of women, racial and ethnic minority, and lesbian, gay, bisexual, and transgender (LGBT) veterans. We then describe how institutional structures, not only in the military, but in higher education as well, may produce different outcomes along these dimensions of identity, benefiting some and disadvantaging others. Finally, we delineate recommendations for practice and mechanisms for evaluating the success of one's efforts to support student veterans in higher education.

Expanding Our Awareness of Veterans

In this overview of women, racial and ethnic minority, and LGBT veterans, we draw heavily on literature centered on the military context. We do that in part because research on these populations is very limited, but we also believe it is important to understand the military context, for it is this culture to which student veterans have been socialized. First, however, a definitional consideration: as we use the term "student veteran," we recognize that some individuals who present to campus offices as "veterans" are in fact active-duty military personnel, National Guard, or active Reservists, among other designations. For the purposes of this chapter, we use the term "veterans" to represent the very broad category of individuals who are serving or have previously served in the U.S. military.

Women

Women have served in the military in every war the United States has fought dating back to the Revolutionary War, but it was not until 1948 that women were granted permanent status in the military and were entitled to veterans' benefits (Huynh-Hohnbaum, Damron-Rodriguez, Washington, Villa, & Harada, 2003). Women had largely served in positions ranging from kitchen workers to nurses until the 1990s, when hundreds of thousands of new positions in the military opened to women (McSally, 2011). Women now constitute 14 percent of the active military force and 8 percent of the total force deployed to Iraq and Afghanistan; over 150,000 women have served in Iraq and Afghanistan since 2002 (McSally, 2011). This growth in the active force translates into higher numbers of women veterans attending college; roughly 26 percent of all veterans enrolled in higher education are women (Radford, 2009). Though higher percentages of male and female veterans have completed some college education when compared with nonveterans, women veterans as a group have greater educational attainment than male veterans (Holder, 2011). For instance, since 2002, a higher percentage of women veterans than male veterans have completed bachelor's degrees (Holder, 2011).

A primary issue typically identified when describing the experiences of women veterans is sexual assault, which the U.S. Department of Veterans Affairs (VA) has termed "military sexual trauma" (MST). In addition to sexual assault, MST includes "repeated, threatening sexual harassment occurring during military service" (Hyun, Pavao, & Kimerling, 2009, p. 1). According to the National Center for Posttraumatic Stress Disorder (2007), 1 in 5 women (20 percent) and 1 in 100 men (1 percent) met the VA's criteria for MST. Other studies have reported even higher rates of MST. In their survey of former reservists, Street, Stafford, Mahan, and Hendricks (2008) found that 60 percent of women and 27 percent of men had experienced repeated or severe sexual harassment, and sexual assault was experienced by 13 percent of women and 1.6 percent of men during their

U.S. military service. Lipari, Cook, Rock, and Matos (2008) found that 9 percent of military women reported experiencing some form of sexual coercion, 31 percent reported experiencing unwanted sexual attention, and 52 percent reported experiencing other offensive sexual behaviors. In a study of factors associated with women's risk of rape in the military, Sadler, Booth, Cook, and Doebbeling (2003) found that 27 percent of participants experienced sexual harassment, 54 percent reported unwanted sexual contact, and 30 percent experienced one or more completed or attempted rapes during their U.S. military service. Of note, perpetrators of rape were "identified as male, non-commissioned officers, and peers of similar rank" (Sadler et al., 2003, p. 266).

It is not uncommon for a person to develop posttraumatic stress disorder (PTSD) from rape or sexual assault; yet, women veterans "are not as likely to be diagnosed with PTSD as men" (Baechtold & De Sawal, 2009, p. 37). As DiRamio, Ackerman, and Mitchell (2008) observed, "sexual assault [is an issue] that many 'civilian' women students face as well" (p. 96); consequently, MST may be dismissed by veterans offices as "women's issues" instead of PTSD. Further, the psychological effects of combat that often yield PTSD diagnoses for men are treated as depression and as anxiety in women. This is believed to be due to "cultural views that do not easily recognize women as combatants" (Baechtold & DeSawal, 2009, p. 37). PTSD and MST may be underreported among women veterans and the underlying causes of the trauma may not be understood.

U.S. Department of Defense policy continues to ban women from serving in ground combat positions (McSally, 2011). However, women are "involved in ground combat and are necessary to the success of the mission, but are denied the open acceptance of their service in this capacity" (McSally, 2011, p. 153). These combat experiences have been chronicled in the documentary film *Lioness* (Benello, Ettinger, Helfand, McLagan, & Sommers, 2008), where women Army personnel participated in cordon and search operations, ran with firing teams carrying Squaw Automatic Weapons (SAWs), and engaged in direct exchange of fire with insurgents (Perry, 2008). Female Engagement Teams (FETs), originally developed by the Marine Corps, now used in Special Operations, are assigned to accompany male troops on missions that may begin as routine searches of households, but can explode into deadly combat incidents (Bumiller, 2010; Jordan, 2011). Today's higher education administrators will hear, if they have not already, stories of female gunners atop armored vehicles and instances in which women veterans were in positions of engaging and killing enemy combatants. Thus, viewing women veterans' psychological issues as *solely* sexual assault ignores the increasing scope and complexity of PTSD among today's veterans.

Exacerbating the transition from military to civilian life is the disconnect some women veterans experience when beginning to access VA medical and psychological services (Fontana & Rosenheck, 2006). Returning women veterans face a general public that often does not understand or recognize their service, and they encounter VA personnel who misinterpret their experiences and potentially disqualify them for benefits and treatments to which they should be entitled (Hefling, 2009). This systemic erasing of women veterans' military experiences creates or exacerbates senses of isolation and invisibility that may contribute to women's detachment from veteran identity postservice (Baechtold & De Sawal, 2009). This information presents a caution to higher education administrators as women veterans may harbor low expectations for assistance beyond simple educational benefit processing.

Racial and Ethnic Minorities

The proportion of racial and ethnic minorities enlisting in the military has grown, and much of the increase can be attributed to the growing numbers of women (National Center for Veterans Analysis and Statistics, 2011). In the 2000 U.S. Census, 83 percent of male veterans identified as white, non-Hispanic (compared with nearly 65 percent of nonveterans), and 9 percent identified as black, non-Hispanic; in contrast, nearly 30 percent of all women veterans identified as members of racial minority groups, with most identifying as black, non-Hispanic (U.S. Department of Veterans Affairs Office of Policy & Planning, 2007). The proportion of Hispanics in the military has also increased, and by 2020 the proportion of women veterans who are Hispanic is projected to grow to 9 percent (VA Office of Policy & Planning, 2007).

Although President Truman mandated equal racial treatment in the military in 1948, the military remained segregated until the Korean War (Wilson, 1994). The Servicemen's Readjustment Act, known as the GI Bill, was signed into law in 1944 and has been "widely celebrated as a benchmark of opportunity for Americans who have served in the armed forces" (Herbold, 1994, p. 104). Yet, as Cooney, Segal, Segal, and Falk (2003) observed, the benefits afforded for service in the military vary greatly by race. Several scholars have explored the impact of the GI Bill and whether it has expanded access and increased educational attainment, in particular, for African Americans (Herbold, 1994; Turner & Bound,

2003; Wilson, 1994). Herbold (1994) noted, "though Congress granted all soldiers the same benefits theoretically, the segregationist principles of almost every institution of higher learning effectively disbarred a huge proportion of black veterans from earning a college degree" (p. 107). Thus, the benefits of the GI Bill after World War II went largely unfulfilled; black veterans were largely limited to the South in their educational choices (Turner & Bound, 2003). Herbold (1994) further observed that while the GI Bill "broke down class lines in higher education," the Black middle class failed to keep pace and "inequities of race remained" (p. 106).

Lesbian, Gay, Bisexual, and Transgender Persons

In her study of LGBT veterans of recent U.S. conflicts, Garland (2007) provided a time line of U.S. policy on "homosexuals" in the military (the U.S. Department of Defense uses the word "homosexual" in its Homosexual Conduct Policy). This time line predates World War I and cites the Uniform Code of Military Justice, signed by President Truman in 1950, as the codification of regulations and penalties concerning homosexuality (Garland, 2007). In 1982, President Reagan issued a defense directive stating that "homosexuality" is "incompatible with military service" and poses a security risk (Garland, 2007). In response to this policy, many academic institutions sought to bar military recruiters from campuses or to eliminate Reserve Officer Training Corps (ROTC) programs (Burrelli & Feder, 2009). Although there are advantages to having military officers trained on college campuses, these are offset by "severe homophobia and heterosexism encouraged by present policy, counteracting attitudes of free inquiry" (Card, 1994, p. 120). In 1993, President Clinton issued a defense directive that military applicants and personnel should not be asked about their sexual orientations; this policy became known as "Don't Ask, Don't Tell" (DADT). In December 2010, legislative action was passed to repeal DADT, and in July 2011, President Obama, the Secretary of Defense, and the Chairman of the Joint Chiefs of Staff certified that the repeal will not harm military readiness (Bumiller, 2011). The repeal of DADT went into effect on September 20, 2011. The effect of this repeal remains to be seen.

The actual number of gay, lesbian, and bisexual persons serving in uniform is unknown, as the military does not track these figures. However, O'Keefe (2010) estimated that roughly 2 to 3 percent of all military personnel are gay or lesbian. Further, the 2000 U.S. Census reported that 2 percent of veterans are gay men and 1 percent are lesbians (Gates, 2003). The data on transgender veterans are even more limited; however, Grant,

Mottet, and Tanis (2011) reported that 20 percent of all adult transgender people in the U.S. are military veterans.

The oppressive and silencing environment of the military leaves many service members in the closet until after discharge. This isolation occurs on military academies and with gay and lesbian students in ROTC programs as well. Estes (2007) conducted interviews with gay alumni who attended the U.S. Naval Academy, U.S. Military Academy (West Point), the U.S. Coast Guard Academy, and the U.S. Air Force Academy, or were in ROTC between the 1960s and 1990s. None were "out" while on campus, but they sought support and networking as alumni. One gay Naval Academy alumnus created a gay alumni chapter that also served as a support network for gay and lesbian cadets (Estes, 2007).

Those who "come out" after leaving the military can experience great distress related to belonging to an oppressed group (Meyer, 2003). In general, they use little support and access few services (such as veteran services) because they fear needing to return to the closeted roles they were forced to play in the military (Frank, 2004; Garland, 2007). Many who "come out" in personal relationships remain closeted in their work environments, which, like the military, are often heterosexist or homophobic work spaces (Garland, 2007). However, these spaces can change.

Estes (2007) noted that the integration of women and racial minorities into the military academies is part of a "continuum of change" that, he posited, will "ultimately lead to changes in the [military] policy toward gays and lesbians" (p. 95). He underscored this point with a quotation from a West Point faculty member: "When we deny their [gays' and lesbians'] right to military service, we improperly restrict the franchise of citizenship and give in to homophobic prejudice very like the unreasoned racial and gender prejudices of the past" (p. 95). We are amidst change, and campus administrators have a unique opportunity to create affirming spaces for LGBT veterans.

Structural Inequalities

The preceding section provided an overview of the historical and contemporary status of women, LGBT, and racial and ethnic minority veterans. Despite the fact that women have gained access to some (not all) military positions, racial minorities have broken the color barrier in the military, and LGBT service members can now serve openly, discrimination, barriers, and inequities persist. This section seeks to illuminate how institutional and interpersonal barriers derive from a broader ideology that privileges masculinity, whiteness, and heterosexuality in the military and U.S. society at large. Examining this can improve our understanding of the experiences of women, LGBT, and racial and ethnic minorities in the military and of their roles in other settings, such as higher education. We also seek to understand the ways in which our institutional practices are embedded in this broader ideology that may unwittingly sustain or reproduce inequalities.

Several authors have explored the ways in which gender operates to sustain the prevailing image of the military as a male-only environment, even as the numbers of women serving continues to grow. Some have suggested that the "long history" of the military and military academies as single-sex institutions is "potentially related to [current] problems regarding the integration of women" (Robinson Kurpius & Lucart, 2000, p. 255). Others analyzed how dominant "ideological values subordinate women to men in military and civilian contexts" (Prividera & Howard, 2006, p. 29). These authors further argued that the "continued essentializing of soldiers as 'masculine men' calls into question the very legitimacy of the female soldier" (p. 30). Thus, even as women have gained ground in their military representation, they continue to be excluded from some roles (such as combat) that are "defined in terms of men and masculinity" (Herbert, 1998, p. 14). Further, the male-dominated culture creates pressures on women to prove their heterosexuality, or rather avoid "the threat or the label of 'lesbian'" (Herbert, 1998, p. 19); consequently, women "strategize around gender" (p. 54) to avoid penalties that exist if one is perceived as "too feminine" or "too masculine" (p. 53). For instance, Herbert (1998) found that some women "adopt male mannerisms" (p. 106), but some of these behaviors, such as "swearing and drinking may heighten perceptions of masculinity, but have other repercussions" such as "being seen as a lesbian" and facing "not only the informal homophobia ... but also the threat of being forced out of the military" (pp. 105–106). Women would offset "masculine strategies" with "feminine props" such as earrings, perfume, and makeup (Herbert, 1998, p. 105), yet then risked being perceived as "incompetent, heterosexual slut[s]" (p. 106). Thus, many adopted a "neuter" persona to "render notions of either feminine and masculine absent from one's presentation" (Herbert, 1998, p. 108). Six out of every ten women in Herbert's (1998) study tried to be "asexual," and Herbert noted that it is "more difficult to attack that which we cannot see" (p. 109).

The ideological system that constructs maleness and masculinity as the archetypal military service-member also produces a "racialized framing" that privileges whiteness (Prividera & Howard, 2006, p. 30). Again, this extends beyond the bounds of the military. Fendrich (1972) described this in his study of black Vietnam veterans' readjustment to civilian life, noting that the black male did not reap the sociocultural benefits of being a veteran, but was instead relegated back into a racist system. For instance, the VA kept many black veterans "from receiving unemployment benefits" and others were "denied their educational benefits" (Herbold, 1994, p. 105). While serving in the military, these men developed a set of expectations for the rewards and recognitions due to them as veterans; they expected to be granted the same benefits as their white peers, including access to jobs, housing, and education. Yet, "the black veteran returns to a society that is racist" and "is faced with the prospect of second-class citizenship" (Fendrich & Axelson, 1971, p. 248). In the decades since the Vietnam War, others have continued to illustrate how racial/ethnic minorities cite negative military experiences, from racist comments to racial segregation (Huynh-Hohnbaum et al., 2003; Moore & Webb, 2000), and face postservice disadvantages related to education and income (Cooney et al., 2003; Harada et al., 2002). This disparity is even more pronounced for non-white women than it is for men, as women veterans face "the 'double whammy' phenomenon: disadvantaged because of both their race and gender" (Moore & Webb, 1998, p. 99).

Finally, sexuality intersects with these gendered and racialized hierarchies. Segal (1999) noted, "exclusion of homosexuals is another way to maintain the military as a province of heterosexual males" (p. 576). Hawthorne (2011) found that for a male recruit, being gay resulted in more negative perceptions, but not for a female. In her study, "the woman who was gay experienced some prejudice compared to the man who was straight but not to the degree that the man who was gay did" (Hawthorne, 2011, p. 54). Paradoxically, women are disproportionately the targets of homosexuality-related military discharges (Anderson & Smith, 1993). Some suggest that women and gay men are not "real men" and thus are more likely to be targets of harassment (Thomas & Thomas, 1996). Further, as Francke (1997) found in her study of West Point cadets, the integration of women into military training shifted attention from African American men to women as the primary targets of discrimination. As one white male cadet at West Point told his African American classmate, "You belong in the Corps ... It's the women we don't want" (Francke, 1997, p. 217). Campus administrators must examine these interlocking hierarchies that sustain difference based on gender, race, and sexuality—not only in the military, but in higher education as well. We must "un-gender" and "e-race" those practices and structures that produce, support, and maintain divisions and hierarchies (D'Amico & Weinstein, 1999, p. 260).

Implications for Practice

As the number of post-9/11 veterans increases on U.S. campuses, services for veterans are becoming more streamlined and integrated. For example, in 2010 the VA certifying official at Kent State University (KSU) moved from the Student Financial Aid office into the Adult Student Center (ASC), which was renamed the Center for Adult and Veteran Services (CAVS) to reflect the expanded range of services. The decision to combine veteran benefit processing with adult students is supported by Grimes and colleagues (2011) who found that student veterans identify with their older peers because of their maturity and life experiences. However, as the new CAVS department at KSU increased services and programs for veterans, it became apparent that initiatives for veterans were attracting primarily, and at times exclusively, white male student veterans. The CAVS department sought to address this concern through intentional outreach to women veterans on campus. Although gains are being made, gaps persist, including the challenge of involving veterans of color on a predominantly white campus, and the need to address the marginalization of LGBT veterans. In this section, we offer suggestions for how practitioners might create friendly campuses for *all* veterans.

Campus and Community Collaborations

Women who served in the military are less likely to identify themselves as veterans after they complete their service (Baechtold & De Sawal, 2009). Thus, women student veterans may not view campus veterans' offices as useful resources. Intentional outreach with other identity-based groups and offices, such as the women's center, multicultural center, LGBT center, Black Studies faculty, and disability services affords collaborative opportunities for programming, leadership development, and other initiatives. At KSU, intentional outreach yielded a multioffice partnership that brought Shoshana Johnson, a black female prisoner of war, to campus for a speaking engagement and visit with the campus veterans' club members.

The American Council on Education's (ACE) Office of Women in Higher Education advocates campus and community collaborations as ways that administrators can respond to the high rates of sexual assault experienced by women service members (Burns Phillips, 2010). ACE suggests that campuses collaborate with nearby colleges and universities to provide women counselors trained to work with PTSD and sexual assault issues, and that administrators seek out "appropriately trained practicing female therapists in the community willing to do *pro bono* work with returning women veterans" (Burns Phillips, 2010, p. 1).

Campus administrators should also facilitate new connections and collaborations so they can be proactive in supporting LGBT veterans following the repeal of DADT. Veterans' offices and LGBT centers should initiate conversations about how they can provide welcoming spaces for LGBT veterans on campus (Leets, 2011). Further, it is important to understand that transgender service members still cannot serve openly in the U.S. military, even following the DADT repeal; practitioners should consider the implications of this exclusion in their outreach to transgender veterans (Leets, 2011).

Child Care

Although all parenting veterans may grapple with child care, social expectations continue to situate the responsibility largely upon women. Further, a higher percentage of women veterans are divorced compared to non-veteran women and male veterans (National Center for Veterans Analysis and Statistics, 2011). Not all of these divorced women have children, yet it is reasonable to infer that those who are parents are more likely to be the primary, if not the sole, caregivers. Thus, administrators can anticipate the need for child-care services among single parents, and single mothers in particular. Campus programs that cater to single parents by providing access to parenting education, child-care referrals, and peer mentoring may prove to be particularly appealing to women veterans returning to civilian life who are potentially overwhelmed by single parenting responsibilities (Burns Phillips, 2010). By example, the KSU CAVS office provides a single parent program in order to attract women veterans with children. Those campuses with single parent programs should make a concerted effort to recruit and invite participation of women veterans with children.

ACE identified that women veterans returning to campus need "child care services that are not only affordable, but also within walking distance of the campus so they can make brief visits to their children during the school day" (Burns Phillips, 2010, p. 1). Though having affordable child-care services on campus is ideal, less than 60 percent of the campuses surveyed by ACE had campus day-care programs (Burns Phillips, 2010). For those with day care, campuses could set aside a few spaces for last-minute registrations for children of returning veterans and review policies to ensure sensitivity to early departure without penalty, should a student be (re)deployed (Burns Phillips, 2010). For those campuses without day care, starting a program is an option, but alternatives are available. A campus can collaborate with nearby institutions, local places of worship, or other community organizations to create affordable child care. Campuses are also encouraged to host visiting days for children so they can familiarize themselves with the campus (Burns Phillips, 2010) and offer children free admission to campus programs.

Career Services

Only about 38 of the 123 campuses surveyed by ACE have individuals in their career services offices who are knowledgeable about the military-to-civilian translation of skills for a résumé (Burns Phillips, 2010). This is an issue for all student veterans, and campuses would be wise to provide training for career services personnel in this area. However, some particular considerations relate to veterans, such as negotiating for wages and benefits. In the military, wages and benefits are standardized: "regardless of race/ethnicity or gender, service-members of the same rank receive the same military pay" (Moore & Webb, 2000, p. 217). The authors noted that this is not the case in the civilian sector "where, for example, men and women in the same jobs, at the same level, sometimes receive different salaries, often lower for women" (p. 217). Thus, student veterans benefit from career counseling on how to negotiate effectively for wages and benefits, as well as knowledge about pay inequities that persist for women and minorities. Additionally, career counselors should educate LGBT graduates (veterans and nonveterans alike) about negotiating for same-sex and domestic partner benefits.

Health and Counseling

Several authors have emphasized the need for campuses to better support the mental and physical health of student veterans, and, more specifically, many have identified the unique needs and circumstances of women veterans (Burns Phillips, 2010; DiRamio et al., 2008). As described above, the rates of MST are high for women veterans, and researchers report that long-term emotional and physical effects of MST can include substance abuse as well as "anxiety, depression, headaches, sleep disturbances, gastrointestinal disorders, nausea, and sexual dysfunction" (Skinner et al., 2000, p. 291). Thus, campus health and counseling personnel should be trained and prepared to support women veterans around these issues. Such knowledge can be acquired by initiating or attending VA- and community-sponsored mental health summits on topics such as PTSD, MST, anxiety disorders, and depression.

Some have observed that VA health care systems were designed for and are still geared to treat men, and this may be a contributing factor in lower rates of women veterans' use of VA health services (Hoff & Rosenheck, 1998). By contrast, one study reports that black and Hispanic veterans (not disaggregated by gender) are more likely to use VA inpatient and outpatient care. Harada and colleagues (2002) reported, "black veterans were more than three times as likely, and Hispanic veterans two times as likely, as white veterans to use VA ambulatory care" (p. 126). Harada and colleagues' study (2002) of the aspects of veteran identity that influence use of VA outpatient care found that racial minority veterans prefer the VA to other systems of care, and they suggested this may be related to high identification with their veteran status and higher rates of being uninsured. Campus health and counseling entities should target all student veterans, including veterans of color, in education and outreach efforts, but these findings provide some context for understanding what might influence veterans' relative use (or lack of use) of these campus resources.

Fontana and Rosenheck's (2006) study of trauma, change in strength of religious faith, and use of mental health services among veterans treated for PTSD suggested that spirituality should perhaps be more central to treatment, either in the form of a greater role for pastoral counseling or a wider inclusion of spiritual issues in traditional psychotherapy. This invites opportunities for campus personnel and local houses of worship to collaborate on outreach and services to veterans. The needs of LGBT veterans on campus also warrant greater attention by health and counseling offices. These student veterans may be harder to identify and will likely be more cautious about "outing" themselves; however, targeted outreach is important and timely. As DADT becomes a military relic, and with evidence that some LGBT veterans are more likely to "come out" postservice (Estes, 2007; Meyer, 2003; Pope, 2011), campus health and counseling programs should prepare to meet the needs of this population. However, the U.S. Department of Defense and the VA have been slow to provide post-DADT training resources on their web sites or through in-person training opportunities; thus, higher education administrators have the opportunity to develop and design germane mental health training for practitioners working with veterans on college campuses. Collaboration, for instance, between LGBT center staff and campus mental health officials would be a welcome start. For those campuses with graduate programs, campus administrators can tap the resources among their graduate-level student body, especially those in the helping fields who are also veterans. Some graduate students may wish to enhance their career-related experiences by creating and administering trainings based on research, collaboration, and personal experiences. Kent State, for instance, tapped such resources to develop a Veteran Suicide Prevention program.

Campus mental health officials should also learn more about U.S. military policy in order to understand the historical and current contexts, restrictions, and consequences that have resulted in veterans' reluctance to seek services. For instance, current military regulations medically disqualify transsexual men and women from service (*Documenting Courage*, 2010). The risks for disqualification leave most silenced, and many do not seek health care. Even after discharge, some gay and lesbian veterans do not utilize VA inpatient or outpatient services due to fear and mistrust (*Documenting Courage*, 2010; Mizock & Fleming, 2011); transgender veterans share this reluctance. Campus administrators might consider required training for their mental health providers on military culture and policies in order to help them more effectively connect and reach out to the student veteran population. For example, college and university counselors could take courses on military history or attend conferences that provide workshops and program sessions that address military culture and student veterans' transitions to the higher education environment.

Grant and colleagues (2011) found that 30 percent of the transgender adult study respondents reported having a physical disability or mental health condition that substantially affected a major life activity. Yet Bryant and Schilt (2008) found that at least 10 percent of transgender veterans reported being turned away from the VA because they are transgender. These respondents also described a dearth of clear and consistent practice, lack of respect from health personnel, and organizational and interpersonal discrimination (Bryant & Schilt, 2008). In 2011, the VA released a new directive on providing health care "without discrimination" for transgender veterans (Sandeen, 2011). Campus health and counseling offices should review policies and protocols and facilitate sensitivity training for staff members to ensure that they, too, are prepared to provide physical and mental health care "without discrimination" for transgender student veterans (Mizock & Fleming, 2011).

Suicide is a significant health care issue facing student veterans. Veterans, especially males aged 30 to 79 and females aged 40 to 59, are at higher risk of suicide than their nonveteran peers (McCarthy et al., 2009). (The broad age range for men serves to indicate that male veterans, of all age categories from 30 to 79, had increased risk relative to similarly aged men in the general population; the highest suicide rates were found in male veterans aged 30 to 39). LGBT persons, in the broader society, are more likely to attempt suicide than their heterosexual counterparts (Boarts, 2008; D'Augelli & colleagues, 2005), from which we can infer that LGBT veterans are at increased risk of suicide. Further, higher rates of suicide are discovered among individuals experiencing MST (Valente & Wight, 2007) or PTSD (McCarthy et al., 2009), and among African American LGBT individuals (Boarts, 2008). Effective suicide prevention interventions on campus are urgently needed.

Social Support and Networking

Researchers report that developing social supports is an important strategy for veterans dealing with the emotional content of trauma and war, and is associated with well-being (Hunt & Robbins, 2001). Equally notable, the lack of social support can lead to isolation or detachment (Loo, 1993). Thus, when developing social support initiatives for student veterans, campus personnel should consider how to best involve and support women veterans, veterans of color, and LGBT veterans. Intragroup dialogue is one strategy that can enable specific populations, such as LGBT veterans, to build cohesiveness, understanding, and mutual support. However, campus personnel should be cautious about appearing to only or primarily address the needs of women veterans, veterans of color, and LGBT veterans through "special" programming or social support, as such efforts risk reinforcement of out-group perceptions.

Women veterans, veterans of color, and LGBT veterans may also benefit from mentoring opportunities. One model initiative is the "Dear Jane" campaign, a letter-writing initiative developed by the Business and Professional Women's Foundation (see the list of resources at the end of this chapter for more information about this campaign). "Dear Jane" connects deployed military women readying for separation from the service with current veterans to share what worked and what did not work in their transition efforts. Student orientation staff could adapt this campaign to design mentoring opportunities during orientation that pair new student veterans with upper-class student veterans. Similarly, leadership development staff could assign a seasoned student leader with an emerging student leader. Practitioners could match upper-class student veterans with veteran alumni, not only to provide outlets for reflecting on the campus experience and how to negotiate particular challenges, but also to network and prepare for the anticipated transition to professional life after graduation. In addition to serving as mentors and resources, alumni may be at points in their identity developments (racial, sexual, or gender) that allow them to assist the development of other social support initiatives. For instance, an alumnus of The Citadel who was closeted as a student founded the Citadel Gay and Lesbian Alliance, an alumni association that "connects gay or gay-friendly students, faculty, and alumni" (Estes, 2010, p. 61).

Addressing Structural Inequalities

Implementing these recommendations without addressing the sociocultural and organizational practices that produce discrimination, marginalization, and isolation would be "folly" (Houser, 2007, p. 969). Additional efforts are needed to ameliorate the systemic sociocultural factors that perpetuate the structural inequalities discussed above. One starting place for change is training and education. Researchers found, for example, that training on sexual harassment for military personnel is associated with more favorable attitudes toward women (Vogt, Bruce, Street, & Stafford, 2007). Campus personnel should develop educational initiatives that explore, with students *and* staff, attitudes that normalize aggressive masculinity as the "necessary foundation of the military [and other social organizations] rather than being an unfortunate hangover of patriarchy" (Jeffreys, 2007, p. 16). Awareness gained through such efforts has the potential to challenge conceptions of women veterans as victims of MST, LGBT veterans as victims of homophobia, and veterans of color as victims of racial discrimination; it also encourages consideration of how some people choose to perpetuate abuse and discrimination because they have the power to do so, and because it is tacitly sanctioned.

Attitudes are heavily influenced by one's environment (Vogt et al., 2007). In a study of lesbian, gay, and bisexual people, Waldo (1999) found that if those in supervisory roles give the impression that heterosexism is not tolerated, it is less likely to occur. Further, in interviews with Army, Air Force, Marine, and Navy service members who were deployed to the Middle East, Frank (2004) discovered that lesbian and gay service members who were "out" experienced greater degrees of unit cohesion, and that those who remained in the closet about their sexual orientations faced more isolation, fear, and uncertainty. Thus, academic leaders who set expectations for a campus culture that will not tolerate sexism, racism, or heterosexism can begin to cultivate an inclusive environment for *all* student veterans.

Measuring Success

As campus personnel develop and implement initiatives, they should ask: "How will I know if these efforts are successful?" Participation rates in programs and services are one measure: how many and which groups of veterans take advantage of various initiatives? Although rates of participation are a seemingly simple measure, if a particular demographic has not been in attendance, the lack of participation is a telling data point. Correspondingly, campus personnel should seek to learn about participants' satisfaction with any given experiences, such as mentoring activities, orientation programs, or counseling sessions. Point-of-service satisfaction surveys can be developed and administered to gather immediate feedback from participants, and practitioners can identify the areas in which they are performing well and the areas with room for improvement.

More generally, administrators need to acquire a better picture of their populations of enrolled veterans. Recent changes in the Post-9/11 GI Bill require basic exit data on benefit recipients (U.S. Department of Veterans Affairs, 2011). For instance, legislators may increasingly ask if GI Bill benefits result in veterans' persistence and graduation. The VA predicts that state legislators will also request data in the coming years to determine the success or failure of public universities in addressing the needs of this key constituency (U.S. Department of Veterans Affairs, 2011). Data pertaining to veterans on college campuses are too often so broadly aggregate as to severely limit usefulness. Data should be collected at the point of college application to include veterans who are using VA benefits, veterans who are not using benefits, applicable GI Bill chapter, gender, race, and ethnicity so that a profile of the campus veteran population can be generated. The veteran benefit certification process requires specific sets of data to be transmitted based on each veteran's discharge papers and GI Bill application. Both sets of data are useful and can inform campus administrators about the numbers of veterans on campus overall, demographic information, and the numbers of veterans who served in prior military conflicts.

These efforts require the collection of new data as well as new or improved analyses of existing data. We may know the average rates of enrollment and graduation among veterans and nonveterans, but it can be difficult to examine trends among different groups of veterans based on demographic or background characteristics. Bensimon (2005) called for administrators to disaggregate all student outcome data by race and ethnicity, and by gender within race and ethnicity categories, in order to reveal possible patterns of unequal outcomes; this call applies to student veteran data as well. At present, campuses combine multiple identity-based groups in the category "veteran," which effectively masks any subgroup differences. Disaggregating data can illuminate discrepancies as well as inequities and can prompt conversations about unequal outcomes. Useful, complete data "can intensify learning, confirm or refute untested hypotheses, challenge preconceived ideas, motivate further inquiry, and provide the impetus for change" (Bensimon, 2005, p. 106).

Conclusion

Even in our media-rich culture that circulates images of veterans embodying a broad range of demographics, the image of a veteran as male, white, and heterosexual continues to dominate. This stereotype can hinder the acculturation and success of women veterans, veterans of color, and LGBT veterans on campus, and can further exacerbate the barriers that veterans may encounter while transitioning to campus life. Investing the administrative energy, focus, and synergy necessary to deconstruct structural barriers holds the potential to bear noticeable and measureable outcomes for *all* veterans on campus and the student body overall.

We note a few points and cautions that warrant future exploration. We have described women veterans, veterans of color, and LGBT veterans as discrete populations, yet they are not mutually exclusive. For example, lesbian and gay veterans are not without gender, and women are not without race or ethnicity. Thus, as universities develop initiatives and interventions to support veterans returning to campus, it is essential to recognize the complexity and multidimensionality of veteran identity.

Further, this chapter did not explore varied types of institutions and how institutional type may influence the experience of student veterans. For example, whereas many veterans of color may feel isolated at predominantly white institutions in rural areas, their experiences would likely be different at urban, demographically diverse community colleges.

For-profit and online colleges, which are currently under scrutiny for questionable recruitment practices targeting veterans (Lipton, 2010), are another context that warrants consideration. Administrators are encouraged to consider the institutional type, geography, and demographic makeup of their individual campuses and translate the information in this chapter in ways that makes sense to their unique institutional contexts.

Finally, we must be cautious not to frame conversations about student veterans disproportionately in terms of shortcomings or deficiencies. Hermann, Rayback, and Wilson (2008) emphasized student veterans' challenges, such as academic preparedness, denial of academic credit for military training, and physical and mental illnesses; yet, student veterans also bring assets and strengths to campus and to their individual lives. Hassan, Jackson, Lindsay, McCabe, and Sanders (2010) called for administrators to "broaden the paradigm of the student veteran from deficits to strengths, from shortcomings to possibilities, and from isolation to community" (p. 32). We echo this call. Respondents in our qualitative study of the experiences of women veterans (Iverson & Anderson, 2010) were quick to note that if women veterans are described predominantly as in need of more support, we risk reifying dominant images of women as weak or vulnerable, and they would be less likely to respond to invitations for their participation in such research projects as they reject essentialized characterizations of their identities.

In the post–World War II era, "no one anticipated the tidal wave of veterans who would go to college after the war" (Wilson, 1994, p. 35). Now, as President Obama continues plans to withdraw troops from combat zones, colleges certainly should anticipate a substantial influx of returning veterans (Hassan et al., 2010). Campus administrators have the opportunity with the Post-9/11 GI Bill to be strategic and inclusive in institutional efforts to provide welcoming, friendly, and affirming spaces for *all* veterans on campus.

Resources

American Council on Education (ACE), *The Female Veteran-Friendly Campus*
> http://www.acenet.edu/Content/NavigationMenu/Programs Services/OWHE/Female_Veteran-Friendly_Campus_issue _brief.pdf

The ACE Office of Women in Higher Education (OWHE)
published an issue brief (2010) addressing issues women veterans
face and offering practical options for institutions serving these
students.

American Veterans for Equal Rights (AVER)

http://aver.us/aver/

AVER is a nonprofit, chapter-based association of active, reserve
and veteran service members dedicated to full and equal rights and
equitable treatment for all present and former members of the U.S.
armed forces.

American Women Veterans

http://www.americanwomenveterans.org/

American Women Veterans is the nation's preeminent,
nonpartisan, 501(c)3 nonprofit organization that serves, honors
and empowers women veterans and their families from all eras and
branches of service.

Black Veterans for Social Justice

http://www.bvsj.org/

This group is committed to fighting injustices suffered by
individuals at the hands of the military and society at large, and to
assisting military personnel in making a smooth transition from
active duty to civilian life.

Business and Professional Women's Foundation (BPW), Joining Forces for Women Veterans' Mentorship Program

http://www.bpwfoundation.org/index.php/issues/women_
veterans/

BPW has developed a "Blueprint for Action" to support women
veterans and their families as they return to their civilian lives. In
particular, they focus on providing mentorships and have
developed a "Dear Jane" campaign that connects women members
of the military to benefits and resources as they transition into
civilian life.

Kent State University, Center for Adult and Veteran Services

http://www.kent.edu/cavs/index.cfm

GI Jobs Military Friendly School 2011, 2012 that offers programs,
services and a Facebook page for women veterans.

National Alliance on Mental Illness (NAMI)

http://www.nami.org/

NAMI has a veterans' resource center with a section dedicated to "veterans of culturally diverse populations"; this includes a comprehensive list of culturally specific resources, with links to reports, videos, and other web sites.

National Association for Black Veterans (NABVETS)
http://www.nabvets.com/
This professional organization provides strategic advocacy on behalf of its membership with Congress, the Federal Administration, State Administrations and other agencies and organizations; personal advocacy on behalf of veterans; advocacy for youth and on behalf of families; and historical advocacy to generate and preserve the historical record.

Ohio Department of Veterans Services, Women Veterans Advisory Committee
http://dvs.ohio.gov/committees/women_veterans_advisory_committee.aspx
This site has information about an annual conference on women veterans in the state of Ohio.

The Palm Center
http://www.palmcenter.org/
A leader in commissioning and disseminating research in the areas of gender, sexuality, and the military.

Servicemembers Legal Defense Network (SLDN)
www.sldn.org/
SLDN is devoted to assisting those affected by "Don't Ask, Don't Tell, Don't Pursue."

The Society of Hispanic Veterans
http://www.hispanicveterans.org/
This organization, located in Florida, was created to help and assist veterans in need. The Society is also an official supporter of the Veterans History Project, collecting personal recollections of Hispanic veterans.

A Soldier's Heart
http://www.soldiersheart.net/index.shtml
A Soldier's Heart addresses the emotional, moral, and spiritual needs of veterans, their families, and communities, including a support program specifically for women veterans.

Transgender American Veterans Association (TAVA)

http://www.tavausa.org/about.html

TAVA acts proactively with other concerned LGBT organizations to ensure that transsexual and transgendered veterans will receive appropriate care for medical conditions.

United Mexican-American Veterans Association (UMAVA)

http://umava.org

This association promotes understanding, appreciation, and respect for the sacrifices and commitment given by the Hispanic/Mexican-American veterans; toward this end, they record oral and written histories, compile documentaries, and create memorials honoring Hispanic/Mexican-American veterans.

United States Department of Veteran Affairs, Center for Women Veterans

http://www.va.gov/womenvet/

This site includes information on the National Training Summit on Women Veterans in Washington, DC, July 2011.

References

Anderson, C. W., & Smith, H. R. (1993). Stigma and honor: Gay, lesbian, and bisexual people in the U.S. military. In L. Diamant (Ed.), *Homosexual issues in the workplace* (pp. 65–89). Washington, DC: Taylor & Francis.

Baechtold, M., & De Sawal, D. M. (2009). Meeting the needs of women veterans. In R. Ackerman & D. DiRamio (Eds.), *Creating a veteran-friendly campus: Strategies for transition success*. New Directions for Student Services, 126, pp. 35–43. San Francisco: Jossey-Bass.

Benello, J. P., Ettinger, W., & Helfand, J. (Executive Producers), & McLagan, M., & Sommers, D. (Directors). (2008). *Lioness* [Motion picture]. United States: Room 11 Productions & Chicken & Egg Pictures.

Bensimon, E. M. (2005). Closing the achievement gap in higher education: An organizational learning perspective. In A. Kezar (Ed.), *Organizational learning in higher education*. New Directions for Higher Education, 131, pp. 99–111. San Francisco: Jossey-Bass.

Boarts, J. M. (2008). *Psychological predictors of health risk behaviors in minority lesbian, gay, bisexual, and transgendered adolescents*. (Doctoral dissertation). Kent State University, Kent.

Bryant, K., & Schilt, K. (2008). *Transgender people in the U.S. military: Summary and analysis of the 2008 Transgender American Veterans Association survey*. Santa Barbara: The University of California Palm Center & the Transgender American Veterans Association.

Bumiller, E. (2010, October 2). For female Marines, tea comes with bullets. *The New York Times*. Retrieved from http://www.nytimes.com/2010/10/03/world/asia/03marines.html

Bumiller, E. (2011, July 22). Obama ends "Don't Ask, Don't Tell" policy. *The New York Times*. Retrieved from http://www.nytimes.com/2011/07/23/us/23military.html

Burns Phillips, D. (2010, July). *The female veteran-friendly campus*. Washington, DC: American Council on Education Office of Women in Higher Education. Retrieved from http://www.acenet.edu

Burrelli, D. F., & Feder, J. (2009). *Homosexuals and the U.S. military: Current issues*. Washington, DC: Congressional Research Service.

Card, C. (1994). The military ban and the ROTC: A study in closeting. *Journal of Homosexuality, 27*(3–4), 117–146.

Cooney Jr., R. T., Segal, M. W., Segal, D. R., & Falk, W. W. (2003). Racial differences in the impact of military service on the socioeconomic status of women veterans. *Armed Forces & Society, 30*, 53–86.

D'Amico, F., & Weinstein, L. (1999). *Gender camouflage: Women and the U.S. military*. New York: New York University Press.

D'Augelli, A. R., Grossman, A. H., Salter, N. P., Vasey, J. J., Starks, M. T., & Sinclair, K. O. (2005). Predicting the suicide attempts of lesbian, gay, and bisexual youth. *Suicide and Life-Threatening Behavior, 35*(6), 646–660.

DiRamio, D., Ackerman, R., & Mitchell, R. L. (2008). From combat to campus: Voices of student-veterans. *NASPA Journal, 45*(1), 73–102.

Documenting courage: Gay, lesbian, bisexual and transgender veterans speak out. (2010). Washington, DC: American Veterans for Equal Rights, Human Rights Campaign & Servicemembers Legal Defense Network.

Estes, S. (2007). *Ask and tell: Gay and lesbian veterans speak out*. Chapel Hill: University of North Carolina Press.

Estes, S. (2010, spring). The long gay line: Gender and sexual orientation at The Citadel. *Southern Cultures*, 46–64.

Fendrich, J. M. (1972). The returning Black Vietnam-era veteran. *Social Service Review, 46*(1), 60–75.

Fendrich, J. M., & Axelson, L. J. (1971). Marital status and political alienation among Black veterans. *American Journal of Sociology, 77*(2), 245–261.

Fontana, A., & Rosenheck, R. (2006). Treatment of female veterans with posttraumatic stress disorder: The role of conflict in a predominantly male environment. *Psychiatric Quarterly, 77*(1), 55–67.

Francke, L. B. (1997). *Ground zero: The gender wars in the military*. New York: Simon & Schuster.

Frank, N. (2004). *Gays and lesbians at war: Military service in Iraq and Afghanistan under "Don't Ask, Don't Tell, Don't Pursue."* Santa Barbara: University of California, Santa Barbara Center for the Study of Sexual Minorities in the Military. Retrieved from http://www.palmcenter.org/system/files/Frank091504_GaysAtWar.pdf

Garland, K. (2007). *An exploratory study of lesbian, gay, bisexual, and transgender veterans of recent U.S. conflicts*. (Master's thesis). Northampton, MA: Smith College School for Social Work.

Gates, G. (2003). *Gay veterans top one million*. Washington, DC: The Urban Institute. Retrieved from http://www.urban.org/publications/900642.html

Grant, J. M., Mottet, L. A., & Tanis, J. (2011). *Injustice at every turn: A report of the National Transgender Discrimination Survey.* Washington, DC: The National Gay and Lesbian Task Force and the National Center for Transgender Equality.

Grimes, A., Meehan, M., Miller, D., Mills, S. E, Ward, M. C., & Wilkinson, N. P. (2011). Beyond the barricade: A holistic view of veteran students at an urban university. *Journal of the Indiana University Student Personnel Association,* 62–74.

Harada, N. D., Damron-Rodriguez, J., Villa, V. M., Washington, D. L., Dhanani, S., Shon, H., … Anderson, R. (2002). Veteran identity and race/ethnicity: Influences on VA outpatient care utilization. *Medical Care, 40*(1), I117–I128.

Hassan, A. M., Jackson, R., Lindsay, D. R., McCabe, D. G., & Sanders III, J. E. (2010). The veteran student in 2010: How do you see me? *About Campus, 15*(2), 30–32.

Hawthorne, L. M. (2011). *A few good (straight) men: Uncoupling the effects of gender roles and sexual orientation on sexual prejudice toward Army personnel.* (Master's thesis). Montana State University, Bozeman.

Hefling, K. (2009, December 14). Female veterans struggle for acceptance. *The Huffington Post.* Retrieved from http://www.huffingtonpost.com/2009/12/14/female-veterans-struggle-_n_390951.html

Herbert, M. S. (1998). *Camouflage isn't only for combat: Gender, sexuality, and women in the military.* New York: New York University Press.

Herbold, H. (1994). Never a level playing field: Blacks and the GI Bill. *Journal of Blacks in Higher Education, 6,* 104–108.

Hermann, D., Rayback, D., & Wilson, R. (2008, November 21). College is for veterans, too. *The Chronicle of Higher Education, 55*(13), A99.

Hoff, R. A., & Rosenheck, R. A. (1998). Female veterans' use of Department of Veterans Affairs health care services. *Medical Care, 36*(7), 1114–1119.

Holder, K. A. (2011). *Educational Attainment of Veterans: 2000 to 2009.* Washington, DC: U.S. Department of Veterans Affairs National Center for Veterans Analysis and Statistics. Retrieved from http://www.va.gov/

Houser, K. (2007). Analysis and implications of the omission of offenders in the DoD care for victims of sexual assault task force report. *Violence Against Women, 13*(9), 961–970.

Hunt, N. & Robbins, I. (2001). World War II veterans, social support, and veterans associations. *Aging & Mental Health, 5*(2), 175–182.

Huynh-Hohnbaum, A. T., Damron-Rodriguez, J., Washington, D. L., Villa, V., & Harada, N. (2003). Exploring the diversity of women veterans' identity to improve delivery of veterans' health services. *Affilia, 18*(2), 165–176.

Hyun, J. K., Pavao, J., & Kimerling, R. (2009). Military sexual trauma. *PTSD Research Quarterly, 20*(2), 1–3.

Iverson, S. V., & Anderson, R. (2010, May 27). *"You don't look like you were in the service": The experiences of women veterans on campus.* Presentation at conference Ohio University Serving Those Who Serve, Kent, Ohio.

Jeffreys, S. (2007). Double jeopardy: Women, the U.S. military and the war in Iraq. *Women's Studies International Forum, 30,* 16–25.

Jordan, B. (2011, February 14). Spec Ops needs a few good women. *Military.com.* Retrieved from http://www.military.com/news/article/spec-ops-needs-a-few-good-women.html

Leets, C. (2011, Fall). How will the DADT repeal affect our campuses? *Out on Campus.* Retrieved from http://www.myacpa.org/sc/sclgbta/newsletter/Fall2011Newsletter .pdf

Lipari, R. N., Cook, P. J., Rock, L. M., & Matos, K. (2008). *2006 gender relations survey of active duty members.* Arlington, VA: U.S. Department of Defense Manpower Data Center.

Lipton, E. (2010, December 9). Profits and scrutiny for colleges courting veterans. *The New York Times,* A1.

Loo, C. M. (1993). An integrative-sequential treatment model for posttraumatic stress disorder: A case study of the Japanese American internment and redress. *Clinical Psychology Review, 13,* 89–117.

McCarthy, J. F., Valenstein, M., Kim, H. M., Ilgen, M., Zivin, K., & Blow, F. C. (2009). Suicide mortality among patients receiving care in the Veterans Health Administration health system. *American Journal of Epidemiology, 169*(8), 1033–1038.

McSally, M. E. (2011). Defending America in mixed company: Gender in the U.S. armed forces. *Daedalus, 140*(3), 148–164.

Meyer, I. H. (2003). Prejudice, social stress, and mental health in lesbian, gay, and bisexual populations: Conceptual issues and research evidence. *Psychological Bulletin, 129*(5), 674–697.

Mizock, L., & Fleming, M. Z. (2011). Transgender and gender variant populations with mental illness: Implications for clinical care. *Professional Psychology Research and Practice, 42*(2), 208–213.

Moore, B. L., & Webb, S. C. (1998). Equal opportunity in the U.S. Navy: Perceptions of active-duty African American women. *Gender Issues, 16*(3), 99–119.

Moore, B. L., & Webb, S. C. (2000). Perceptions of equal opportunity among women and minority Army personnel. *Sociological Inquiry, 70*(2), 215–239.

National Center for Posttraumatic Stress Disorder. (2007). *Military sexual trauma.* Washington, DC: United States Department of Veterans Affairs. Retrieved from http://www.ptsd.va.gov/public/pages/military-sexual-trauma-general.asp

National Center for Veterans Analysis and Statistics. (2011, January). *Profile of veterans: 2009.* Washington, DC: United States Department of Veterans Affairs.

O'Keefe, E. (2010, January 27). Estimate: 66,000 gays in the military. *The Washington Post.* Retrieved from http://voices.washingtonpost.com/federal-eye/2010/01/eye_opener_estimate_66000_gays.html

Perry, T. (2008, November 13). Women on Iraq's front lines. *Los Angeles Times.* Retrieved from http://articles.latimes.com/2008/nov/13/entertainment/et-lioness13

Pope, A. A. (2011). "Don't Ask, Don't Tell"—except in a job interview: The discriminatory effect of the policy on a veteran's employment. *Washington College of Law Legislation and Policy Brief, 3*(1), 87–103. Retrieved from http://digitalcommons.wcl.american.edu/lpb/vol3/iss1/4

Prividera, L. C., & Howard, J. W. (2006). Masculinity, whiteness, and the warrior hero: Perpetuating the strategic rhetoric of U.S. nationalism and marginalization of women. *Women and Language, 29*(2), 29–37.

Radford, A. W. (2009). *Military service members and veterans in higher education: What the new GI Bill may mean for postsecondary institutions.* Washington, DC: American Council on Education.

Robinson Kurpius, S. E., & Lucart, A. L. (2000). Military and civilian undergraduates: Attitudes toward women, masculinity, and authoritarianism. *Sex Roles, 43*(3/4), 255–265.

Sadler, A. G., Booth, B. M., Cook, B. L., & Doebbeling, B. N. (2003). Factors associated with women's risk of rape in the military environment. *American Journal of Industrial Medicine, 43,* 262–273.

Sandeen, A. (2011, July 28). Good news for trans veterans: New VA health care guidelines. *On the Issues Magazine.* Retrieved from http://www.ontheissuesmagazine.com/cafe2/article/165

Segal, D. R. (1999). Diversity in the American military. In J. S. Chafetz (Ed.), *Handbook of the Sociological of Gender,* (pp. 563–582). New York: Springer, 1999.

Skinner, K. M., Kressin, N., Frayne, S., Tripp, T. J., Hankin, C. S., Miller, D. R., & Sullivan, L. M. (2000). The prevalence of military sexual assault among female veterans' administration outpatients. *Journal of Interpersonal Violence, 15*(3), 291–310.

Street, A. E., Stafford, J., Mahan, C. M., & Hendricks, A. (2008). Sexual harassment and assault experienced by reservists during military service: Prevalence and health correlates. *Journal of Rehabilitation Research and Development, 45*(3), 409–419.

Thomas, P. J., & Thomas, M. S. (1996). Integration of women in the military: Parallels to the progress of homosexuals? In G. M. Herek, J. B. Jobe, & R. M. Carney (Eds.), *Coming out in force: Sexual orientation and the military* (pp. 65–85). Chicago: University of Chicago Press.

Turner, S., & Bound, J. (2003). Closing the gap or widening the divide: The effects of the GI Bill and World War II on the educational outcomes of Black Americans. *Journal of Economic History, 63,* 145–177.

United States Department of Veterans Affairs Office of Policy & Planning (2007, September). *Women veterans: Past, present, and future.* Washington, DC: Author.

United States Department of Veterans Affairs. (2011). *School certifying official handbook.* Washington, DC: Author. Retrieved from http://gibill.va.gov/documents/job_aids/SCO_Handbook_v1.pdf

Valente, S., & Wight, C. (2007). Military sexual trauma—Violence and sexual abuse. *Military Medicine, 172*(3), 259–265.

Vogt, D., Bruce, T. A., Street, A. E., & Stafford, J. (2007). Attitudes toward women and tolerance for sexual harassment among reservists. *Violence Against Women, 13*(9), 879–900.

Waldo, C. R. (1999). Working in a majority context: A structural model of heterosexism as minority stress in the workplace. *Journal of Counseling Psychology, 46*(2), 218–232.

Wilson, R. (1994). GI Bill expands access for African Americans. *Educational Record, 75*(4), 32–39.

VIGNETTE

Annie Rose Badder

Student, University of West Georgia

The original idea of the "college experience" is one that I will never be able to fully appreciate. When I think about the college experience, the first things that come to mind are parties and carefree attitudes. I will not be able to experience either of these things. I am a 29-year-old female. I have two children ages five and four, and I am a veteran. I do not have the luxury of some college students to make bad decisions or party from sun up to sundown on the weekends. I have responsibilities and no room for mistakes.

I served in the Navy for eight years, and though I have never been on a "real" deployment (such as Iraq or Afghanistan), I've seen and experienced things that other people my age would not be able to relate to. I started my college experience at a community college in January 2009. My father had passed away two weeks before the start of school, my husband was serving on the front line in Afghanistan, and my children were both under the age of three. I have to admit, it was less than a conventional start to my college "career."

Starting at a community college was better than rushing into a full-blown university. The people around me were a little closer to my age. Though I chose to keep primarily to myself, I noticed that many had both families and jobs. I, fortunately, had the luxury of not working while trying to go to school. Though I didn't have a paying job, I was still a married-single parent; my husband still had six more months in Afghanistan before I would get any help with the kids. I have to admit, I did not start my college career well; I scraped by with the rare A or B, but mostly Cs.

During that time, I felt alone and that nobody could possibly understand what I was going through. Overnight, I went from military acronyms to civilian jargon. Instead of stepping out of my comfort zone, I had taken a flying leap! I no longer belonged to the military life that was so familiar. I was now part of the group of people who "once were" ... military police, corpsman, helicopter mechanics, scout snipers, or other roles that are not recognizable in civilian society as valid jobs unless you have that little piece of paper—a degree.

I transferred from out of state to the University of West Georgia. I've completed my associate's degree and now I'm finishing up my bachelor's degree in criminology. My GPA is currently a 2.7, but I am striving to bring that up to at least a 3.0 before I saunter across the graduation stage. I've already picked out a graduate program to pursue a master's in forensic psychology with an emphasis in criminal investigation and behavior analysis. I have to say, my experience has been pretty good so far. I enjoy coming to school and observing the style of the "kids" nowadays. I have to admit, though, that I feel so old! Listening to my fellow students say things like, "don't sweat my swag" and "that's fire" makes me laugh. What happened to saying, "that's awesome?"

Even though I miss the military lifestyle, every day I learn more about myself and others around me. I become a better person, and I hope that the younger students around me can learn from my experiences in order to enrich their lives. I continue to expand my comfort zone, and eventually I will be able to fully accept and appreciate the college experience that is available to me.

CHAPTER SIX

UNDERSTANDING DISABILITY IN THE STUDENT VETERAN COMMUNITY

Amanda Kraus and Nicholas A. Rattray

In recent years, higher education has experienced a spike in the enrollment of veterans (Church, 2009). Although student veterans have had a presence on college campuses since World War I, current veterans have unique characteristics that shape their experiences in higher education. Compared to veterans from previous eras, improved equipment and advances in medical technology have led to higher survival rates, but also much higher rates of injury. Greater attention is being paid to invisible or hidden injuries that have only recently begun to be legitimated by the U.S. Department of Veterans Affairs (VA). Student veterans' unfamiliarity with the processes tied to campus disability services, such as self-disclosure and documentation, and discomfort in identifying as "disabled" complicates their integration into campus communities (Burnett & Segoria, 2009). Although higher education professionals have developed robust models for understanding student diversity, the unique experiences that veterans bring to campus pose new sets of challenges. In order to contribute to the success of disabled veterans in higher education, practitioners must develop authentic understandings of the complex intersection of disability and veteran status.

Disability is a rich experience for many students. For veterans, this experience becomes further complicated as they negotiate newly acquired disabilities with their transitions out of the military, reintegration into their communities, and their integration to higher education. To begin to understand how to create effective campus programs and services for disabled student veterans, we must consider the factors that shape how individuals conceptualize disability, and how a new injury may affect one's sense of self. This chapter presents resources and replicable models of practice that seek to inform the development of campus-based programs and services, suggests new approaches to connecting with student veterans, and identifies meaningful ways for disabled veterans to connect with their campus communities. (Note: The language used in this chapter reinforces the sociopolitical nature of disability and is also representative of the preferences of veterans. The following terms are used interchangeably: disabled veterans, injured veterans, and veterans with injuries. Person-first language, such as "veterans with disabilities," is also appropriate.)

To better understand the experiences of disabled veterans in higher education, in 2008 the University of Arizona (UA) was awarded a federal grant through the U.S. Department of Education to fund qualitative research, outreach, academic courses, and direct disability and wellness services to better understand the experiences of disabled veterans in higher education. Through this project, our research team explores how student veterans make meaning of disability and identifies barriers that disabled veterans experience in accessing and integrating successfully to higher education. Implications from this research illustrate the richness and complexity of disability identity relevant to student veterans and can inform practice in higher education. This chapter draws from the UA's research, current literature, and national models of practice to provide recommendations for connecting with disabled student veterans and creating programs and services that contribute to their success on campus. We argue that reframing disability in the contexts of language, trust, partnership building, health, wellness and direct services enables us to serve this emerging population holistically.

Disability Experiences Among Student Veterans

This generation of veterans is experiencing a higher rate of disability or injury than previous generations. Whereas Vietnam-era veterans experienced an injury-to-casualty rate of three-to-one, for veterans of Operation Iraqi Freedom (OIF) and Operation Enduring Freedom (OEF) the rate is sixteen-to-one (Stiglitz & Bilmes, 2008). U.S. Department of Defense (DOD) statistics indicate that up to 20 percent of injuries involve the spinal cord, and the number of amputations has surpassed those during the Vietnam era (Bilmes, 2007). Of the 2 million veterans expected to enroll in higher education (Radford, 2009), one quarter will have some type of disability (Tanielian & Jaycox, 2008), and are twice as likely as nonveteran students to have at least one disability (National Survey of Student Engagement [NSSE], 2010). Often mis- and underdiagnosed, this generation of veterans has a high rate of hidden or invisible injuries that include posttraumatic stress disorder (PTSD), traumatic brain injuries (TBIs), and other cognitive or mental effects of service that have an impact on their educational experiences, such as learning disabilities, hearing loss, or chronic pain (Glover-Graf, Miller, & Freeman, 2010).

Student veterans indicate the following as major health concerns relevant to PTSD and TBI: disrupted sleep, insomnia, nightmares, pain, uncontrollable anger, anxiety, depression, flashbacks, difficulty focusing, loneliness, and hypervigilance (Kraus, 2010). Many self-medicate with alcohol or drugs, and very often personal and professional relationships are negatively affected by these symptoms. In addition to the effects of PTSD and TBI, veterans are also grappling with issues of disclosure. Unlike their visibly disabled counterparts, those with psychological disabilities must negotiate how and when to disclose to friends, family, faculty, and staff. Veterans may choose not to pursue treatment for a number of reasons: they may be fearful of the associated stigma or of jeopardizing their future military careers; they may not consider themselves disabled or eligible for disability-related accommodations on campus; or they may experience shame or fear associated with psychological disabilities (Burnett & Segoria, 2009; Kraus, 2010). The ways in which veterans become injured or disabled further complicate how they identify. It is erroneous to assume that the injuries of today's veterans are combat-connected—many veterans have sustained disabilities that are service-connected or are completely unrelated to their service. These veterans may not consider themselves worthy of attention or services and often prioritize those with combat-connected injuries.

Other disabilities highly prevalent among the current generation of veterans include mobility, hearing, and vision impairments. Amputations are the most common physical disability connected to service (Bilmes, 2007). Visual and hearing losses occur at higher rates than in previous eras due to increased vulnerability from accidents or injuries (such as motor vehicle accidents, gunshot or shrapnel, assault, falls, or anoxia), and may also be connected to TBI (Goodrich, 2007). Furthermore, the increasing prevalence of multiple deployments has led to higher rates of physical and mental issues (Kline et al., 2010): in part, this is due to exposure to environmental risks such as poor air quality, biohazards, and depleted uranium (Helmer et al., 2007). When learning to live with new sensory or physical disabilities, veterans undergo extensive rehabilitation processes and may need to relearn everyday behaviors and habits; some will use wheelchairs, prosthetics, orthotics, or sensory aids to maintain autonomy and mobility. It takes time and resources to become independent. The VA may provide medical treatment and associated equipment, including clothing for amputees, sports wheelchairs, and state-of-the-art prosthetics, but deciphering the complex processes of eligibility in procuring medical and education benefits can be confusing for many veterans.

Another phenomenon specific to this generation is that of polytrauma (Lew et al., 2009). Many veterans acquire multiple disabilities as a result of one traumatic event. For example, after a service member's truck is hit with an improvised explosive device (IED), he or she may be diagnosed with PTSD, TBI, burns, and physical and sensory disabilities. VA hospitals have dedicated polytrauma units and staff to offer comprehensive care to these individuals. It is important for higher education professionals to be aware of these situations because many veterans identify with several disabilities, which presents implications for campus programs and services and for academic course instruction.

It is common for injured service members to be released to rehabilitation facilities run by the DOD based on their primary disabilities, and many of these service members wish to return to service or to combat postinjury. Although disability does not always preclude a return to service, for many service members, new disabilities can prompt their separation from the military. Rehabilitation often generates the unrealistic expectation that disabilities can be fixed or cured, especially in light of advances in medical technology and procedures. An extreme version of rehabilitation proposes that veterans will be rendered more capable than they were prior to injury. As we reach out to veterans recently released from rehabilitation centers, we should be aware that they may have varying conceptions about higher education and their places in it. Subsequently, one of the challenges in our interactions with newly disabled student veterans is to develop strategies to normalize their experiences and reframe disability, rather than focus on fixing it.

As part of the dialogue surrounding service-related injuries, we must not forget that some veterans have learning disabilities as well. For many veterans, learning disabilities that were diagnosed in adolescence influenced their decisions to enter the military; many had decided that higher education was not an option for them. Today, as they choose to pursue higher education, the persistence of learning disabilities makes it necessary to educate student veterans on strategies and accommodations that may increase their chances of academic success.

We do not present detailed information on various disabilities in order to reinforce clinical or negative thinking on the topic; rather, we offer some insight into the recent experiences of disabled student veterans. Though we espouse disability as a source of culture, community, and pride, it is clear that many student veterans would not share those concepts. In response, higher education professionals may need to engage in more personal outreach efforts to explain processes associated with eligibility, disclosure, and services. Unlike many of their undergraduate counterparts, student veterans may be newly disabled, may not have the benefit of experiences with resources in their primary and secondary (K–12) educational pursuits, and may not have had parental involvement in their pursuits of accommodations. As veterans choose to request disability-related services, higher education professionals ought to consider different approaches in practice and in the development of effective campus resources than those that are used with the general student population.

Concepts of Disability

As we develop programs and services on campus to support the success of disabled veterans, it is important to explore how they make meaning of disability. Like many of us, veterans have been socialized to think about disability in certain ways. Traditionally, disability is represented through a medical lens in which it is conceived as an impairment or bodily abnormality belonging to an individual with the obvious intervention to fix or cure the problem (Albrecht, Seelman, & Bury, 2001). The "problem" is situated within the individual. The media reflect this frame (Haller, 1997, 2010; Longmore, 2003); newspaper headlines, television sit-coms, and movies present disability in negative, damaging ways. For example, disability is often portrayed as tragic or pitiful, a fate worse than death (Haller 1997, 2010). Disabled individuals are also presented as inspirational, magical super heroes, or as villains or threats—rarely as ordinary, regular people for whom disability is one piece of multidimensional identities. Beyond the media, we receive messages about disability through design and policy. The Americans with Disabilities Act (ADA) Standards for Accessible Design (1991, 2010) puts forth parameters by which access is often defined. Though this landmark legislation provides visibility and recourse for disabled individuals, it also sustains a minimal concept of access—one that is often limited, separate, and not equitable to the nondisabled experience. Both disabled and nondisabled people alike are socialized to understand disability through these disempowering messages. These ideas shape not only our personal assumptions and beliefs about disability, but our policy and practice as well.

In addition to these ubiquitous societal cues, veterans have also been heavily influenced by their service in the military in that they have learned the value of disability from the DOD and the VA. In the military, service members are trained not to admit weakness; their careers depend on being fit for duty. We must keep in mind that veterans are negotiating various systems and, therefore, concepts of disability. As they integrate into higher education, they retain concepts of disability based on medical rehabilitation that are reinforced by continued treatment at VA hospitals aimed at "fixing" bodies. It is important to consider the complex array of concepts that influence the meanings attached to disability.

Although identifying and reporting disabilities is crucial to receiving services at universities, many veterans learn to suppress and hide injuries and frequently experience trepidation in disclosing even insignificant injuries for fear of repercussion. Left untreated, even seemingly small injuries can worsen, causing permanent injury or disability. Many veterans and other service members indicate that they equate disability with failure or incapacity (Kraus, 2010). During their service, members of the military are often encouraged to minimize or hide injuries, or as one person put it, "take lots of ibuprofen" (Kraus, Rattray, & Standage, 2010); by identifying their injuries, they risk compromising their military careers. The DOD (U.S. Department of Defense, 2011) reports incidents of injury with its casualty statistics, indicating who is fit to return to duty. This fear or reluctance to personally identify as disabled or with disability remains prevalent and has direct implications for our practice on campus.

The VA rating system plays an important role in how veterans conceptualize disability. Upon exiting the military, each service member is required to complete an assessment and identify any injuries as part of the Transition Assistance Program (TAP). The VA uses this assessment as a way to determine eligibility for medical benefits; a veteran can be given multiple ratings for various disabilities or injuries, and the overall rating determines medical compensation. However, conflicts arise when an individual seeks a higher rating to procure increased compensation, but does not truly identify with the rating. For example, a certain disability or combination of disabilities could yield a disability rating of 100 percent. Individuals with multiple injuries may receive disability ratings that are greater than 100 percent. The complexity of the VA's classification system can result in a situation in which a veteran's disability rating does not match his or her self-concept.

A promising development in the way disability is conceived in higher education has emerged with the field of disability studies. As an interdisciplinary field, disability studies focuses on the rich histories of disabled individuals and the representation of disability across various areas, promotes greater understanding of the experience of disability, and advocates for social change (Albrecht et al., 2001). Disability scholars and activists argue that disability is a sociopolitical construct created and perpetuated by an environment with barriers that exclude disabled people from access and participation. This concept minimizes the impact of an individual's impairment and locates the problem, or burden of responsibility, within the environment. These ideas are increasingly espoused by educators, designers, and policymakers.

The idea of quantifying a disability, as in the approach used by the VA, is contrary to newer, more progressive ways of conceiving of disability. During their work in the military, veterans have been trained to fight for justice. Introducing veterans to a concept of disability that focuses less on individuals' impairments and more on equitable and usable physical space, policy, and curricula appeals not only to their prior training, but also helps them identify more readily with disability on personal levels (Branker, 2009). It is important to consider that we in higher education interact with disabled student veterans who have been socialized to think about disability in ways that affect disability identity formation and challenge ideas of disability community or culture. Disabled student veterans readily acknowledge disability as an important aspect of their communities, but display ambivalence in how they identify personally (DiRamio, Ackerman & Mitchell, 2008). Higher education practitioners cannot assume that they know how individual disabled veterans identify. We must be cognizant of this very personal and complicated process as we reach out to veterans; building trust and rapport is critical.

Student veterans use an informal, unspoken hierarchy to assign value to acquired disabilities (Kraus et al., 2010). This hierarchy is informed by the variety of disabilities and the concepts previously discussed; the circumstances that cause disablement are of critical importance to this schema. According to this hierarchy, a combat-related injury garners more respect than other injuries. Injuries sustained in combat or combat theater are more highly valued than injuries sustained stateside, during military trainings, or those not connected to combat or service. For example, a service member who loses a leg in combat is considered more deserving of respect and services than one who is involved in an automobile accident that occurred in the United States. An individual who sustained an injury unconnected to service may not believe that he or she is as deserving of accommodations as a friend injured in combat. Similarly, hidden injuries tend to receive less validation than loss of body parts or more visible impairments. As a personal identifier, the value that an individual places on his or her own injury may determine whether or not he or she feels deserving of certain recognition or the right to access particular campus services. As we in higher education seek to connect with disabled student veterans, knowledge of group dynamics, such as this hierarchy, are useful in understanding how disability is conceptualized within the student veteran community. This type of insight can be used to inform professional practice.

Best Practices

As veterans have become more visible across campuses, many universities have created new programs or modified support and outreach for students with military experience. For instance, the University of Minnesota established a "One Stop Veterans Office" at the Twin Cities campus aimed at consolidating services. In addition, they have also created a veteran-specific orientation, developed new policies such as waiving late fees, established a "Veterans Transition Center," and instituted a reintegrated program for faculty and staff. The University of California-Berkeley (UC), has built on the UC-wide "Troops to College" initiative to foster a welcoming programs for student veterans including the "Cal Veterans Group," a designated academic course called "Veterans in Higher Education," and other services that are part of the Transfer, Re-Entry, and Student Parent Center. These institutions incorporate disability resources into their programs, demonstrating an understanding that disability is an important aspect of the experience of returning veterans. The Association of Higher Education and Disability (AHEAD) has a special interest group dedicated to Wounded Warriors. This professional association provides excellent resources on national best practices. The National Association of Student Personnel Administrators (NASPA) Veterans Knowledge Community is also composed of higher education professionals who work to improve the experiences of student veterans. This group is well versed on campus-based disability resources for veterans.

The practices discussed in this section represent a holistic approach to conceptualizing disability and veteran status. These models of practice encourage professionals to think broadly about ways to build rapport with this student population and create meaningful opportunities for disabled student veterans to connect with campus. Drawing upon research, established practice, and infusing the values of student veterans into our work, these recommended practices inform one another and encourage flexibility, openness, and innovation in our campus approaches. We draw upon the UA's pilot project, including data from a professionals' roundtable that convened representatives from over thirty-five institutions and organizations for two annual meetings, as well as national organizations such as the American Council on Education (ACE), AHEAD, and NASPA.

Veterans arrive in higher education through various nontraditional paths. Some chose military service as an alternative to higher education because of their dislike for school. Others aspire to higher education and chose the military as a way to finance future education. And some plan for careers in the service, but because of disability are forced to separate from the military. For those who planned to have military careers, higher education is a bittersweet opportunity. Unlike their undergraduate counterparts, newly disabled veterans do not approach campus disability services with prior experience with K–12 individualized education plans (IEPs) or with the involvement of their parents. They are familiarizing themselves with their new disability identities as they learn about the resources and services available to them, hence the need to reenvision campus programs and services.

One of the central challenges in working with veterans on campus stems from reluctance on the part of individual veterans to identify as having disabilities. Often, the primary way that veterans think about disability stems from their VA-assigned "disability ratings." Individuals' VA ratings can be contentious, as previously mentioned. There is a contradiction for individuals who are reluctant to identify with disability, but will often need to fight for disability ratings in order to procure necessary compensation. A second meaning of disability relates to student status in the university. Are individual students registered and do they receive services from disability services in the form of reasonable accommodations? This model, familiar in higher education, is framed around trying to make the experience of disabled students in the classroom commensurate with that of nondisabled students. Research indicates that most veterans initially resist being labeled as "disabled" and avoid initiating contact with disability services (Burnett & Segoria, 2009).

Often, student veterans with invisible injuries downplay their injuries or try to pass as nondisabled. In a survey of student veterans conducted at the UA in 2011, 52 percent of respondents had disability ratings from the VA, yet fewer participants (45 percent) reported sustaining service-related injuries or disabilities. When asked about identifying as persons with disabilities, the figure dipped to 15 percent. The reluctance of veterans to identify as disabled in ways that make them identifiable to the campus community was made clear during an interview with Antoine (pseudonym), 28, who has served three tours in Iraq as a Navy corpsman (Kraus et al., 2010). Although Antoine indicated in a questionnaire that he had sustained a service-related injury, he minimized its impact and declined to discuss disability in general until the end of the interview. When asked again, Antoine explained that in fact he had a number of VA ratings for disability: "Well, I got PTSD. They gave me that last year or so. Back and knees and just basic joint stuff. Well, I got actually—not too long ago I got diagnosed with a mild TBI just from getting tossed around the back of a truck, hit with a couple explosions, but that's about it. No puncture wounds or gun shots or anything like that" (Kraus et al., 2010, data set). Despite not indicating disabilities on the questionnaire, Antoine had serious physical and psychological injuries that merited disability ratings from the VA. However, his nonchalance underscores the attitude that many veterans have toward their injuries—they lean toward nondisclosure unless circumstances require identification (Church, 2008). Experience also suggests that over time, many students become more comfortable and more positive in their thinking about disability after they have connected with campus disability services and other veterans who actively adopt disability identities.

Building Relationships with Student Veterans

There is a need to reach out to disabled student veterans to introduce available resources and the disability community and culture. Often, it does not occur to student veterans to access disability services on campus, or they are reluctant to do so because they do not readily identify with the term "disability." Further, disabled student veterans tend to be unfamiliar with disability-related policy and practice on college campuses. This section offers models that may inform outreach and marketing efforts and provide insight on how to build rapport and trust with disabled student veterans.

Because of the ambiguity many disabled student veterans experience when thinking about disability, higher education professionals—specifically those who work in veterans services or disability services offices—must engender strong, trusting relationships with disabled student veterans. There are many ways to build solid relationships with this population. Because veterans value peer-to-peer connections and trust the community of veterans, it would be helpful to identify a student veteran who has been successful in utilizing accommodations or disability-related resources and is willing to serve in an ambassador role. The ambassador can speak directly with other student veterans and essentially vouch for or lend credibility to campus resources. One misconception that student veterans have when pursuing accommodations is that they may be taking services away from others with greater need (Kraus, 2010); having this key contact with a peer can mitigate the tendency veterans have to prioritize others' needs before their own. Furthermore, the peer-to-peer relationship the ambassador holds with student veterans can help cultivate healthy relationships with staff.

An effective way to build trust with student veterans is through intentional listening. We must listen to their stories without framing them around disability. We cannot assume the salience of disability for students, or that we share common definitions or language around injury. Because of the tenuous nature of veterans' relationships with their disabilities, we should avoid overlabeling and check our personal biases around veteran and disability status. As the example with Antoine demonstrates, veterans will disclose pertinent information as they are ready. We should strive to engage veterans, and all students, in interactive processes in which we listen and learn.

A key element in how student veterans value individuals is the level of trust. Fellow veterans are nearly always trusted implicitly, whereas nonveterans are treated with skepticism. A select group of civilians or nonveterans who have earned the trust of the larger group of veterans are often referred to as "allies" or "friendlies." Friendlies are dependable, helpful, and trustworthy staff dedicated to advocacy on behalf of the unique issues and needs of student veterans. Staff and faculty who demonstrate loyalty and respect for student veterans' diverse experiences tend to earn the trust of the student veteran community; trusted nonveterans are vetted informally by leaders within the student veteran community over time.

In building relationships with disabled veterans, it may be helpful to reframe disability. As we discussed earlier in the chapter, veterans have been socialized to think about disability in very stigmatizing, negative ways.

In our practice, we can reframe our notions of disability and relocate the problem. In the case of classroom or physical accommodations, we locate the problem in the environment as opposed to within the individual. By identifying a barrier in the learning or physical environment, we alleviate the sense that a veteran with a disability is the source of the problem. Veterans report that an important value integral to military training centers on fighting for justice and equity (Kraus, 2010). When we approach disability as a social responsibility, the issue becomes less about an individual and more about a fair and just community. By working to eliminate environmental barriers and utilize principles of good design, we work toward access and equity—two ideals that resonate with many veterans.

Language in Outreach

Representing disability in our communications with student veterans is crucial to reinforce disability as a significant element of diverse campus communities. As veterans transition into higher education, they may not be familiar with language we commonly use in our practice. Also, as veterans learn to make meaning of disability, the language with which they choose to identify is important. "Person-first" language (such as "persons with disabilities") became popular in the 1990s to emphasize how people should not be defined by their disabilities. Disability scholars and activists offer an alternative to "person-first" language in naming disabled individuals as disabled. This choice emphasizes the collective experiences within the disability community and also reinforces the idea that disabled individuals are disabled by barriers in the environment. However, research conducted at the UA (Kraus, 2011) found that 32 percent of respondents indicated that they avoid using the term "disabled" to identify themselves, 19 percent avoid the term "wounded warrior," and 18 percent avoid the term "wounded." In a similar vein, some leaders in the veteran community purposely try to take the "disorder" out of posttraumatic stress as a way of normalizing their experiences. Disability services offices, by their very title, may be off-putting to student veterans. Intentional language plays a key role in communicating with student veterans. In order to make them feel more comfortable in their pursuits of accommodations, it is important to target programs and services to student veterans as a group rather than focusing on disabled veterans specifically. This approach also increases the likelihood of reaching out to veterans with invisible disabilities.

At the UA, staff initially marketed the "Disabled Veterans Reintegration and Education Project," but soon eliminated "disabled" from the title so as not to make assumptions about identity. Fostering rapport with the larger community was necessary to engender a sense of trust for the project. Though the project remains focused on disability, this broad approach allows students to disclose information about their disabilities more organically, when they feel safe to do so. In light of this decision, we removed "disabled" from program marketing and signage, and also became a major player in developing a comprehensive series of initiatives that contribute to the overall success of veterans on campus.

Partnerships and Collaboration

Partnerships across campus are critical in creating a culture that is welcoming and inclusive of disabled student veterans. We must infuse broad concepts of disability into campus practice by introducing universal design and incorporating disability resources, news, and information on mental health, wellness, and athletics into the student veterans' center. This type of relationship can be helpful in blurring the boundaries of disability on campus, as disabled veterans should have seamless access to all campus resources. Veterans have indicated that regardless of how one personally identifies, disability is an important element of their community. Hence, there is a need to have disability services staff involved in campus efforts to incorporate disability consistently. One promising model was recently developed among community colleges in California (see *Veterans and the Community College: A Training Guide* in the list of resources at the end of this chapter). In partnership with the U.S. Department of Education and the San Francisco Office for Civil Rights, the collaborative effort resulted in an online training program that includes best practices, legal responsibilities, and case studies of programs serving disabled veterans delivered through interviews, video footage, and key articles. The program can be incorporated into in-service trainings for faculty, staff, and administrators at colleges and universities.

Accommodations

Higher education practitioners should become familiar with the multitude of resources that may benefit disabled veterans both academically and socially. This section outlines potential accommodations to address barriers in the academic environment and also the potential benefits of connecting with the disability community. There is a need, as discussed above, to create relationships with disabled student veterans and educate them on available programs and services. Many colleges and universities have dedicated disability services staff members who serve as the "point persons" for veterans. Having a consistent point of contact on campus may help veterans feel more comfortable approaching the disability services office as they are more likely to trust that the person has sensitivity to and awareness of veterans' issues. Identifying this point of contact is a step that most institutions can take despite limited budgets or resources. Staff may wish to provide regular office hours in the student veterans' center in order to be more accessible to students. Eliminating the need for student veterans to physically access the disability services office may alleviate some of the burden or anxiety associated with this experience. Spending time with student veterans outside of the disability services office may also benefit professionals by providing direct insight into their experiences on campus.

Many veterans indicate that due to PTSD or hypervigilance, they find it difficult or impossible to concentrate in class (Glover-Graf et al., 2010). This may compromise their abilities to recall information, take notes, or complete examinations. These students would benefit from connecting with their campuses' disability services offices to pursue accommodations that may include note taking, extended test-taking time, or private or low-distraction space to take examinations. Disability services staff or other campus staff who work with veterans may be able to dialogue with individual students about disclosing their disabilities to instructors. If students feel safe, these types of conversations can strengthen their relationships with instructors and improve the classroom experience.

It may be appropriate to consider a new classification of accommodations specific to veterans. Because of the ambiguity associated with symptoms related to PTSD and TBI, staff and faculty may need to expand their thinking on accommodations. Many symptoms are triggered by common classroom experiences. For example, a student veteran who identifies with hypervigilance may feel uncomfortable sitting with his or her back to the classroom door. It is important for that student to sit near the door and identify a clear exit route. This may not be a traditional accommodation, but it forces us to think differently about the how to best offer equitable access for students with unique experiences. In addition to the multitude of accommodations available on campus, connecting with the disability services office may provide social outlets for disabled veterans. Veterans who have newly acquired disabilities may benefit from meeting other disabled individuals through casual interactions and formal programs, such as wheelchair or adaptive athletics.

Mental Health

When considering how to work effectively with disabled veterans on campus, we must use a broad definition of disability. Because of the high rate of hidden or invisible injuries specific to this generation of veterans, campuses must consider how to support mental health and promote wellness among student veterans. In surveys conducted with student veterans at the UA, a majority of participants rated several health issues as either "moderate" or "high" concerns: anxiety, depression, hypervigilance, stress, and sleeping problems. PTSD was noted as a major issue, and its characteristics were described by one respondent as "anxiety, depression, anger/frustration, and rigidity." Other respondents suggested that PTSD is "rampant" and that many students may be unaware that they are suffering from its effects. The survey results also indicate that many veterans who do not have disability ratings for PTSD still are experiencing symptoms that affect their academic success. Thus, inconsistencies in the way that disability or injuries are defined by the VA, the institution, and in common usage may present barriers to offering services.

Disability services offices may not be adequately equipped to serve students with mental health issues, so it is crucial to link to campus psychological and counseling services or community-based services. In response to the need for on-campus mental health services for enrolled veterans, it is necessary to cultivate links with the local VA office, which can be a critical community-university partnership (Burnett & Segoria, 2009). VA counselors may come to campus to offer on-site individual counseling or group therapy sessions. Because of the unique experiences of women veterans and other diverse subpopulations, it may be prudent to develop group counseling opportunities for specific groups.

Flexibility and open-mindedness to new approaches have proven to be important in reaching out to veterans. For example, some veterans at the UA have participated in energy therapy as a way to cope with symptoms associated with PTSD. Energy healing falls into the area of complementary therapies, or natural approaches, that promote health restoration and healing (Wardell & Weymouth, 2004), and has been found to result in positive effects for mental health (Taylor, 2001). Based on a pilot study with practitioners trained in the "Healing Touch" approach, student veterans at the UA have reported improvements in depression and anxiety levels, and in their sleep patterns. Despite initial hesitancy to participate in alternative approaches, several students have noted progress in their abilities to cope with stress. Students also described learning new techniques for maintaining concentration and noted increased abilities to monitor hypervigilance and other symptoms of PTSD.

In coping with the consequences of mental health issues on campus, many students have emphasized peer-to-peer support and have pinpointed the crucial role played by the student veterans center. "Having fellow veterans that you can talk to about things has made a huge difference," one respondent wrote. "There are things that veterans encounter that many of the younger students just don't get or care to understand." Safe spaces like the student veterans center or veterans-only academic courses can function as outlets for coping with the effects of PTSD. Higher education professionals may want to consider creating a peer support group so that veterans can share and build on their collective knowledge.

Sports and Recreation

We should not underestimate the need for wellness in our work with student veterans. Sports and recreation can provide the outlets necessary for exercise, fitness, teamwork, and stress management for veterans with physical and nonphysical injuries. Veterans and athletes share many characteristics; veterans describe themselves as competitive, healthy, strong, and team-oriented, all of which are qualities we attribute to athletes. Collegiate intramural sports are a way for veterans to connect with campus and foster a team experience that facilitates their wellness. In fact, the advent of wheelchair sports was influenced heavily by disabled World War II veterans who were interested in competitive sports (Wheelchair & Ambulatory Sports, USA [WASUSA], 2011). Those who acquire physical disabilities may believe that they can no longer participate in athletics. The wheelchair and adaptive sports communities are large and provide opportunities for disabled veterans to pursue athletics.

The term "wheelchair sports" refers to sports traditionally played by nondisabled athletes that have been modified to allow for wheelchair users to compete. Wheelchair sports may have modified rules, but the overall play is rigorous and the integrity is high. Adaptive sports encompass sports for those with sensory disabilities, such as goalball, where a ball emits sound to indicate its proximity to the player. Adaptive sports may better accommodate those with brain injuries or strength and dexterity challenges. For example, adaptive tennis uses larger racquets and larger tennis balls and the court size is modified. In contrast, the only major modification for wheelchair tennis is that the player may choose to hit the ball after two bounces instead of one. Competitive wheelchair athletes travel internationally and some seek to qualify for the Paralympics. The VA sponsors many sports clinics throughout the year and also hosts the annual National Veterans Wheelchair Games. The list of resources at the end of this chapter includes national organizations for wheelchair and adaptive sports and listings of collegiate and community programs. We recognize that not every college and university has the resources to support wheelchair sports, but many local communities already have established programs for disabled athletes.

The UA has hosted four sports camps for disabled veterans across the country interested in pursuing sports and higher education. Not only have the participants been impressed with the level of competition and community associated with wheelchair sports, they also found it helpful to connect with other veterans who share similar experiences with disability. Some veterans derive personal motivation for higher education through their commitments to collegiate teams. If it were not for sports, these individuals may not have pursued or completed their programs of study. Although collegiate wheelchair and adaptive sports programs are rare, it may be possible to collaborate with VA rehabilitation counselors' initiatives, community-based teams and programs, and VA-sponsored sporting events.

Tracking and Assessment Practices

Assessing the impact of campus initiatives can be challenging given difficulties in tracking students through institution information systems. A significant percentage of veterans and other active duty students take leaves of absence for personal and professional reasons. Figures for students making use of educational benefits through the GI Bill can offer approximations of the campus population, but do not include veterans who are not using benefits and who may not self-identify. To supplement these data, the UA tracks usage of its Student Veterans Center through an electronic reader that recognizes students through use of their identification cards each time they enter the office. In addition, an e-mail listserv for those certified to use GI Bill benefits can be developed and data can be collected on basic demographics and information about academic, extracurricular, and health activities.

Due to limited tracking mechanisms, accessing rich data on disabled or injured veterans can be problematic. Many institutions use figures for recipients of veteran education benefits (commonly known as the GI Bill) as a limited proxy for student veterans. To isolate the number of disabled veterans on your campus, you may choose to track those who use the VA

Vocational Rehabilitation and Employment (VR&E) VetSuccess Program (commonly called the "Chapter 31 program") or work to capture data on veteran status students who register in the disability services office. It may be difficult to recruit disabled veterans to campus or even identify them upon their arrival because symptoms associated with various disabilities manifest themselves differently in college settings and veterans may not self-identify.

Conclusion

Although there is growing urgency and attention to meet the needs of student veterans in higher education, professionals continue to grapple with how to incorporate an understanding and appreciation of disability into practice. This chapter seeks to familiarize readers with the experiences of disabled veterans so that higher education professionals may appreciate how the acquisition of disabilities affects veterans' experiences as students new to higher education. In order to do so, it is important to approach veterans with a holistic perspective and keep abreast of national best practices. This chapter presents many strategies to consider and potentially employ in our work, but to make our practice effective, we must understand students' personal experiences of disability. Not only is this information presented to challenge practitioners to think broadly about effective practice, but also to expand our thinking about disability and the importance of disability in shaping identity and experiences in college. Once we begin to understand the complex and sensitive situations that disabled veterans are negotiating, our practices will require flexibility and appropriate innovation in order to be effective.

No two individuals will have the same experience with disability, and no two veterans will describe disability in the same terms—hence the importance of building rapport with disabled student veterans. Because veterans tend to identify with disability more tentatively than other disabled students, a personal relationship with disability services or student affairs staff and faculty is necessary to connect students with resources that can foster their success as college students.

Another recommendation for practice worth highlighting is the reframing of disability. Disability is traditionally regarded as an individual's impairment or "problem." However, disability scholars and activists position disability as a sociopolitical phenomenon, created and perpetuated by the environment. In practice, rather than directing our intervention at individual students, we can relocate the "problem" into the environment and work at eliminating barriers to access and participation at a systemic level. This work will reduce the need for innumerable requests for individual accommodations and yield more sustainable change. Veterans have long played roles in changing disability policy. Like their predecessors, today's veterans are motivated by the idea of leaving a legacy and affecting change for future generations of student veterans. Perhaps their unique cause will include fighting for good design, access, and incorporation of new paradigms of disability into the culture of higher education.

The intersection of disability and veteran status is sensitive and complicated. Higher education plays a critical role in the overall reintegration and wellness of student veterans. With the severity and frequency of mental health issues following return from deployment, there is great need for peer-to-peer connection and the opportunity to become involved with a community. Higher education can provide this community for veterans, whether through personal connections with faculty and staff, the support of fellow student veterans, or adaptive athletics. Given recent reports indicating that suicide among veterans is accounting for more casualties than military deployment (U.S. Department of Defense, 2010), support in coping with the consequences of posttraumatic stress and acquired disabilities is paramount for higher education professionals.

Following is a list of disability-related resources, information, and opportunities for student veterans and those who work with student veterans. Though we recognize that disability services and resource centers vary across institutional type, this list may present ideas and examples to innovate practice on your campus, or regional or national opportunities for student veteran involvement.

Resources

Accommodating Student Veterans with Traumatic Brain Injury and Posttraumatic Stress Disorder: Tips for Campus Faculty and Staff
http://www.acenet.edu/Content/NavigationMenu/Programs
Services/MilitaryPrograms/serving/AccommodatingStudent
Veterans_06222011.pdf

Adaptive Sports Center
http://www.adaptivesports.org/

American Association of Adapted Sports Programs
http://www.adaptedsports.org/

Association of Higher Education and Disability (AHEAD) Special Interest Group: Wounded Warriors
http://ahead.org/sigs#veterans

Center for Universal Design
http://www.ncsu.edu/project/design-projects/udi/

Healing Touch International
http://www.healingtouchinternational.org/index.php

NASPA Veterans Knowledge Community
http://naspa.org/kc/veterans/

National Wheelchair Basketball Association
http://www.nwba.org/

National Veterans Wheelchair Games
http://www.va.gov/opa/speceven/wcg/index.asp

Paralympic Games
http://www.paralympic.org/index.html

Society for Disability Studies
http://disstudies.org

United States Department of Veterans Affairs, Vocational Rehabilitation and Employment (VR&E) VetSuccess Program
http://www.vba.va.gov/bln/vre/

United States Quad Rugby Association
http://www.quadrugby.com/

University of Arizona Disabled Veterans Reintegration and Education Project
http://drc.arizona.edu/veterans

USA Goalball
http://www.angelfire.com/hi5/usa-goalball

Veterans and the Community College: A Training Guide
http://www.galvin-group.com/training/veterans-and-the-community-college-a-training-guide.aspx

Veterans in Higher Education National Clearinghouse
http://vets.arizona.edu/clearinghouse/

Wheelchair and Ambulatory Sports USA
http://www.wsusa.org/

Wheelchair Tennis—United States Tennis Association
http://www.usta.com/Play-Tennis/Wheelchair-Tennis/Wheelchair/

References

Albrecht, G. L., Seelman, K. D., & Bury, M. (2001). *Handbook of disability studies.* Thousand Oaks, CA: Sage.

Americans with Disabilities Act Standards for Accessible Design. (1991). 28 CFR. (Revised 1994).

Americans with Disabilities Act Standards for Accessible Design. (2010). 28 CFR.

Bilmes, L. (2007). *Soldiers returning from Iraq and Afghanistan: The long-term costs of providing veterans medical care and disability benefits* (John F. Kennedy School of Government Working Paper Series RWP07–001). Retrieved from http://web.hks .harvard.edu/publications/workingpapers/citation.aspx?PubId=4329

Branker, C. (2009). Deserving design: The new generation of student veterans. *Journal of Postsecondary Education and Disability, 22*(1), 59–66.

Burnett, S. E., & Segoria, J. (2009). Collaboration for military transition students from combat to college: It takes a community. *Journal of Postsecondary Education and Disability, 22*(1), 53–58.

Church, T. E. (2008). Helping student-veterans poses unique challenges. *Disability Compliance in Higher Education, 13*, 4.

Church, T. E. (2009). Returning veterans on campus with war related injuries and the long road back home. *Journal of Postsecondary Education and Disability, 22*(1), 43–52.

DiRamio, D., Ackerman, D., & Mitchell, R. L. (2008). From combat to campus: Voices of student-veterans. *NASPA Journal, 45*(1), 73–102.

Glover-Graf, N. M., Miller, E., & Freeman, S. (2010). Accommodating veterans with post-traumatic stress disorder symptoms in the academic setting. *Rehabilitation Education, 24*(1/2), 43–56.

Goodrich, G. L. (2007). Visual function in patients of a polytrauma rehabilitation center: A descriptive study. *Journal of Rehabilitation Research and Development, 44*(7), 929–936.

Haller, B. A. (1997). *Images of disability in news media: Implications for future research.* Paper presented at the meeting of the National Communication Association, Chicago.

Haller, B. A. (2010). *Representing disability in an ableist world: Essay on mass media.* Louisville, KY: Advocado Press.

Helmer, D. A., Rossignol, M., Blatt, M., Agarwal, R., Teichman, R., & Lange, G. (2007). Health and exposure concerns of veterans deployed to Iraq and Afghanistan. *Journal of Occupational and Environmental Medicine, 49*(5), 475–480.

Kline, A., Falca-Dodson, M., Sussner, B., Ciccone, D. S., Chandler, H., Callahan, L., & Losonczy, M. (2010). Effects of repeated deployment to Iraq and Afghanistan on the health of New Jersey Army National Guard troops: Implications for military readiness. *American Journal of Public Health, 100*(2), 276–283.

Kraus, A. (2010). Disability dynamics within the student veteran community. *NASPA NetResults.* Retrieved from http://www.naspa.org/membership/mem/pubs/nr/ default.cfm?id=1718

Kraus, A. (2011). *Disability dynamics within the student veteran community.* Paper presented at the meeting of the Association of Higher Education and Disability, Seattle, Washington.

Kraus, A., Rattray, N., & Standage, D. (2010). *Operation Integration: The culture of student veterans* [Data set]. Tucson: University of Arizona.

Lew, H. L., Tun, C., Otis, J. D., Kerns, R. D., Clark, M. E., & Cifu, D. X. (2009). Prevalence of chronic pain, posttraumatic stress disorder, and persistent postconcussive symptoms in OIF/OEF veterans: Polytrauma clinical triad. *Journal of Rehabilitation Research and Development, 46*(6), 697–702.

Longmore, P. K. (2003). *Why I burned my book and other essays on disability.* Philadelphia: Temple University Press.

National Survey of Student Engagement. (2010). *Major differences: Examining student engagement by field of study—annual results 2010.* Bloomington: Indiana University Center for Postsecondary Research.

Radford, A. W. (2009). *Military service members and veterans in higher education: What the new GI Bill may mean for postsecondary institutions.* Washington, DC: American Council on Education.

Stiglitz, J. E., & Bilmes, L. (2008). *The three trillion dollar war: The true cost of the Iraq conflict.* New York: Norton.

Tanielian, T., & Jaycox, L. H. (2008). *Invisible wounds of war: Psychological and cognitive injuries, their consequences, and services to assist recovery.* Santa Monica, CA: Center for Military Health Policy Research.

Taylor, B. (2001). The effects of healing touch on the coping ability, self esteem and general health of undergraduate nursing students. *Complementary Therapies in Nursing and Midwifery, 7*(1), 34–42.

United States Department of Defense. (2010). *The challenge and the promise strengthening the force, preventing suicide, and saving lives* (Report of the Task Force on the Prevention of Suicide by Members of the Armed Forces). Washington, DC: Author.

United States Department of Defense. (2011). *U.S. casualty status* [data set]. Retrieved from http://www.defense.gov/news/casualty.pdf

Wardell, D. W., & Weymouth, K. F. (2004). Review of studies of healing touch. *Journal of Nursing Scholarship, 36*(2), 147–154.

Wheelchair & Ambulatory Sports, USA. (2011). *About Wheelchair & Ambulatory Sports, USA* [web page]. Retrieved from http://www.wsusa.org/index.php?option=com _content&task=view&id=1&Itemid=439

VIGNETTE

Amanda Irish
Student, University of Iowa

When I first came to the University of Iowa in 2006, I was married and had been out of the area for four years. I'm originally from Cedar Rapids, but most of my friends from high school had moved or had families of their own. I felt very disconnected. I decided that the best course of action was to put myself out there and make friends the best way I knew how, so I rushed a sorority.

I thought that I had more in common with the average college student than any other veteran. After all, I left the military, in part, to get away from the military culture. I had heard about the University of Iowa Veterans Association (UIVA), but figured it would be "a bunch of old guys telling their war stories" and I wanted no part of it.

My sorority experience was fine, but certainly not exceptional. I met a few friends with whom I still maintain relationships, but overall I never really felt like I fit in. Most of the girls were 18–21, single, and had little life experience. I was 21, married, and a veteran suffering with PTSD. For some of the girls, it was a big deal that I was married and that I had been in the military. I just wanted to feel accepted.

It took me three years to attend a UIVA event—Veterans Day lunch at Applebee's in 2009. I had signed up for and planned to attend several events prior to that one, but I always found "better" things to do. But that day, I said "Why not?" and went to see what UIVA was all about. I was shocked. When I arrived, I was greeted by a few of the student members. They asked the usual questions about who I was, where I was from, and in what branch I had served. I looked around and quickly discovered that everyone was just like me—young, some married, some single, with the same dry sense of humor, and I felt a sense of camaraderie with them that I had been missing since separating from the Marines. I was hooked.

In the two years following my return to Iowa, after being medically discharged 10 days early (from my four-year contract) for endometriosis, I had been diagnosed with PTSD, depression, anxiety, and a slew of other conditions warranting a 70 percent service-connected rating, and had gotten divorced. I was alone and hurting, but UIVA helped to heal my wounds. The social support I received through UIVA gave me the courage to pursue treatment for my mental health problems and brought my protective wall down.

As the current president of UIVA, it is my job to help veterans and returning reservists at the University of Iowa adjust to and integrate into university life. Additionally, it is UIVA's charge to support persons still serving, as well as their families, and to raise awareness among fellow students of the daily sacrifices made on their behalf by service members. Every student veteran who steps foot on our campus has a unique set of needs and defining experiences. It is my hope that not one has to feel alone or lost as he or she attempts to transition and integrate into the university community.

The people I've met in UIVA are lifelong friends. Some of the old guard have moved away, and some are still in the area, but I've never met a group of more genuine, kind, interesting, or motivated people anywhere. I hope someday, someone will write these same things about how UIVA was there for them. That's how I'll know I did my job.

CHAPTER SEVEN

ENROLLMENT, TRANSFERS, AND DEGREE COMPLETION FOR VETERANS

John D. Mikelson and Kevin P. Saunders

This chapter discusses the need to provide support as veterans enter, matriculate through, and graduate from colleges and universities. We first identify some of the unique challenges that military personnel and veterans face at different stages in the process. Then we provide strategies that individual offices and institutions might implement to address these challenges. Finally, we turn our attention to ways that institutions can use assessment to better understand and meet students' needs. Because the Post-9/11 GI Bill provides a designated and short time frame for veterans to use educational benefits, attention to the factors that influence active duty and student veterans' entrance, persistence, and completion is particularly important.

It is clear that the new Post-9/11 GI Bill represents a dramatic expansion of veterans' education benefits. One year after the new bill took effect, just over 300,000 individuals used the benefits to enroll in higher education (Steele, Salcedo, & Coley, 2010), and veterans and service members comprise a growing number of undergraduate and graduate students.

> In 2007–2008, approximately 657,000 undergraduates were veterans and another 215,000 were military service members on either active duty or in the reserves. Among 2007–08 graduate students, 107,000 were veterans and 38,000 were military service members. To put these numbers

in context, military students represented about 4 percent of both the undergraduate and graduate student populations. (Radford, 2011, p. 4)

Colleges across the nation are reporting increases in enrollments of student veterans and service members who are using military education benefits to fund their college tuition and living expenses. Arizona State University (ASU), for example, reported that its student veteran population jumped from 874 student in 2008, to 1,269 students in 2009, and 1,767 students in 2010 (Sabo, 2010).

Despite the growing numbers of student veterans and service members participating in the Post-9/11 GI Bill, recent data from the U.S. Department of Veterans Affairs (VA) show that only a small percentage of veterans use all of their federal education benefits. In addition to this possible underuse of available benefits, we have limited information about the overall success of the GI Bill because the federal government does not track veterans' higher education retention or completion rates (O'Herrin, 2011). In short, although the Post-9/11 GI Bill represents an increase in available education benefits for veterans and service members, these data suggest that students may face barriers in their educational progress.

Institutions will continue to encounter the potential for a significant increase of veterans on campus for many years. Military personnel and veterans represent a distinct group of adult learners who often have unique challenges that have an impact on their educational experiences. The transition to the civilian college environment may present individuals with social, cognitive, physical, and psychological readjustment challenges. In addition, though government and institutional policies seek to reduce barriers to education, individuals can face bureaucratic, informational, and reenrollment hurdles (Cook & Kim, 2009). Institutions should consider these unique needs as they support military students in the enrollment, transfer, and degree completion processes. This chapter provides guidance to improve the programs, services, and policies at colleges and universities that support students before, during, and after deployment.

Enrollment

The GI Bill is a powerful incentive for many individuals who enlist in the military. According to the U.S. Department of Defense's Youth Attitude Tracking Survey (YATS), in 1999, 32 percent of males and 37 percent

of females between 16 and 24 years of age reported that the top reason they sought to join the military was educational funding (Wilson et
al. 2000). In addition to the motivating influence of education benefits,
veterans increasingly receive targeted attention from the higher education institutions in which they later choose to enroll. A 2008 survey of
723 institutions revealed that more than half reported implementation
of marketing and outreach strategies specifically designed to attract military members and veterans. Such efforts include targeted print and Web
materials, participation in recruiting events on military installations, and
highlighting of campus veterans services in catalogs (Cook & Kim, 2009).

Despite the multiple incentives for military personnel to continue their
educations, several barriers persist that may complicate or limit their enrollment decisions. Some veterans may not be able to gain admission to highly
selective institutions. "Boredom or frustration with high school—often
accompanied by mediocre transcripts and SAT scores—led many into the
military in the first place" (Alvarez, 2008, para. 17). Once veteran and military personnel gain offers of admission, they face additional challenges
that can affect their enrollment decisions related to financing education
(Radford, 2009), balancing family responsibilities with school (Winston
Group, 2008), and navigating course standards and expectations that
may align more closely with the needs of traditional residential students
(Brown & Gross, 2011).

Military personnel and veterans may also face financial challenges that
interfere with or preclude enrollment. Individuals who expect that the GI
Bill will cover all expenses associated with education can be surprised when
faced with the need to pay tuition costs in advance of applied benefits,
the need to pay penalties associated with late tuition payments, delays in
reimbursements, or the need to supplement benefits with student loans
(Radford, 2009; Steele et al., 2010). For example, under new rules (as of
September 2011), payments through the Post-9/11 GI Bill must be applied
after all other aid is considered, which can delay payments through the VA
as other forms of financial aid are processed.

Many institutions provide financial assistance designed specifically
for veterans. The most common forms include eligibility for in-state
tuition rates at public institutions and discounted tuition rates at private
institutions (Cook & Kim, 2009). Although there are several forms of
federal and institutional financial assistance, students may have varied
levels of financial aid awareness. One study found that whereas some
veterans and service members understand the various types of financial
aid, others are unaware or confused about Title IV programs, campus-based

aid, and relevant eligibility, or mistakenly think that GI Bill benefits will cover all costs, which is not always the case (Scott, 2008). (For more information about Title IV financial aid programs, see the list of resources at the end of this chapter.) In a different study, 38 percent of respondents reported having difficulty understanding their GI Bill benefit options (Steele et al., 2010).

The ability of college and university representatives to adequately address questions about academic programs likely has an important impact on veterans' enrollment decisions. For example, one study reported that a highly desired service from institutions was information about whether specific degrees or certificates would provide meaningful credentials for students after completion (Cook & Kim, 2009). As O'Herrin (2011) described, veterans are typically older and often bring credit earned through courses completed in the military. Many seek to enhance their employment prospects after military service and want assurances that their institution and program selections will support their employment goals.

In addition to awareness of financial barriers and student veterans' needs for assurance of the benefits of degrees and academic programs, institutions need to recognize the challenges associated with student veterans who stop out or drop out due to military service. Military personnel and veterans who are called to service and subsequently return to campus face unique challenges when they seek to return to their institutions. Cook and Kim (2009) noted that of responding institutions that offered programs or services for veterans or military personnel, only 22 percent had expedited reenrollment processes to help students return to their academic pursuits. The authors also reported that a majority of responding institutions with services (62 percent) required students returning from deployment to complete standard reenrollment processes. Finally, a small number (16 percent) of institutions with specific programs for military personnel required returning students to reapply and be readmitted in order to enroll. While some of these efforts may represent standard administrative practices that are applied consistently to students who drop out or stop out for various reasons, these administrative barriers may delay students' reengagement with their institutions and send unintended but clear messages regarding the campus climate for returning veterans.

Before we turn attention to the process of transferring academic credit for military students, we offer a brief note of how enrollment decisions can be shaped by the type of institution (for example, public versus private, two-year versus four-year, nonprofit versus for-profit). Veterans likely bring different needs to their enrollment decisions, which may influence their decisions about the types of institution they attend. Field (2008) reported findings from a study of enrollment trends at the top 500 institutions that served military personnel and veterans based on the number of students enrolled who used Post-9/11 GI Bill benefits. The study noted that while 6 percent of all college students chose for-profit institutions, 19 percent of students using GI Bill benefits chose for-profit institutions. In 2007, close to three out of every five students who used GI Bill benefits at the top 500 institutions serving such students enrolled in a community college or a for-profit institution (Field, 2008).The top 500 institutions are defined by the VA as "those institutions [that] enrolled 84 percent of the 343,751 people who used the GI Bill benefits" (as cited in Field, 2008, sidebar). This enrollment trend remained consistent following implementation of the Post-9/11 GI Bill, which was designed to improve access to four-year institutions through increased benefits and allowances for housing and textbooks. In 2010, of the 15 institutions that enrolled more than 1,000 students using GI Bill benefits, 7 were for-profit institutions and 5 were 2-year institutions (Sewall, 2010).

Regardless of institutional type, many military members participate in distance learning. For example, in fiscal year 2010, 64 percent of all tuition reimbursements through the Post-9/11 GI Bill supported online courses (Brown & Gross, 2011). Veterans' institutional choices are influenced by several factors, including location, convenience, cost, and support systems. Veterans may seek academic institutions that permit them to build on specific skills gained in the military and allow them to balance work, studies, and family commitments. Taken together, the trends in both institutional type and course format indicate the influence of student veterans' needs on their selections. Although course offerings and cost are important factors, campus location is often a primary influence on student veterans' enrollment choices as well (Radford, 2009).

Transfer

Earning transferrable academic credit for military service or for coursework completed prior to or during deployment is a key factor and a potential barrier to student veterans' college enrollment and degree completion. Service members may find it difficult to understand transfer credit evaluation and acceptance processes, and may be unsure of how to find the right institutional contacts who can assist them. According to Cook and Kim (2009), almost three-fourths of responding institutions with services for military personnel award credit for military training and experience. In addition to surveying institutions, their study included follow-up focus groups with veterans and service members who noted difficulty finding institutions that recognize training and experience gained during military service. Many respondents in the Cook and Kim (2009) study believed that transfer credit was largely based on institutional attitude toward the military or the institutions' levels of "military friendliness."

Higher education administrators acknowledge challenges in determining the amount of credit to be transferred and how transfer credit should be categorized (elective courses versus core courses), utilizing partial credit recommendations, distinguishing credit *acceptance* from degree requirement *reduction*, applying standardized caps, and underscoring policies to implement the practice and transfer of credits (American Council on Education [ACE], 2010, emphasis added). These challenges are reflected in students' perceptions of the transfer experience. An online survey of veterans and other GI Bill beneficiaries found that of those who attempted to transfer credit, only 47 percent were satisfied with the results (Steele et al., 2010).

In addition to the challenge of transferring credit from military training and experience, several students face challenges when looking to transfer credits between institutions. Many active duty service members find it difficult to transfer credits to local educational institutions following their reassignments to different bases or installations (DiRamio, Ackerman, & Mitchell, 2008). Veterans become frustrated when they have to repeat coursework, experience increased time to graduation due to course duplication (which has an impact on financial aid eligibility if time extends beyond the expiration date for benefits), or perceive lack of recognition of their prior experiences (ACE, n.d.). Also, veterans note that poor advising and lack of communication about credit transfer resources and processes can be barriers to their success (Cook & Kim, 2009).

Institutions participating in the *Success for Veterans Award Grants* (ACE, n.d.) identified several challenges that institutions face in managing the credit transfer process. The 20 grantee institutions noted struggles with several aspects of awarding credit, due in part to challenges in identifying material that is covered, evaluating student mastery of course material, and determining instructor qualifications. Some noted the inability to award credit when there are no complete one-to-one course substitutions (that is, only partial material is addressed) or when courses do not align with the institutional degree programs.

Institution type may also influence the ease of credit transfer for veterans and service members. In one study, individuals attending private institutions described more satisfaction with the credit transfer process compared to those attending public institutions. In particular, individuals at public four-year institutions reported inconsistencies in credit transfer rules (Steele et al., 2010).

Completion

Currently, no consistent tracking of completion rates for students using GI Bill benefits exists. In part, the difficulty in understanding completion rates is that there is no single database that can calculate annual, comprehensive graduation rates for all institutions and students enrolled in higher education in the United States. Although several data sources exist to help understand completion rates (including institutional and noninstitutional databases), this information is often incomplete because of the difficulty in tracking individual students across multiple institutions (such as those who transfer) or who enter with various degree or program goals (such as certificate, associate's, bachelor's, or graduate-level studies) (Cook & Pullaro, 2010). Groux (2011), citing U.S. Bureau of Labor statistics, reported that "in 2009, about 33 percent of veterans had completed some college or an associate's degree, while about 27 percent had earned a credential such as a bachelor's degree" (para. 1). Some research suggests that veterans may underuse their earned benefits. For example, Field (2008) reported that only 6 percent of veterans have used the entire 36 months of educational benefits, suggesting that many veterans drop out, stop out, complete technical training, or earn associate's degrees, but may not use the benefits to earn bachelor's degrees. It is important to note, however, that many veterans may be able to earn bachelor's degrees in less than 36 months or may already have bachelor's degrees.

Although national data may not provide a clear picture of degree completion or educational progress for veterans, the literature notes several challenges that can either delay or interfere with educational progress. One significant challenge facing military students is the possibility of active duty responsibilities. Ongoing duties can cause students to drop courses, change schedules, or miss classes. With constant travel demands, frequent training exercises, and possible deployments, active members of the military find themselves in unique circumstances that diminish their academic experiences and reduce the likelihood of sustained connection to their campus communities. For example, deployment or active duty assignments can take students away from educational resources, including Internet access, which may limit access to instructional materials, thwart the ability to respond to course requirements in a timely manner, and make engaging in group work difficult (Brown & Gross, 2011). A recent study found that 80 percent of all colleges and universities reported that they had a student or students who needed to withdraw for military service, and about two-thirds of all institutions implemented policies regarding tuition refunds or academic transition provisions related to withdrawal for service (Woo, 2006). Despite institutions' attempts to ease the transitions for students who withdraw, student veterans can experience extended time to degree completion due to the need to wait to take infrequently offered courses or because they miss sequenced courses during deployment.

Especially at the time they first enroll, veterans may experience feelings of isolation on college campuses. For veterans who are reentering civilian life, taking on the student role can make adapting even more difficult. It is not uncommon for new student veterans, particularly individuals with mental or physical injuries, to feel overwhelmed by the choices and rhythms of college life. Returning combat veterans bring to campus with them heightened sensory awareness of sights, sounds, and smells. Individuals who experienced high degrees of identification with their military identities or who experienced high levels of cohesion in the military may miss the closeness they experienced among their units and their structured routines. Some may find reconnecting with friends to be more difficult than expected, and that challenges arise in trying to generate a "new normal" (DiRamio et al., 2008).

Similar to the enrollment and transfer processes, we note possible differences in support structures that can encourage program completion by institution type. Cook and Kim (2009) found that more public than private institutions are likely to have programs specifically designed for veterans; private not-for-profit institutions were less likely to have dedicated departments that offer services to veterans (26 percent) compared to nearly 60 percent of public two- and four-year institutions. Even though private four-year institutions have smaller numbers of military personnel and veterans enrolled, there remains a need to provide services and support for students. One recommendation is for smaller institutions to develop partnerships with other institutions to share best practices and develop additional support structures.

Strategies

The ACE publication *From Solider to Student: Easing the Transition of Service Members on Campus* (Cook & Kim, 2009) records several best practices that lead to veterans' success (for example, creating veteran service offices, streamlining admissions and registration processes, and offering training for faculty and staff). Here we describe strategies that individuals and institutions might implement to enhance veterans' success as they progress through the enrollment, transfer, and degree completion processes.

Enrollment

Because financing of education is one of the first issues military students encounter (DiRamio et al., 2008; Radford, 2009), institutions should consider providing financial guidance directly to student veterans. One strategy employed by the Madison Area Technical College, a *Success for Veterans Award* grantee (ACE, n.d.), was to hire a coordinator who provides one-on-one GI Bill assistance to student veterans. In addition to the personalized assistance, the coordinator also hosts workshops to help students understand their benefits and how changes in the Post-9/11 GI Bill affect their benefits (ACE, n.d.).

One of the most direct ways that schools can help student veterans is by making comprehensive financial aid and enrollment information available on their web sites. Focus group participants in the Cook and Kim (2009) study indicated that prospective students often turn to web sites for relevant information; difficult web site navigation, incomplete information, or inaccurate information can dissuade military students from enrolling at an institution. For example, Fairleigh Dickinson University publishes an online tool that includes a preadmission checklist to help veterans prepare for benefits processing. This feature extends beyond support for current students and also serves as a recruiting tool that produces high levels of comfort and confidence among prospective students (ACE, 2011).

In addition to assistance through professional staff and communication tools, institutions can consider policies that reduce financial stress for student veterans. The availability of fee deferments when education benefits such as GI Bill funds or tuition assistance are delayed beyond payment due dates addresses a significant concern for incoming student veterans. Delays in receiving veteran benefits can create financial burdens for students and may discourage some individuals from pursing further education despite the benefits offered in the Post-9/11 GI Bill. Institutions may choose to adopt policies similar to the State of Minnesota Higher Education Fairness Statute (2011), which prohibits the assessment of late fees or other charges for veterans who are eligible to receive, have applied for, and are waiting to receive federal assistance; the policy also prohibits institutions from preventing eligible students from registering for subsequent academic terms.

Many veterans are launching into their formal education endeavors from different places in their lives than their peers who are recent high school graduates. As a result, they may not have current college entrance exam scores and their earlier scores may not reflect their actual levels of readiness for higher education after years of service and formal military training and education. Institutions can reduce enrollment barriers by developing admission processes to accommodate veterans whose academic credentials do not reflect their academic potential. Another policy that can benefit veterans is offering conditional admittance to provide access to education for those who want to attend. Other practices, such as the University of Iowa's ReStart Program (in which students who stop out or drop out can request removal of academic sessions), may help veterans and other students who have experienced struggles in academic settings to continue their educational pursuits (see the list of resources at the end of this chapter for more information). Institutions may also consider accepting older college entrance exam scores and determining whether military service should positively affect admissions decisions.

The unique circumstances of military personnel and veterans can create additional challenges in the enrollment process. For example, military students may be considered transfer students because of the number of potential transfer credits earned during military service. In 2010, ACE hosted an online dialogue called *The Veteran Success Jam,* which brought together veterans, service members, campus leaders, nonprofit organizations, and government agencies. One discussion during the conference noted that some institutions were freezing transfer admissions, which resulted in an automatic barrier for military students who earned previous credit in the military. Although some institutions created strategies to work around this barrier, this case illustrates the potential implications of institutional policies regarding transfer students that may have unintended consequences for student veterans and military personnel (ACE, 2010). In short, institutions should review their policies and practices with regard to designation of student veterans as transfer students, which has implications for several areas including admissions decisions, campus housing eligibility and placements, and class standing. In these cases, it is important to consider students as individuals as well as the unique issues that surround their lives and affect their abilities to attend college.

Several best practices shared by *Success for Veterans Award* grantees (ACE, n.d.) are useful to consider as tools that not only support veterans' enrollment decisions, but also provide critical foundations that can encourage success to completion. Several of the grantees developed special orientation sessions for student veterans to help them obtain information and begin the transition to college. California State Polytechnic University, Pomona, provides an online version of orientation that has modules on specific areas useful to veterans, including time management strategies and applying for GI Bill benefits. Other institutions provide breakout sessions for veterans as ways to deliver customized information on financial aid, available campus and community resources, and potential courses of interest (ACE, n.d.).

Transfer

Accepting and applying earned credits will vary depending on factors such as institutional policies and students' academic majors. The process is not, nor should it be, a one-size-fits-all model. For example, a sailor with a nuclear technician rating in the Navy will likely see few of the earned technical credits applied to the undergraduate degree in history that he or she has decided to pursue. The process varies by individual student as appropriate to degree requirements. Depending on institutional policy and practice, credit transfer decisions may be based on the judgment of academic advisors, transcript evaluators, faculty members, or other academic department representatives. The goal of the decision process is to find the "best fit" without devaluing the degree, and to give credit where credit is due.

Individual advisors and institutions should be familiar with the publication *A Transfer Guide: Understanding Your Military Transcripts and ACE Credit Recommendations* (ACE, 2011). This guide is addressed to service members and veterans, and its purpose is to help make the application and transfer processes more understandable for them when they are preparing to start college. It provides simple, straightforward guidance on understanding military credit recommendations and transcripts, including definitions of common terms, answers to frequently asked questions, and a transfer credit checklist. In some cases, state policies offer additional support, such as the State of Minnesota Higher Education Fairness Statute (2011) mentioned earlier in this chapter, which requires institutions to recognize coursework and award educational credits for a veteran's military training and service if the courses or training meet ACE standards. It is important to note, however, that recognition of coursework and provision of credits does not necessarily mean that credits align with students' intended certificate or degree programs.

Institutions should clearly articulate academic credit transfer policies, and place policies where veterans and service members can easily find them. It can be difficult to find complete information about institutions' credit transfer policies on their web sites. Information clarity and accessibility can go a long way toward reducing confusion and allows service members to make educated decisions based on the available information. This point should not be overstated, however, noting that in one study, only 14 percent of respondents indicated that credit transfer policies were major factors in choosing their institutions (Steele et al., 2010).

Admissions staff and academic advisors can also help veterans and service members better understand their military transcripts and ACE credit recommendations. These individuals also serve as ongoing sources of support during the transfer process. Dedicated student veteran advisors can build institutional capacity to standardize the process and also offer personalized advising. Dedicated advisors are better able to address the needs of a growing student veteran population, make appropriate recommendations to deans and department chairs, and help build tools and infrastructures to support consistent, accurate advising of prospective veterans.

Veterans, service members, and academic advisors agree that there must be an individualized approach to evaluating military credit and transcripts (ACE, 2010). Reviewing transcripts is extremely labor intensive. Practices that are emerging to reduce the burden include helping military students develop academic portfolios, creating and regularly training advising teams to assist military students, and identifying contact persons who can support students throughout the transfer process. In order to address these hurdles, institutions should develop programs to educate college and university personnel by clarifying the ACE review process and assisting faculty and staff to develop better understandings of military transcripts. Specific steps could include having institutions sponsor in-house trainings and fund staff members' attendance at ACE workshops.

Institutions can also move beyond advising support to consider ways of streamlining curricula in ways that benefit student veterans and service members. Clackamas Community College, a *Success for Veterans Award* grantee (ACE, n.d.), identifies programs that can be condensed when coupled with certain types of military training and experiences. In addition, the institution highlighted experiences that correlate with degree programs and examined the associated learning outcomes in ACE credit recommendations to develop a series of bridge courses that filled curricular gaps. Credit transfer is combined with coursework to accelerate degree progress in areas such as law enforcement, business administration, human services, and humanities (ACE, n.d.).

On the other hand, accepting military transfer credit may not always support veterans' success. In the ACE *Veteran Success Jam* (2010), institutional representatives raised a number of concerns: for example, credits that exceed the amounts required to graduate may generate additional fees; also, some schools are reluctant to award credit for fear that it will result in the devaluation of degrees. In some cases, coursework, training, or experiences do not meet the postsecondary criteria, the materials provided for transfer credit consideration are not comprehensive enough to make determinations, or assessment tools are inadequate. Sometimes courses may be too narrow in scope to be eligible for transfer, such as training focused on specialized military topics that are not taught in postsecondary education.

Also, accepting too much military training for college credit may shortchange veterans in that they may then rush to the finish line. As a result, college or university transcripts may look thin or be perceived as less rigorous, especially for individuals who plan to apply to competitive, rigorous graduate or professional schools in pursuit of advanced degrees. Veterans mentioned that Post-9/11 GI Bill benefits should not be about simply getting diplomas; rather, the benefits should be about how we set veterans up for success by allowing them to explore new ideas, paths, and interests during college (ACE, 2010).

In order for the credit award process to be successful and judicious, institutions should follow clear, consistent processes and policies. For example, the University of Iowa clearly specifies military service credits that will not be accepted for transfer, such as basic training or career-technical training courses. Also, the University of Iowa Office of Admissions has the authority to evaluate military transcripts according to recommendations contained in the ACE *Guide to the Evaluation of Educational Experiences in the Armed Services* (see the list of resources at the end of this chapter for information about the *Guide*).

Completion

Beyond the enrollment and transfer process, institutions have the responsibility to support military students' successful progress to program completion. This work begins before students arrive, in that institutions continually develop the necessary infrastructures to meet students' needs. One important aspect of this type of infrastructure is the provision of professional development opportunities for staff and faculty. Institutions participating in the *Success for Veterans Award Grant* (ACE, n.d.) agreed that training for faculty and staff is important and supports a better understanding of student veterans and their needs. Cook and Kim (2009) found that although most institutions in their study indicated clear focuses on improving services for military service members, less than half of the institutions with existing programs offered relevant professional development opportunities for faculty and staff. Of note is the New Jersey Association of State Colleges and Universities (NJASCU), which developed a training program for faculty and staff that includes modules on GI Bill benefits, community resources, national trends, mental health, and more (ACE, n.d.).

In addition to prearrival structural needs, institutions should develop programs and policies that attend to the transition needs of arriving military students. Targeted orientation programs (as mentioned earlier in this chapter) and the development of coursework that aids veterans in the transition from military to civilian life are beneficial. For example, Park University offers a series of five courses open only to student veterans, such as "Orientation to Learning and Life Skills," which are taught by veterans or instructors who are familiar with military culture. Park University realizes a 100 percent continuation rate for veterans who complete the series (ACE, n.d.). Another example of an innovative program is a partnership between Fresno City College, Pacific Gas and Electric (PG&E), and the Fresno County Workforce Investment Board. Together these organizations developed a curriculum to address projected workforce vacancies in the Fresno area. This program boasts a 99 percent completion rate, measured by graduation, the number of individuals who pass the PG&E employment test, and gainful employment with PG&E or one of its competitors (ACE, n.d.). Both of these examples demonstrate how direct attention to transition needs and intentional design of curricula can promote student success to completion.

Institutions should identify multiple strategies to enhance student veterans' engagement in the campus community. One strategy is to facilitate peer-to-peer interaction for service members and veterans through designation of space for gathering and networking, sponsorship of student clubs, or organization of student activities. For example, the University of Maine at Augusta has a peer mentor program that operates out of its veteran lounge where experienced student veterans help newly enrolled veterans adjust to academic life and find available resources. Similarly, the University of California, Santa Cruz has a vet-to-vet mentoring program through which mentors provide information on campus resources, community support, university policies, and career transition assistance. At California State University, Sacramento, veterans receive strong encouragement to engage on campus. A Veterans Success Academy provides summer leadership training to incoming veterans with the expectation that they provide leadership service on campus during their academic careers. The program actively engages student veterans as campus leaders, which fosters a welcoming and supportive campus environment (ACE, n.d.).

Another strategy to promote student engagement on campus is to designate a highly visible office that offers a single point of contact, coordinates services, provides advice, creates programs, and advocates for students. This is one of the campus strategies recommended to help make an institution veteran-friendly in the ACE (2008) publication *Serving Those Who Serve: Higher Education and America's Veterans*. Not only does this point of contact help students navigate when they first arrive on campus, it also offers continued support through administrative processes and the removal of retention obstacles that may arise throughout student veterans' educational experiences.

Assessment

It is important to determine the impact of various institutional structures, policies, practices, and structures on the student veteran experience as these individuals enter, transition through, and complete their educational experiences. The purpose of assessment is to collect information, make meaning of it, and use it to make changes that will enhance effectiveness (Walvoord, 2004). Assessment supports higher education professionals' abilities to have meaningful conversations about ways to better meet students' needs.

An important first step when thinking about assessment of institutional programs is to develop a shared understanding of the purpose of assessment, the intended program goals, the constituents who contribute to the programs, the current and needed sources of information, and how assessment information will be used (Walvoord, 2004). We suggest that institutions develop work groups consisting of various campus representatives who gather to discuss the assessment needs of the institution; work group members could include individuals from units such as admissions, registrar, student affairs, disability services, counseling center, veteran services, institutional research, academic affairs, community partners, and student veteran offices. Other chapters in this handbook recommend the development of support or advisory groups for veteran services. In order to ensure an emphasis on assessment, it may be useful to either charge a small subcommittee with specific assessment responsibilities or to develop a different group for assessment work. Building a designated structure that can devote attention to assessment will prevent the tendency of implementation or planning groups to think of assessment at the conclusion of their efforts.

When identifying the assessment needs of the institution, one useful starting point is to consider the relevant set of questions ACE developed for campus leaders (Radford, 2009). Although there are many possible uses for assessment information (such as reporting requirements for outside agencies, demonstrating accountability of resource allocation, determining veterans' needs and the quality of services provided by the institution, or measuring achievement of intended programmatic outcomes), these questions allow the institution to focus its attention on areas where assessment information may prove most useful in supporting program improvements. Some questions from the set include:

- How many veterans and military personnel use VA benefits to attend the institution? How does that compare to other institutions in the area?
- What financial aid is available to veterans and service members?
- What has the institution done to as a result of the new Post-9/11 GI Bill and what work remains?
- What efforts has the institution made to meet service members' needs?
- Does the institution have the necessary services to meet students' needs (for example, advising, counseling, peer support network)? Or, are there other campuses or community partners that could collaborate to provide services?
- Does the institution have veteran-friendly academic policies (for example, awarding credit for training, expediting re-enrollment)? What does the institution know about the implementation of these policies and their impact?
- Has the institution established or considered establishing a dedicated office to serve as a primary point of contact?
- Does the institution currently provide programs and services specifically designed for enrolled or prospective service members and veterans?

- Are services for military service members and veterans part of the institution's long-term strategic plan?
- Does the institution offer opportunities for faculty and administrators to acquire information about the unique needs of military student populations?
- What existing campus resources and promising practices help to create a positive campus environment for student veterans and service members? [Radford, 2009, p. 23]

Many of the assessment strategies provided in this chapter can serve as examples of best practices for work groups to consider. It is important to recognize that not all questions will necessarily apply, and that institutions will need to prioritize the various areas addressed in these questions. This initial effort is similar to a SWOT analysis (strengths, weaknesses, opportunities, threats) or an environmental scan in which the institution considers current efforts and resources that seek to meet student veterans' needs (Wolf, 2007). It is important to take the time for this step at the outset so that there is a shared, comprehensive view of campus programs and how they intersect with respect to serving veterans and service members.

After this step, the work group will need to focus its attention on how the current efforts and resources align with the needs of military personnel and veterans at the institution. The next priority should be implementing a needs assessment process so that these sets of needs can be identified and explored. Institutions might consider using survey instruments to measure student perspectives on university experiences and identify those they view favorably, areas in which they have concerns, and what suggestions they have to improve the university's response to particular needs. Areas of service that the instrument should consider include the following:

- Outreach and recruitment (such as marketing efforts, web site information, and admissions processes)
- Financial guidance and resources (support for understanding benefits and institutional financial aid)
- Academic services (such as academic advising, credit transfer information, orientation, career counseling, and tutoring and academic support)
- Student services (such as medical services, counseling, support groups, housing, transportation, benefits for family members, connections with military bases and units in community, and community resources)

Work group members should consider review of needs assessment instruments used at other institutions as a foundation for developing in-house instruments (Cook & Kim, 2009; Lokken, Pfeffer, McAuley, & Strong, 2009). See the resource list at the end of this chapter for information about needs assessments conducted by American River College; University of Nevada, Reno; the University of Texas at San Antonio; and by Rand Health on behalf of the New York State Health Foundation.

Needs assessment instruments should focus on general student perspectives on university experiences that they view favorably, areas in which students have concerns, and what students would like implemented to improve the university's response to their particular needs. Given this focus, institutions might consider directing attention to currently enrolled students who either have identified themselves as service members or are currently using VA benefits. Survey instruments are most easily administered through online tools, but may be most effective if introduced in personalized manners (for example, through personalized letters or e-mail messages from known institutional contacts). Dillman, Smyth, and Christian (2009) provide best practices for the design and administration of survey instruments, including online tools.

In addition, institutions may realize great benefits from conducting focus groups with current military students. These conversations provide more in-depth understandings of the unique experiences of military students and may generate ideas for future developments. Institutions should consider the focus group protocols used in several recent studies as tools for needs assessment activities (Cook & Kim, 2009; Steele et al., 2010). As Steele and colleagues (2010) noted, survey questions can provide useful information about the perceptions and experiences of students, but do so in less depth than focus group discussions. For example, their survey data indicated that over one-third of respondents reported having difficulty understanding their GI benefits. Focus group results, however, offered additional insight when participants shared that they would like an online accounting system that shows total benefit balances as well as an accounting of dates and purposes of pending and previous payments.

After conducting needs assessments, institutions should develop assessment activities that can help determine the impact of current or future programs designed to address the range of needs identified in the needs assessment process. In other words, though needs assessment efforts provide institutions with useful information about elements needed to enhance the learning environment for student veterans, additional information is needed to determine the quality or impact of current practices designed to meet those needs.

Participating institutions in the *Success for Veterans Award Grants* (ACE, n.d.) noted the difficulty in identifying and tracking their student veteran populations. Many of the grantees asked veterans to self-identify on their admissions applications and suggested that institutions ask students whether they have ever served in the armed forces as a way to identify the larger population of service members and ensure that services are made available to help those individuals achieve their educational goals.

Assessment data are important when trying to provide explanations of program impact. For example, the Los Angeles City College uses a robust assessment effort to demonstrate increased average grade point averages (GPAs), successful completion and transfer rates, and improved satisfaction for student veterans. This institution, and others participating in the *Success for Veterans Award Grants* (ACE, n.d.), noted that important next steps include the development of models to track outcomes and the collection of outcome data to take programs to the next level. As institutions look to develop robust assessment practices that track outcomes and use outcomes information to improve programs, they might consider ways of implementing intentional assessment cycles.

We offer two conceptual tools to assist the assessment group in meeting its challenge. The first tool is an overview of the assessment cycle, but is presented in a way that also considers its role in overall program planning and implementation. Figure 7.1 is based on assessment and curriculum design models (Huba & Freed, 2000; Wiggins & McTighe, 2005). In order for institutions to begin exploring the impact of their programs, it is important to start at the top of the cycle and first identify clear results (for example, learning outcomes and broad programmatic goals) that serve as guideposts for programs and activities. Wiggins and McTighe (2005) described this as a backward design process, where we begin with the intended end results. Without this important foundation, it may be more likely to start at the bottom of the cycle as institutions design programs and then try to apply various assessment tools to determine if they worked.

A second important message contained within Figure 7.1 is that the cycle relies on the discussion and use of results to improve the program. In other words, this is an ongoing process that requires that campus officials discuss and use information to consistently revise efforts. The cycle explains that this is a systematic and ongoing effort, rather than a data collection exercise that simply stops. We encourage the assessment group to use this model as they develop an assessment plan. We also note that once the work group identifies the assessment plan and proposes a cycle of implementation (for example, focusing on one or two specific goals at a time), subsequent assessment work will be less difficult as the process matures and useful tools are developed. Walvoord's *Assessment Clear and Simple* (2004) is a helpful guide for this process and provides a short and direct overview of how to design and implement an assessment plan.

The second tool that the assessment work group can use is a general planning table to guide and track implementation of the assessment plan (Walvoord, 2004). Table 7.1 provides a condensed format that represents the items in the cycle portrayed in Figure 7.1.

FIGURE 7.1. ASSESSMENT CYCLE FOR PROGRAM IMPROVEMENT.

TABLE 7.1. ASSESSMENT PLANNING TABLE.

Assessment Measure	Goal 1	Goal 2	Goal 3	How Data Are Used for Improvement
Current student survey	X		X	Working group reviews results, develops summary, shares with key groups, and develops recommendations for future practices.
Current student focus group	X	X		Working group reviews, presents summary to key groups, recommendations for practice considered broadly across campus.

It is critical that institutions engage in efforts to assess the effectiveness of their programs and services to ensure the success of enrolled veterans and service members, and the VA should be able to track these student-level trends as well. Consider the following statement made in by Michael Dakduk (2010), executive director of Student Veterans of America (SVA): "Degree attainment should be a student veteran's mission and the VA needs to track how well that mission is being completed ... The question remains: How many of our veterans have successfully transitioned into a college atmosphere and have gone on to attain their college diploma? The numbers will tell the story and they remain to be seen" (para. 4). SVA is a coalition of campus-based student veteran organizations in the United States that engages in advocacy efforts to assure that the voices of student veterans are heard by policymakers and stakeholders. Information about SVA's work is provided in the list of resources at the end of this chapter.

Conclusion

Cook and Kim (2009) reported that three-fourths of institutions that participated in their study recognized student retention and persistence toward degree completion as top, pressing issues facing student veterans. Institutions will need to engage in systematic and ongoing assessment in order to check where successes and failures occur, disseminate information, improve programs, and ultimately, to support individual students as they enter institutions and complete their educations.

Resources

American Association for Adult and Continuing Education (AAACE) Commission for Military Education and Training (CMET)
http://www.aaace.org/index.php?option=com_content&view=article&catid=20%3Aaaace-content&id=52%3Acmet&Itemid=85

American Council on Education (ACE), A Transfer Guide: Understanding Your Military Transcript and ACE Credit Recommendations
http://www.acenet.edu/Content/NavigationMenu/Programs Services/MilitaryPrograms/TransferGuide_Updated2011.pdf

American Council on Education (ACE), Guide to the Evaluation of Educational Experiences in the Armed Services

http://www.militaryguides.acenet.edu/

American River College Veterans Needs Assessment Survey
http://arcveteransclub.blogspot.com/2010/02/veterans-needs-assessment-survey.html

Association of Veterans Education Certifying Officials (AVECO)
http://www.aveco.org/

California State University, Sacramento Veterans Success Center
http://www.csus.edu/vets/

Council of College and Military Educators (CCME)
http://www.ccmeonline.org/

National Academic Advising Association (NACADA) Clearinghouse for Advising Veterans
http://www.nacada.ksu.edu/clearinghouse/advisingissues/military.htm

National Association of Veteran's Program Administrators (NAVPA)
http://www.navpa.org/

New Jersey Association of State Colleges and Universities (NJASCU), Operation Promise for Servicemembers
http://www.operationpromiseforservicemembers.com/

Park University Success for Veterans Program
http://www.park.edu/Military/success.shtml

Rand Health, Needs Assessment of New York State Veterans
http://www.rand.org/content/dam/rand/pubs/technical_reports/2011/RAND_TR920.pdf

Student Veterans of America, Creating a Veteran-Friendly Campus: A Guide for College and University Administrators
http://www.studentveterans.org/resourcelibrary/documents/CreatingaVeteranFriendlyCampus_AGuideforCollegeandUniversityAdministrators.pdf

Student Veterans of America, Combat to College: A Guide for the Transitioning Student Veteran
http://www.studentveterans.org/resourcelibrary/documents/Combat_to_College_Guide.pdf

United States Department of Education Title IV Programs
http://federalstudentaid.ed.gov/about/title4_programs.html

University of California, Santa Cruz Veteran Students
http://stars.ucsc.edu/veteran.html

University of Iowa College of Liberal Arts and Sciences ReStart Program

http://clas.uiowa.edu/students/handbook/restart

University of Maine at August Veterans Services

http://www.uma.edu/veteranservices.html

University of Nevada, Reno Needs Assessment

http://www.unr.edu/uvc/documents/FINALUNRVetReport.pdf

University of Texas at San Antonio Student Veterans Needs Assessment

http://utsa.edu/va/survey/

Western Association of Veterans Education Specialists

http://www.uswaves.org/

References

Alvarez, L. (2008, October 30). Continuing an education: Combat to college. *New York Times*. Retrieved from http://www.nytimes.com/2008/11/02/education/edlife/vets.html?_r=1

American Council on Education. (n.d.). *Promising practices in veterans' education: Outcomes and recommendations from the Success for Veterans Award Grants*. Washington, DC: Author. Retrieved from http://www.acenet.edu/AM/Template.cfm?Section=serving&TEMPLATE=/CM/ContentDisplay.cfm&CONTENTID=42786

American Council on Education. (2008). *Serving those who serve: Higher education and America's veterans* [Issue brief]. Retrieved from http://www.acenet.edu/Content/NavigationMenu/ProgramsServices/MilitaryPrograms/serving/Veterans_Issue_Brief_1108.pdf

American Council on Education. (2010). *Veteran success jam*. Washington, DC: Author. Retrieved from http://www.acenet.edu/AM/Template.cfm?Section=Home&TEMPLATE=/CM/ContentDisplay.cfm&CONTENTID=37400

American Council on Education. (2011). *A transfer guide: Understanding your military transcript and ACE credit recommendations*. Washington, DC: Author. Retrieved from http://www.acenet.edu/Content/NavigationMenu/ProgramsServices/MilitaryPrograms/TransferGuide_Updated2011.pdf

Brown, P. A., & Gross, C. (2011). Serving those who have served—managing veteran and military student best practices. *Journal of Continuing Higher Education, 59*, 45–49.

Cook, B. J., & Kim, Y. (2009). *From soldier to student: Easing the transition of service members on campus*. Washington, DC: American Council on Education. Retrieved from http://www.acenet.edu/AM/Template.cfm?Section=HENA&Template=/CM/ContentDisplay.cfm&ContentID=33233

Cook, B., & Pullaro, N. (2010). *College graduation rates: Behind the numbers*. Washington, DC: American Council on Education. Retrieved from http://www.acenet.edu/AM/Template.cfm?Section=Home&TEMPLATE=/CM/ContentDisplay.cfm&CONTENTID=38399

Dakduk, M. (2010, October 8). Secretary Shinseki has a message for student veterans: Graduate! *Veteran Journal*. Retrieved from http://www.veteranjournal.com/shinseki-message/

Dillman, D. A., Smyth, J. D., & Christian, L. M. (2009). *Internet, mail, and mixed-mode surveys: The tailored design method* (3rd ed.). Hoboken, NJ: Wiley.

DiRamio, D., Ackerman, R., & Mitchell, R.L. (2008). From combat to campus: Voices of student-veterans. *NASPA Journal, 45*(1), 73–102.

Field, K. (2008). Cost, convenience drive veterans' college choices. *Chronicle of Higher Education, 54*(46), A1. Retrieved from http://www.tcc.edu/news/stories/documents/FromtheissuedatedJuly25.pdf

Groux, C. (2011, July 13). Campus-based and online education strive to meet veterans' needs. *U.S. News University Connection*. Retrieved from http://www.usnewsuniversity directory.com/articles/campus-based-and-online-education-strive-to-meet-v_11604 .aspx

Huba, M. E., & Freed, J. E. (2000). *Learner-centered assessment on college campuses: Shifting the focus from teaching to learning*. Boston: Allyn & Bacon.

Lokken, J. M., Pfeffer, D. S., McAuley, J., & Strong, C. (2009). A statewide approach to creating veteran-friendly campuses. In R. Ackerman & D. DiRamio (Eds.), *Creating a veteran-family campus: Strategies for transition success*. New Directions for Student Services, 126, pp. 45–54. San Francisco: Jossey-Bass.

O'Herrin, E. (2011). Enhancing veteran success in higher education. *Peer Review, 13*(1), 15–18.

Radford, A. W. (2009). *Military service members and veterans in higher education: What the new GI Bill may mean for postsecondary institutions*. Washington, DC: American Council on Education. Retrieved from http://www.acenet.edu/Content/NavigationMenu/ProgramsServices/CPA/Publications/MilService.errata.pdf

Radford, A. W. (2011). *Military service members and veterans: A profile of those enrolled in undergraduate and graduate education in 2007–08*. Washington, DC: U.S. Department of Education, National Center for Education Statistics. Retrieved from http://nces.ed.gov/pubs2011/2011163.pdf

Sabo, R. (2010, November 15). Veteran student enrollments spike. GIBill.com. Retrieved from http://www.gibill.com/news/veteran-student-enrollments-spike-299.html

Scott, G. A. (2008). *Veteran students received similar amounts of Title IV aid as nonveterans but more total aid with GI benefits* (Report GAO-08–741). Washington, DC: United States Government Accountability Office.

Sewall, M. (2010, June 13). Veterans use new GI Bill largely at for-profit and 2-year colleges. *Chronicle of Higher Education, 56*(38), A20. Retrieved from http://chronicle.com/article/Veterans-Use-Benefits-of-Ne/65914/

State of Minnesota Higher Education Fairness Statute. 197.775 Subdivisions 1–4. (2011). Retrieved from https://www.revisor.mn.gov/statutes/?id=197.775

Steele, J. L., Salcedo, N., & Coley, J. (2010). *Military veterans' experiences using the Post-9/11 GI Bill and pursuing postsecondary education*. Washington, DC: American Council on Education. Retrieved from http://www.acenet.edu/AM/Template.cfm?Section=Programs_and_Services&TEMPLATE=/CM/HTMLDisplay.cfm&CONTENTID=38956

Walvoord, B. E. (2004). *Assessment clear and simple: A practical guide for institutions, departments, and general education.* San Francisco: Jossey-Bass.

Wiggins, G., & McTighe, J. (2005). *Understanding by design* (2nd ed.). Upper Saddle River, NJ: Pearson.

Wilson, M. J., Greenlees, J. B., Hagerty, T., Helba, C. V., Hintze, D. W., & Lehnus, J. D. (2000). *Youth attitude tracking study 1999: Propensity and advertising report* (C-DASW01–96-C-0041). Arlington, VA: Defense Manpower Data Center.

Winston Group. (2008). *GI Bill focus group analysis for American Council on Education.* Washington, DC: Author.

Wolf, P. (2007). A model for facilitating curriculum development in higher education: A faculty-driven, data-informed, and educational developer–supported approach. In P. Wolf & J. C. Hughes (Eds.), *Curriculum development in higher education: Faculty-driven processes and practices.* New Directions for Teaching & Learning, 112, pp. 15–20. San Francisco: Jossey-Bass.

Woo, S. (2006, November 2). GAO report urges Education Department to complete overdue study on student aid to service members. *Chronicle of Higher Education.* Retrieved from http://chronicle.com/article/GAO-Report-Urges-Education/117782/

VIGNETTE

Jonathan Miller
Student, University of West Georgia

I joined the Army shortly after the war in Iraq started. I was 21, had a year of college under my belt, and a good job. At the time, the attacks on the World Trade Center and the Pentagon were still fresh in the nation's mind. I remember not knowing how to express myself as I watched protesters marching and politicians and celebrities debating each other. The only way I knew how to speak out about what I believed was to join the military in the defense of our country and those I loved. I served for seven years in the 101st Airborne Division as an aviation operations specialist. I wouldn't trade my time in the Army for anything; it made me who I am today. I met some of the most amazing people, developed a better understanding of the world, and learned a lot about myself.

I also learned that I didn't know very much. Every day in the Army was a learning experience. I learned from my drill sergeants, my officers, soldiers under me, and from the Afghanis and Iraqis. I took college courses online while I was in the Army. I struggled with maintaining passing grades while working 60–80 hours a week, but I managed to complete most of my basic courses in preparation for my reentry to the civilian world.

After seven years of military service, I decided I needed to do something different. During the process of departing the military, I underwent the same series of classes and instruction that all veterans go through. They made me feel prepared for reentry to civilian life. The adjustment was much more difficult than I anticipated.

Thanks to the Veterans Administration and the Post-9/11 GI Bill, I didn't have to worry about paying for college. Getting into college was another matter. While I was applying to colleges in our area, I continued taking online courses with the university in which I was enrolled. I managed to improve my grades during my first months out of the Army, but it wasn't enough to impress the colleges and universities to which I was applying. I was discouraged at how little assistance I was getting from universities in the enrollment process. I was used to being afforded a certain level of respect, even from my superiors. My new mission was to attain a college degree, and the people who I believed should be interested in helping me were not. I wrote college faculty members, deans, and admissions officials, and was growing more and more frustrated by the lack of assistance from these officials.

I couldn't understand why I wouldn't be an ideal candidate for any of these institutions. The schools should have known that my tuition was assured through the VA. Military veterans are hard workers, good learners, and self-disciplined. What I found I lacked was the knowledge or assistance in getting back into college. We don't have the high school advisors helping us with application processes. We are out of touch with registration procedures and orientation schedules. We may be able to work for days with only a few hours of sleep, put together a battle strategy under fire, but we have difficulty navigating the bureaucracy that is higher education.

Finally, I was accepted to the University of West Georgia and resumed my education. I was able to push myself to make the dean's list. Some of my professors encouraged me to try new things, and I found new talents and developed new skills. I have worked to earn the same respect from my peers and instructors that I earned in the military, and am beginning to see the fruits of that labor. Last Veterans Day I was honored and moved to be invited to read names during a ceremony honoring the war fallen. Faculty members in the college student affairs and counseling programs have shown that there are civilian educators who care about veterans. Their thoughtfulness and concern has been important in keeping me motivated to meet my goals in higher education.

CHAPTER EIGHT

OFFICES OF VETERANS AND MILITARY SERVICES

Stephen G. Abel, Robert J. Bright, and R. M. Cooper

September 11, 2001 and its aftermath brought to the forefront once again the sacrifices that service men and women make during war. Over the past decade, many college and university students have been called to active duty in the United States military, either through existing enlistment obligations (such as the National Guard) or decisions to serve as a result of the effect that 9/11 had on them. These service members and veterans are now returning to finish their college degrees or, in some cases, are enrolling in college or university courses for the first time.

Abraham Lincoln, in his second inaugural address in 1865, highlighted the commitment and the responsibility of care that the United States owed its veterans (U.S. Department of Veterans Affairs [VA], n.d.). Today, U.S. colleges and universities share in that same responsibility to serve the large and growing number of service members and veterans on college campuses who have made tremendous sacrifices in serving the nation.

In this chapter, we describe the mission and role of Offices of Veterans and Military Services (OVMSs) on college and university campuses, and we recommend organizational models and arrays of support services for working successfully with student veterans and service members. The configuration of such an office, as well as the services offered, will no doubt vary among institutions, as will resources made available for veterans services. Although not all institutions will have the same levels of funds, we strongly recommend OVMSs as the best way to organize services and coordinate effective outreach to student veterans and prospective students. We also discuss needs assessment strategies that can be tailored to individual campuses to help identify the type and range of support services for veterans appropriate to the campus. Finally, we discuss how campus-based veterans services can be evaluated to determine their effectiveness in serving the needs of student veterans.

The Mission of the OVMS on College Campuses

OVMSs frequently offer and coordinate a wide range of support services, many of which are discussed in more detail later in this chapter. However, the overarching mission of the OVMS should center on serving student veterans and service members directly and indirectly in ways that foster their success. Ultimately, the mission of any OVMS should reflect the mission of the individual college or university. OVMS should also serve the principal purposes of identifying service members and veterans and increasing their enrollments (outreach and recruitment), increasing the breadth and depth of campus awareness of the needs and issues facing these students, increasing their retention and persistence rates through support services, and increasing their graduation rates. At the most basic level, OVMSs provide central contact points for student veterans service members who are enrolled or are seeking to enroll, and OVMS staff work to ensure that individuals have access to the services and resources needed for their success.

In 2010, the Council for the Advancement of Standards in Higher Education (CAS) released a set of standards and guidelines for campus-based offices of veterans and military programs and services, and readers are advised to review that document carefully for more information. To meet CAS standards, OVMSs should, among other efforts, employ at least one dedicated staff member, assure ready and equal access to programs and services by *all* enrolled veterans and service members, serve multiple liaison roles, and systematically assess and evaluate the unit's effectiveness (CAS, 2010).

OVMSs should assist all veterans and service members, of all wars, of all generations. However, the establishment of the Post-9/11 GI Bill, comprising the most robust education benefits package since World War II, has resulted in large numbers of veterans attending undergraduate and graduate degree programs across the United States. Since 9/11 and the subsequent increase in military personnel called to active duty, the number of veterans on college campuses in the United States has more than doubled from 397,589 in 2000 to 819,281 in 2010 (VA, 2010). This trend grew slowly at first, but then jumped dramatically. From 2009 to 2010, the number of veterans enrolled and utilizing educational benefits on college and university campuses across the nation grew from 541,439 to 819,281 (VA, 2010). Equally noticeable is the increase of veterans on college campuses who have sustained physiological or psychological service-related injuries (Chapter Six of this handbook provides a detailed discussion about serving veterans with disabilities). Total and proportional enrollments of veterans differ from campus to campus—even leading to recent attempts to characterize and categorize campuses in terms of the relative presence of veterans and service members—as a way to understand this phenomenon.

Cook and Kim (2009) reported that institutions with less than 1 percent veteran enrollment were characterized as low veteran-enrollment schools. The authors noted that in general, these schools had no strategic plans focused on programming and services for veterans. On the other hand, institutions with veteran enrollments of 3 percent or higher were defined as high veteran-enrollment schools. The majority of these institutions had developed long-term strategic plans and broad ranges of programs and support services designed for military veterans (Cook & Kim, 2009). Institutions of higher education that purposefully plan for and address the challenges facing veterans who are transitioning from active duty and perhaps back again to college campuses tend to attract larger numbers of veterans to their campuses. Moreover, Cook and Kim (2009) concluded, "institutions with a dedicated [OVMS] were more likely to make programmatic changes than institutions without" (p. ix).

In order to support and assist student veterans in their pursuits of higher education, several steps should be taken. These include identifying student veterans and service members within the campus community, recruiting veteran applicants to the campus, determining the level of campus awareness of student veterans' needs, providing myriad support services specific to the needs of student veterans, and assessing the impact of an OVMS and campus community in meeting the needs of student veterans. OVMSs can be central resources in these efforts and frequently are charged with taking the lead in these areas. In the remaining sections of this chapter these measures and the OVMS's role in each are reviewed.

How Can Institutions Identify Student Veterans on Their Campuses?

Far from a simple head count, identifying all veterans and service members on campus can present a significant challenge. Individuals who receive VA educational benefits are readily identifiable as they must self-identity to receive those benefits. However, Keith Wilson, director of educational benefits at the VA's headquarters in Washington, DC (personal communication, June, 2010), estimated that only 60 to 65 percent of veterans on the average college campus are accessing their VA educational benefits at any given time, and the remaining 35 to 40 percent may or may not choose to self-disclose. For example, veterans who intend to enroll in graduate or professional programs after completing their undergraduate degrees may save their benefits for graduate school, which is usually more expensive than undergraduate study, and tap other sources to finance their undergraduate educations. Other enrolled veterans may not be using VA educational benefits because their benefits were insufficient to fund their entire degree programs or because of failure to complete their degrees within the VA's tight time limits (36 months in the case of the Post-9/11 GI Bill).

The easiest way to attempt to identify prospective student veterans is to include a series of voluntary questions on admissions applications. Applicants for admission may be asked to identify their branches of service (Army, Navy, Air Force, Marine Corps, or Coast Guard), component of service (Active, Guard, or Reserve), combat service, and plans to use VA educational benefits to finance any portions of their educations.

An aggressive outreach campaign to *current* students will assist administrators at colleges and universities currently lacking comprehensive sets of application questions or those in the early stages of outreach. These campaigns can include print media, such as campus newspaper articles, announcements, advertisements, flyers, posters, and stories and advertisements on campus and local television stations. The OVMS web site and social media sites like Facebook and Twitter can also be used in outreach. The key is that university administrators take comprehensive steps to identify and serve all of veterans and service members, not just those receiving educational benefits from the VA, or in the case of some active duty service members, the U.S. Department of Defense.

How Can OVMSs Assist Institutions Seeking to Increase Enrollments of Student Veterans?

Increasing veteran enrollments requires a great deal of collaboration with numerous offices throughout the university and community. Beginning with the student admissions process, OVMS staff, in conjunction with enrollment management offices, should be actively involved in recruiting veterans from local military units and, for OVMSs at four-year institutions, community colleges. Participating in job, education, and degree program transfer fairs is an excellent way to advertise an institution's commitment to enrolling student veterans and supporting their success. Collaborating with the university's marketing or public relations representatives to advertise the veteran-friendliness of the campus is also important in attracting service members and veterans to apply and enroll. This outreach could include speaking directly to individual veterans, groups of veterans, and nearby National Guard and reserve units regarding the ease of admissions and enrollment processes, prompt evaluation of prior transcripts, reliable estimates of financial aid packages, availability of online courses, and the presence of an OVMS.

The protracted transition of leaving the security and camaraderie of military service and moving first into the civilian world and then enrolling or reenrolling in college represents a challenging and serious commitment for many student veterans. Thus, it is likely that veterans will choose to enroll in schools that have made significant commitments to their success. Establishing an OVMS that can provide a central point of contact and assist applicants as they seek information or negotiate admissions and enrollment processes is a significant, concrete demonstration of an institution's commitment to veterans. A proactive, strongly networked OVMS can have a direct influence on increasing the numbers of enrolled student veterans. OVMSs also can make significant contributions in the retention rates of student veterans by facilitating campus awareness of veteran issues, developing and implementing a number of programmatic support services for veterans, and in some cases, offering veterans opportunities to work with individuals who understand military culture from their own prior experiences and can help provide a "bridge" for moving into the college environment.

When Secretary of Veterans Affairs Eric K. Shinseki met with veterans at Fort Dix, New Jersey, in October 2010, he highlighted his concern about the low student veterans' persistence rate from first year to second year, which at that time was just 50 percent nationally. At a Student Veterans of America Leadership Summit eight months later, Secretary Shinseki (2011) reported: "Early indications suggest graduation rates for student veterans are lower than [the graduation rate for all students entering four-year institutions]—perhaps significantly lower" (para. 11). There is currently a dearth of solid, reliable data on enrollment patterns and academic outcomes among veterans. If colleges and universities reported specific, uniform data annually to the VA, such data could be analyzed and published, allowing institutions to gain comparative knowledge and allowing prospective students to make more informed decisions about institutional choice.

Providing direct services to student veterans should be a major objective of OVMSs as these support services can assist student veterans with acclimating to the campus environment (for example, orientation programs specifically geared to veterans) as well as persisting to graduation (for example, on-site advising, peer support, intervening when there are problems with accessing benefits, and so forth). Later sections in this chapter describe and discuss OVMS services for student veterans.

How Can OVMSs Facilitate Campus Awareness?

Administrators and student services staff can design and conduct campus audits to determine the levels of awareness in their campus communities pertaining to student veterans, and inventory the services, programs, and issues concerning student veterans that are currently present at their institutions. Furthermore, administrators may wish to conduct needs assessments of student veterans themselves to determine principal issues to address. By identifying the specific needs of student veterans and service members, institutions can make better use of available resources, and current students may be able to reap the benefits of their own input. More detailed suggestions for conducting such a needs assessment are presented at the end of this chapter.

Potentially untapped advocates for student veterans may include current campus community members with relatives or close friends who are service members or veterans. For example, at Rutgers University, a senior administrator had a relative serving in the military during the post-9/11 combat campaigns. The administrator's awareness and knowledge of his relative's experiences as a student veteran prompted him to take proactive steps in making the campus community more veteran-friendly. On campuses that already have established OVMSs (or committed individuals who may be serving as ad hoc advocates in the absence of OVMSs), to bring attention to the challenges that returning veterans encounter on campus, university administrators can succeed in accommodating student veterans in their schools, departments, and classrooms.

Because of their familiarity with the issues and needs of student veterans and their direct roles as resources for student veterans, OVMSs can more effectively intervene or pursue policy and changes in practice as they become better known on their campuses. Facilitating awareness in campus communities of the issues that service members are dealing with as they pursue their higher education goals is a principal objective of OVMSs. This awareness can make campuses more welcoming places for veterans and communicate that their success is a priority of the administration, staff, and faculty. In other words, OVMSs have a reciprocal mission such that OVMS staff pursue campuswide changes and work with individual student veterans to address their issues and problems. Efforts in both of these areas exemplify the commitment by the campus to the success of student veterans. Creating awareness is also important for those campuses that do not currently have OVMSs, but are seeking support to develop dedicated offices and programs that will serve the needs of their student veterans.

Establishment of a university-wide advisory committee is one way that universities can create awareness among the campus community and identify specific veterans' needs and issues. This advisory committee can serve as a strong symbolic and practical indication that an institution is taking the needs of veterans seriously and is carefully exploring steps to address those needs. As one example, in 2008 the president of Rutgers University created the Committee on Veterans' Services, which was tasked with identifying difficulties that veterans encountered when accessing university services. This committee issued 14 recommendations. One recommendation was to have a single point of contact at the university and on each campus to deal with veterans; as a result, the OVMS was created. The committee is broadly representative and includes senior academic administrators, student affairs administrators, a range of university operations office representatives, and enrolled student veterans. Because the director of the OVMS works most closely with student veterans, the director sets the meeting agendas with the approval of the committee chair, who is a senior vice president of the university. Involvement and leadership of senior administrators reinforces the high institutional priority placed on these issues and this campuswide undertaking. Additionally, these senior-level administrators have the authority and resources to implement committee recommendations that result from meeting discussions. The committee meets periodically during the academic year to provide policy-level guidance and continues to share information regarding veteran issues and concerns as well as veteran success stories. This committee (or a committee like this) can be a significant instrument in promoting better understanding and awareness among the campus community of student veterans and their specific needs.

In creating and fostering awareness, it is helpful for those who work directly in the campus environment with student veterans (such as faculty, administrators, residence hall directors or advisors, academic advisors) to have better understandings of the military culture of which the veterans have been (or are) part. This military culture is based on duty, honor, and country (the motto of the U.S. Military Academy) and encompasses such personal characteristics as discipline, camaraderie, and integrity. One very small symbol of military culture that may translate well into campus settings is the awarding of a commander's coin to recognize the superior performance of an individual under a high-ranking officer's command. The tradition of awarding coins is currently present in all military branches as well as some federal government officials and agencies, including the Commander-in-Chief and Cabinet, the Central Intelligence Agency, and the National Security Agency. Accordingly, a small way that a university can acknowledge and demonstrate respect for the military culture of its student veterans and service members is by establishing a recognition coin that the president of the university and the director of the OVMS can present to honor the contributions and accomplishments of students who are veterans, and current members of the military, ROTC, National Guard, and U.S. Reserve. For example, the president's recognition coin may be awarded to recognize student veterans with exemplary academic achievements, or outstanding records of campus service, or those who have mentored other student veterans.

Additional opportunities that will help facilitate campus awareness and at the same time recognize the contributions that student veterans have made through their service to the nation is to host an appreciation reception or dinner for all veterans affiliated with the campus. Such a major event, held in honor of faculty, staff, alumni, and students who are military members and veterans, would be a clear indication to the entire university community that service to the nation is valued and appreciated.

Stereotypes. An important part of facilitating campus awareness of student veterans is identifying and addressing the prevailing negative stereotypes of veterans. Rather narrow and sensationalistic stereotypes of veterans and the military can be found in mainstream media, such as portrayals of service members with posttraumatic stress disorder (PTSD) as threats to themselves and others. However, student veterans with PTSD may find that their greatest difficulties come with maintaining concentration and focus, and devices such as "smartpens" issued by the VA or campus disability services office can help.

One goal of an OVMS should be working with staff, faculty, and students to dispel often widely held negative images of veterans. OVMS staff members' and advisory board members' participation in committees and groups at all levels of the university provides opportunities to educate and better inform community members. Opening OVMS and student veteran organization events to the community at large can also aid in this ongoing effort. For example, to commemorate holidays like Veterans Day, in addition to conducting a solemn, formal ceremony honoring all veterans, OVMSs can sponsor or cosponsor events that enhance understanding and promote discussion of issues related to veterans, the military, and global affairs.

In November 2010, Rutgers University Veterans Services, in coordination with SERVS (Rutgers Veteran Students, the student veterans organization at the New Brunswick/Piscataway Campus), hosted a lecture and panel discussion on *The Role of the Military in a Democracy* to address the awareness goal. Equally effective was a student veterans organization–sponsored *Civilian/Veteran Dialogue* held at the Newark Campus of Rutgers, which provided an opportunity for interaction and dialogue between nonveteran staff, faculty, and students and members of the student veteran community.

Essential Services, Programs, and Campus Relationships

To maximize responsiveness and efficiency, the OVMS should be the initial contact—if not the principal continuing point of contact—for veterans and service members with questions or who are experiencing difficulties. As a result, OVMS staff should be prepared to field or directly deal with issues related to admissions, enrollment, registration, housing and residence life, veteran's benefits, academic advising, tutoring, career advising, disability services, student health, counseling services, financial aid, and student accounting. This section of the chapter includes a discussion of key support services and programs, the importance of developing strong working relationships with campus units and representatives, and considerations for OVMSs or student veterans' representatives (in cases where institutions do not have designated OVMSs) to address when planning or providing assistance to student veterans.

School Certifying Official

The school certifying official is frequently affiliated with the registrar's office, student accounts office, or in some cases, with the OVMS (Steele,

Salcedo, & Coley, 2010). Larger campuses may employ more than one school certifying official, and OVMS staff will likely have the most day-to-day interaction with these individuals. School certifying officials verify each veteran's eligibility for VA educational benefits and ensure that courses in which a veteran enrolls represent progress toward the intended degree, which is a VA criterion for maintaining access to benefits. Because of their role, school certifying officials have direct access to the VA regional processing offices, which is also helpful for OVMS staff in their work to support student veterans.

OVMS staff members who are also officially recognized as school certifying officials have access to the regional offices and can facilitate helping students find important information. However, the work of certifying VA benefits for veterans, the core responsibility of the school certifying official, represents a significant time commitment which increases as the numbers of enrolled veterans increase. Consequently, although the school certifying official may be housed within the OVMS, individual OVMS staff members should not be expected to provide or coordinate comprehensive support services and simultaneously undertake the responsibilities of the school certifying official.

Fees, Tuition, and Grants and Scholarships

Universities and colleges should consider waiving or refunding admission application fees for veterans and active duty personnel. Student service members often face mid-semester academic withdrawals and subsequent reenrollments due to activation or deployments (Rumann & Hamrick, 2010). In these situations, institutions should consider providing refunds for semester or term tuition and fees. Under current provisions of the Post-9/11 GI Bill, the VA pays 100 percent of the educational benefit only if the veteran was on active duty for 36 months. Individuals with less than 36 months of active duty service pay the difference between the educational benefit offered to them and total costs. The VA will not pay tuition for someone who withdraws from the institution. If the institution does not waive the VA's portion of the tuition, or if the institution does not return the veteran's portion, the veteran is left to pay out of his or her own pocket.

Additionally, institutions should consider implementation of reenrollment processes that ease veterans and service members' transitions to student status. At Rutgers University, reenrollment processes for veterans have been streamlined and the OVMS works with the admissions office to aid student veterans. Other financial considerations include institutional participation in the Yellow Ribbon Program, which provides additional educational funding for veterans (see the list of resources at the end of this chapter for more information), and institution-specific grants or scholarships for veterans and military members.

Campus Housing for Student Veterans

Some campuses offer learning communities and special-interest housing options for student veterans. For campuses with resources for these options, OVMS staff can work with the individuals responsible for developing these programs (such as the directors of residential life, housing, and learning communities) to assess student interest and collaborate to tailor learning communities or other themed campus housing opportunities for student veterans.

Housing or residence life administrators can review existing housing policies with OVMS staff to determine how they affect student veterans differently from nonveteran undergraduate students. For example, on some college campuses undergraduate student veterans are permitted to live in graduate student housing (where specific student veteran housing is not available). The establishment of this policy addresses an issue raised by student veterans who are often reasonably close in age to first-year students, but because of their service and life experiences are much less interested in living environments designed for first-year undergraduate students.

The availability of designated campus housing can be a pivotal consideration for student veterans, especially, but not only, in cases where off-campus housing is either limited or prohibitively expensive. OVMS staff members should establish very strong, collaborative relationships with senior residential life administrators so that quick, appropriate actions can be taken as individual situations arise.

Mentoring for Student Veterans

Ongoing acclimation to the campus environment and transition to academic life can be facilitated through a mentoring program for student veterans coordinated through the OVMS. Mentors for incoming student veterans may be upper-class peers or staff and faculty who have had prior military experiences (or who have sincere commitments to assisting student veterans). One example of a comprehensive mentoring program could incorporate two levels of mentors: peers and staff or faculty members. Upper-class student veterans and service members can mentor incoming veterans and service members with regard to skills and resources for acclimating to the university or college. OVMS staff, faculty, and alumni can be valuable mentors and coaches for helping students persist to graduation and make workforce or graduate school contacts.

Veteran Service Support Team

Establishment of a campuswide Veterans Services Support Team can be helpful in providing comprehensive, direct support for student veterans. This team approach is useful in efficiently coordinating the varied offices and support services with which student veterans come in contact. This team works with the OVMS on a daily basis to provide support for individual issues; whereas, the Committee on Veterans' Services mentioned earlier in this chapter meets once or twice a semester to deal with institutional policy issues.

To create a comprehensive campus team, representatives should include delegates from every office on campus that in some way interacts with student veterans during their educational endeavors. Key members of the support team should at a minimum include representatives from admissions, the registrar, financial aid, student accounting, housing, physical health care, counseling, disability services, and career services. Representatives from other offices might include multicultural student affairs, campus recreation services, and academic advising units. When possible, team representatives should be upper-level administrators (such as deans, associate deans, and directors) because of their job responsibilities and abilities to address changes or needs quickly. When senior administrators are not available, representatives should be, at minimum, a full-time professional staff member within the unit who can facilitate the flow of information and ensure continuity in team membership.

With this team in place, questions are answered quickly, issues are resolved expeditiously, student veterans' anxieties are minimized, and retention rates increase. This team is analogous to the members of a symphony orchestra. In order for the team to play in harmony and achieve the desired results, the orchestra must have a conductor. For this support team, the conductor is generally the OVMS director or the designated campus veteran representative.

Centralized "In-House" or "In-Office" Services

For universities or colleges that have the available resources, the creation of a centralized services hub that gathers together a range of services under the same program area or in a shared building provides student veterans access to confidential, personalized "in-house" services. Key services or programs to include are tutoring, counseling, academic advising, disability services, and access to state or veteran organization claims and benefits officers. Access to these individuals does not require full-time representation at the OVMS, but can be accomplished through establishment of weekly office hours. At many institutions, several of these services are already provided for all students. When these services can be provided under one roof at a "friendly location," easy access is provided and serves to break down any kind of stigma associated with accessing services. For example, the stigma of walking into a building with the word "counseling" over the door is virtually eliminated when walking into a building called Veterans House.

One way to create an in-house service hub without additional costs is to establish regular, publicized times in which representatives from these offices are available to student veterans at the OVMS. Another option, where appropriate, could include identification of on-call staff members from each designated office who are available to come to the OVMS to meet with student veterans who have approached the OVMS seeking specific services or information. For example, a student veteran who would not visit the university's disability services office or the mental health clinic agreed to meet—albeit reluctantly—with clinicians from those two offices during their scheduled office hours at the OVMS. For this student veteran, meeting at the OVMS provided a safe, more comfortable, and less stigmatizing environment in which to explore and access these services. After meeting with the clinicians, he recognized and acknowledged his need for these services, and he continued to receive regular services from these offices at the OVMS because of his anxiety about the social stigma (discussed later in this chapter) associated with his conditions and their treatment. This example highlights the advantages of coordinating "in-house" services for veterans as it demonstrates the importance of trust, confidentiality, and student control that may be necessary for student veterans to access campus services that can help them succeed. This also demonstrates the critical need for OVMS staff to seek and retain the confidence and trust of each individual student veteran they are charged to serve.

Although the ideal situation is to provide these services at a central "in-house" location that is convenient for student veterans, it is most important that veterans are aware of the services that are available on campus, know how to access them, and receive the encouragement and assistance to do so.

OVMS as a Campus Resource

Via the veterans services support team discussed earlier, OVMS staff members are able to draw together experts across the campus and within the community to better serve veterans and service members. As colleagues, OVMS staff should also volunteer their time and expertise to help units study, revise, or streamline policies and services to more effectively serve all students including veterans and service members. As examples, OVMS staff could serve on an advisory group for the office of disability services, a campuswide enrollment services task force, or on academic policy committees or working groups. Additionally, OVMS staff should function as a resource for individual administrators, staff members, and faculty members who seek assistance or guidance to resolve situations or work effectively with student veterans. Just as a faculty member might contact an office of disability services for guidance in working with a student disability-related concern, OVMS staff members can provide consultation to members of the campus community seeking guidance in addressing concerns related to student veterans. The OVMS web sites, brochures, and other information should identify the OVMS as a resource available to faculty, staff, and administrators.

At the same time, a number of related campus and community offices and organizations should be encouraged to make the OVMS their first contact for questions or information regarding student veterans. These offices could include, but are not limited to, the ROTC departments on campus, student veteran organizations, and local or regional National Guard and Reserve units, as well as veteran organizations such as Veterans of Foreign Wars (VFW), American Legion, and other state and local veteran groups. A new OVMS should make it a priority to reach out to these offices and organizations to develop this broad network of contacts and potential constituencies.

OVMS staff should anticipate that the inquiries they will receive from faculty, staff, administrators, or community organization representatives will be many and varied. In addition to their content expertise, OVMS staff should be prepared to assist and advocate for student veterans (and potential student veterans) who experience wide varieties of concerns or situations. Responding to students' problems or situations case by case can reveal potential problems or holes in existing institutional policies and procedures, which can then be addressed, perhaps in conjunction with the university-wide advisory committee. Some of the situations that OVMS staff members face may involve high-stakes consequences for the students involved, and many turn into empowerment or educational opportunities for students. Depending on the particular circumstance, advocating for students may thus encompass strategies ranging from helping them identify appropriate contact persons, to assisting them as they initiate and prepare for informal meetings or formal appeals, to making direct contacts on students' behalf.

Developing an Office of Veterans and Military Services

This section presents information on factors to consider when developing OVMSs on university or college campuses. Topics covered below include OVMS staff, professional development, and location and size of the facility.

Although the size, scope, staffing, and focal emphases of an OVMS will likely reflect the size, resources, and students' documented needs at the individual college or university, it may be helpful to identify and examine various models and examples. One leading information source is the *Military Times EDGE* magazine, which publishes annual rankings of OVMS at colleges and universities across the nation. The survey instrument is based on an initial poll of student veterans to identify the most important features and services sought by students (Standifer, 2011). The rankings include two-year and four-year institutions; online, nontraditional, and bricks-and-mortar colleges; and public, private, not-for-profit, and for-profit institutions. Reviews of program rankings, explorations of individual programs' web sites, and discussions with program staff may help readers identify a range of models and approaches for further examination and consideration.

Veteran Services Office Staff

At a minimum, institutions of higher education should provide one full-time staff member whose sole responsibility is to assist veterans and service members enrolled at the institution. Unless hiring policies preclude an institution from designating this position as a veteran hire, there are significant advantages to having this position filled by a veteran who meets the established hiring criteria. A veteran in this position is preferable because he or she will have an understanding of veterans' service and sacrifice and the unique challenges they face, which may not be well understood elsewhere in the campus community. The additional benefit of having a veteran in this position is his or her ability to educate, train, and inform nonveteran staff, faculty, and students about the nuances and culture of the military.

In our judgment, institutions that make this role an additional duty for a current staff or faculty member, or hire a part-time person, do not provide adequate services to resolve issues effectively and in timely manners. One illustration of potential problems involved a prospective student veteran who sought answers to enrollment and benefits questions, only to be told that someone would return his call once the part-time veteran services employee returned the following week. The prospective student decided that a university that offered support to veterans only two days a week did not make his success as a priority, and he immediately chose a university with full-time staff focused on his educational success.

If only a single individual can be hired, the primary responsibilities of this full-time staff person should be to ensure that policies, programs, activities, and services are in place that will assist and support veterans at the institution. Furthermore, the OVMS staff person will need to develop and implement plans for evaluating the policies, programs, activities, and services to determine their impact on student veterans' successful educational experiences. In addition, he or she would coordinate recruitment and outreach efforts of the OVMS and serve as the principal point of contact for student veterans seeking assistance in navigating campus processes.

When resources are available, whether through appropriations, grants, or private funding, a college or university should increase OVMS staff to include (in order of priority):

- An administrative assistant who, in addition to providing the full scope of administrative duties, is capable of referring student veterans to other campus services as well as advising veterans about basic educational benefits.
- An assistant OVMS director, especially once the campus's student veteran population numbers in the hundreds. In this case, the assistant director could be the primary point of contact for outreach, enrollment, and individual student issues. With this addition to the staff, the director's role would shift to include a larger focus on policy development and improvement of existing policies and procedures, and to cultivate strong working relationships with outside agencies and offices whose work affects the lives of student veterans.
- A second or third assistant director, or program coordinators, or related professional staff designations (depending on resources and staffing patterns) could be added for those colleges or universities with even larger

student veteran populations. In these cases, each professional staff member may develop special expertise in one or more areas involved in working with student veterans (for example, tutoring and advising services, or mentoring and networking programs). A multicampus veteran services coordinator should be established for those universities and colleges with two or more campuses located some distance from each other, and each individual campus should employ at least one full-time OVMS staff member (see previous discussion).

Wherever possible, arrangements should be made with the state or county government or a service organization (such as the VFW or American Legion) to provide a VA-certified Veterans Service Officer (VSO)—who is capable of assisting veterans with the full range of federal veteran benefits, processing service-related injury claims, and representing the veteran during appeals or hearings (Kreter, n.d.). This person's hours on campus can best be determined by the workload created by the size of the campus's veteran and service member population.

Finally, in every case, regardless of available resources, colleges and universities should take advantage of the VA Work-Study Program. It is not required that campus resources be expended, and funding levels are based on the number of enrolled student veterans who receive VA educational benefits. Through this work-study program, the VA will fund student veterans to work up to 20 hours per week during the academic year, but not more than 1,300 hours annually. The VA pays the state or federal minimum wage rate, whichever is higher, directly to the student. The only requirement is that a designated institutional representative must be accountable for supervising students and reporting their hours to the appropriate VA Regional Processing Center. (See the resource list at the end of this chapter to access more information about the VA Work-Study Program.) To the college or university, this is an invaluable resource representing tens—if not hundreds—of thousands of dollars of support to the OVMS, and is ancillary income for student veterans, many of whom are in need of additional income or financial aid. VA work-study students assigned to the OVMS can share some of the responsibilities involved in serving student veterans.

When resources are limited, another option to augment OVMS staff is the use of undergraduate student interns identified through individual academic departments or career services offices and the use of graduate students seeking practicum or field experience credit. Although these students may not be able to help with the daily operations of the OVMS, they can prove very valuable in completing special projects. For example, an intern from the Rutgers School of Information and Communications created a video series for the university's OVMS that highlighted, in conjunction with a number of academic deans, the stature of the university, unique academic programs, and the exceptional services available to student veterans on campus.

OVMS staff should also reach out to their institution's alumni and development offices, as the planning or presence of a campus-based OVMS may attract volunteer interest as well as targeted contributions to supplement the resources dedicated by the college or university. Stories and profiles of student veterans and service members that appear in alumni magazines, in development office literature, and on institutional web sites can help inform prospective volunteers and donors.

OVMS Staff Professional Development

Ongoing professional development is essential to ensuring that high-quality, effective OVMS staff and services are available for student veterans. However, given the relative newness of OVMSs and designated staff members, professional development opportunities and standards for practice are evolving. Generally speaking, professional development for OVMS staff should focus on the areas of awareness and skill development. All OVMS staff must be aware of and understand, in broad and reasonably comprehensive terms, the range of potential issues that may affect service members or veterans in their transitions to college as well as factors that promote veterans' success. Individual OVMS staff members must also develop skills to work effectively with student veterans who struggle with transitions, life circumstances, or additional issues that affect persistence and success.

Given the wide range of student veterans' needs, the training agenda for OVMS staff is appropriately ambitious. Institution of higher education may offer internal trainings, symposia, and workshops for the university community focused on working with students in transitions. OVMS staff should investigate what their institutions have to offer and take advantage of these cost-effective training opportunities. One example of these types of initiatives is a comprehensive suicide prevention effort that was part of a university-wide campaign to address this critical issue. Supervisors and managers received extensive training on identifying risk factors as well as training materials to share with employees they supervised. We recommend that the OVMS be housed in the division of student affairs, and that OVMS staff have opportunities for professional development that are similar to those offered to other student affairs professionals. Attendance at student affairs conferences (such as NASPA, Student Affairs Administrators in Higher Education or ACPA, College Student Educators International) is helpful. Additionally, institutions and professional staff should consider affiliating with NAVPA (National Association of Veterans' Programs Administrators) to take advantage of its networking and professional development opportunities.

Affiliating with national, regional, and state-level organizations and associations should be a priority of OVMS personnel. State-level organizations often conduct subject-specific training throughout the year that permits staff members to stay current on emerging issues. For example, the New Jersey Association of Veterans Program Administrators hosts quarterly training sessions that include representatives from all of New Jersey's university and colleges. Attendees represent campus offices that interact with veterans, including veteran services staff, certifying officials, financial aid personnel, student accounting, and others. These training sessions are usually half days at the quarterly meetings and full days at the annual meeting. There is no cost for the quarterly meeting and a modest cost to cover handout materials at the annual training.

Government and not-for-profit organizations also conduct regional and national conferences and symposiums. These meetings provide opportunities for OVMS staff to hear from prominent, nationally recognized leaders on topics specific to working with student veterans. The American Council on Education (ACE) has taken the lead in dealing with issues confronting service members, which includes publication of *From Soldier to Student: Easing the Transition for Service Members on Campus* (Cook & Kim, 2009) and *From Combat to Campus: How Universities and Colleges Are Helping Veterans Succeed* (Myers, 2009). Attending these meetings and conferences also provides opportunities for OVMS staff members to network with OVMS professionals from other campuses in order to share information, brainstorm, and problem solve. Also, trainings, symposiums, and conferences hosted by other institutions and government agencies with broad missions should not be overlooked. For example, one medical school's behavioral health care division recently held a conference on traumatic brain injury, posttraumatic stress, and suicide awareness and prevention where preeminent authorities from the U.S. Department of Defense and the VA addressed clinical dimensions of mental health issues among returning veterans.

Facility Size and Location

As previously highlighted, the size of an institution's veteran population should guide staffing and space decisions for the OVMS. At a minimum, the office should be easily accessible to students, and ideally it should be located toward the center of the campus. It will require an adequate reception area, at least one private office space where OVMS staff can discuss confidential material and personal information with student veterans, and, wherever possible, a multipurpose area or lounge where veterans can relax, study, and socialize. This meeting space should be open to student veteran organizations on campus as well as other organizations engaged in supporting veterans and military service personnel on campus, in the community, and around the world.

OVMS spaces should be facilities that student veterans and service members—as well as their family members—can identify as their own. Offices, office suites, lounges, or stand-alone facilities (analogous to Greek letter organization houses or [multi-] cultural centers) may be appropriate depending on the size of the student population and the number and type of services offered. For example, Veterans House at Rutgers University New Brunswick, dedicated in Fall 2010, is an eight-room former home adjacent to the main campus that was converted into office spaces, a student lounge, and a small kitchen and dining area. Many institutions do not have stand-alone facilities, however, and OVMS "offices" may consist of individuals in student accounting or registrar offices who have additional job responsibilities to work with student veterans and who often serve as their institutions' school certifying officials.

Whatever the size, the OVMS should have dedicated space, rather than temporary or multiuse space, and its location on campus should be chosen where possible based on proximity to offices and units with which OVMS staff and students work closely, as well as other strategic considerations. In addition, OVMS staff should closely monitor the student traffic in their centers, perhaps especially if the facilities are stand-alone, to ensure that students' sense of ownership and affiliation is not isolating for those students and fostering lower levels of participation in the broader campus community.

Organizational Placement of the OVMS

The organizational placement of an OVMS within an institution should make sense for that institution; two logical affiliations are student services and enrollment management offices. Although OVMS staff members should have regular contact with campus VA certifying officials who are typically affiliated with registrar offices, those interactions may well be limited to specific processes, such as certifying benefits through review of military discharge certificates (DD214), completing veteran certification requests, and obtaining certificates of eligibility. (For more information about military service records, see the U.S. National Archives and Records listing in the list of resources at the end of this chapter.) The OVMS role in these processes is reasonably minor—to ensure that students provide these documents to certifying officials, and in some cases, to assist students with obtaining appropriate documentation. However, as a matter of mission, enrollment management offices are typically not focused on addressing and resolving individual student veterans' issues or circumstances.

Enrollment management office representatives should collaborate closely with OVMS staff to ensure successful recruiting programs for veterans and military members. Veterans and service members seek to identify people on campus who understand their needs, the processes by which they access their earned educational benefits, and can assist them in the enrollment process; OVMS staff members are that resource and can help students navigate more effectively and efficiently through enrollment services processes. However, depending on campus processes, substantive enrollment services interactions with students may end once students accept offers of admission and enroll. In comparison, student affairs divisions typically provide broad ranges of services to enrolled students. Student affairs units address a wide range of student needs, from daily support activities to complex issues; these offices include, but are not limited to, student health, student counseling, disability services, residential life, academic student support services and tutoring, judicial affairs, multicultural student services, student activities, recreational student services, and in some cases, campus security and enrollment management. Resolving individual veterans' challenges related to these and other areas constitutes the bulk of the work performed on a daily basis by the OVMS, and thus situating the office within the division of student affairs positions OVMS staff to work efficiently with colleagues in student support offices and departments.

Assessment and Evaluation of the OVMS

As previously discussed in this chapter, a principal mission of the OVMS is to increase student veteran enrollment, retention, and graduation rates. Assessment and evaluation can help the OVMS staff determine the extent to which the OVMS is successful in achieving its mission. Assessment and evaluation can also provide evidence to support increases in funding resources (for example, additional staff members or programs). Numerous assessment and evaluation models can provide guiding frameworks for conducting assessments and evaluation. In addition, the 2010 CAS standards and guidelines for veterans and military programs and services may be helpful with respect to benchmarking best practices and designing and conducting self-studies.

The assessment model presented here is grounded in Schuh's *Assessment Methods for Student Affairs* (2009), and readers are urged to consult that volume for more details on designing and conducting assessments.

Needs Assessment

As the first step, campuses must identify their enrolled student veterans, understand their varied backgrounds, and determine the support services needed to aid in their persistence to degree attainment. In some cases, the decision to establish a program or develop a service may seem intuitive. However, an initial needs assessment followed by deliberate and focused planning in the development of programs and services will help maximize resources. For example, a number of the services that have been recommended and reviewed in this chapter were based on conclusions reached after evaluating one year's worth of data collected primarily from students who sought assistance from the Rutgers Veterans Services, the university's OVMS. Based on a review of fiscal year 2010–11 staff calendars, records, and case notes, 427 individual student veterans dealing with 1,552 issues were served. The varied services provided by a OVMS are illustrated in this detailed list of topics related to transition issues accessed by students at Rutgers (in descending order) (see Table 8.1).

In some situations, these data were used as the catalyst for establishing a specific service or program. For example, in reviewing data midterm, it was clear that the academic advising and tutoring functions at the university were not meeting veterans' needs. Again, individual veterans must ensure that every class taken is in the pursuit of a degree, and that the degree is completed within the VA's relatively small window for benefits eligibility. To address these shortcomings, the Rutgers University vice dean of the School of Arts and Sciences volunteered to become the academic advisor for student veterans, and a student organization, RU-for-Troops (RU for Rutgers University), created a comprehensive and successful peer-tutoring service.

TABLE 8.1. RUTGERS VETERANS SERVICES PROVIDED BY OVMS, FISCAL YEAR 2010–11

Transition Issues	No. of Students Helped
Veteran benefits	256
Enrollment	243
General information and referrals	194
Academic advising	193
Transfer credits	171
Housing/residential life	143
Disability services	88
Special programs	78
Distance learning	73
Financial distress	42
Work-study	37
Tutoring/student support services	34

Needs assessments should be conducted on campuses for which data related to services offered to student veterans have not previously been collected, or that lack current or systematic data on student veterans' needs for services, or that want to ensure that they are addressing all the needs of the student veteran population. Gupta (1999) defined a needs assessment as a process for "pinpointing gaps in performance or a method for identifying new and future performance needs" (p. 4). Information collected through needs assessments can assist OVMSs in purposeful planning for programming and support services specific to the needs of student veterans on their campuses. Needs assessment should be carefully planned and designed, and should address data sources (from whom data will be collected), how to contact data sources, methods for collecting data, budget, time line, data analysis, and reporting of final results (with whom the information will be shared and the preferred format). Another step is the determination of the key information to collect. It is helpful to be purposeful in data collection; collecting only data that are relevant to the topic will maximize budget and personnel resources and encourage higher response rates from participants.

Types of Data Collected in a Needs Assessment

Topics that should be considered for inclusion in a needs assessment are related to information that helps the OVMS learn more about members of the student veteran population and their needs with respect to higher education. Accordingly, data collection should focus on the following topics, although additional topics may be appropriate on specific campuses:

- Characteristics and demographics of the student veteran population
- Current services offered and levels of adequacy
- Needs of the student veteran population in the campus environment (such as housing, academics, financial aid, disability resources, health and wellness, and student activities)
- Barriers (potential and real) to implementing services, programs, and activities
- Barriers (potential and real) to accessing services, programs, and activities
- Resources for implementing services, programs, and activities
- The priorities or most important issues and needs to be addressed

In addition to conducting a needs assessment, OVMS staff should develop a plan for evaluating current services, programs, and activities.

Evaluation

Evaluation provides a systematic process of inquiry that allows for conclusions to be reached about the merit and worth of the program, policy, person, or activity that is being evaluated (Mathison, 2005). OVMS staff members should conduct regular evaluations to determine their offices' impact on achieving their missions and working with student veterans. Similar to needs assessments, evaluation reports are valuable resources in guiding future program planning and support services for student veterans. Here we address two types of evaluation: process evaluation (formative) and outcome evaluation (summative); each is focused on a different aspect of assessing the OVMS.

Process Evaluation

The process evaluation highlights specifics of what the program (that is, the OVMS) does and who participates or receives services from the program or activity. Process evaluations are focused on assessment of the processes, methods, or procedures associated with the program, activity, or policy and the extent to which the program, activity, or policy reaches the intended audience(s). Several questions can guide the development of a process evaluation plan, such as:

Program or Activity Process Questions:

- What programs or activities are being implemented?
- How is the program or activity implemented?
- Are the programs and activities being delivered as intended?
- How many sessions were held for the program or activity?
- How effective were the sessions?
- What was the quality of the activity or program?
- What went well? What could be improved?

Participant Process Questions:

- How many individuals are being served? What proportion of student veterans on campus are being reached and are accessing the services?
- What are the demographics of individuals who are reached and who are not reached?
- Are the participants being reached as intended?
- What are participants' responses to the program activities? What are their levels of satisfaction and perceptions of effectiveness of the program or service?
- How did participants access the service, program, or activity? How did they learn about it?

For each of the process questions listed above, it is important to establish "how" the question will be answered and appropriate data source(s). Evaluation *indicators* are useful in identifying the information needed to answer the question. Examples of indicators include number of support services, programs, or activities delivered; number of students served in each program or activity; number of contacts with each student in each program or activity; number of referrals made for students, faculty, and administrators; adequacy or accessibility of the services, programs, and activities; length of time for the activity or program; and how quickly referrals were served. Data related to these indicators can be collected using numerous methods, including surveys, open-ended questionnaires, focus groups, one-on-one interviews, observations, documents (such as reports or logs), and essays (for example, asking veterans to describe what the OVMS has done to support them as students). More recently, visual methods and evidence (such as photographs and videos) are used in qualitative data collection.

Process evaluations can be ongoing with data analyzed and reported at different times throughout the academic year. For some activities, particularly those services or programs that occur more frequently or are accessed more frequently, data may be monitored on a daily or monthly basis. With other activities and programs, a semiannual or annual basis may be more practical. The key is to have a systematic evaluation plan and process in place rather than regarding evaluation as an afterthought, or simply as a means of collecting data to justify or examine an activity, service, or program.

Outcome Evaluation

Outcome evaluations focus on the results of the program, activity, service, or policy. OVMSs are encouraged to use their individual missions, goals, and objectives as focuses in the outcome evaluation stage. Findings from outcome evaluations specify the actions that have taken place as a result of—or in the aftermath of—the program, activity, service, or policy. For example, at the institutional level, student veteran retention and graduation rates may be evaluated to identify potential increases or decreases. At the unit or program level, an activity, service, or program result may be evaluated to determine if it increased awareness, knowledge, skills, motivation or changes in behavior, practice, decision making, or policies. Several questions can guide the development of an outcome evaluation plan and data collection strategies, such as:

- To what extent are programs, services, and activities meeting their specific goals?
- Did retention and persistence rates increase among student veterans and service members?
- What delivery method was most effective (for example, social media or e-mail messages to advertise a program)? What delivery method was most often used?
- Are all sectors of the student veteran and service member population being served (for example, women, veterans with disabilities, veterans of color, and lesbian, gay, bisexual, and transgender veterans)?
- What are unintended outcomes?

Once again, it is important to establish the information and data needed (in other words, evidence indicators) to answer the questions posed. A good deal of institutional data (including retention and graduation rates) are routinely collected and can be accessed through the institution's office of institutional research or academic compliance. Other sources of data may already exist on campus within other departments and offices that are serving students, including student veterans, on a daily basis. As discussed earlier in this chapter, veterans who utilize educational benefits are identifiable through registration records, and institutions can make it easier for veterans to voluntarily disclose their statuses early in the admissions application process. The ability to identify all veterans and service members (not only those using educational benefits) at the early stages of contact with the college or university will permit more comprehensive analyses of students' enrollment patterns and educational outcomes. State and federal laws impose institutional reporting requirements on special populations, including veterans; in collaboration with appropriate campus offices, OVMS staff may be able to obtain access to individual-level data, or at a minimum, obtain aggregated data.

Organizing and Planning for Evaluation

In order to conduct the evaluations listed above and to answer the types of questions addressed by each type of evaluation, it is useful to develop an evaluation planning spreadsheet. The first column of the spreadsheet should be labeled "evaluation question," with each evaluation question listed in a new row of the spreadsheet. Then, across the top of the spreadsheet, individual columns can be created to organize the information needed to answer each evaluation question. These columns should include:

1. *Methods* that will be used to collect data to answer the evaluation question (such as surveys or focus groups).
2. *Data sources* from whom data will be collected (such as student veterans, faculty, staff, or administrators).
3. *Evaluation tools* and measures that will be used (such as a OVMS student survey for advising or faculty focus group questions and protocols for levels of awareness).
4. *Time line* intended for collection and analysis of data to answer the evaluation questions with benchmark dates identified.
5. *Budget* and corresponding costs.
6. *Task responsibilities* for individuals who have responsibilities for the tasks associated with the evaluation.
7. *Comments or notes* for additional information (such as contacts).

Once the column headers are organized, for each evaluation question, complete the information prompted by the column headings. This is an example of what this might look like for one question:

- *Question:* How many individuals were served by the OVMS in the academic year?
- *Data Source:* OVMS administrative records
- *Evaluation Tool:* None for this question
- *Time Line:* Two weeks before annual report is due (with date specified)
- *Budget:* Administrative support staff can complete; no additional costs
- *Task Responsibility:* Administrative support staff

Finally, when considering and developing assessment and evaluation plans, OVMS staff members should first make contact with their division heads or the offices responsible for institutional accreditation to determine whether there are specific OVMS requirements for institutional (or divisional) accreditation and self-studies. This will help align the OVMS's assessment and evaluation plans with institutional expectations, needs, and requirements. OVMSs may also find that there is assistance available on their campuses for assessment and evaluation practices.

Conclusion

Colleges and universities have a unique opportunity to serve student veterans and service members effectively via the creation and support of OVMSs tailored to the needs and sizes of their student veteran populations. Staffing, resources, facilities, and collaborations can have an impact on the relative effectiveness of these offices. As OVMSs are created or expanded, staff members should continually seek to meet the needs of individual student veterans and build campus awareness about student veterans' experiences and circumstances. Tapping resources in the form of advisory committees, support teams, and community or agency representatives can maximize the impact and reaches of OVMSs, and OVMS staff should identify and engage in appropriate training and professional development opportunities. Finally, OVMS staff should regularly and systematically evaluate their services to ensure that student veterans are, in fact, well served.

Resources

APCA—College Student Educators International
http://www2.myacpa.org/

American Council on Education, Serving Those Who Serve: Higher Education and America's Veterans
http://www.acenet.edu/Content/NavigationMenu/Programs Services/MilitaryPrograms/serving/Veterans_Issue_Brief_1108.pdf

American Legion
http://legion.org/

Chronicle of Higher Education, Cost, Convenience Drive Veterans' College Choices
https://www.tcc.edu/news/stories/documents/Fromtheissuedated July25.pdf

Council for the Advancement of Standards in Higher Education (CAS), Veterans and Military Programs and Services (VMPS) Standards
http://www.cas.edu/index.php/updates/press-release/cas-announces-the-release-of-the-newest-standard/

Inside Higher Ed, Campuses as Vet-Friendly Zones
http://www.insidehighered.com/news/2009/06/05/veterans

Kennesaw State University, An Exploration of a First-Year Experience Course to Meet the Needs of Veteran and Other Nontraditional College Students
http://digitalcommons.kennesaw.edu/cgi/viewcontent.cgi?article =1452&context=etd

Military Times EDGE monthly magazine
www.MilitaryTimesEDGE.com

Minnesota Department of Veterans Affairs Higher Education Veterans Programs, *Institutional Readiness: Guidelines for becoming a Veteran Friendly Campus*
http://www.mnveteranservice.org/documents/Institutional _Readiness.pdf

Minnesota State Colleges and Universities, Military-Friendly Policies
http://www.mnscu.edu/military/policies.html

NASPA—Student Affairs Administrators in Higher Education
http://www.naspa.org/

National Association of Veterans' Program Administrators (NAVPA)
http://www.navpa.org/pages/membership.html

Student Veterans of America, What Makes a School Veteran-Friendly?
http://www.studentveterans.org/?p=1192

United States Department of Veterans Affairs, Work-Study Program
http://www.gibill.va.gov/resources/education_resources/
programs/work_study_program.html#HOW MUCH MAY I EARN

**United States Department of Veterans Affairs, Yellow Ribbon
Program**
http://gibill.va.gov/documents/pamphlets/Yellow_Ribbon_
Pamphlet.pdf

**United States Archives and Records Administration, Veterans' Service
Records**
http://www.archives.gov/veterans/military-service-records/about-
service-records.html

Veterans of Foreign Wars (VFW)
http://www.vfw.org/

References

Cook, B. J., & Kim, Y. (2009). *From soldier to student: Easing the transitions of service members on campus*. Washington, DC: American Council on Education. Retrieved from http://www.acenet.edu/AM/Template.cfm?Section=HENA&Template=/CM/ContentDisplay.cfm&ContentID=33233

Council for the Advancement of Standards in Higher Education. (2010, November 12). *New standards provide a framework for establishing and assessing college veterans service programs* [Press release]. Retrieved from http://www.cas.edu/wp-content/uploads/2010/12/FOR-IMMEDIATE-RELEASE1.pdf

Gupta, K. (1999). *A practical guide to needs assessment*. San Francisco: Jossey-Bass.

Kreter, H. S. (n.d.). *The role of a county veteran's service officer* [web site]. Retrieved from http://www.co.genesee.ny.us/departments/veterans/veteranserviceofficer.html

Mathison, S. (Ed). (2005). *Encyclopedia of evaluation*. Thousand Oaks, CA: Sage.

Myers, V. (2009). *From combat to campus: How universities and colleges are helping veterans succeed*. Washington, DC: American Council on Education. Retrieved from http://intraweb.stockton.edu/eyos/veteran_affairs/content/docs/From%20Combat%20to%20Campus.pdf

Rumann, C. B., & Hamrick, F. A. (2010). Student veterans in transition: Re-enrolling after war zone deployments. *Journal of Higher Education, 81*(4), 431–458

Schuh, J. H. (2009), *Assessment methods for student affairs*. San Francisco: Jossey-Bass.

Shinseki, E. K. (2011, June 15). Address delivered at the Student Veterans of America leadership summit. Retrieved from http://www.studentveterans.org/?p=1473

Standifer, C. (2011, November). Schools that serve. *Military Times EDGE*, 30–37.

Steele, J. L., Salcedo, N., & Coley, J. (2010). *Service members in school: Military veterans' experiences using the Post-9/11 GI Bill and pursuing postsecondary education.* Washington, DC: American Council on Education. Retrieved from http://www.acenet .edu/AM/Template.cfm?Section=Programs_and_Services&TEMPLATE=/CM/ HTMLDisplay.cfm&CONTENTID=38956

United States Department of Veterans Affairs (n.d.). *The origin of the VA motto: Lincoln's second inaugural address.* Washington, DC: Author. Retrieved from http://www.va .gov/opa/publications/celebrate/vamotto.pdf

United States Department of Veterans Affairs. (2010). *Annual benefits report: Fiscal year 2010.* Washington, DC: Author. Retrieved from http://www.vba.va.gov/ REPORTS/abr/2010_abr.pdf

VIGNETTE

Kathy Meyers

Veterans and Military Personnel, Western Illinois University

When asked to assume additional responsibilities for coordinating services for student veterans almost five years ago, I was ready for change and very enthusiastic about meeting new challenges. The first objective was to streamline services for student veterans and military personnel; they would no longer be shuffled to multiple offices to complete admission applications and enrollment forms. My role was to serve as the primary point of contact to assist the student veteran population in completing these processes, respond to inquiries, and resolve issues or concerns. My colleagues and I quickly learned that the demand to streamline services and expand programming efforts was much greater than I was able to manage on a part-time basis because I had assumed veteran-related responsibilities in addition to my initial job duties. Providing quality services and resources to more than 600 enrolled veterans and military personnel required my full-time attention.

Shortly thereafter, I was relocated to a new center dedicated specifically to serving this student population. Although the center was spacious and met our needs at the time, the competition for limited internal resources left us with a serious lack of funding to furnish the center. The hustle to "beg, borrow, and steal" furniture and equipment from various campus departments was on! The remaining challenge was to provide adequate staffing without a budget for additional full-time personnel. Through the assistance of the Department of Veterans Affairs Work Study Program, we were able to open the Veterans Resource Center on Veterans Day in 2009.

In reality, the initial lack of funding served as a catalyst in facilitating many of our successes. There aren't words to adequately describe the significant value of these peer work-study student employees and their impact on the development of services for the student veteran population. Though the student veteran employees have assumed a significant and integral role in meeting the needs of their peers, an inherent challenge continues with the constant need to train and retrain student employees. It took a strong network of committed individuals, departments, and agencies for the Veterans Resource Center to be successful. A core group of professionals willingly banded together to share their knowledge and time to establish collaborative and innovative services; student veterans hit the ground running by participating in focus groups, volunteering for programs, and serving as peer mentors; and veteran-related agencies agreed to develop partnerships with the campus community.

The Department of Veterans Affairs volunteered its services by providing staff members who maintained office hours every other week to provide additional health care and related assistance. Additional partnerships with the Veterans Administration Health Care System and the Veterans Health Administration Office of Rural Health have evolved. The resulting outcomes include an array of on-campus experts, services, resources, and programs designed specifically to meet the emerging needs of a growing student veteran population. Once we were able to establish a track record, it was time to move forward in enhancing and improving the educational opportunities that would enable student veterans to succeed.

External resources were accessed to enable the VRC to expand its outreach, enrollment, and retention efforts. Our veteran-specific orientation programs and services expanded with the 2012 launch of an online orientation guide. Regardless of their geographic locations, veterans and military personnel are able to gather relevant academic, student services, financial, personal, and healthcare information in a timely manner. Another important retention initiative is Project STRIVE—Students Transitioning and Reintegrating in Veterans Education. STRIVE provides early outreach and intervention to newly enrolled and returning students designed to increase the retention and graduation rates of student veterans.

Based on student surveys and program evaluations, our veteran and military student population has responded positively to our initiatives. Student veteran enrollment rates continue to climb; our students are increasing awareness of veteran-specific issues; and our student veterans are, individually and collectively, serving as facilitators to ease the transitions of their comrades. Our continued success will likely be dependent upon the campus community to be flexible, proactive, and willing to change as we move forward in fostering a climate that will enable our returning service men and women to share their stories.

CHAPTER NINE

FOCUSED LEARNING ENVIRONMENTS FOR STUDENT VETERANS

Sarah Minnis, Stephanie Bondi, and Corey B. Rumann

Veterans and service members need a wide range of support systems at institutions of higher education to feel welcome and be successful on campus. Creating a veteran-friendly environment takes the concerted effort of everyone on campus to identify the resources and mechanisms that need to be put in place to address the needs of this population. In addition to creating policies and procedures and establishing strategies to meet the transition needs of student veterans, the environment should promote student learning and engagement. Institutions of higher education are increasingly called to account for student learning (Schmidtlein & Berdahl, 2005). Although many approaches to supporting student veterans discussed in this handbook may be planned and implemented primarily by staff members at colleges or universities, focused learning environments are initiatives that call most directly for faculty involvement, and on some campuses will need to be led by individual faculty members or groups of faculty. At some institutions, staff may already be working closely with faculty on collaborative initiatives, but on other campuses, supporting student veterans' success through focused learning environments may be an opportunity to build partnerships across academic and student affairs. Depending on the nature of the learning environment, faculty members' involvement in planning and facilitation is imperative because of their control over awarding academic credit and designing and approving curriculum additions. As noted in Chapter Seven of this handbook, the degree completion and academic success of student veterans—and of all students—should be primary objectives of any college or university.

This chapter addresses the ways in which focused learning environments can be designed to facilitate student veterans' and service members' academic successes. We begin by discussing two theoretical perspectives (adult learning and social learning) that can be used to help conceptualize student veterans' academic learning and successes and to strengthen learning environments designed for military service members. We discuss types of learning environments, including orientation programs and learning communities; offer examples of promising practices at different colleges and universities; and describe one institution's process for establishing a student veteran learning community on campus. Next, we describe assessment approaches to document and measure student learning and success. Finally, the chapter concludes with implications, recommendations, and a list of resources.

Adult Learning Theories

Understanding the experiences and learning perspectives that student veterans bring to campus can be strengthened by drawing on relevant theories. When considering the development of specific learning opportunities tailored for veterans, it is most helpful to turn to adult learning theories that emphasize how interactions and involvement can affect college students' social and academic experiences. Although student veterans may share a number of characteristics with their traditional-aged student counterparts, the combination of age and life experience suggests that structuring different types of learning environments would be appropriate. Two theoretical bases that hold promise for shaping curricular and cocurricular learning opportunities for student veterans are Malcolm Knowles' theory of andragogy (1977) and Jack Mezirow's theory of transformative learning (1981). Both theories provide frameworks for addressing the unique needs of veterans through academic and cocurricular programs.

Knowles' theory (1977) of adult learning—andragogy—grew out of the study of pedagogy, or the way in which children learn. Knowles realized that the ways in which adults learn differ significantly from those of children, and he described different expectations about learning processes and environments characteristic of adult learners. A key focus of andragogy is on the learner's ability and willingness to be self-directed in the learning process. Additionally, the self-directed learning advocated by Knowles encourages adult learners to incorporate their life experiences into their learning and meaning-making processes.

Andragogy is different from many traditional learning approaches that center on digesting concepts offered by a textbook or instructor. Although instructors often fail to encourage students to integrate personal experiences into their classroom learning (Palmer & Zajonc, 2010), the salience of the lived experiences of adult learners, including veterans and service members returning to campus after active duty, can be an important anchor for structuring their learning environments. For student veterans, this could mean structuring focused learning environments so that students are invited to draw upon their military experiences. For example, in courses dealing with world history, cultures, or religions, faculty could require students to research topics of their choices (relevant to course content) and encourage them to rely on their personal experiences and curiosities, including their experiences in the military, to guide the direction of their research. In this type of assignment, students are given structure about specific expected outcomes and elements of the assignment, but they are also encouraged to pursue learning in ways meaningful to them and based on their own experiences and interests.

Relying on a traditional content delivery approach such as lecturing may leave students disconnected from classroom learning and could contribute to distraction and a lack of engagement (Palmer & Zajonc, 2010). For example, student veterans may be engrossed in processing salient military experiences, which may distract from their engagement in the classroom if not intentionally incorporated into the learning process. Though instructors should be cautious to avoid making assumptions about what student veterans have gone through, they should not necessarily shy away from inviting student veterans—indeed, all students—to voice and process their experiences relevant to the subject matter. A skilled instructor (faculty or staff) will not make assumptions about student veterans' military service history (for example, that they have PTSD or have experienced combat) or expect them to speak on behalf of all veterans. Skilled instructors utilizing andragogy will afford opportunities for veterans to reflect upon, share, and make meaning of their military service as a vehicle that also fosters meaning making related to course content. Faculty and staff working with student veterans should educate themselves about student veterans' experiences so they can avoid making inappropriate, insensitive, or stereotyped remarks in the learning environment.

In order for students to be engaged in self-directed learning, instructors must create conducive environments (Doyle, 2008). Knowles (1977) noted the critical importance of "establishing a climate that is conducive to learning, which is dominated or characterized by trust, by informality, by openness, by mutuality, by mutual respect, warmth, caring" and so forth (p. 209). Especially if students have not participated in such learning environments before, they may be unfamiliar with the approach and practices of self-directed learning and may need coaching to engage in it (Doyle). This tenet of Knowles' andragogy (1977) can guide instructors' efforts to engage student veterans in learning.

Another adult learning theory is Mezirow's theory (1996) of transformative learning. This theory explains how individuals come to make sense of and learn from their life events, such as military and educational experiences. Transformative learning focuses on how individuals interpret the events they have experienced as well as the important roles played by those with whom they can share and process those events (Mezirow, 1996). Two learning capabilities that are central to transformative learning are critical reflection and reflective judgment (Mezirow, 2009). During critical reflection, students think about their values and assumptions while considering alternative perspectives. Reflective judgment is a process of making decisions while considering the epistemic and value origins of various perspectives (Mezirow, 2009). In general, transformative learning highlights the ways in which people make sense of their worlds and "construct knowledge ... as part of the transformative learning experience ... [and appreciate] a culturally relevant and spiritually grounded approach" (Taylor, 2008, pp. 8–9).

Using transformative learning approaches, instructors should provide student veterans (and all students) opportunities to explore their values, ideals, cultural perceptions, and connections to others. Specifically, veterans examine and challenge their current and prior worldviews by considering the military culture, deployment experiences, and new relationships along with associated values. Through engaging in transformative learning, students "reassess the structure of assumptions and expectations which frame [their] thinking, feeling, and acting" (Mezirow, 2009, p. 90). For example, student veterans in a political science class would be expected to reflect on their personal military experiences and attitudes when considering, for instance, contemporary political events, trends, and structures. Faculty would guide students to examine their own assumptions about military service in light of a variety of additional political perspectives, inviting students to reconsider and modify, if appropriate, their frames of reference and related values and assumptions. Transformative learning opportunities invite students to reconfigure their assumptions and frameworks for understanding the world through this process, and then use the new framework for understanding and decision making.

Social Learning Theory

Social learning suggests that people learn through their interactions with others "in the context of . . . lived experience of participation in the world" (Wenger, 1998, p. 3). In other words, people learn from and with each other in social contexts, making meaning from new information presented in light of their lived experiences. Wenger (1998) described *communities of practice* as one way of understanding and promoting learning. Coming together with others who share cultural practices can contribute to a sense of belonging on campus. Although a sense of belonging is important in itself, belonging fosters engagement in interactions that facilitate learning. For instance, student veterans in a community of practice focused on writing would share and gain individual insights about writing, contribute to a collective ideal of writing, and participate in making meaning of what is important among this group of student veterans.

Within communities of practice, newcomers learn expectations of practice from more established community members (Wenger, 2009). For student veterans, more experienced community members could be advanced undergraduate or graduate student veterans, faculty, or staff. Learning about important elements of community participation happens individually as students bring their prior experiences into the community of practice and participate in the community with others. Plus, learning occurs socially as the group makes meaning of collective group experiences. Learning in communities that include established community members such as faculty or staff offers opportunities for these established members to contribute their own expectations and experiences of what it means to be members of the university or college community and the community of degree holders.

Social interactions are key to the success of communities of practice. The motivation to belong to the community becomes a factor in engaging community members in learning (Wenger, 1998). For example, student veterans who are part of a community of practice (such as a student veteran learning community or orientation program) are motivated to participate in the learning activity (such as learning how to take full advantage of veteran benefits, or learning course content) because learning how to participate affords them more access to that community of practice through shared understanding and experiences. Understanding the behaviors expected of college and university students and feeling a sense of belonging affords student veterans more access to participate in the university community. A two-pronged motivational system—learning content or practices and gaining a sense of belonging—is one benefit of viewing learning through the lens of communities of practice.

Communities of practice composed of veterans create specialized spaces and opportunities for veterans to learn through social interactions with each other. Creating spaces for veterans to connect is important when social interactions and the attached learning are likely to come more easily and quickly among students who can relate to each other's experiences. Next, we describe two settings—orientation programs and learning communities—that can constitute focused learning environments for student veterans by employing adult and social learning theories. Examples of each setting are also provided.

Orientation Programs for Veterans

For many veterans and service members, an orientation program may be the first exposure to resources available on campus, the first introduction to those who assist veterans on campus, and perhaps the first time to meet other students and veterans. Orientation programs should provide access to caring faculty and staff, as faculty and staff play critical roles in adult and social learning theories. For example, transformative learning can more readily occur when students are connected with faculty and staff who encourage critical reflection and trying on new perspectives. On some campuses, the initial resource person for veterans is the staff member who assists them with accessing their GI Bill benefits and confirming their college enrollment. For some student veterans, this staff member may be the only person they approach with subsequent questions and concerns related to the college or university experience (Rumann, 2010). Without broader introduction to specific unit-level and person-level resources for veterans on campus, or without introduction to other new and returning veterans, student veterans new to the institution can feel isolated, neglected, and confused (DiRamio, Ackerman, & Mitchell, 2008).

Many student veterans also have questions and concerns regarding financial aid, course transfer credits, and veteran-specific support services on campus. A veteran-only orientation program offers the opportunity to address specific questions and issues of interest to service members and veterans in an environment where others likely have similar questions, concerns, and circumstances. Creating a focused learning environment, such as a veteran-only orientation, is also about connecting student veterans with people who can support their learning by providing a framework for critical reflection, guiding self-directed learning, or offering opportunities for interactions that promote learning. Such a proactive effort to providing information and connecting student veterans with faculty, staff, and other students can help ease the transition to college life (DiRamio, Ackerman, & Mitchell, 2008). An added bonus is that orientation sessions also provide avenues to identify student veterans and service members on campus who may not otherwise self-identify as such so that they may be invited to participate in subsequent learning opportunities.

In and of itself, an orientation program is not necessarily an environment that fosters learning. For example, an orientation program designed to introduce students to faculty and staff with little opportunity for interaction would not necessarily be a focused learning environment informed by adult learning and social learning theories. Similarly, an orientation program that features a procession of staff members speaking at a podium about resources on campus for student veterans does not necessarily provide a focused learning environment. To provide learning opportunities, an orientation would incorporate time and space for meaningful student-student and staff/faculty-student interactions. It could also offer opportunities for student veterans to begin to reflect upon their military experiences as they come to understand the process of transitioning to college.

Example of an Orientation Program

At first, the "Boots to Backpacks" orientation program for student veterans at Texas A&M University was an optional session held the week prior to the start of the fall term when most campus welcome programs are held. All veterans and service members new to campus were invited to attend this combination information session and veteran social. The U.S. Department of Veterans Affairs (VA) certifying official, Student Veterans Association president, and vice president of Student Affairs each welcomed students and presented information about veterans' benefits and campus involvement opportunities. Representatives of key service offices on campus and the local VA clinic attended the social to provide resources and guidance regarding adjustment and academic services. This format allowed staff to share information, but because attendance was limited to newly enrolled veterans, the program did not meet an intended goal of connecting new student veterans with returning ones.

Despite careful planning for the second year of the program, the social designed to help all student veterans on campus connect was hampered by low attendance. The program was revised the following year with the bulk of the resources and advising information delivered through new student conferences and individual advising sessions held in the campus Office of Veteran Services. The social program was moved to an evening during the second week of classes. With heavy promotion by the Student Veteran Association to encourage returning and incoming student veterans' attendance, the social was well attended by new and returning student veterans. Senior administrators as well as faculty and staff members also welcomed student veterans at the social. Via formal remarks and informal interactions, institutional leaders also expressed their commitment to student veterans' success. This two-phase orientation model will be used at A&M going forward to offer student veterans information related to resources and services critical to their success on campus and to promote networking with other student veterans, including members of the Student Veteran Association.

Student veteran–only orientation programs offer a number of potential advantages such as providing tailored financial aid information, bringing student veterans together early on, addressing course transfer processes and issues, creating an environment where student veterans feel recognized and involved, asking individual student veterans what they need, and connecting student veterans with faculty and staff across campus. However, developing this may not be the best or only model for achieving the goals and setting the stage for continued learning. Depending on the needs of each specific campus and the levels and types of resources available, orientation programming and information sharing can be provided in different ways. For example, Kent State University holds an open house a few weeks after classes have started to give student veterans an opportunity to connect and to address questions that have arisen for them during the beginning of the semester. Also, after discovering that a number of incoming veterans and service members missed important information relevant to their success, Kent State developed student veteran-only semester-long orientation courses as part of the first-year experience courses for adult learners (R. Anderson, personal communication, Octobern 5, 2011).

Learning Communities for Student Veterans

Social learning, andragogy, and transformative learning theories all advocate for learning environments that purposefully connect faculty, staff, and students with one another. One strategy implemented on a number of campuses is learning communities for student veterans. Student veterans' involvement in learning community environments has been recommended as one way to help ease academic and social transitions (DiRamio & Jarvis, 2011).

Academic learning communities can be designed around a common curriculum (Goodsell Love & Tokuno, 1999; Lenning & Ebbers, 1999; Shapiro & Levine, 1999) in which a group of students takes two or more classes together (Brower & Dettinger, 1998). Learning communities typically are composed of students who share similar academic or social interests, and they may share common characteristics, such as military experiences. The academic component of learning communities is reasonably straightforward, but the social aspects of learning community environments should not be ignored (Brower & Dettinger, 1998), especially for student veterans who may be trying to connect with other veterans on campus. Faculty involvement is also an important part of the learning community design. Most learning community designs encourage faculty interaction with students as a strategy to facilitate learning (Goodsell Love & Tokuno, 1999; Shapiro & Levine, 1999). The social aspects of learning communities where students and faculty have regular interactions, form relationships, and share in generating and moving towards common goals might be found in any given classroom, but are not necessarily part of the traditional classroom experience. Any learning community—regardless of model or framework—should be designed to promote social interactions that are the foundation for learning (Wenger, 1998).

One of the more common types of learning communities for student veterans is veteran-only courses that cover topics relevant to enrolling veterans and service members, such as a course at the University of Iowa that focuses on postdeployment challenges. Some institutions offer series of courses in which only student veterans may enroll. Another example is the recently established learning community at Texas A&M described in more detail in the section that follows. (See Chapter Four of this handbook for descriptions of courses offered at Lane Community College and Park University).

The benefits of learning communities have been well documented (Lenning & Ebbers, 1999; MacGregor & Smith, 2005; Shapiro & Levine, 1999; Smith, MacGregor, Matthews, & Gabelnick, 2004; Tinto, 1998). Learning community participation is positively related to student engagement in learning (Tinto, 1998; Zhao & Kuh, 2004), retention (Lenning & Ebbers, 1999) and academic performance (Zhao & Kuh, 2004). Currently, there is a dearth of information about the effect of learning communities on student veterans' learning and college experiences, so the need for careful assessment and evaluation studies is great.

Learning communities are often designed to build connections among students and, in many cases, with faculty members as well (Shapiro & Levine, 1999). They also create opportunities through faculty and staff interactions to encourage the active and reflective learning that is central to the transformative learning approach. For example, faculty and staff involved in learning communities can create opportunities for student veterans to reflect upon their military experiences in environments where other community members are likely to relate to military culture and to offer different perspective on similar experiences. This sharing and critical reflection are key components of the transformative learning approach.

Social learning theories suggest that learning communities for student veterans not only help student veterans achieve academic goals but also serve as an instrumental way for them to connect with other veterans on campus. Individuals within communities of practice, such as learning communities, benefit from the inclusion of a variety of perspectives and levels of experience provided by teaching assistants, program staff, or advanced students who are members of the learning community or invited as guests. Advanced students, faculty, and staff convey expected behaviors and attitudes to students (such as developing study skills, seeking campus resources, and exercising critical thinking) who learn to perform them through participating in the community (Wenger, 1998).

Overall, learning communities provide the environment for social interaction paramount to the effectiveness of learning described in social learning theories and necessary for the framing of critical reflection and reflective judgment required for transformative learning and andragogy. Creating these programs also provides additional evidence that the institution is committed to meeting the needs of student veterans. Two illustrations of veterans' learning communities are provided in the next section.

Examples of Learning Communities

As noted previously, institutions have created learning communities for student veterans. Two examples of those types of focused learning environments are presented here, one at Texas A&M University and the other at Eastern Kentucky University.

Texas A&M University. The Veteran Services Office set a goal of improving student veteran academic achievement and transition success, and the campuswide committee for veteran-friendly initiatives identified the learning community model as a promising strategy. Engaging new student veterans and service members in a common academic learning environment was the first intended objective of the learning community. However, Texas A&M students are expected to complete only a few basic requirements before proceeding to courses relevant to the academic major, meaning there were few courses they could take as a group. Therefore, the committee collaborated with the College of Geosciences to identify a world geography course that met several different academic degree requirements. Additionally, a faculty member who is a Marine Corps veteran agreed to teach the course. A smaller veteran-only section of the geography course was established with special grant funding from the provost's office designated to develop veteran-friendly academic practices.

The second objective of the learning community was to address new student veterans' transition challenges. The majority of enrolled student veterans came to the university as transfer students, and most had little to no experience on a traditional university campus with a large population of traditional undergraduate students. The transition component of the learning community was particularly relevant in helping the new student veterans adjust and identify key resources necessary to their academic and social success. As such, a new cocurricular transitions course was designed to introduce key campus resources, address study and tutoring strategies, and provide opportunities for the student veterans to interact in a less structured environment around transition themes and topics for discussion on alternate weeks. Guest speakers were asked to present information about services and resources available in their offices on campus and to solicit input from the enrolled students on how to make services and resources more veteran-friendly. Within this learning community, student veterans were connected with each other, engaged with a faculty member, and performed the practices of successful college students by discussing how campus resources can support their learning.

Eastern Kentucky University. Eastern Kentucky University (EKU) takes the veteran-only course one step further and has established a cohort program for student veterans based on their military experiences and placement test scores prior to enrollment (B. Morris, personal communication, February 28, 2012). Student veterans who score low on the tests and require remediation are enrolled together in one section of a college transition class while veterans who score higher and do not need remediation enroll in a standard orientation course not specifically tailored to student veterans. The section of the course for student veterans is more focused on their specific needs and is taught by veterans who are faculty, staff, and teaching assistants. The course for student veterans focuses on critical and creative thinking skills and is designed to address a broad range of transition issues and concerns that veterans often experience during transitions from military service to college. Following adult learning theory, instructors of the veterans-only section incorporate salient military experiences into the learning environment. For example, the book *Tears of a Warrior* (Seahorn & Seahorn, 2008), written by a Vietnam veteran and his wife, is used in the course, and students also write their own stories and prose or create art. Student veterans with two or more academic deficiencies are also enrolled in student veteran-only refresher courses in English, mathematics, and reading; members of the EKU Veterans Education and Transition Support (VETS) Club provide tutoring to help these students make successful transitions.

Other Focused Learning Environments

Additional spaces in higher education could be constructed as focused learning environments for student veterans. Student organizations such as student veterans associations, physical spaces such as veterans' lounges, online discussion boards, and mentoring programs could be designed and implemented in ways consistent with principles of adult learning and social learning theories. However, the creation of any of these spaces for student veterans does not automatically ensure that learning will be promoted or fostered. Rather, opportunities that engage student veterans with each other, staff, and faculty in meaningful ways and that promote critical thinking, sharing of experiences, incorporating new perspectives, or reflective judgment are some key characteristics of effective learning environments.

Assessment

Assessments of learning environments for veterans should be conducted on an ongoing basis to identify challenges, strengths, and gaps in resources and learning opportunities for student veterans. The information gained through assessment processes can be analyzed to evaluate needs, satisfaction with the programs, the extent to which the programs meet established learning outcomes, and to communicate the need for and the importance of the programs when proposing that faculty invest in these initiatives. Additionally, assessment results showing contributions to student veteran success can be used to make a case for additional or continued funding for programs and subsequent initiatives.

Conducting the Assessment

Begin by setting out a plan for the assessment, which should include identifying who should be on the assessment team as well as those who should oversee the assessment process (Caffarella, 2002). Consider including someone who connects regularly with student veterans and understands their needs (on some campuses this person may be the VA certifying official), faculty member(s) with interests in student veterans' experiences and success, someone with expertise in designing learning environments, and representatives from the student veteran population. The evaluation and assessment strategies should be intentionally planned with clear and specified objectives in mind (Smith et al., 2004). Objectives could be geared toward understanding the *needs* of student veterans or determining the *outcomes* of particular initiatives utilizing elements of andragogy, social learning, and transformative learning. A detailed time line for the assessment also should be part of the plan. Allow time for assessment, follow-up, and adjustments needed in anticipation of program development or change. Keep in mind the academic calendar and deadlines for communication with incoming students, orientation staff, instructors, and registration staff. Committing organizational resources including individuals' time for the assessment process is a significant part of the program review and planning processes. Consider possible overlaps in assessment needs with existing assessment processes, such as course evaluations, so that efforts may be streamlined where possible.

Use of multiple sources of data is important in strengthening validity of assessment results (Creswell, 2003). Data collection methods might include participation statistics, document review, surveys, open-ended questions, or individual interviews (Schuh, 2009). Additionally, focus groups (Krueger & Casey, 2009) should be strongly considered because they can also help advance purposeful reflection and interaction among students. Degree completion and persistence rates of student veterans who participate and those who do not participate in focused learning environments can provide information about to what extent participation in focused learning environments may be linked to academic success.

Once gathered, the data must be analyzed to determine implications and recommendations, including needs, challenges, benefits, and opportunities for change. If needs or specified learning outcomes are not being met, then the learning environment and perhaps the learning outcomes should be adjusted as part of the planning phase to either clarify the learning outcome or to identify the practices that are best aligned with the desired outcomes. Benefits of focused learning environments should be highlighted in reports to program stakeholders including participants, faculty members targeted for involvement, and current and potential funding sources. Following a systematic assessment cycle—where goals frame assessment and results inform changes in curriculum and programming—is key to fulfilling internal needs for program improvement and external needs for accountability (Volkwein, 2009).

Implications and Recommendations

Because of student veterans' and service members' unique needs as students and their increasing prevalence on college campuses, institutions of higher education should design and implement veteran-specific learning opportunities for student veterans. Educators and administrators should begin assessing current resources and capabilities to develop and offer these programs.

A number of idiosyncratic factors must be considered, including institutional resources, size of student veteran enrollment, institutional type, and campus culture. For example, at a campus with a predominantly full-time student body and a large population of student veterans, a targeted orientation program may be the best way to meet students' initial needs for information and resources, including contact with other veterans and service members. On a commuter campus with mostly part-time students who may not be interacting on campus in other ways, a veteran-only course may provide a welcome, ongoing opportunity to interact. From another perspective, a campus with a predominantly full-time student body may be better prepared to offer a learning community, perhaps with a residential component, where students are expected to gather regularly than another institution with mostly part-time students where convening a group on a regular basis may be less feasible. To begin, existing programs and services should be assessed, and enrolled student veterans should be asked about their transition and educational experiences thus far. Additionally, a campus' existing resources including staff, faculty, and current programs should be considered in the context of institutional type. For example, an institution with many faculty members who are interested or experienced in military culture may have an easier time implementing a series of veteran-only courses taught by current faculty members than another campus with few or no interested faculty.

From a theoretical perspective, faculty-student and student-student interactions are paramount. Understanding how social and educational interactions among students can best be facilitated on campus can assist the planning team in determining how to establish or improve learning environments for student veterans. Additionally, transformative learning theories suggest that students benefit from interactions with faculty and staff who can assist them in envisioning and incorporating new perspectives, so understanding how and in which settings faculty and staff currently interact with students in these ways, and perhaps with student veterans specifically, is important information to consider.

Some student veterans may feel pressure to complete their degree as quickly as possible before their GI Bill funding runs out, so many hesitate to become involved in these "extra" programs when they may not initially realize the benefits to their educational pursuits. Faculty and staff may need to spend additional effort encouraging student veterans to participate in orientation programs and learning communities that can enrich their educational experiences and possibly also contribute to timely degree completion. The investment that the institution puts into such veteran-specific educational opportunities can have a significant impact on student veterans' success in higher education as well as improve the institution's ability to recruit and retain future student veterans.

In addition, faculty and staff should be flexible in how they structure student learning opportunities (that is, they should consider social and transformative learning models). Learning theories and approaches to education employed for traditional student populations may still prevail on many campuses, so shifting to approaches that reach student veterans more effectively may pose formidable challenges for faculty and staff.

Faculty and staff are commonly more comfortable with their established teaching methods and practices than they are learning and implementing different approaches (Bok, 2008). Yet teachers employing nontraditional approaches, such as these advocated for student veterans, need not reduce the rigor of the academic experience or their expectations of students.

As an initial step, faculty and staff who are familiar with and interested in student veterans or military culture should be identified on campus. The academic vice president or provost could convene a task force or advisory board of these faculty members. However, despite experience and interest, these individuals may need and seek training and resources to learn about serving this new group of students. Recognition and reward structures for those who develop and lead student veteran learning environments should be implemented institutionally so that faculty and staff may focus appropriate shares of their energy and time on serving this population. Finally, identifying needs for additional funding, securing sources of funding, and obtaining additional resources such as staff time and training materials must be considered when creating and improving focused learning environments for student veterans.

Conclusion

Creating focused learning environments for student veterans is one promising way in which institutions of higher education can meet the academic needs of student veterans and foster their success. These programs can also facilitate social interaction between student veterans and faculty and staff in the campus community—all of which can yield greater learning. The faculty-student and student-student connections function to provide support and motivation for student veterans to succeed both academically and socially.

Resources

ACE Military Programs
http://www.acenet.edu/AM/Template.cfm?Section=Military_ Programs

National Association of Veterans Upward Bound
http://www.navub.org/

National Resource Center for the First-Year Experience and Students in Transition
http://www.sc.edu/fye/index.html

SERV Program
http://servprogram.com/default.aspx

Servicemembers Opportunity Colleges
http://www.soc.aascu.org/

Toolkit for Veteran-Friendly Institutions
http://www.vetfriendlytoolkit.org/

Washington Center for Improving the Quality of Undergraduate Education
http://www.evergreen.edu/washcenter/home.asp

References

Bok, D. (2008). *Our underachieving colleges: A candid look at how much students learn and why they should be learning more.* Princeton, NJ: Princeton University Press.

Brower, A. M., & Dettinger, K. M. (1998). What is a learning community? Toward a comprehensive model. *About Campus, 3*(5), 15–21.

Caffarella, R. S. (2002). *Planning programs for adult learners.* San Francisco: Jossey-Bass.

Creswell, J. W. (2003). *Research design: Qualitative, quantitative, and mixed methods approaches* (2nd ed.). Thousand Oaks, CA: Sage.

DiRamio, D., Ackerman, R., & Mitchell, R. (2008). From combat to campus: Voices of student-veterans. *NASPA Journal, 45*(1), 73–102.

DiRamio, D., & Jarvis, K. (2011). Veterans in higher education: When Johnny and Jane come marching to campus. In K. Ward & L. Wolf-Wendel (Series Eds.), *ASHE Higher Education Report: Vol. 37*(3). San Francisco: Jossey-Bass.

Doyle, T. (2008). *Helping students learn in a learning-centered environment: A guide to facilitating learning in higher education.* Sterling, VA: Stylus.

Goodsell Love, A., & Tokuno, K. A. (1999). Learning community models. In J. H. Levine (Ed.), *Learning communities: New structures, new partnerships for learning* (Monograph No. 26) (pp. 9–17). Columbia: University of South Carolina, National Resource Center for the First-Year Experience and Students in Transition.

Knowles, M. S. (1977). Adult learning processes: Pedagogy and andragogy. *Religious Education, 72*(2), 202–210.

Krueger, R. A., & Casey, M. A. (2009). *Focus groups: A practical guide to applied research* (4th ed.). Thousand Oaks, CA: Sage.

Lenning, O. T., & Ebbers, L. H. (1999). The powerful potential of learning communities: Improving education for the future. *ASHE-ERIC Higher Education Report, 26*(6). Washington, D. C.: The George Washington University.

MacGregor, J., & Smith, B. L. (2005). Where are learning communities now? National leaders take stock. *About Campus, 10*(2), 2–8.

Mezirow, J. (1981). A critical theory of adult learning and education. *Adult Education Quarterly, 32*(1), 3–24.

Mezirow, J. (1996). Contemporary paradigms of learning. *Adult Education Quarterly, 46,* 158–172.

Mezirow, J. (2009). An overview on transformative learning. In K. Illeris (Ed.), *Contemporary theories of learning* (pp. 90–105). New York: Routledge.

Palmer, P. J., & Zajonc, A.S.M. (2010). *The heart of higher education: A call to renewal.* San Francisco: Jossey-Bass.

Rumann, C. B. (2010). Student veterans returning to a community college: Understanding their transitions. (Doctoral dissertation). Iowa State University, Ames. Available from ProQuest Digital Dissertations. (AAT 3403830)

Schmidtlein, F.A., & Berdahl, R. O. (2005). Autonomy and accountability: Who controls academe? In P. G. Altbach, R. O. Berdahl, & P. J. Gumport (Eds.), *American higher education in the twenty-first century: Social, political, and economic challenges* (2nd ed., pp. 71–90). Baltimore, MD: Johns Hopkins University Press.

Schuh, J., & Associates. (2009). *Assessment methods for student affairs.* San Francisco: Jossey-Bass.

Seahorn, J. J., & Seahorn, E. A. (2008). *Tears of a warrior: A family's story of combat and living with PTSD.* Ft. Collins, CO: Team Pursuits.

Shapiro, N. S., & Levine, J. H. (1999). *Creating learning communities: A practical guide to winning support, organizing for change, and implementing programs.* San Francisco: Jossey-Bass.

Smith, B. L., MacGregor, J., Matthews, R. S., & Gabelnick, F. (2004). *Learning communities: Reforming undergraduate education.* San Francisco: Jossey-Bass.

Taylor, E. W. (2008). Transformative learning. *New Directions for Adult and Continuing Education, 119,* 5–15.

Tinto, V. (1998). Colleges as communities: Taking research on student persistence seriously. *The Review of Higher Education, 21*(2), 167–177.

Volkwein, J. F. (2009). Assessing student outcomes: Why, who, what, how? *New Directions for Institutional Research, Assessment Supplement 2009.* San Francisco: Jossey-Bass.

Wenger, E. (1998). *Communities of practice: Learning, meaning, and identity.* New York: Cambridge University Press.

Wenger, E. (2009). A social theory of learning. In K. Illeries (Ed.), *Contemporary theories of learning* (pp. 209–218). New York: Routledge.

Zhao, C. M., & Kuh, G. D. (2004). Adding value: Learning communities and student engagement. *Research in Higher Education, 45*(2), 115–138.

VIGNETTE

Paul F. Tschudi

Faculty, The George Washington University

I have worked at The George Washington University (GWU) for 25 years, and am also a Vietnam veteran who served as a medic in 1969–1970. I began my career at GWU in 1986 as the administrator for military contract programs. The programs were designed so that active duty military personnel could earn college credits while in training for medical-related jobs within their branches of service.

"Back in the day," being a Vietnam veteran and going to college was not a congenial mix. Not until 1979 did I feel welcomed enough to attempt to earn a college degree. I also grappled with conflicted feelings about that war, the trauma, and the challenges I faced upon returning home. I found myself avoiding anything related to my own identity as a veteran until accepting the administrative position in 1986. Now I am fully engaged and committed to playing a role in assisting our Operation Enduring Freedom (OEF) and Operation Iraqi Freedom (OIF) veterans in smoothing their transitions from combat to campus. There is no way that I want them to face what my generation of veterans had to endure.

In 2005, I accepted an appointment at GWU as assistant professor. My current role as both a veteran and faculty member benefits our student veterans in a number of ways, including serving as faculty advisor to our Student Veterans Group and as the faculty mentor to a service learning group whose project involved the creation of an orientation and resource web site for new student veterans. In addition, the group developed a course entitled "Life Beyond War." The course is offered in two sections; one is for graduate students in counseling who are interested in working with the military community, and the other is open to student veterans to provide instruction on facilitating peer support groups held on campus. Midway through the semester, the two sections merge into a blended learning experience.

I have served our student veterans for almost three years now and have enjoyed the experience immensely. Student veterans are smart, goal-oriented, insightful, mature, and grateful for opportunities to earn college degrees in ways that many students are not.

Student veterans often attend college to continue to serve this country and create a better world, but the transition is not always easy. They enter a campus culture that is very different from military culture. They are usually older, they have more life experience, they have held leadership roles with high levels of responsibility, and they have often been exposed to traumatic events. Also, they are used to working cooperatively with their fellow soldiers—they come from supportive and even loving environments to one in which they perceive a great deal of self-absorption.

In my experience, enrolled veterans are not expecting to be treated either as victims or as heroes. They do not want to be marginalized or have others make assumptions about who they are. They want to be treated as individuals who happen to be veterans and who, as individuals, do not necessarily represent the views, experiences, and challenges of all veterans. Yet what veterans deserve is to have their military service honored and to be provided with the services and support on the college campuses they attend. These should include academic advising, administrative support, mental health, disability, and career services as well as opportunities for community service. Such services should be administered by qualified people who understand and appreciate the unique needs and gifts our student veterans bring to campus. Only recently have I appreciated that my status as an "old soldier" would have such value. In offering my experience to assist in their growth, I also grow.

I call upon my colleagues to join me in serving and supporting our student veterans. You and your college community will reap much more than you sow.

CHAPTER TEN

STUDENT VETERANS ORGANIZATIONS AND STUDENT SELF-ADVOCACY

Brian A. Hawthorne, Mark C. Bauman, and Leah Ewing Ross

Each year, new student veterans organizations form on campuses throughout the nation, especially as service members and veterans flock to campus in response to the generous Post-9/11 GI Bill benefits and as a result of the drawdown of military operations in Iraq and Afghanistan. Veterans and service members form their own organizations for many reasons, but mostly because they want to connect with other individuals with military experience who understand what they are going through and want to connect with others who represent their interests. The presence of student veterans organizations on college campuses has historical roots in prior postwar periods, and some of these original organizations remain in place today. The importance of contemporary student veterans organizations on campus as well as the beneficial outcomes associated with these organizations are highlighted in this chapter.

Brief History of Student Veterans Organizations

Summerlot, Green, and Parker (2009) noted the evolution and eventual decline of student veterans organizations from the post–World War II and Korean Conflict eras. They explained that many such groups were localized to college campuses and were thus oriented toward issues specific to those institutions, "such as housing and the transition to college life" (p. 71). Goodier (1946) provided evidence of this localized effort in the World War II era at Illinois State Normal University (now Illinois State University):

> Early in the present school year veterans on campus felt the need of an organization. After considerable correspondence and deliberation, it was decided ... not to seek affiliation with any existing groups but to petition the faculty for permission to set up a local organization to be known as the "Golden Eagle." The organization is proving a definite asset both to the members and to the University ... it has helped entering veterans feel at home on the campus ... and it is quite evident that the Golden Eagle will become increasingly prominent and helpful in the coming months. (p. 230)

On the national front, one organization—the American Veterans Committee (AVC)—was founded in 1943 by University of California, Los Angeles (UCLA) alumni and counts Franklin D. Roosevelt and Ronald Reagan among its former members (Schmadeke, 2008; *Time Magazine*, 1945). As was the case with other small veterans groups at the time, the AVC was formed in an effort to provide an alternative to the community-based, not-for-profit American Legion, which was not integrated and offered only segregated chapters (Schmadeke, 2008), and the Veterans of Foreign Wars (VFW), which was not open to women (*Time Magazine*, 1945). With the motto "Citizens first, veterans second," the AVC was considered more progressive than other veterans' organizations of the time because it included women and "championed civil rights and government-financed low cost housing, and was the first national veterans group to be racially integrated" (Schmadeke, 2008, para. 4).

Campus Climates

Early AVC members included student veterans who were supported by the first GI Bill on campuses throughout the United States (Tyler, 1966). The organization's membership peaked during the post–World War II era, but soon thereafter it was caught in the struggle between "progressive members and communists who sought to take it over even before the rise of U.S. Senator Joseph McCarthy" (Schmadeke, 2008, para. 14). Though it was "branded as a Communist front in its early days, AVC survived significant organizational turbulence to become a small but influential, internationally oriented advocacy organization—the American veteran's voice for civil rights and equal rights" (American Veterans Committee Records, n.d., para. 1).

The Second World War has been characterized as "The Good War" (Terkel, 1984; Wynn, 1996), yet perceptions of the Vietnam conflict were and continue to be largely negative. Modell and Haggerty (1991) explained that "many returning veterans apparently felt a lack of closure of the morally confusing phase of life just completed, partly because of the ... blame directed to the veteran by their fellow citizens" (p. 213). The overarching result was that campus climates were less than hospitable for the almost 60 percent of Vietnam era veterans who used the GI Bill for postsecondary education (Mettler, 2005). Unwelcoming campus environments meant that many students in that era decided they were "better off not identifying as veterans" (Summerlot, Green, & Parker, 2009, p. 71), and student veterans organizations gained little traction.

Collectively, the inhospitable climates at many colleges were not offset by campus organizations formed by or for veterans—unlike the post–World War II era. That is not to say, however, that no such groups formed during that period. For example, The Pennsylvania State University traces the founding of its group, Penn State Veterans Organization (PSUVO), to 1968 (PSU, n.d.). A national group emerged in 1968 as well—the National Association of Collegiate Veterans (NACV)—partly in response to the rise of Post Vietnam Syndrome (now known as posttraumatic stress disorder) on college campuses (NACV, n.d.). The organization changed its name to the National Association of Concerned Veterans (and maintained the NACV acronym) in 1972 and expanded its scope with a goal of ensuring that "todays [original] veterans never have to experience what the Vietnam era veterans experienced upon their return" (NACV, n.d., para. 2). NACV is a "grass roots advocacy and direct services organization" (NACV, n.d., para. 1) committed to military issues with particular attention to transition challenges from military to civilian life.

Contemporary Student Veterans Organizations

During the Cold War, campuses realized enrollment declines among military personnel, which resulted in an overall campus climate that was characterized as "indifference to the military" (Summerlot, Green, & Parker, 2009, p. 72). Yet the rise of contemporary student veterans organizations at national and local levels may reflect renewed interest surrounding the needs of undergraduate and graduate students who have been deployed. Though initially slow to respond, many campuses across the country have made efforts to address the unique needs of student veterans, including the establishment or renewal of student veterans organizations. However, it would be inaccurate to suggest that these efforts come solely from institutions. Summerlot, Green, and Parker (2009) found that "most commonly, the idea of starting an SVO [student veterans organization] originates with student veterans themselves, typically in response to the need to identify with others on campus and work together to enhance the academic success of veterans" (p. 75).

Rumann, Kraus, and Bauman (2011) explained that much of the movement to form student organizations seems to be of a grass-roots nature, often requiring prospective advisors of these groups to "meet students where they are"—meaning to take the notions of "gathering," "meeting," and "advising" into the forums in which students communicate. In contemporary times, individual students make extensive use of social networking in their personal lives and as a tool through which to gather and organize groups of people. For example, a Facebook search for student veterans at a specific college or university is likely to produce results. At institutions with prolific social networking communities, administrators should consider visiting this place—this virtual place—to form preliminary connections with students and explore possibilities for expanded use of social networking to reach veterans. This is a simple way for faculty, staff, and administrators to make efforts to connect with student veterans on their campuses.

Numerous student veterans groups formed on college campuses throughout the United States in the 2000s (Sabo, 2010); this may lead the casual observer to conclude that these groups are flourishing and that higher education is rapidly meeting the needs of the growing student veteran population. However, in a study for the American Council on Education (ACE), Cook and Kim (2009) found that only 32 percent of college campuses hosted student veterans organizations at that time; campus leaders at all colleges and universities should consider "meeting student veterans where they are"—whatever that means for their campuses—and initiate dialogues about forming organizations. As Summerlot, Green, and Parker (2009) stated, "student veterans, once they are on campus, will look to replace the cohesion of their unit by seeking out others who have had similar experiences. An active student organization for veterans can become this point of connection" (p. 72). Colleges and universities can show tremendous support for current and future military personnel through provision of resources and advisement necessary to begin or improve student veterans organizations.

Types of Student Veterans Organizations

Student veterans organizations are unique and varied, reflecting the size of the veteran populations, the student enrollment demographics, and the environments of the campuses they serve. However, they are not necessarily limited to individuals with military experience. For example, the University of California, San Diego (UCSD) group welcomes "any UCSD student who supports our missions of improving life for student veterans at UCSD and [of] community service" (UCSD Student Veterans Organization, 2011, para. 1). To date, no empirical studies have explored the intricacies of student veterans organizations, including organizational structures, governance, participation, and satisfaction. The characteristics presented below are knowledge and insight gained through the collective experience of SVA (chapter author Brian Hawthorne serves as a member of the SVA board of directors). This information is not presented as empirical data; rather, it is shared so that it can serve as a starting point for conversations among individuals who work with student veterans, and it is also an example of an area in which there is a dearth of information about the student veteran experience.

Residential Campuses

Some student veterans organizations may resemble and function like traditional student organizations. Key characteristics of these groups may include elected leadership, funding streams (such as those from the institutional coffers, small donors, or dues), regular meetings and events, strong member presences and influence on campus, and consistent access to campus leaders. However, it appears that the bulk of veterans enrolled at residential institutions do not participate. This is not unusual due to the range of student veterans' ages and personal situations, and the fact that many are likely unaware of the ways in which student veterans organizations can assist them (Hamilton, 2011). Yet these challenges should not discourage those who have the time and interest in being part of this movement from continuing their efforts.

Community College or Commuter School Chapters

There is growing evidence that a large portion of the veteran population attends community colleges, commuter schools, or for-profit institutions immediately following discharge from the service (Cutright, 2011; Sewall, 2010). This trend presents challenges and opportunities for student veteran advocacy. Community colleges in particular are challenging environments for student veterans organizations because of the high turnover among student leaders who only remain for one or two years. However, due to the large populations of veterans at these institutions, and the fact that many of these campus communities are looking to improve student engagement (Center for Community College Student Engagement, 2009), student veterans may have opportunities to make significant and immediate differences through student veterans organizations at their individual campuses or through organizations in their communities.

Online Chapters

The concurrent rise of social media and online education has prompted the growth of organizations that are exclusively devoted to veterans enrolled in online schools, such as the Student Veterans of Bryant and Stratton College Online (Seegert, 2011). Some of these online groups have large, disconnected memberships that include active duty members; little, if any, leadership or structure; little to no direct contact with university leadership; and few common demands or needs. However, some colleges and universities are utilizing student interest in social networking to foster their connections to the institutions and reach out to students. For example, Brandman University has 26 campuses and a large number of online students, including veterans and deployed military personnel. The institution implemented Inigral's "Schools App" (Inigral, 2011) for Facebook to foster social networking among Brandman community members: "[Our students] don't have the same opportunities to build a social network that students at traditional schools enjoy. But it's really important that students feel connected to their school community and having a strong support network is critical to their success . . . Our goals are to increase retention, build community, strengthen support systems, and . . . engage potential students" (Stoller, 2011, para. 2–3).

Advantages of Organizing

Following military service, many student veterans continue to seek and enjoy leadership experiences in college before moving on to their next careers. Astin (1984, 1999) asserted that this type of campus involvement is an important component of students' overall success in college in that leads to increased rates of satisfaction, which results in increased rates of retention. However, involvement opportunities can be hard for student veterans to secure, especially for undergraduate veterans who are competing with civilian, traditionally aged peers for leadership positions, and for older students who live off campus and have myriad obligations, such as family and work commitments. These challenges are similar to those experienced by the overall population of nontraditional students, including transfer students and adult learners (DiRamio & Jarvis, 2011; Kilgore & Rice, 2003; Whitt, 1994). Participation in campus veterans groups affords students a number of advantages, including occasions to meet and network with other veterans, and opportunities for leadership involvement in an area that is important to service members.

Student veterans organizations pair the mission of helping veterans with the development of campus networks, which, in turn, contributes to the success of their educational endeavors. As a result of connecting in this manner, group members are able to seek help with coursework, learn about employment openings, and develop social outlets. The benefits of student veterans formally organizing on campus can be significant. Although not always the case, recognized student groups often receive financial support from institutional or student activity fees, such as The George Washington University's (GWU) SEVEN (GWU Center for Student Engagement, n.d.) and outside donations, such as the Military Family Research Institute's (MFRI) Operation Diploma (Purdue University News Service, 2011). Student veterans groups may also benefit from affiliation with national organizations, such as Student Veterans of America (SVA), which is a "coalition of student veterans groups on college campuses" with 490 chapters throughout the United States (SVA, 2011, para. 4). SVA chapters must be institutionally recognized student groups with clearly stated purposes, such as outreach and advocacy, social support, counseling, new student orientation, or community service (SVA, n.d., pp. 6–7). The benefits of SVA affiliation include scholarship opportunities, employment-seeking assistance for graduates, and the support of the association's executive staff in Washington, DC that "enables communication between chapters, connects chapters with resources from outside their campuses, develops and implements new programs, and provides a voice for all veterans at the state and national level" (SVA, 2011, para. 5).

Registering as an official campus organization provides recognition that, in turn, grants access to institutional decision makers and advocates that students may not otherwise have opportunities to meet or know.

Specific benefits vary by campus, but when student veterans organize official campus groups, they have increased opportunities to advocate for members, voice their concerns and needs to campus decision makers, network with other student groups, and gain momentum for their goals and objectives—the same features that benefit all registered student groups on campus. Furthermore, it is often easier for registered organizations to reserve meeting and event space, access equipment and supplies, and utilize campus services such as catering. These types of support allow students to maximize on the benefits and opportunities that result from gathering for a common purpose, interest, or cause. On individual and group levels, student veterans organizations allow members to learn what challenges fellow veterans are facing in their college experiences and to share information about resources and benefits. This is an essential component of advocacy—in order to work on behalf of student veterans on campus, group leaders must know what members need and want.

It is essential for group leaders to regularly conduct needs assessments to ensure that their efforts are responsive to members' needs. As O'Herrin (2011) explained, "veterans are a diverse population with an incredibly wide range of experiences, [and] it is impossible to take a one-size-fits-all approach to serving them. Thus, one of the most important steps that campus leadership can take is to gauge the specific needs of veterans at their institution before devoting resources to new initiatives. Both student veterans and campus administrators have spoken to the success of efforts that have been crafted with direct input from the enrolled student veteran population and have emphasized this is the best approach to designing supportive programs" (para. 10). This advice also pertains to establishing or maintaining organizations for student veterans. As with all attempts to serve students, the simple action of creating organizations without regard for students' actual needs is not optimal.

In the same vein, formally organizing student veterans allows them to share information about opportunities on and off campus that affect various parts of their personal, professional, and academic lives. Veterans have inherent trust in one another, such as the kinship among "box buddies"—a term used among military members to refer to those who have served in Afghanistan or Iraq (Bauman, 2009). As such, veterans may be more likely to talk to other veterans about their problems and concerns, refer each other to Department of Veterans Affairs (VA) services, and hire fellow veterans. The presence of student veterans organizations is critical in that they help to ensure that there are continued networks of veterans helping veterans on college and university campuses and that students' efforts are maintained and extended to future student veterans. This type of campus engagement can form lifelong relationships, business opportunities, and support networks that enrich the student experience, though these appeals and benefits are likely realized disproportionately by students who are satisfied with their military or postmilitary experiences or are interested in identifying with their statuses as veterans while enrolled in college. In addition, there is a contingent of organization members who are not student veterans, yet benefit from these relationships as well, such as relatives and partners of military members. Student veterans organizations are not particularly difficult to form, yet the benefits are significant, and they are excellent avenues through which individuals can join student veteran advocacy efforts, such as those led by SVA.

Institutional Perspective

From an institutional perspective, there are several advantages to the organization of student veterans. DiRamio, Ackerman, and Mitchell (2008) noted that sometimes student veterans represent an "invisible group" on campus, flying under the radar. The presence of an organized group on campus provides administrators with a point of contact for this population and substantially aids in their abilities to deliver services, listen to feedback about veterans' issues, and advance veterans' academic and social success in an efficient manner. Also, a student veterans' group allows for the further development of kinship among veterans and simultaneously moves them onto the campus radar screen. As noted earlier, the almost immediate bond that exists among people in uniform can be palpable. Higher education institutions should tap into this kinship, both in terms of veterans helping their campuses and veterans helping each other. Consider, for example, a program in which newly enrolled student veterans are paired with returning student veterans who can help answer questions, orient them to campus, and shed light on available resources.

Many institutions commit substantial funds for veteran centers and other forms of support for veterans. In addition, there are many free or inexpensive ways to assist student veterans, including tapping into the expertise of currently enrolled student veterans. For example, administrators can work with members of student veterans organizations to create and update publications that include pre- and postdeployment checklists and other pertinent information for this group of individuals. Although simple, this type of project engages student veterans on campus, provides a useful service, and ensures that information is relevant and up to date.

This work can also be expanded to include institutions' outreach efforts to recruit, enroll, and retain veterans. There is a deep kinship among student veterans, and their formal and informal networks can make institutions' efforts in these arenas more robust. Veterans' success is likely to lead to more veteran interest, and therefore more veteran enrollment and increased rates of veteran satisfaction.

The reciprocal nature of this relationship is not unlike the nature of other student networks in higher education. For example, in 2009 administrators at American University (AU) did not involve student veterans in conversations about and plans for the allocation of Yellow Ribbon funds. (Established by the Post-9/11 Veterans Educational Assistance Act of 2008, the Yellow Ribbon Program "allows institutions ... to voluntarily enter into an agreement with VA to fund tuition and fee expenses that exceed the highest public in-state undergraduate tuition and fee rate in their state. The institution can contribute a specified dollar amount of those expenses, and VA will match the contribution—not to exceed 50 percent of the difference" [U.S. Department of Veterans Affairs, 2010, para. 1]). Student veterans enrolled at AU felt that they were being treated unfairly because the process through which they had to compete for limited funds made it seem as though some students' military experiences were more valuable than others (Anderson, 2009). AU has since increased its participation in the Yellow Ribbon Program, in 2011 was recognized by *GI Jobs* magazine as one of the top military friendly institutions in the United States (Stankorb, 2011), and serves as a model for student veterans at nearby Georgetown University who are urging the administration to further increase its Yellow Ribbon funds and devote a full-time staff position to the undergraduate veterans affairs office (Gillis, 2011).

Types of Advocacy Efforts on Campus

College and university faculty members, administrators, and staff members play key roles in supporting all students and, as such, have opportunities to attend to issues surrounding student veterans, including the development of student veterans organizations. In so doing, campuses should first endeavor to discuss and define the term "veteran" in a way that most appropriately describes their communities. The federal government provides a reasonably succinct definition of the term "veteran" as "a person who served in the active military, naval or air service, and who was discharged or released therefrom under conditions other than dishonorable" (Veterans

Benefits, Title 38, 2009). Although this definition may be appropriate for legal or other purposes, it is likely too restrictive for colleges and universities with undergraduate and graduate students who are members of the military and do not fit the federal definition. These students can include Reserve Officers' Training Corps (ROTC) cadets, who may concurrently be enlisted members of the military, as well as National Guard and Reserve personnel who recently graduated from basic training or advanced training schools, and personnel who have served one or more contract periods (generally four years per period) and are still members of the military. According to the federal definition, none of these students would qualify as "veterans," yet these select examples are representative of the students who should be included in institutions' definitions of student veterans; the fact that they are still members of the military does not change the reality that their needs are similar to those who have fulfilled their military duties and have been released or discharged.

Once the *concept* of student veterans and the *community* of student veterans are better understood, campuses can more easily develop or expand their initiatives and programs to include awareness, education, and action surrounding student veterans. Institutional leaders—including presidents, deans, and directors—are critical in creating campuswide movements related to these efforts. Ruth J. Person, chancellor of the University of Michigan-Flint (UM-Flint) and her colleagues are examples of the positive impact that institutional leaders can have in this regard. In 2011, Chancellor Person was invited to testify before the Michigan House of Representatives regarding the programs initiated on the UM-Flint campus. UM-Flint made service to student veterans a "signature priority" in 2008, and in 2009 opened the Student Veterans Resource Center, which hosts a faculty advisor, offers veterans-only classes, and holds orientation programs for student veterans, among other efforts (Mostafavi, 2011).

Certainly large-scale advocacy efforts like those at UM-Flint are both needed and important and can go a long way toward creating campuswide awareness. But in the end, connecting with student veterans—as one would connect with *all* students—is the result of intentional cultivation of interpersonal relationships. It is at this level in particular that an individual faculty, administrative, or staff (FAS) member can become involved in a thoroughly meaningful, helpful, and supportive fashion. Although many campuses will have current or former military members in their FAS ranks, not all prospective or effective FAS advisors of student veterans organizations have connections to the military (Rumann, Kraus, & Bauman, 2011). Yet individuals who have no specific ties to the military (either themselves or their family members) seem to hesitate when it comes to volunteering to engage with student veterans. Despite their interest, FAS members without military experience or connections often perceive that student veterans might simply prefer other advisors or supporters who have similar backgrounds and can "understand" implicitly what it means to be a veteran. In order to address this concern, consider parallel populations on college campuses that benefit from the support of allies. In particular, the lesbian, gay, bisexual, transgender, and queer (LGBTQ) community is a relevant example for how nonmilitary FAS members might consider any concerns regarding authenticity among student veterans. The LGBTQ community receives meaningful support from allies who do not personally identify as LGBTQ, but are open and committed to forming meaningful relationships and collaborations and become social justice allies (Reason, Broido, Davis, & Evans, 2005). Similarly, FAS members need not be concerned that student veterans groups will reflexively reject offers of assistance or service; an authentic desire to assist this group of students will often outweigh the lack of military experience. True allies of student veterans are community members who are genuine, committed, available, and perhaps most important, nonjudgmental in their desires to assist student veterans.

The Advisory Role

The following suggestions are offered for individuals considering service as advisors to existing or newly forming student veterans organizations. This guidance is not meant to be exhaustive; rather, it offers starting points for consideration of engagement with student veterans. In order for these ideas to be truly useful, readers are encouraged to reflect on the individuality of their campuses and their campus cultures, including the climates for student veterans. When in doubt about how to help, administrators are encouraged to simply reach out to student veterans and "ask them what they need. Ask them what they're missing" (Lipka, 2011, para. 15). This can be done through contact with individual students and by hosting simple interest meetings on campus.

As a place to start, administrators can reach out to the VA certifying official on campus to obtain lists of veterans utilizing their GI Bill benefits on campus. It can be useful to search Facebook and other social media sites to learn about informal student veterans groups that have formed on campus or in the area. Also, neighboring campuses or other institutions within the same university system may be interested in sharing resources to form student veterans organizations or to expand existing efforts to include a broader reach. Furthermore, it may be useful to reach out to alumni veterans for assistance in serving in advisory roles and for honest feedback and reflection on their campus experiences.

Learn What Is Known About Student Veterans

The literature base specifically related to student veterans is growing. DiRamio, Ackerman, and Mitchell (2008) published one of the first empirical works, and a handful of studies have been produced since (such as Rumann & Hamrick, 2010). Several doctoral dissertations have explored topics related to student veterans as well (Bauman, 2009; Livingston, 2009; Pattillo, 2011; Rumann, 2010). These largely qualitative works reflect the authentic voices of the students themselves and are thus good sources of genuine insight into the student veteran experience and culture. Reports from nonprofit organizations, including ACE's *From Soldier to Student* (Cook & Kim, 2009) provide thorough details about the current picture of student veterans on U.S. college campuses. The popular higher education press, including the *Chronicle of Higher Education* and *Inside Higher Ed*, frequently highlight articles related to student veterans (such as Berrett, 2011; Lipka, 2011; Scorza, 2011). More comprehensive publications are beginning to emerge as well, including Ackerman and DiRamio (2009), DiRamio and Jarvis (2011), and Madaus (2009).

Collectively, these works represent current knowledge about student veterans, but this knowledge is far from complete. Campus administrators should consider these works as useful contributions to professional and personal understandings of this population, but they are not exhaustive. In order to become effective advocates for student veterans, campus administrators can begin their work by learning from advisors at other institutions. For example, each year the University of Louisville hosts the Veteran Symposium for Higher Education at which higher education professionals who work with student veterans share ideas, learn about policy and legislation updates, and discuss numerous topics and issues that affect this population. Also, a variety of higher education meetings and conference agendas include sessions on topics related to student veterans, such as those sponsored by ACE, the American College Personnel Association (ACPA), the National Academic Advising Association (NACADA), the National Association of Student Personnel Administrators (NASPA), and the New England Conference for Student Success.

Do Not Reflexively Accept "What Is Known"

Review of the literature about student veterans and their campus experiences provides readers with academic insight, but it is not a substitute for becoming familiar with the lived experience of individual student veterans enrolled at individual colleges and universities. To that end, prospective student group advisors should read with critical eyes and should never automatically apply research findings or implications directly to their own campuses or to student veteran populations. Rather, insights and findings presented in the literature should serve as the foundation for campus administrators, faculty members, and staff to study, reflect on, and learn from the student veteran populations on their campuses. Advisors and prospective advocates should share what they have learned with student veterans and ask if it "rings true" or resonates with them. Much of what advisors learn about student veterans comes from their individual and group interactions with veterans themselves; that type of knowledge cannot be gleaned solely from information presented in articles, books, reports, and conference sessions.

Avoid Basic Errors

Current and prospective advisors who are new to working with student veterans may make some basic interpersonal missteps as they begin to interact with students due to misinformation, nervousness, desires to "break the ice," or any number of other reasons. Though this example seems obvious, one should never ask a veteran if he or she has fired a weapon, shot at people, or harmed anyone. The alienation that results from this type of inquiry can obstruct or even prevent the formation of personal relationships, including achieving desired rapport between advisors and service members and veterans. Similarly, it is important to separate politics, political opinions, and personal perspectives on war and military conflict from the individual; student veterans have (and many continue) to do the jobs they are told to do.

General guidance for current or future advisors is actually quite simple: allow veterans to disclose information about their experiences in the military. When getting to know student veterans, ask open-ended, nonjudgmental questions to which individuals can freely respond in ways that make them comfortable, respect the wide variety of answers students provide, and avoid the inclination to compare, contrast, or group students. Never call a veteran out in class, or in some other group format, even if the intention is benign or positive. It is not appropriate to expect a student veteran to speak on behalf of all student veterans or of all veterans in general. Also, it should not be assumed that a veteran is "Republican" or "conservative" or "prowar" solely because of his or her military affiliation. In short, do not allow one's own discomfort—if such discomfort exists—to become a wedge.

When a student veteran or service member enters a campus office, the individual greeting him or her should stand up (if able), shake hands, and offer appreciation for his or her service. Doing so instantly sets the tone and creates an atmosphere in which the individual knows that he or she is respected. (In the same vein, an individual's preference to eschew recognition for his or her military service should be respected as well.) Initiate dialogue with open-ended questions guided by genuine interest in the student and his or her experience, such as: What is your position in the military? Why did you enlist? How was your service? Where did you serve and what was it like? What skills did you learn in the military that are helpful in what you are doing now? How are you doing here on campus? What is it like to move from one culture to another? Is the military understanding of your college demands, and is the college understanding of your military commitments?

Advisors should endeavor to form genuine and meaningful relationships with individual student veterans and within student veterans organizations. It is important to remember that student veterans' experiences are varied, as are their opinions and feelings about those experiences. Not unlike other advisory roles on campus, advisors of student veterans organizations and others interested in building rapport with student veterans should simply be available to these students. They can show interest in student veterans through continual relationship-building efforts, such as offering to continue conversations over coffee, or by setting times to meet regularly. Participation in events that are meaningful to veterans is also important, such as assistance in organizing memorials, fundraisers, tours of military museums, or visits to veteran hospitals.

Well-intended advisors can appear insensitive simply by trying to do too much, especially without prior coordination with student veterans. For example, many student veterans would be honored to speak of their experiences, but they may not be comfortable doing so on the spur of the moment without an invitation and advance notice; prompting a veteran to engage in this way in passing can make him or her very uncomfortable. Also, an area of insensitivity is the assumption that all student veterans "need help" or struggle with issues like binge drinking. Continual overemphasis of available counseling, PTSD, and TBI services can give the impression that administrators think that every student veteran on campus is in immediate need; the trick is to balance appropriate and necessary advertisement of services and resources without making assumptions about what students need.

Be Prepared

Although it is inappropriate to stereotype veterans based on what one reads or hears in literature or popular media, or to assume that all veterans have had similar experiences in the military, it is clear that some student veterans face serious challenges. Rudd, Goulding, and Bryan (2011) studied the psychological challenges that student veterans face, including the risk of suicide. Of particular concern was that among the student veterans who participated in the study, 46 percent had thought about suicide, 20 percent had plans for suicide, 10.4 percent thought about suicide on a frequent basis, 7.7 percent had attempted suicide, and 3.8 percent believed that suicide would take place. Suicide and suicidal thoughts are among the most severe challenges that student veterans face, and although not all student veterans are at risk of suicide, many issues potentially affect them.

Regardless of the nature of the particular challenge at hand, advisors who have developed strong, positive, and trusting relationships with student veterans are clearly in better positions to render assistance when students struggle. At times, this assistance may simply involve listening without judgment. In other instances, assistance could mean providing referrals to campus offices or community resources that are specifically equipped to address the presenting concerns. Although challenges vary among individual veterans, advisors must be sufficiently well versed in knowledge of resources and be aware of their own limits so that the best and most effective services are provided to student veterans on campus. In addition to awareness of campus resources (an overview can be provided by the dean of students or similar), advisors should know how to get outside help when needed, such as those available from the VA. At the most basic level, advisors should know how to get in touch with the local VA office and know what services are offered there. Of greater benefit is to make visits to the local VA office to establish rapport with colleagues there and to gain the knowledge necessary to properly refer students when necessary.

Consider Specialized Programs

There exists among veterans a sense of collective identity, and campuses could truly benefit by tapping into this unique bond. However, well-intentioned institutions risk taking these efforts too far, inadvertently segregating groups of individuals who may already feel marginalized. Each campus's environment should dictate conversations and plans related to specialized programs for veterans. For example, while special orientation programs for veterans, including those planned and conducted by or with members of student veterans organizations, have been successfully implemented on many campuses throughout the country (such as Ball State University, n.d.), institutions should also consider including veterans in portions of general orientation programs to help them feel part of the general campus community. Although veterans appreciate connecting with other veterans on campus, students are most successful when fully engaged on campus (Kuh, Kinzie, Schuh, & Whitt, 2010).

Focus on the Relationship

The success of advising student veterans organizations relies heavily on the presence of meaningful and supportive relationships. However, advisors may be unsure of how these relationships will unfold given the unique and sometimes life-changing experiences of student veterans (Ackerman, DiRamio & Mitchell, 2009). To that end, advising student veterans organizations may involve more time and personal energy than advising other student groups. In their work with student veterans, advisors should endeavor to form meaningful, individual relationships with each member, recognizing that many have experienced life-changing events to which most people on campus cannot relate. Advisors should devote the time and energy necessary to educate themselves about the types and significance of the unique challenges faced by student veterans. This kind of advising relationship should not be entered into lightly. Certainly the core elements of student development, including building rapport and addressing challenges, are consistent across groups. Yet what is different here is the collection of stories and the life experiences accumulated by these individuals in what is often a short amount of time; this accelerated maturation can fundamentally shift individuals' worldviews (Livingston, 2009; Vien, 2010). Advisors should be aware of this phenomenon and embrace the mature, often thoughtful, and reflective nature of many student veterans.

Avoid Assumptions

The need to avoid assumptions when working with student veterans seems obvious, yet assumptions often creep into advisory relationships. As noted earlier in this chapter, one such assumption is that all military personnel or veterans are "conservative," "Republican," or "prowar." Much like other undergraduate and graduate students, military personnel are diverse in their political perspectives and take varied stances on global issues. In fact, Bauman (2009) found that student veterans went "to the box" (as noted above, "the box" is a term used among military members to refer to those who have served in Afghanistan or Iraq; literally, the sandbox) not for war, or oil, or politics, but rather for each other, so that the persons next to them in uniform need not be there alone; it is this strong and powerful bond among military members that provides a great deal of the motivation to serve. The reasons people choose to join the military are varied (Ackerman, DiRamio, & Mitchell, 2009; Kleykamp, 2006; Naylor, 2011). Thus, to stereotype or prejudge student veterans, or to allow assumptions to creep into evolving relationships, is inappropriate and unfair.

From Advisor to Advocate

At times, veterans feel disconnected, and perhaps marginalized, from the overall student body and also from the institution itself (Schwartz & Kay, 2010; Summers, 2010). In their roles as advocates, advisors play substantial roles in assisting student veterans in finding their voices, and when those voices are silent or go unheard, advisors serve as voices on behalf of the students. In many ways, advocacy in this arena means moving from grassroots efforts, to organized student veterans, to more institutional, regional, and national perspectives. To be successful advocates, individuals must first understand their institutional cultures, climates, and openness to the issues at hand (Sue, 1998; Whitt, 1997). Advocates must thoughtfully reflect on the individual nuances of their campuses and devise plans that are most likely to be successful while maintaining focus on serving those who have served the nation. For example, a potential advocate should tune into other sources of support for student veterans, or be aware if he or she is a trailblazer on campus with regard to student veterans, serving as the first and only voice of advocacy. It is also helpful to anticipate how well one's leadership will be received on campus when discussing and implementing programs related to this population. Relevant political and social climates that surround this topic on campus should be explored, and any potential voids with regard to the student veteran experience should be acknowledged. To a great degree, these and related areas require the advisor to assess the overall campus climate as it relates to the military in general and student veterans in particular.

Summerlot, Green, and Parker (2009) identified three types of campus climates with regard to student veterans: supportive, ambivalent, and challenging. The supportive climate is characterized by "institutionally based efforts to support veterans" (p. 73) while in the ambivalent climate, "veterans receive little recognition, if any, and minimal campus-based support services" (p. 73). Yet most difficult is the challenging climate, where any "links between the campus community and the military" (p. 74) are strained. This strain causes veterans to minimize or even conceal their identities as members of the military (Summerlot, Green, & Parker 2009) even though their roles in the military are often large parts of their identities (Bauman, 2009).

Current and prospective advisors should take time to reflect on these broad categories. It is also helpful to discuss these topics with colleagues who have experience working with student veterans, and perhaps most important, to talk to current veterans. Areas worthy of effort may include the following types of efforts: If the climate appears at least open to the idea of a student veterans organization, harness the energy and bring focus to disjointed efforts on campus. Bring together individuals acting on their own in order to collectively and collaboratively serve the student veteran population. Seek external funding for a veteran center. Partner with area colleges to provide a smooth transfer process from a local or regional two-year institution to a four-year institution.

Suggested Outcomes of Advocacy by and for Student Veterans

Advocacy efforts on behalf of and by student veterans can be informed by the experiences of student veterans organizations around the nation. This list of advocacy efforts is not exhaustive, but provides a place to start for student veterans and supporters of student veterans engaging in advocacy on campus.

Policy Revisions

The policies that affect veterans should be examined in tandem with members of the student veterans organization. Institutional settings, governance, and cultures differ, yet several areas benefit from examination with a "veteran lens" to determine if they are meeting the needs of this population. This also serves as an assessment activity in which student veterans organizations can play an active role.

Potential areas of exploration include greater flexibility in housing policies. Veterans and service members should be issued waivers from requirements that all students live on campus, or they could be invited to live in graduate student housing, apartment-style housing, or adult/family communities rather than in traditional undergraduate residence halls. Recruitment and admissions practices that identify veterans early in the recruitment process facilitate outreach and monitoring of subsequent progress. Course withdrawal time frames and class attendance policies should acknowledge and work to accommodate nonnegotiable duties and training requirements to which military service members are subject. Financial aid policies and student account deadlines should accommodate possible delays in VA payments and make emergency bridge funding available. Academic credit should be granted for military experiences and training to the extent that is practicable. This list is not exhaustive, but it is likely to generate further discussion about the unique challenges student veterans face on individual campuses and how they can be addressed.

Priority or Privileged Registration

Many colleges already offer priority or early registration opportunities for select groups of students such as athletes, ROTC cadets, and students with disabilities who face unique sets of barriers like time constraints and benefit availability. Student veterans may face similar constraints, such as limited duration of GI Bill benefits, yet they are not usually afforded early registration privileges that could mitigate these problems. Access to courses is a crucial component of veterans' abilities to effectively utilize their earned benefits in the strict timeframes that are imposed. Campus administrators could work with the student veterans organization to determine the best ways to maximize enrolled students' opportunities to achieve degree completion before their GI benefits expire.

Veterans' Memorials

Some schools have built or expanded memorial sites for veterans on their campuses. These spaces can be used to recognize students, alumni, and campus community members who have served in the military, been killed in war, and all individuals who have fallen in battle. The development or expansion of a veterans' memorial is an excellent way to involve members of the student veterans organization in a community-building project while also bringing attention to their experiences and providing connections to other veterans.

Veterans' Lounge

The acquisition of dedicated lounge and meeting space is a common request of campus groups, and it is a logical step in an institution's effort to support veterans' organizations. Dedicating a place for veterans to network, study, and receive assistance in a "safe" space that is free of distractions or intrusions helps ensure that they are accessing campus resources, including counseling and veteran-specific services. This concept is extended to include other offices on campus that serve as vet-friendly zones, such as offices on the California State University at Sacramento campus that are identified by stickers, where student veterans can "expect to find at least basic knowledge of posttraumatic stress disorder and traumatic brain injury, as well as the understanding that those conditions are not stigmatizing or unique to veterans" and comfortably ask questions and seek services in supportive environments (Lipka, 2011, para. 6).

Commitment

Regardless of the goals of self-advocacy efforts, it is critical to have buy-in from the majority of student veterans organization members. These efforts are, in effect, campus lobbying work, and it is necessary for student veterans to be organized and articulate. In order to be successful advocates, decision makers must understand the needs and requests of student veterans, and they are more likely to take such efforts seriously if members present their needs in professional and persuasive manners, which may involve different strategies at different campuses. An example of this type of localized effort was the reaction of student veterans at GWU when it was announced that the current Veterans Memorial Park would be removed for construction of a new building. In response to the university's plans, student veterans gathered input from members about relocation of the park, developed ideas, and presented options to the administration. As a result, student veterans had substantial input on the design of the new (future) park and collaborated with university officials to ensure their needs and interests were addressed (chapter author Brian Hawthorne completed his undergraduate degree at GWU as a student veteran).

Collaboration with On- and Off-Campus Organizations

It can take a lot of work for new or revamped student organizations to develop presences on their campuses and become well known among students. In order to become established and effective, and to provide networking opportunities for members, student veterans organizations frequently partner with other groups on and off campus.

Other Student Organizations

Members of student veterans organizations can find strong advocates and allies among members of other student groups that can provide guidance with regard to paperwork, fundraisers, and navigating campus policies and key personnel. It is advantageous for members of student veterans organizations to become familiar with how student government operates on campus. Of particular benefit is the attainment of a resolution from student government to support student veterans on campus, which may include the sharing of student fees and the inclusion of veterans' concerns in overall student advocacy efforts. Examples of other groups with which to collaborate include community service organizations and others that engage in service efforts, such as fraternities, sororities, and political societies. In addition, student veterans organizations can benefit from relationships with groups of other underrepresented students on campus, such as LGBTQ and racial and ethnic minority students, who are also working to bring attention to their unique needs and experiences.

External Organizations

Nonprofit groups, veteran organizations, and local businesses can be extremely helpful in moving student veterans' efforts forward. Members of external organizations are frequently willing to help student veterans fundraise, search for jobs, apply for and access benefits, lobby university and community leaders, and partner to plan and organize special events. For example, American Legion or VFW posts can be approached for use of meeting space or collaboration on mutual fundraising activities. Local high schools can provide student veterans with opportunities to talk about their experiences with teenagers who are exploring options for their futures, and may collaborate for fundraising and athletic events. Local government agencies often provide support for campus events through the provision of guest speakers, such as area mayors or city and county council members. Student veterans may ask to participate in career and networking events sponsored by the local chamber of commerce and related agencies.

It is essential to understand other groups' goals and priorities when planning to collaborate, though successful relationships do not necessarily require shared agendas in order to be mutually beneficial. For example, many organizations want to help veterans and be recognized for doing so, which is a powerful force for philanthropy and political partnerships. However, it is important to understand what each organization is trying to accomplish before long-term or formal agreements are reached.

Broader Involvement

Student veterans groups' connections to other student veterans groups in their regions and around the country can be extremely beneficial for networking purposes, collaboration, and individual and group support. Student veterans can easily meet peers from across the country if they become involved with national organizations, such as SVA or Iraq and Afghanistan Veterans of America (IAVA), which have memberships comprised of predominantly younger, post-9/11 veterans. SVA, IAVA, and similar organizations have access to myriad resources, provide scholarships, and host networking events. They are also excellent sources of best practice ideas, funding partnerships, and public recognition opportunities, and they sponsor events throughout the year to connect veterans and provide opportunities for them to learn from experts and from each other.

For example, SVA supports chapters with fundraising initiatives and helps them make connections with members of large organizations, such as the VA and the U.S. Congress, who are able to assist with events and job searches, and who want to hear from individual student veterans about their military and college experiences. Additionally, SVA hosts multiple conferences throughout the year at which chapter leaders learn from and with one another. SVA provides chapters with access to the national media, which garners attention for their efforts beyond their local areas. Membership dues for SVA and similar groups are low or free, and involvement can help student veterans organizations take advocacy efforts to the next level of effectiveness and awareness in that their interests are represented on the national stage. It is difficult for individual campus student veterans organizations to achieve audiences within the U.S. Congress and the White House, whereas national organizations synthesize the concerns of multiple chapters throughout the country and use their voices on Capitol Hill to be heard.

Assessing Student Veterans Organizations

"The importance of showing that we know when, how, and under what conditions students learn will be superseded only by the importance of showing that we can use that information to improve what we do for them" (Hanson, 1990, p. 270). Students form the core of student veterans organizations, and to a great extent assessment in this area should include a heavy emphasis on student learning, which is a fundamental purpose of any college or university. More specifically, the *Student Learning Imperative* (ACPA, 1996) emphasized that student learning and personal development are the central goals of student affairs programs and services. When assessing the value of student veterans organizations and the quality of advising, the learning that accompanies students' participation in the organization becomes a key focus. That is, how is this learning shaped (or not) by participation in the organization?

Assessment of Student Learning

Hanson (1990) explicated "broad questions that drive the research agenda for [the next generation of] student affairs" (p. 277) and provided a comprehensive framework for assessing student learning that has a clear beginning, middle, and end. Questions related to this type of assessment are presented below in modified form to address the specific needs of student veterans organizations.

Beginning. How can we describe students in meaningful ways when they first enter college? What do we know about student veterans who participate in student veterans organizations? How are they different from other students? How are they similar? How might involvement in a student veterans organization influence or affect student veterans, including their learning and development?

Middle. How can we describe what students learn while they are still involved and active in the organization and by the time they leave the institution? More specifically, how might we describe the learning that occurs within the student veterans organization both during the time they are involved and after their participation has ended?

End. How can we describe the process of how students learn and develop? How does involvement in a student veterans organization influence this process? Is what they learn, in part, due to their involvement in a student veterans organization? Are there connections between their individual development and their involvement in the organization?

Hanson's framework (1990) requires that advisors (or other stakeholders) seeking to assess student learning start early so that they begin the quest to understand the student veterans organization experience from the moment members join. Early collection of data, when coupled with insights from the "middle" and "end" phases, allows for the depiction of student learning and growth (or lack thereof) over time. In the presence of demonstrated growth, this type of assessment provides opportunities to understand whether it was due, at least in part, to involvement in the student veterans organization.

The application of Hanson's framework (1990) suggests that assessment should continue as students become more engaged in the organization—a period that could span one or more years. The potential challenge with student veterans organizations is that some of these members might stop out due to military obligations and may therefore be invisible until they seek to return. However, advisors and others are encouraged to remain connected to these students during their time away. More specifically, *the student veterans organization and its leadership should endeavor to keep these individuals as fully functioning members of the organization.* The "middle" phase of Hanson's framework (1990)—the phase that relates to learning during one's involvement—can present unique challenges in the assessment of student learning in cases where students are moving between college and active duty service. If individuals are deployed, but are still active members of the organization, those conducting assessments must consider unique ways to capture their learning and the overall impact of involvement on their learning, such as via e-mail or interactions on Facebook or Skype.

The final phase of this framework is akin to an exit point. That is, as student veterans finish their time with student veterans organizations (ideally, but not necessarily, at the same time they receive their degrees), those conducting assessments should seek insight as to the learning and development that occurred as a result of their involvement. The areas of focus will differ from campus to campus and should tie directly to institutional learning outcomes as well as the goals of the individual student veterans organization, which would be defined in part by assessing student veterans' demonstrated needs. It is important to note that a student's decision to leave the organization is not necessarily negative; rather, it may be a sign of transition and engagement with the larger nonveteran community.

At the most basic level, however, is evaluation of whether the students involved with the organizations have been successful in their educational pursuits. Student veterans organizations exist to support students and help facilitate their success. Do the students involved with the groups reach their goals and objectives, whether they are degree attainment, job training, or preparation for the pursuit of advanced degrees? Any insight gathered in this type of assessment would help to fill the dearth of information about the student veteran experience, as emphasized by Ackerman, DiRamio, and Mitchell (2009): "There is an urgent need to share best practices, exchange ideas, and to conduct research that will provide campuses with the information needed to promote the academic achievement of veterans who are students" (p. 13).

Assessment of the Organization

The assessment of student learning is critical, yet assessment of the overall functional health, progress, and outcomes of an organization is equally worthwhile. As Terenzini and Upcraft (1996) noted, "outcomes assessments attempt to answer the most important questions of all . . . is what we are doing having any effect, is that effect the intended one, and how do we know?" (p. 218). It is therefore insufficient for assessments of student veterans organizations to simply record the numbers of members or track the numbers of individuals who participate in programs. There is a need to dig deeper in order to understand how the groups' members are learning, developing, or are engaging in robust experiences.

Many models with varying degrees of complexity can be employed in assessments of student veterans organizations. In an effort to simplify assessment, concepts and ideas presented by Terenzini and Upcraft (1996) have been adapted for a suggested framework. (Note, however, that entire book volumes and a plethora of articles are dedicated solely to the topic of assessment in student affairs and higher education. Advisors should consult these sources for a more thorough treatment of assessment strategies.) The framework focuses on the overall functional health, progress, and outcomes related to a student veterans organization; with some adjustment, it can be applied to other areas of interest, such as individual programs and fundraising initiatives. Subsequent findings can inform advisors, group leaders, and others who work with and support the student veterans organization.

Define the Problem or Challenge. The student veterans organization should have a clearly articulated, succinct mission. SVA (n.d.) asserts that a "group needs a purpose and the best way to define that is through establishing at least one formal program," such as outreach and advocacy, social support, counseling, new student orientation, and/or community service (pp. 6–7).

Define the Goals or Outcomes. There is, at times, a tendency to write dozens of outcomes for a particular program. Although there is no universal "right" number, the overabundance of outcomes can lead to subsequent assessment strategies that are unnecessarily complex and convoluted. As outcomes for student veterans organizations are considered, a handful of succinctly worded outcomes, constructed by members of the organization will likely serve members well. For example: *The organization will expand its membership by 10 percent in the first year.* Or: *The organization will sponsor one event each semester to welcome newly enrolled student veterans.*

Define the Assessment Strategy. This is the "how" in the framework. As with other ideas presented in this brief assessment guide, think simple. In many cases, the results will stay within the organizations or within the institutions. Therefore, before strategy is determined, the audience should be identified in order to inform the selection of the assessment strategy; the selection will, in turn, determine the types of data that are needed.

Collect and Analyze Data; Reflect on and Apply Conclusions. Too often, assessment reports remain filed away in drawers, never to be fully or even partially used. Results should be interpreted and discussed as a group, allowing the conclusions to form collectively. Beyond this aspect of assessment, however, findings should be applied in a way that is reasonable and with the group's improvement in mind. For example, has the group expanded? Sheer numbers are not measures of health, especially in light of small student veterans' populations on many campuses, and the fact that student veterans are deployed during their collegiate experiences and therefore are not always "counted" as group members. However, one measure of the health of a student veterans organization is its presence on campus and whether or not student veterans are accessing or involved with the group. Has the group collaborated with other organizations on campus to provide speakers, programming, or other events on topics relevant to student veterans? Do members utilize campus resources in efforts to improve the group's activities or expand its reach? Does the student veterans organization have relationships with agencies in the area?

Are student veterans' voices heard on a campuswide level? In this way, insights and conclusions from the data cycle back into the organization and its efforts in a fashion that allows for positive change.

Conclusion

Individuals who share similar backgrounds and experiences are drawn to one another for support and understanding. This holds true for the many thousands of veterans enrolled in institutions of higher education across the United States. The presence of student veterans organizations speaks to the unique characteristics of this population on our campuses. The organization, scope, and goals of student veterans organizations are as diverse as the institutions at which they reside and the individuals who comprise their memberships, yet they share a common goal of supporting the men and women who have provided service to this country and, in turn, need assistance in their educational pursuits. With support from campus stakeholders and allies, student veterans organizations can be powerful vehicles through which the voices of student veterans are heard and their needs acknowledged and addressed.

Resources

American Council on Education, Military Programs
  http://www.acenet.edu/AM/Template.cfm?Section=Military
  _Programs
Iraq and Afghanistan Veterans of America
  http://iava.org/
Student Veterans of America
  http://www.studentveterans.org/
Veteran Symposium for Higher Education
  http://stuaff.org/veterans/

References

Ackerman, R., & DiRamio, D. (Eds.). (2009). Creating a veteran-friendly campus: Strategies for transition and success. *New Directions for Student Services, 126.* San Francisco: Jossey-Bass.

Ackerman, R., & DiRamio, D., & Mitchell, R. L. (2009). Transitions: Combat veterans as college students. In R. Ackerman & D. DiRamio (Eds.), *Creating a veteran-friendly campus: Strategies for transition and success.* New Directions for Student Services, 126, pp. 5–14. San Francisco: Jossey-Bass.

American College Personnel Association. (1996). *Student learning imperative: Implications for student affairs.* Washington, DC: Author. Retrieved from http://www.acpa.nche.edu/sli/sli.htm

American Veterans Committee Records. (n.d.). *Guide to the American Veterans Committee records, 1942–2002* (MS2144). Special Collections Research Center, The George Washington University, Washington, DC. Retrieved from http://www.gwu.edu/gelman/spec/ead/ms2144.html#ref1352

Anderson, L. (2009, October 4). AU vets waiting for GI Bill funds. *The Eagle.* Retrieved from http://www.theeagleonline.com/news/story/au-vets-waiting-for-gi-bill-funds/

Astin, A. W. (1984). Student involvement: A developmental theory for higher education. *Journal of College Student Personnel, 25*(4), 297–308.

Astin, A. W. (1999). Student involvement: A developmental theory for higher education. *Journal of College Student Development, 40*(5), 518–529.

Ball State University. (n.d.). *Student veteran orientation program* [web site]. Retrieved from http://cms.bsu.edu/AdmissionsLanding/ScholarshipsandFinancialAid/Typesof Aid/VeteransandDependentsEducationalBenefits/OrientationProgram.aspx

Bauman, M. C. (2009). *Called to serve: The military mobilization of undergraduates.* (Doctoral dissertation). The Pennsylvania State University, State College.

Berrett, D. (2011, April 8). Words from wartime. *Inside Higher Ed.* Retrieved from http://www.insidehighered.com/news/2011/04/08/veterans_in_college_have _vexed_relationship_to_writing_assignments

Center for Community College Student Engagement. (2009). *Making connections: Dimensions of student engagement (2009 CCSSE findings).* Austin: University of Texas at Austin Community College Leadership Program.

Cook, B. J., & Kim, Y. (2009). *From soldier to student: Easing the transition of service members on campus.* Washington, DC: American Council on Education.

Cutright, M. (2011, February 4). Ready for the transfer wave? *Inside Higher Ed.* Retrieved from http://www.insidehighered.com/views/2011/02/04/cutright

DiRamio, D., Ackerman, R., & Mitchell, R. L. (2008). From combat to campus: Voices of student-veterans. *NASPA Journal, 45*(1), 73–102.

DiRamio, D., & Jarvis, K. (2011). Veterans in higher education: When Johnny and Jane came marching to campus. *ASHE Higher Education Report, 37*(3). San Francisco: Jossey-Bass.

George Washington University Center for Student Engagement. (n.d.) *Benefits of registering a student organization* [web site]. Retrieved from http://studentorgs.gwu.edu/register/orgbenefits/

Gillis, J. (2011, April 29). Advocacy creates resources for student vets. *The Hoya.* Retrieved from http://www.thehoya.com/advocacy-creates-resources-for-student-vets-1.2213038#.Tp9bXt6Ike4

Goodier, F. T. (1946). A teachers college adjusts to the war and postwar periods. *Peabody Journal of Education, 23*(4), 227–231.

Hamilton, R. (2011, September 10). On campus, studying the needs of veterans. *New York Times*. Retrieved from http://www.nytimes.com/2011/09/11/us/11ttscience .html?pagewanted=all

Hanson, G. R. (1990). Improving practice through research, evaluation, and outcomes assessment. In M. J. Barr & M. L. Upcraft (Eds.), *New futures for student affairs: Building a vision for professional leadership and practice* (pp. 270–292). San Francisco: Jossey-Bass.

Inigral. (2011). Schools App [web site]. Retrieved from http://www.inigral.com/

Kilgore, D., & Rice, P. J. (Eds.). (2003). Meeting the special needs of adult students. *New Directions for Student Services, 102*. San Francisco: Jossey-Bass.

Kleykamp, M. A. (2006). College, jobs, or the military? Enlistment during a time of war. *Social Science Quarterly, 87*(2), 272–290.

Kuh, G. D., Kinzie, J., Schuh, J. H., & Whitt, E. J. (2010). *Student success in college: Creating conditions that matter* (Rev. ed.). San Francisco: Jossey-Bass.

Lipka, S. (2011, March 8). To support student veterans, be visible and engage other students, grant winners advise. *Chronicle of Higher Education*. Retrieved from http://chronicle.com/article/Grant-Winners-Offer-Tips-on/126653/

Livingston, W. G. (2009). *Discovering the academic and social transitions of re-enrolling student veterans at one institution: A grounded theory*. (Doctoral dissertation). Clemson University, Clemson, South Carolina.

Madaus, J. W. (Ed.). (2009). Veterans with disabilities [Special issue]. *Journal of Postsecondary Education and Disability, 22*(1).

Mettler, S. (2005). *Soldiers to citizens: The G.I. Bill and the making of the greatest generation*. New York: Oxford University Press.

Modell, J., & Haggerty, T. (1991). The social impact of war. *Annual Review of Sociology, 17*, 205–224.

Mostafavi, B. (2011, May 17). Michigan House to hear about University of Michigan-Flint efforts to serve student veterans. *Flint Journal*. Retrieved from http://www.mlive.com/news/flint/index.ssf/2011/05/michigan_house_to_hear_ about_u.html

National Association of Concerned Veterans. (n.d.). [web site]. Retrieved from http://concernedveterans.org/

Naylor, B. (Host). (2011, July 5). *Service just one reason to join the military* [Radio broadcast]. Washington, DC: National Public Radio. Retrieved from http://www.npr.org/ 2011/07/05/137627844/service-just-one-reason-to-join-the-military

O'Herrin, E. (2011). Enhancing veteran success in higher education. *Peer Review, 13*(1). Retrieved from http://www.aacu.org/peerreview/pr-wi11/prwi11_oherrin.cfm

Pattillo, S. P. (2011). *Are student veterans a traditional, nontraditional, or special population? A study of veterans on the Auburn University campus*. (Doctoral dissertation). Auburn University, Auburn, Alabama.

Pennsylvania State University. (n.d.). Penn State Veterans Organization [web site]. Retrieved from http://www.clubs.psu.edu/up/psuvo/

Purdue University. (2011, February 3). Purdue institute awards $9,400 to student veteran organizations. *Purdue University News Service*. Retrieved from http://www .purdue.edu/newsroom/outreach/2011/110203HittDiploma.html

Reason, R. D., Broido, E. M., Davis, T. L., & Evans, N. J. (Eds.). (2005). Developing social justice allies. *New Directions for Student Services, 110*. San Francisco: Jossey-Bass.

Rudd, M. D., Goulding, J., & Bryan, C. J. (2011, August 15). Student veterans: A national survey exploring psychological symptoms and suicide risk. *Professional Psychology: Research and Practice (Online First)*. Retrieved from http://psycnet.apa.org/index .cfm?fa=browsePA.ofp&jcode=pro

Rumann, C. B. (2010). *Student veterans returning to a community college: Understanding their transitions.* (Doctoral dissertation). Iowa State University, Ames.

Rumann, C. B., & Hamrick, F. A. (2010). Student veterans in transition: Re-enrolling after war zone deployments. *Journal of Higher Education, 81*(4), 431–458.

Rumann, C. B., Kraus, A., & Bauman, M. C. (2011, March). *Past, present, and future: Student veterans on campus.* Preconference workshop presented at the NASPA Annual Conference, Philadelphia, Pennsylvania.

Sabo, R. (2010, December 8). Student veterans organizations and support on the rise at college campuses. *GI Bill.* Retrieved from http://www.gibill.com/news/student-veterans-organizations-on-the-rise-308.html

Schmadeke, S. (2008, February 7). American Veterans Committee to close last chapter, based in Park Forest. *Chicago Tribune.* Retrieved from http://articles.chicagotribune .com/2008–02–07/news/0802061200_1_avc-american-veterans-committee-veterans-group

Schwartz, V., & Kay, J. (2010, September 2). Caring for vets in college. *Huffington Post.* http://www.huffingtonpost.com/victor-schwartz/caring-for-vets-in-colleg_b_704115.html

Scorza, J. (2011, April 4). Student veterans [Audio podcast]. In WAMC (Producer), & Mount Holyoke College (Producer), *Academic Minute.* Albany, NY: Northeast Public Radio. Retrieved from http://www.insidehighered.com/audio/academic_pulse/ student_veterans

Seegert, M. (2011, May 31). Bryant and Stratton College Online forms student veterans group. *Bryant & Stratton* College [Blog]. Retrieved from http://onlineblog .bryantstratton.edu/bryant-stratton-college-online-forms-student-veterans-group/

Sewall, M. (2010, June 13). Veterans use benefits of new GI Bill largely at for-profit and 2-year colleges. *Chronicle of Higher Education.* Retrieved from http://chronicle .com/article/Veterans-Use-Benefits-of-Ne/65914/

Stankorb, S. (2011, September 28). AU among nation's top military friendly schools. *American Today.* Retrieved from http://observer.american.edu/americantoday/ 20110927-AU-among-Top-Military-Friendly-Schools.cfm

Stoller, E. (2011, April 18). Creating community when you don't have a "quad." *Inside Higher Ed.* Retrieved from http://www.insidehighered.com/blogs/student_affairs _and_technology/creating_community_when_you_don_t_have_a_quad

Student Veterans of America. (n.d.). *How to start an SVA chapter.* Washington, DC: Author. Retrieved from http://www.studentveterans.org/resourcelibrary/ documents/ HowtoStartanSVAChapter.pdf

Student Veterans of America. (2011). *About SVA* [web site]. Retrieved from http: //www.studentveterans.org/about/

Sue, S. (1998). In search of cultural competence in psychotherapy and counseling. *American Psychologist, 53*(4), 440–448.

Summerlot, J., Green, S.-M., & Parker, D. (2009). Student veterans organizations. *New Directions for Student Services, 126,* 71–79.

Summers, L. (2010, January 30). Student veterans find strength in numbers. *Daily News Online*. Retrieved from http://tdn.com/news/local/article_812a8fc0–0df7–11df-845b-001cc4c002e0.html

Terenzini, P. T., & Upcraft, M. L. (1996). Assessing program and service outcomes. In M. L. Upcraft & J. H. Schuh (Eds.), *Assessment in student affairs: A guide for practitioners* (pp. 217–239). San Francisco: Jossey-Bass.

Terkel, S. (1984). *"The good war": An oral history of World War II*. New York: Pantheon.

Time Magazine. (1945, December 3). Veterans: Peace Campaign. Retrieved from http://www.time.com/time/magazine/article/0,9171,852459–1,00.html

Tyler, R. L. (1966). The American Veterans Committee: Out of a hot war and into the cold. *American Quarterly, 18,* 419–436.

University of California, San Diego Student Veterans Organization. (2011). *Welcome to UCSD SVO*. [web site]. Retrieved from http://studentvets.ucsd.edu/

United States Department of Veterans Affairs. (2010, January). *The Post-9/11 GI Bill Yellow Ribbon program*. Washington, DC: Author.

Veterans Benefits, Title 38 (2009). United States Code. 38 USC § 101, Part 1, Chapter 1. http://www.law.cornell.edu/uscode/pdf/uscode38/lii_usc_TI_38_PA_I_CH_1_SE _101.pdf

Vien, C. (2010, January 27). Repaying the debt: How institutions of higher education can serve our student veterans. *University of Phoenix Knowledge Network*. Retrieved from https://www.phoenix.edu/uopx-knowledge-network/articles/working-learners/ institutions-higher-education-serving-veterans.html

Whitt, E. J. (1994). Encouraging adult learner involvement. *NASPA Journal, 31*(4), 309–318.

Whitt, E. J. (Ed.). (1997). *College student affairs administration* (ASHE Reader Series). Needham Heights, MA: Ginn Press.

Wynn, N. A. (1996). The 'good war': The Second World War and postwar American society. *Journal of Contemporary History, 31*(3), 463–482.

VIGNETTE

Joseph R. Sorge
Student, University of Nevada, Las Vegas

I served five years in the Air Force Security Forces. When I first joined the Air Force, I had two goals in mind. One was to get my experience as a police officer, and the other was to complete my college degree. I spent five years in the military and gained many experiences from the military way of life, including how to have discipline, how to be proactive, and how to persevere in everything I do. I was 19 years old when I enlisted, so I quickly learned about becoming independent. Although I did not complete as much college as I hoped, my military experiences developed my personality and taught me teamwork, how to perform my job, and leadership skills. In the military I had multiple duties. I started as an Armory Official and then worked as an Entry Controller. When I received my security clearance, I worked as a Response Team Leader, became a member of a SWAT team, and finally earned the privilege of becoming a base Patrolman. After serving honorably in the military, my service obligation was complete, and it was time for me to reintegrate back into the civilian world.

After four years in the workforce, the Post-9/11 GI Bill came into effect and I was able to return to college. I started at the University of Nevada, Las Vegas (UNLV) in September 2009 as a criminal justice major. As I began taking my classes, I applied my military experiences and work ethic to do my best. I have worked hard to be successful throughout my college career. I am an active member in my campus community and maintain a high GPA. I have also served as the president of student organizations. I attribute those accomplishments to the military's lesson of being proactive. Since I have been an active member on my campus, I've noticed that many of the nonmilitary students are complacent and tend to complain about issues that involve collegiate responsibilities. I hear nonmilitary students complaining about doing their homework, reading their chapters, having to show up for class, their boyfriends acting like jerks, they don't have time for school and work ... blah, blah, blah. I don't mean to rant, but that is what I hear literally every day. I never hear those complaints from other military service members and veterans in the room. Normally, they just turn and look at me and shake their heads in disgust. We just "know." Military tend to understand military. When a person experiences the military lifestyle, the words *complacent* and *military* never go together in the same sentence. This experience was a culture shock for me. However, I applied the perseverance I learned in the military and I continue to progress toward my degree. I did find one refuge, however, in the Student Veterans Organization (SVO).

When I was president of SVO, I felt that I could make a difference in the lives of the other service members on campus and create a place for military veterans to call home. When I started at UNLV, I did not know about SVO. I had to learn everything myself about my campus. When I stepped up to the SVO presidency, I wanted that to change. Today, with the help the Office of Veterans Services, veterans have a place to come for answers.

As I complete my degree, I feel very humbled to have accomplished much in my life. However, there is far more to achieve. If I had to give advice to incoming veterans on how to make their transitions from the military to college life easier, I would say to join the campus student veterans organization first. That should give veterans common ground with other veterans and a place to start learning about their campus communities. From there, I would recommend that veterans apply their military instincts, get involved as much as they desire, and enjoy their college experiences until they accomplish the new mission ... to graduate.

CHAPTER ELEVEN

INSTITUTIONAL LEADERSHIP ON SERVING STUDENT VETERANS AND SERVICE MEMBERS

Tom Jackson Jr., Charles J. Fey, and Leah Ewing Ross

Colleges and universities throughout the United States are seeking to become more supportive of veterans and service members, yet many campuses have been generally underprepared to effectively meet these individuals' needs. Although much was learned about student veterans' needs during the 1960s and 1970s, some of the practices and knowledge useful in that era are outdated and counterproductive for contemporary students. If higher education administrators wish to increase the presence of service members and veterans on their campuses—and foster their success—they need to provide adequate support services for these students (Baechtold & De Sawal, 2009). There are differing perspectives on what those services might include, the related costs, and the types of support that should be offered both inside and outside of the classroom. Yet to institutional leaders, supporting veterans and service members is simply expected and is considered the "right thing to do." Many state legislatures have lowered or eliminated tuition for veterans attending public colleges and universities; private institutions have also found that supporting student veterans is patriotic, developmental, and fiscally prudent. In almost all instances, support for veterans and service members is paramount and is in the best interests of these individuals and the nation—simply put, there is honor in serving those who have served our country. This chapter discusses the roles, responsibilities, and potential strategies for higher education administrators to help support and serve the student veteran population. It also identifies appropriate institutional objectives and recommended strategies to create a veteran-campus.

Developing Services and Support

Institutional leaders, from presidents and provosts to vice presidents and deans, are critical to the successful establishment of and support for student veteran services. With the advent of the Post-9/11 GI Bill, veterans are enrolling in college in numbers not seen since the 1970s: "Approximately 800,000 returned veterans used GI Bill benefits [in 2010], up 40 percent from 2009" (Hughes, 2011, para. 10). The opportunities provided to veterans and service members are extensions of promises made during the World War II era. "The G.I. Bill is a promise we made . . . that those who defend our country should be able to take advantage of America's opportunity . . . This new [Post-9/11 GI] bill fulfills that promise, and will do nothing less than change the course of an entire generation" (Iraq & Afghanistan Veterans of America, 2011, para. 3).

Colleges and university administrators seize opportunities to ensure that individual student veterans and service members have the services and programs necessary to make the most of this potentially life-changing experience. Campuses that enroll increasing numbers of veterans and service members emphasize the development of new services and programs and employ marketing and outreach strategies to recruit these students (Cook & Kim, 2009). In turn, colleges benefit from the presence of these students because their knowledge and wide range of life experiences enrich the classroom and campus communities (O'Herrin, 2011). Overall, higher education opens up a future of promise and fulfillment of the traditional American Dream for all students, including veterans. A college education "is a gateway to the middle class; it gives the United States a more competitive workforce in the global economy" (McSweeney, 2009, para. 4).

Each day, campus leaders make decisions based on myriad variables, including financial concerns, politics, students, institutional and individual relationships, legislative initiatives, and governance. Providing services to veterans and service members who utilize GI Bill benefits may be the right thing to do, but at its root, it is a *decision* based on a legislative opportunity to provide services to students. Veterans are valuable resources to higher education (Katopes, 2009); a compelling reason to provide services for them is the increased enrollment that comes with government funding.

Furthermore, the monies associated with the Post-9/11 GI Bill minimize one significant barrier to retention (funding), which increases students' rates of persistence and allows institutions to direct retention-related funding resources to other students in danger of dropping out. However, student veterans may require additional services at higher levels than other students, such as those related to counseling, accommodation, and accessibility. Institutional leaders must understand the financial costs and benefits of serving veterans and be prepared to commit to initiatives that allow campuses to handle the influx of veterans and service members and maximize the likelihood of degree attainment.

Providing institutional support for veterans and service members requires attention to individuals and to groups of veterans, including formal student organizations such as student veteran associations. In addition, support for symbolic events and activities is essential to the creation of a veteran-friendly campus, such as ceremonies and commemorations on Memorial Day, September 11, and Veterans Day, and celebrations for students, faculty, and staff who have served or are deploying. Honoring student veterans' service to the country demonstrates respect and honor that, in turn, helps them feel part of the campus community.

Role of Institutional Leaders in Policy and Organizational Development

In this chapter, institutional leaders and senior administrators are defined as individuals on college campuses who have significant decision-making authority and control of resource allocation, including presidents, vice presidents, deans, directors, and department chairs. Institutional leaders have obligations to adhere to campus missions and to serve the greater community (Lyons, 1993). They also have obligations to advance their colleges and educate students.

The decision of whether or not to develop veteran services is one that institutional leaders must approach deliberatively:

- Is there a critical mass of student veterans on campus? (Of note: this does not need to be a large number or a sizable proportion of the campus enrollment; rather, this speaks to the threshold of best meeting student veterans' needs on a case-by-case basis versus development of official resources.)
- Is there potential to grow this population?
- Are there military installations nearby, and if so, are there opportunities to collaborate with them?

- Is the state legislature generally favorable to veterans' services and willing to support new services that serve this population?
- Will a decision *not* to provide veteran-specific services negatively affect any students, the campus, or the institution's image or standing within the community or state?

Institutional leaders often approach questions like these through the lens of whether the campus can afford to support more services. The more strategic lens with which to consider these questions is whether the campus should be more veteran-friendly and build services to support these students.

Welcoming more veterans to campus means that more Post-9/11 GI Bill funding will flow to the institution because the funds follow the student. Progressive colleges consider this "found money" and reserve a portion to support the services that veterans need in order to succeed in college. It is then a "win-win" for the veteran and the institution. Improving support services within existing student or academic services to specifically target student veterans and service members is generally not a complex endeavor; often such services are easily modified, adjusted, or enhanced by redefining a department's purpose, shifting or reprioritizing personnel, adding or subtracting specific employees' duties, and collaborating between departments (Greene, 2010). Making these administrative changes will communicate enhanced priorities at the departmental and divisional levels and directly impact services to students.

College campuses should be friendly environments for all students and subgroups of students, including veterans, yet not all institutions are well suited to offer in-depth services and support. A campus, regardless of size, that generally does not attract veterans or service members does not necessarily need to design and implement a fully self-sufficient department solely to serve these students. This would not be cost effective, especially when those services might be better provided by other local colleges that have well-established operations. However, limiting services to just some campuses means that student veterans' higher education choices are more limited than nonveteran students' choices.

One solution to this dilemma is to develop collaborative approaches to share services among geographically close institutions. Such collaborations are successful in other arenas within higher education, such as the regional academic collaborative (RAC) in California with initiatives that "promote a college-going culture and increase eligibility and enrollment at post-secondary institutions" (University of California Regents,

2008). Colleges and universities in Texas are entering partnerships and collaborative relationships as well, including joint degree programs, faculty appointments, and research activities. "Partnerships exist between higher education institutions within the same and between different higher education systems. Such partnerships allow institutions to leverage existing resources to achieve greater efficiencies. Programmatic partnerships are especially important, as they increase student access to degree programs" (Texas Higher Education Coordinating Board, 2008, p. 1). Claremont University Consortium (CUC) in California enjoys particularly extensive academic and administrative collaboration with a vision that includes service "as an international exemplar of the benefits to be gained through consortial practices in higher education" (CUC, 2010).

The examples of collaboration in higher education can prompt creative exploration of ways to make more campuses veteran-friendly specifically, and more student-friendly in general, while eliminating duplicate efforts and reducing institutional overhead. Staff members at each institution that participates in a collaborative agreement need to be well trained to understand the practices and policies of the institutions involved, but such cooperation is not out of the question, and it better leverages limited resources and expertise among partner colleges and universities.

If institutional leaders' decision is to offer student veterans services solely on their own campuses, they should approach the policy decision strategically and with an eye toward their institutions' missions (Lyons, 1993). If the decision is to provide greater opportunities and services for students who are veterans or service members, best practices should be carefully considered while utilizing existing services and departments in order to institutionalize the initiative throughout campus (O'Herrin, 2011). Institutional leaders may look toward academic departments to first address the need for these services in order to engage faculty and the shared governing approach. However, sole use of this approach may not provide the best service, or integration of services, throughout campus. Alternatively, utilizing the leadership of student affairs and enrollment management to address these services can provide more streamlined and cost-effective approaches, especially when those areas are charged to work collaboratively with academic leaders and faculty, resulting in an improved campus climate for student veterans. Generally, campuses with higher numbers of student veterans have designated offices or departments, whereas campuses with fewer numbers of student veterans rely on the registrar's department to provide or coordinate services (Cook & Kim, 2009).

Securing Resources

It is a misconception that in order to develop a new service or program, additional resources and staffing must first be acquired; another option is the reallocation of resources and staffing. As such, the development of veteran services does not necessarily require additional resources and staff if it is perceived as an institutional priority and campus leaders are willing to strategize and shift resources to meet demonstrated need. However, before this happens, campus leaders should determine the basic needs for veterans and service members and whether these services can be provided by existing departments and programs. Cook and Kim (2009) explained that with regard to student veterans, there are three types of institutions: low veteran enrollment campuses have less than 1 percent student veteran enrollment, moderate veteran enrollment campuses have 1–3 percent student veteran enrollment, and high veteran enrollment campuses have more than 3 percent student veteran enrollment. Yet decisions about whether and how to provide services should not be made solely on actual numbers or percentages of students; each campus must weigh the student and community needs in light of available resources, demand, and campus culture. For example, on a very large campus with a wide variety of student services offices and functions where only 300 veterans and service members use benefits, a new department may not be needed. Alternately, a campus with 1,500 veterans and service members using benefits may more efficiently and effectively provide services through a separate department or program office that is integrated within student or enrollment services.

Cook and Kim (2009) suggested that the presence of a dedicated office or department for student veterans and service members demonstrates institutional support for this population, which fits with the natural instinct of institutional administrators to create separate services. If campus leaders perceive a need to initiate or improve veteran services, their efforts should start with redefining the scope of service areas already existing on campus. If the need is to create a larger department to primarily serve student veterans and service members, colleges may identify resources and opportunities for resources in several areas:

- *Redirection of resources.* The redirection of resources is the shifting of budget, personnel, or emphasis from one department to another.
- *A dedicated student fee.* A small flat fee or a per-credit hour fee may be charged to all students, but this may draw criticism from stakeholders that all students are paying for services being utilized by a relatively

small number of students who are themselves being funded through the Post-9/11 or earlier iteration of the GI Bill.

- *Legislative funding.* Legislative funding and student tuition are two of the larger sources of financial support for public colleges; obtaining additional state funding would require this to become a significant institutional and state-level priority and would depend on achieving the requisite legislative support.
- *Department reallocation.* Similar to the redirection of resources, through reallocation institutions can direct a department to provide specific services, or an existing department could be phased out to fund a new office with the primary purpose of serving veterans and service members.
- *Partnerships with local government offices, businesses, and the military.* These types of alliances allow for the sharing of resources and enhancement of services.
- *Gifts.* Grants and gifts in-kind from stakeholders and interested parties may come with relatively fewer restrictions on priorities or expenditures.

As with most initiatives in higher education, data demonstrate success to campus administrators and legislators, which in turn provides leverage for the acquisition of funding and resources to support service members and veterans.

Staffing

When designing services for student veterans, it is essential to avoid the belief that the individuals who serve and work with veterans must also be veterans. In the example that Cook and Kim (2009) shared of many campuses relying on registrar's departments to serve veterans, it is unlikely that the registrar (or the designated staff person) on every campus is a veteran. This is also true of student affairs personnel who are often trained to work with a wide array of students, yet most are not veterans. Furthermore, it is erroneous to believe that every person with prior military service automatically possesses the skills or dispositions to foster and maintain trusting relationships with student veterans. Although some campus personnel who work with student veterans are veterans themselves, and are eager and willing to work with this population, one of the most important needs is for the professional to have expertise in navigating higher education systems and administrative processes. Rumann and Hamrick (2009) explained that it is ideal when campus professionals who work with student veterans have some military experience, or have developed understandings of the military experience through family background, the experiences of close friends or relatives, or study in this area. Although this may help them establish credibility with student veterans and inform their work with community and government organizations, it is not enough—they must also have rich understandings of higher education and be savvy in navigating campus cultures and administrative processes.

Campus Committees and Task Forces

One of the most effective strategies to address student veterans' and service members' needs is the establishment of a campuswide committee or task force (Pembroke, 1993). The group's work should have clearly articulated directives and outcomes, and a limited time frame to accomplish deliberate and focused work. Although it is not necessary that a committee or task force be established by the president, depending on the campus culture, it may be the only way to ensure that the campus community takes seriously the focus on veteran services. It may be more effective for the vice presidents of student affairs and academic affairs to colead the group. Use of this collaborative method encourages multiple perspectives in the consideration of students' needs, existing resources, and potential courses of action.

Committees or task forces charged with determining veteran services should include an appropriate array of campus representatives, such as students, faculty, and support services staff members (Vance, Miller, & Grossman, 2010); offices that should be represented include counseling, disability services, financial aid, admissions, and academic advising. Though it is not necessary to have staff or faculty members who are veterans on the committee or task force, it is extremely important that current student veterans and service members as well as staff and faculty who are veteran-friendly be invited to participate. The committee should be chaired by the dean of students, or a comparable leader who reports directly to the senior student affairs officer and has broad authority to make change and balance institutional priorities with student needs, and who regularly deals with complex campuswide issues.

Initially, the committee or task force should be narrow in its approach. Common areas to review include admission and registration requirements and fees, credit transfer policies, financial aid, campus communication, orientation, meal plans, housing, career services, student and academic services, and campus accessibility. Acquisition of input regarding these areas is similar to the approach used to design and improve services for transfer students (Jacobs & Marling, 2011). Frequently changes that result from this type of committee work improve the campus experience for all students and not just student veterans. For example, one possible change that may result is the extension of offices' operating hours to accommodate student veterans and other students who may need to conduct their business on campus outside of traditional office hours.

Determining the "Feeling" of the Campus Environment

A key component in realizing the success of new initiatives to serve student veterans starts with the vision of institutional leaders. Although relevant data are essential in the *support* for new services on campus, achieving a veteran-friendly atmosphere contributes to the *success* of new endeavors. In determining whether a campus is veteran-friendly—regardless of whether a student veteran organization already exists—it is important to consider how the environment influences student behavior, and to stay in touch with the ways in which students perceive the campus climate, which may be different from the institutional perspective (Kinzie & Mulholland, 2008). Campus leaders should be deliberate in their efforts to reach out to students for feedback on services for veterans and service members. In particular, "management by walking around" (Peters, 2005; Peters & Waterman, 1982; *Economist*, 2008) is an effective way for administrators to gain insight on the campus climate from a variety of perspectives (Kuh, 2000; Kuh, Kinzie, Schuh, & Whitt, 2005; Kuh, Schuh, & Whitt, 1991); a lot can be learned from simply being present and visible on campus. Other approaches to gaining student input and insight include the formation of small focus groups and regular, purposeful interactions with the student government association, student veterans association, and other organizations on campus.

The following questions should guide institutional leaders in their efforts to achieve a campuswide commitment to serve student veterans and service members:

1. Are we presently serving this population?
2. In what ways are we serving this population?
3. What services exist and how are they perceived or used by the students?
4. Are programs and services meeting the needs of the students?
5. How are these programs and services being measured or assessed?
6. Are faculty and staff aware of student veterans' and service members' needs?

7. What departments can immediately improve services to meet student veterans' and service members' needs?

Campus leaders should also be committed and prepared to make practical and symbolic changes. The University of Akron, for example, moved a lounge designated for veterans from one building to another that was preferred by a majority of veterans—the lounge provided the same services in both locations, but the physical change improved overall service to veterans. These types of changes are easy ways to demonstrate that student veterans' and service members' voices are heard and to encourage continued feedback.

Members of the campus community likely have distinct viewpoints regarding a new or renewed emphasis on student veterans, yet as Katopes (2009) reminded us, we must leave behind the old labels and prejudices and look at what the new veteran brings to the classroom. Student veterans and service members comprise one of many subgroups of students on college campuses that faculty and administrators must accommodate and serve (Brown & Gross, 2011). Institutional leaders should consult with faculty and staff to determine the stress points or changes anticipated as the presence of student veterans on campus increases. Brown and Gross explained that some people erroneously believe that all student veterans are combat veterans who require unique, complex, and extended support. Other community members knowingly or unknowingly project their disagreement with federal actions or foreign policy or their opinions about war-related topics onto student veterans. Some colleges and universities do not host military recruiters on their campuses due to philosophical objections on the part of faculty, staff, and students, which in turn may create environments that have a negative impact on the experiences of student veterans returning home and those who are anticipating deployment.

Campus Structures and Coordination of Services

Campuses throughout the United States vary distinctly in mission and support of the student veteran. As an institutional leader, identifying whether to centrally coordinate veteran services or decentralize services throughout multiple offices and departments is critical to the success of the operation. In addition, the organizational framework and structure of services for student veterans and service members, and related reporting lines, have an impact on the general perception and function of the services, as well as how effectively the resources may or may not be used.

Simply put, if oversight of and responsibility for student veteran services are assigned to a high-status position on campus, the function will have more clout.

Vance and Miller (2009) found that many student veterans prefer to attend community colleges near military installations as they are apt to provide the services that foster their success. However, it should not be assumed that all campuses located close to military installations are veteran-friendly. Of utmost importance for student veterans, according to Vance and Miller, is that they desire connections to other veterans, smooth transitions to higher education, efficient coordination of services, elimination of red tape, and support from family and faculty. Many colleges and universities that are not in close proximity to military installations embrace student veterans and service members and offer educational opportunities in various formats in order to provide access for this population. The University of Minnesota, for example, has built a strong online program as well as administrative processes that make it easy for veterans to apply for admission and transfer earned credits. *G.I. Jobs* (a magazine for military personnel in transition) named American University a "Veteran Friendly School for 2011" as a result of its collaborative, cross-campus "Liaison Network" that enhances communication and services to assist returning student veterans (Unger, 2010).

Several publications and agencies have engaged in efforts to identify military-friendly and veteran-friendly colleges and universities. The web site http://www.VeteransBenefitsGIBill.com (2010) assessed the following factors to produce its top-25 list of military-friendly campuses:

- Access to financial aid programs, including military tuition assistance
- Support of education benefits for military spouses and dependents
- Participation in the Post-9/11 GI Bill's Yellow Ribbon Program [a program that extends benefits of the GI Bill]
- Availability of military-friendly distance learning and online degree programs
- Ease of acquiring military student scholarships, discounts, and grants
- Participation in the MyCAA program [military spouse career advancement account]
- Proximity to a military installation
- Academic accreditation

The list of 25 schools includes an array of institutional types, such as public, private, proprietary, and online-only.

Several campuses throughout the United States have developed stand-alone departments, or "one-stop" locations, to serve student veterans. Organizationally, these centers are often in the student services areas of campus and focus on enrollment, articulation, transfer of credit, and support. Administratively, these centers may be the costliest support systems available for student veterans because they involve a designated infrastructure, unshared personnel, and annual operating resources. Despite the challenges in creating and supporting one-stop centers, there are some distinct advantages in that they (a) are places where student veterans may gather, (b) create increased departmental synergy, (c) result in potentially deeper understanding of student needs on the part of staff members, (d) provide deliberate opportunities for community members to advocate on behalf of student veterans, and (e) result in greater continuity of services, including the staff members who work with and know the student veteran and service member community.

Campuses may use several different approaches to serve student veterans and service members. Some, such as the University of South Florida and the University of Kansas, tout centralized models to serve veterans (as described on their web sites, which are included in the list of resources at the end of this chapter, as are other programs services referred throughout the chapter). Such programs may utilize liaisons, or they may fall under the purview of senior administrators (student affairs at both example institutions) who provide oversight for several service departments. Other campuses opt to combine veteran services with other population services. Kent State University combines veteran services with adult services. The University of Akron utilizes several offices, such as the registrar and student life, in combination with a steering committee to address student veterans' needs. Pressures to downsize and cut back the scope of services in the face of budget cuts prompt many institutions to "make do" with existing resources by expanding the scope of operations and combining responsibilities. In these cases, use of collective community approaches to address students' needs can be successful. However, they can require more time and more cooperation and collaboration than other approaches in that representatives across the entire campus community are fully charged with identifying needs and creating approaches to address those needs, versus an administrative top-down approach in which such efforts are incorporated into the fabric of daily institutional operations.

The collaborative, community approach has been successful at The University of Akron. At the urging of two deans, one of whom was a military officer before becoming a faculty member, the provost appointed a Veterans Steering Committee to address the university's approach to handling the needs of student veterans and service members. This group worked (and continues to work) to develop support systems for veterans, service members, and students who are deployed in order to guide them in their transitions into and out of the university (sometimes multiple times) and to assist with general services, socialization, and other veteran-related matters. The committee is comprised of faculty, students, and staff who care about student veterans, and some members are veterans themselves. The group meets regularly and developed a set of goals to guide its work (presented here as a list for clarity; the asterisks indicate items that are important for any college or university seeking to start or improve services for student veterans):

1. Attracting and retaining veterans*
2. Increasing the acceptance of [College Level Examination Program] CLEP credit and working with the colleges across campus to increase transfer for veterans*
3. Supporting and advancing the creation of a student veteran organization within the student government
4. Advocating for individualized advisement for student veterans*
5. Submitting an external national grant application to obtain funding for a coordinator position
6. Improving coordination of services for student veterans *
7. Establishing an external advisory board
8. Establishing The University of Akron as the university of choice for the education of veterans,
9. Exploring opportunities for new educational programming targeted at student veterans
10. Supporting women in the military*
11. Providing training for faculty and staff regarding special issues related to veteran student success (such as suicide prevention programming)*
12. Communicating and marketing veteran related initiatives and services*
13. Promoting establishment of a peer mentoring program*
14. Building relationships with external partners for support and funding*
15. Advancing the university programming for student veterans with Ohio Board of Regents and the university Board of Trustees

16. Remodeling space for a new Veteran-Student Lounge, and
17. Promoting and participating in a campuswide Veterans Day Recognition/Memorial (Belsky & Wineman, 2011)

Regardless of the ways in which colleges and universities organize efforts to meet the needs of student veterans and service members, the asterisked items above are—in our judgment—the baseline critical components of efforts in this arena. Furthermore, institutions should regularly evaluate services and programs for veterans in order to understand which areas are strong and where additional resources are needed. The University of Akron model showcases how the interests and concerns of a small number of very committed faculty, administrators, and staff can result in a campus commitment to student veterans and service members, and the development of services that meet their needs. These types of grassroots efforts garner continual community interest and support.

The institutional-level perspective on serving students may cause higher education professionals to overlook broader system-based approaches that could be beneficial. The State of Minnesota provides a system approach to the provisions and improvement of student veteran services. The Minnesota State Colleges and Universities System has a Web presence dedicated to providing information about higher education in Minnesota for military service members and veterans (Minnesota State Colleges and Universities, 2011). This comprehensive source of information covers topics that range from planning for college to military transfer credit, military education benefits, career and life planning, military-friendly policies, military student bill of rights, and online learning opportunities. Western Michigan University (WMU) offers a similar approach to meeting the unique needs of student veterans and service members in that it coordinates student services from providers across campus and from the local community. The philosophies and practices of the WMU administration, faculty, and staff resulted in WMU's recognition as a "Military Friendly Institution" (Moon & Schma, 2011).

WMU, the campuses in the Minnesota State Colleges and Universities System, and many others throughout the United States are identified as "Beyond the Yellow Ribbon" (BTYR) institutions for their work with student veterans. BTYR "is a comprehensive program that creates awareness for the purpose of connecting Servicemembers and their families with community support, training, services and resources" (BTYR, 2011). Although decisions about whether or not to pursue the BTYR designation or recognition as military-friendly or veteran-friendly campus are unique to each institution, these indicators enhance institutional visibility and reputation among veterans and military personnel.

Institutional Leaders as Advocates for Veterans and Service members

Institutional leaders can be outstanding advocates for veterans and service members (Vance, Miller, & Grossman, 2010). When their messages are combined with those of civic and military leaders, the outcome can be powerful, inspiring, and effective. Virtually every day, campus presidents speak to stakeholders, civic groups, government agencies, media outlets, and families throughout their respective communities. Using these venues to bring attention to the challenges faced by student veterans and service members, and to highlight related initiatives, can help educate the campus and the extended community about the student veteran experience and position the campus as a leader in this area.

Becoming Knowledgeable and Effective Spokespersons

Institutional leaders are well versed in discussing policies, programs, and services on their campuses, and some are experts at addressing these topics on national and international stages. This is emphasized by the fact that as institutional leaders ascend to their positions, they often retain their discipline-specific involvement and expertise (Kuh, Kinzie, Schuh, & Whitt, 2005; Kuh, Schuh, & Whitt, 1991). College and university leaders' training and experience provide insights about the macro-level issues that affect their campuses. Because attention to student veteran services and related concerns is a relatively new (or renewed) subject of campus dialogue, some institutional leaders may not believe that they have the knowledge to articulate relevant information. However, it is not challenging or cumbersome for leaders to become knowledgeable spokespersons and advocates for student veterans in that it is an extension of their everyday work. According to Cook and Kim (2009), the top two changes considered by institutions seeking to become veteran-friendly are professional development opportunities for campus community members who interact with and serve student veterans and the exploration of state and federal funding to support campus programs. Information contained in this handbook and in the chapter reference and resource lists provide numerous resources to help prepare college educators for their work with student veterans.

Large numbers of campus administrators and faculty members probably do not have prior military experience (Rumann & Hamrick, 2009). However, campuses are likely home to some faculty or staff who serve or have served in the military. These individuals can lend their credibility to an institution's message about supporting student veterans and service members. Their involvement also helps to demystify stereotypes about military members and their experiences, including beliefs such as veterans who become leaders are rigid, veterans are militaristic, and all veterans have served in combat (Massad, 2010; National Public Radio, 2007). Finally, however, having prior military experience does not necessarily ensure that the message conveyed is more credible. Despite the benefits of incorporating community members with military experience into campuswide efforts to support student veterans, attention must be paid to the fact that military experiences vary greatly by era, and today's student veterans and service members have likely had very different experiences from those of older veterans on campus. However, there remains a sense of community and understanding among all veterans, and veterans are a source of support and acceptance for other veterans regardless of background, experience, or age.

In educating themselves about student veterans' and service members' experiences, needs, and challenges, institutional leaders should consider the following:

- Do what all academics do when underprepared: read more about the subject and become proficient. The Internet is filled with articles about service members' experiences, and more scholarly works on this topic are beginning to emerge.
- Meet with student veterans on campus to learn about their issues and concerns.
- Meet with faculty and staff from across campus—the people who engage with student veterans and service members on a daily basis in a variety of settings—to glean their insights and solicit ideas for ways to improve services for these students.
- Attend professional development opportunities to learn from and with colleagues in similar roles about how to advocate for and support student veterans.
- Finally, institutional leaders with prior military experience can personalize these efforts to communicate why they care about today's veterans and their success in higher education.

There are a few targeted professional development opportunities available to higher education professionals who work with student veterans and service members or who want to learn how to be better advocates for them. The University of Louisville hosts the annual Veterans Symposium for Higher Education in collaboration with the Servicemembers Opportunity Colleges (SOC). The program was established in 2009 to bring together faculty and staff from campuses throughout the United States to openly discuss best practices and explore ways to improve services and campus cultures in order to better serve student veterans. This symposium offers a range of program offerings, networking opportunities, and access to professionals and scholars from a variety of institutions and organizations who are committed to serving veterans and service members. Also, Purdue University's Military Family Research Institute (MFRI) hosts an annual meeting of Operation Diploma, an initiative that works with colleges, universities, and student veterans organizations throughout Indiana to "make campuses more 'veteran friendly'" and assist "students in their pursuit of their higher education goals" (MFRI, n.d., para. 4). The conference attracts a broad audience; speakers, presenters, and attendees include higher education professionals, government officials, and others who work with student veterans and related services throughout the United States.

Key Strategic Outreach and Collaborative Efforts

Faculty, staff, and students on college campuses are often engaged in civic organizations, professional associations, school districts, religious and community groups, social outlets, and volunteer programs. Each of these avenues of engagement provides opportunities to network and develop relationships with other community leaders (O'Herrin, 2011). Furthermore, these activities may include engagement with family members of student veterans, parents of service members, and citizens with military experience, all of whom may be willing to assist or support student veterans and service members if asked. In addition, many institutional leaders' involvement with local organizations provides opportunities for high-profile work related to the establishment and expansion of networks that benefit the campus, support of community projects, and personalization of the college environment. Many of the local chapters of leadership and service organizations with which senior institutional leaders affiliate, such as Lions Clubs International, Rotary International, and Kiwanis International, count among their members community leaders with prior military experience who are knowledgeable and willing to advocate locally for support of veterans and service members.

Public colleges and strategic private campuses also cultivate personalized working relationships with elected officials and representatives of governmental agencies. Institutional leaders have many opportunities to draft reports, spearhead statewide or local initiatives, and provide information or analyses on issues affecting citizens within the community—including student veterans and service members. Collaborating with key legislators and stakeholders and demonstrating the interests, efforts, and successes achieved by campuses in better supporting student veterans, also can engender external support beyond the campus and local community.

Conclusion

Institutional leaders are in a unique position to make a difference in the way institutions address student veterans' needs and concerns. Not only is there a financial incentive to accommodate student veterans at colleges and universities, but there is also an institutional responsibility to serve those students who have served our country. Higher education administrators can use their influence and positions of power to facilitate campus policies, programs, and initiatives that intentionally create a campus climate that welcomes student veterans and supports their successful academic pursuits.

Resources

Beyond the Yellow Ribbon
http://www.btyr.org/

GI Jobs
http://www.gijobs.com/

Kent State University Center for Adult and Veteran Services
http://www.kent.edu/veterans/index.cfm

Military Family Research Institute at Purdue University
http://www.cfs.purdue.edu/mfri/

Minnesota State Colleges and Universities, Resources for Military Members and Veterans
http://www.mnscu.edu/military/index.html

Servicemembers Opportunity Colleges
http://www.soc.aascu.org/

University of Akron Military Services Center
http://www.uakron.edu/veterans/index.dot

University of Kansas Office of Veterans Services
http://www.registrar.ku.edu/veterans/

University of Minnesota Veterans Services
http://onestop.umn.edu/veterans/

University of South Florida Veterans Services
http://www.veterans.usf.edu/

VeteransBenefitsGIBill.com
http://www.veteransbenefitsgibill.com/

Veteran Symposium for Higher Education, University of Louisville
http://stuaff.org/veterans/

References

Baechtold, M., & De Sawal, D. M. (2009). Meeting the needs of women veterans. *New Directions for Higher Education, 126*, 35–43.

Belsky, M., & Wineman, M. (2011). *Veteran's steering committee annual report academic year 2010–2011*. Akron, OH: University of Akron.

Beyond the Yellow Ribbon (BYTR). (2011). [web site]. Retrieved from http://www.btyr.org/home

Brown, P. A., & Gross, C. (2011). Serving those who have served: Managing veteran and military student best practices. *The Journal of Continuing Higher Education, 59*, 45–49.

Claremont University Consortium. (2010). *Claremont University Consortium mission and values*. Retrieved from http://www.cuc.claremont.edu/aboutcuc/mission.asp

Cook, B. J., & Kim, Y. (2009). *From soldier to student: Easing the transition of service members on campus*. Washington, DC: American Council on Education.

Economist. (2008, September 8). Management by walking around. Retrieved from http://www.economist.com/node/12075015

Greene, D. M. (2010, February 9). Collaborative effort ferries student veterans through launch of new GI Bill. *University of Michigan Record Update*. Retrieved from http://www.ur.umich.edu/update/archives/100209/veterans

Hughes, T. (2011, April 12). Vets go from combat to campus. *USA Today*. Retrieved from http://www.usatoday.com/news/education/2011–04–11-college-vets_N.htm

Iraq and Afghanistan Veterans of America. (2011). *The new G.I. Bill*. Retrieved from http://newgibill.org/post_911_gi_bill

Jacobs, B. C., & Marling, J. L. (2011). Transfer students: How SSAOs can ease the transition process. *Leadership Exchange, 8*(4), 10–15.

Katopes, P. (2009). Veterans returning to college aren't victims, they're assets. *Community College Week, 21*(15), 4–5.

Kinzie, J., & Mulholland, S. (2008). Transforming physical spaces into inclusive multicultural learning environments. In S. R. Harper (Ed.), *Creating inclusive campus environments for cross-cultural learning and student engagement.* Washington, DC: NASPA.

Kuh, G. D. (2000). Understanding campus environments. In M. Barr & M. Desler (Eds.), *The handbook of student affairs administration* (2nd ed., pp. 50–72). San Francisco: Jossey-Bass.

Kuh, G. D., Kinzie, J., Schuh, J. H., & Whitt, E. J. (2005). *Student success in college: Creating conditions that matter.* San Francisco: Jossey-Bass.

Kuh, G. D., Schuh, J. H., & Whitt, E. J. (1991). *Involving colleges: Successful approaches to fostering student learning and development outside the classroom.* San Francisco: Jossey-Bass.

Lyons, J. W. (1993). The importance of institutional mission. In M. Barr, & M. Desler (Eds.), *The handbook of student affairs administration* (2nd ed., pp. 3–15). San Francisco: Jossey-Bass.

Massad, J. (2010, August 2). HR firm helps veterans enter into new careers. *Atlanta Business Chronicle.* Retrieved from http://www.bizjournals.com/atlanta/stories/2010/08/02/focus2.html?t=printable

McSweeney, P. (2009). *Saving and paying for college: Back to school.* Retrieved from http://www.whitehouse.gov/blog/Saving-and-Paying-for-College-Back-to-School

Military Family Research Institute. (n.d.). Inside MFRI. [web site]. Retrieved from http://www.cfs.purdue.edu/mfri/public/about/inside-mfri.aspx

Minnesota State Colleges and Universities. (2011). *Resources for veterans and service members.* Retrieved from http://www.mnscu.edu/military/index.html

Moon, T. L., & Schma, G. A. (2011). A proactive approach to serving military and veteran students. *New Directions for Higher Education, 153,* 53–60.

National Public Radio (Producer). (2007, December 6). *Most soldiers return from war just fine* [radio broadcast]. Retrieved from http://www.npr.org/templates/story/story.php?storyId=16981183

O'Herrin, E. (2011). Enhancing veteran success in higher education. *Peer Review, 13*(1), 15–18.

Pembroke, W. J. (1993). Institutional governance and the role of student affairs. In M. Barr & M. Desler (Eds.), *The handbook of student affairs administration* (2nd ed., pp. 16–29). San Francisco: Jossey-Bass.

Peters, T. (2005). MBWA after all these years. Retrieved from http://www.tompeters.com/dispatches/008106.php

Peters, T., & Waterman, R. (1982). *In search of excellence.* New York: Warner Books.

Rumann, C. B., & Hamrick, F. A. (2009). Supporting student veterans in transition. *New Directions for Student Services, 126,* 25–34.

Texas Higher Education Coordinating Board. (2008). *Joint partnerships among Texas institutions of higher education.* Austin: Author. Retrieved from http://www.thecb.state.tx.us/GeneralPubs/Agenda/AG2008_10/VIH/VI%20H%20Report%20on%20Joint%20Partnerships%209%2030%2008.pdf

Unger, M. (2010, August 16). AU named one of America's most veteran friendly colleges. *American Today.* Washington, DC: American University. Retrieved from http://www.american.edu/americantoday/campus-news/20100816military-friendly-school.cfm

University of California Regents. (2008) *Regional academic collaboratives.* Oakland: Author. Retrieved from http://www.ucop.edu/rac/

Vance, M. L., & Miller, W. K. (2009). Serving wounded warriors: Current practices in postsecondary education. *Journal of Postsecondary Education & Disability, 22*(1), 18–35.

Vance, M. L., Miller, W. K., & Grossman, P. (2010). What you need to know about 21st century college military veterans. *Leadership Exchange, 8*(3), 11–15.

VeteransBenefitsGI Bill.com. (2010). Top 25 military-friendly colleges [web site]. Retrieved from http://www.veteransbenefitsgibill.com/2010/12/15/top-25-military-colleges-for-2011/

VIGNETTE

Nicholas J. Osborne

Veterans Support Services, University of Illinois at Urbana-Champaign

I'm an OIF veteran who served as a law enforcement and intelligence officer in the U.S. Coast Guard. I was assigned to a joint forces intelligence unit and completed a 14-month deployment to the Middle East in 2006–2007. Upon my return to the United States, I left the military and worked as a readjustment counselor with the Department of Veterans Affairs. I hold a doctorate in Educational Leadership and Administration from the University of California-Davis.

I was hired at the University of Illinois at Urbana-Champaign (UIUC) in January 2011 as a result of the Illinois Higher Education Veterans Service Act. My current position is assistant dean of students and director of Veterans Support Services. Approximately 40 percent of my position is devoted to working exclusively with veterans, including active duty, Reserve, and National Guard members, and dependents. I serve as the "neutral zone" or bridge that links incoming veterans to various campus and community-based resources, and I'm typically the first point of contact during their transitions. Additionally, a large part of my job is to enhance visibility of veterans' issues within the campus and local community and to provide professional development training to staff and faculty.

Shortly after being hired, I conducted several focus groups with various segments of the student veteran population, which provided opportunities for veterans to candidly share their experiences transitioning to the university. Among other topics, there was consensus that being identified as a "veteran" made students somewhat vulnerable to inaccurate and exaggerated assumptions about their service. This point was reinforced during several initial professional development workshops I facilitated for faculty and staff, thus prompting me to begin each training with consideration of the questions "How do I view veterans?" and "What are my biases?"

In addition to my work assisting veterans and service members to access the information and services they need to enroll and persist, I decided that we needed to address widespread misconceptions of military culture and minimize the likelihood of viewing student veterans solely through a lens that emphasizes trauma. Several students and I spearheaded a campuswide initiative to raise awareness of veterans' issues. Throughout the past year we've hosted multiple student veteran discussion panels. The panels, often in collaboration with student affairs units, such as the Women's Resource Center, provide opportunities for veterans to "tell their stories" and field questions from faculty, staff, and peers. In addition, faculty members contacted my office to request that student veterans serve as guest speakers in their classrooms, and members of the local media started to include veterans' experiences in their newspaper columns. One large newspaper even provided a seven-week series on veterans' issues; a different veteran was highlighted each week. As visibility increased on campus, we eventually developed and hosted a national diversity conference that focused on veterans' issues in higher education. This experience demonstrated the necessity of creating a context through collaboration rather than a series of isolated events that came exclusively from the "veterans' office."

To more effectively serve our veterans, we must, as educators, reevaluate our biases and misconceptions about military culture and provide students with venues to share their personal narratives. The impending surge of student veterans promises not only increased demands on support services, but also an increased supply of hard-earned and stress-tested talent. In short, these students possess a unique maturity and capability that enhances diversity as well as our institutional missions to cultivate future leaders.

CHAPTER TWELVE

PROMOTING ORGANIZATIONAL CHANGE TO CREATE A VETERAN-FRIENDLY CAMPUS: A CASE STUDY

Jan Arminio and Tomoko Kudo Grabosky

The Council for the Advancement of Standards in Higher Education (CAS) describes "the purpose of Veterans and Military Programs and Services (VMPS) is to provide support for student veterans, military family members, and family member receiving veterans' benefits through the GI Bill" (CAS, 2010, p. 1). Although CAS specifically refers to VMPS, we believe the lynchpin of this support is a systematic and comprehensive approach involving the entire campus. Hence, this chapter focuses on the whole campus climate. This is because of the numerous issues that student veterans and active duty students face as they transition from service member to student (Zinger & Cohen, 2010). These issues could include student veterans and active duty students feeling different from the majority of students around them, functioning in less structured environments, losing their sense of identity, taking care of health and emotional concerns, coping with disabilities, being older, facing discrimination, and being subjected to insensitive comments (Cook & Kim, 2009; DiRamio, Ackerman, & Mitchell, 2008; Zinger & Cohen, 2010).

Addressing these climate issues requires the commitment of a cross-campus comprehensive approach to create processes that not only support these students, but also allow them to graduate at rates at least on par with their peers. Admissions, registration, billing, counseling, advising, and career exploration are such processes. Ethos that ground these processes include well-informed and caring campus members, flexible procedures that accommodate deploying and reenrolling students, and a willingness to alter processes to better serve student veterans and active duty students. For example, admissions and advising personnel must be aware of the relative transferability of academic credits from military service. Deploying students must be able to withdraw or enroll when last-minute changes in deployment schedules occur. Payment schedules must accommodate delays that are associated with disbursements of federal aid. Counseling centers should offer support groups for student veterans as well as significant others and family members of deployed military service members. Furthermore, advisors should work with faculty members and academic programs to advocate for the acceptance of credits for appropriate military experience and education, and they must work with incoming students who may have to miss a summer orientation or advising program due to National Guard or Reserve training. An ad hoc or episodic approach might be able to address scattered instances, but it cannot adequately address larger, underlying cross-campus issues pertinent to ensuring the academic success of student veterans and active duty military students.

Hiring trained staff members to assist veterans was common on college and university campuses decades ago, but on many campuses those positions were eliminated as the numbers of enrolled veterans and service members declined. Moreover, because "contemporary administrators and faculty members are less likely than earlier generations to have personally experienced military or wartime service" (Rumann & Hamrick, 2009, p. 25), and due to the tightening of resources dedicated to public institutions, creating a veteran-friendly campus that effectively serves the growing numbers of student veterans, active duty military personnel, and their families ultimately involves organizational change. In this chapter we present an advocacy model useful in guiding organizational change to create a veteran-friendly campus "where programs and people are in place to assist with the transitions between college and the military" (Ackerman, DiRamio, & Garza Mitchell, 2009, p. 10). This model is promoted by the American Counseling Association (ACA), and its purpose is to guide advocates in transforming organizations so that barriers to personal growth can be eliminated. Just as most campuses have enacted means to better serve diverse student populations with respect to race, ethnicity, gender, sexual orientation, and gender identity, we believe that student veterans, active duty military students, and their families present another multifaceted culture that campuses should genuinely welcome and serve. In this chapter, we discuss this model and demonstrate its applicability through a case study. Finally, we suggest assessment strategies for determining the outcome of such changes.

ACA Advocacy Competencies

The set of ACA Advocacy Competencies (Lewis, Arnold, House, & Toporek, 2002) was developed in response to a growing need for counselors to take advocacy roles in order to effectively address contextual barriers underlying client problems. Toporek and Liu (2001) defined advocacy as "action taken by counseling professionals to facilitate removal of external and institutional barriers to clients' well-being" (p. 387). The goals of advocacy are twofold: (a) to increase a client's sense of personal power, and (b) to foster environmental changes that reflect greater responsiveness to a client's personal needs (Lewis, Lewis, Daniels, & D'Andrea, 1998). Consistent with these definitions and goals, the ACA Advocacy Competency model provides a practical guide for counselors to implement effective and ethical advocacy actions.

Although developed primarily for counselors, this framework can also guide student affairs practitioners and staff members who serve as advocates for students. The model helps student affairs educators and other higher education professionals determine which kinds of advocacy interventions are most effective, which situations require which types of advocacy approaches, and which skills, knowledge, and strategies are necessary to successfully implement advocacy actions to create optimum learning environments for students from diverse backgrounds.

In essence, the model is a culture clash model. Those implementing the model attempt to create and serve as a bridge between two cultures—in this case, military and higher education cultures. The advocate serves as a bicultural liaison interpreting the needs of one cultural group to the predominate culture and interpreting values of each group to the other, which promotes mutual learning. The model empowers those "in the minority" with successfully navigating the educational environment while not forgetting or foregoing the self. This is particularly important for students in the National Guard and the Reserves who constantly traverse the bridge from student to service member, from independence to structure to independence, from an environment of ideas to one of concrete tasks, and from a language of musters, duties, office calls, and briefings, to a language of classes, optional involvements, meetings, and workshops.

FIGURE 12.1. ACA ADVOCACY COMPETENCIES MODEL.

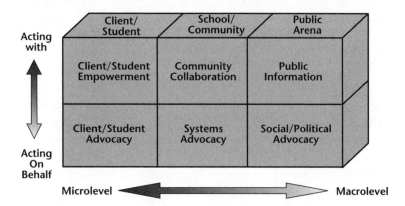

Source: Reprinted from Lewis, Arnold, House, & Toporek, 2002, p. 1. The American Counseling Association. Reprinted with permission. No further reproduction authorized without written permission from the American Counseling Association.

The ACA Advocacy Competency model (Figure 12.1) includes three levels of advocacy: client/student, school/community, and public arenas. Each level of advocacy is divided into two domains according to the degree of the client's involvement, whether advocacy work is *acting with* or *acting on behalf of* a client/student. Consequently, the model consists of six different types of advocacy: client/student empowerment, client/student advocacy, community collaboration, systems advocacy, public information, and social/political advocacy.

A brief overview of each advocacy level and associated competency domains is provided in the following sections. For the purpose of this article, "practitioner" and "student" are used to replace "counselor" and "client" to make it more appropriate for general work with student veterans, active duty military personnel, or their families.

Student Advocacy

Student advocacy takes place at the micro level, focusing on the individual student. The advocacy domains emphasized at this level are student *empowerment* and student *advocacy*. At this level, practitioners become aware of socio-cultural-political issues that negatively affect students' development. Therefore, practitioners utilize empowering strategies to help students understand how contextual issues affect their college experiences and develop skills to advocate for themselves. In addition, practitioners also act as advocates by developing strategies to remove environmental barriers that students face.

School/Community Advocacy

School/community advocacy is focused on systemic and organizational changes. This level of advocacy domain includes *community collaboration* and *systems advocacy*. To implement community collaboration, practitioners become allies to groups or organizations that represent the student in order to resolve problems together. Practitioners use their expertise to collaboratively confront systemic/organizational problems. In addition, apart from the community collaborations, practitioners also take leadership roles in establishing effective strategies and marshaling compelling evidence to advocate for system changes. At this level of advocacy, practitioners conduct environmental assessment through data and systems analysis while collaborating with other stakeholders to create visions for change.

Public Arena Advocacy

Public arena advocacy occurs at the macro level, targeting the general public and society at large. This level of advocacy domain emphasizes *public information* and *social/political advocacy*. To raise public awareness, practitioners, student groups, and the community work together to emphasize macro-systemic issues affecting human rights. The main task in this advocacy is the development of communication strategies on a large scale through the use of media or campaigns. Social/political advocacy is employed when practitioners become aware of a pattern of systemic injustice and oppression, and seek to address issues or advocate for changes at policy or legislative levels.

As described earlier, this model encourages practitioners to initiate interdisciplinary collaboration, confront systemic oppression, maximize multicultural competencies, and work closely with students or community members to establish and achieve advocacy goals (Toporek, Lewis, & Crethar, 2009). Also, this framework guides practitioners to consider and engage in multiple levels of advocacy (Ratts & Hutchins, 2009). The multiple levels of advocacy presented in this model are especially helpful in higher education because they encompass a diverse scope of professional practice and specializations. For instance, senior administrators can draw upon competencies for school/community-level advocacy as they work principally with systems and organizations, whereas practitioners who work directly with students can benefit from student/client-level advocacy. In all respects, this model describes a variety of skills and avenues to implement advocacy work on college campuses.

Case Study

Sheraton State University (SSU) is a comprehensive four-year public institution located in a state with a large veteran population. Chris, a counselor in the University Counseling Center, received a consultation service request from a faculty member who is the spouse of a deployed service member. Because of the professor's familiarity and experience with the military, she has been offering support to student veterans as well as to families and partners of veterans and military service members who are being deployed. Due to the increasing needs and possible mental health issues involved in these cases, the professor became overwhelmed and felt that she could not adequately address these concerns. Therefore, she requested that the counseling center provide additional support to this population. As a result of meeting with this professor, Chris decided she needed to learn more about the university's efforts to address the issues raised by the faculty member.

Upon investigating the university's support services, Chris learned that there were no dedicated services available for the student veteran and service member population on campus. The university did not have a full-time staff person to coordinate services for veterans and active duty military personnel. SSU employs a school certifying official, but many student veterans still express uncertainty about available benefits, application procedures, and their benefit statuses. Chris also discovered that some first-year students serving in the military's reserve component missed summer orientation programs because of schedule conflicts with their annual training duties; consequently, they missed the opportunity to schedule courses in advance and meet with their academic advisors.

In conversations with enrolled students, Chris subsequently discovered that some of their peers on reserve status had dropped courses from their schedules because they could not make up class sessions they had missed to participate in monthly training. Additionally, Chris learned that many student veterans did not feel part of the campus community and had trouble relating to civilian students—some of whom had posed inappropriate questions to veterans and service members, such as ''How many people did you kill?'' In classrooms, they felt uncomfortable when professors or students made critical statements about the military and its missions. In some of their classes, faculty members had raised concerns about veterans' mental health and the high prevalence of posttraumatic stress disorder (PTSD) among contemporary veterans.

Given this situation, Chris consulted the ACA Advocacy Competency model to determine effective ways to address these problems. Because an important aspect of all counselors' responsibilities at the University Counseling Center is outreach (each counselor dedicates approximately one day a week to outreach), Chris chose to focus her outreach on the school/community level of advocacy to collaborate with the student veterans community and to facilitate system advocacy on behalf of student veterans. Chris's supervisor was concerned that her advocacy might not allow sufficient time for her other duties, but Chris emphasized that student veterans and active duty military students merited attention, services, and outreach—as had been the case for international students, students of color, women, and other student populations. Her supervisor offered his cautious support.

In the following sections, an in-depth look at the counselor's advocacy work is described, highlighting the seven ACA Advocacy Competencies within community collaboration and system advocacy as shown in Table 12.1.

Community Collaboration Competencies

Identify environmental factors that impinge upon students' development. The environmental factors underlying student veterans' difficulties were interpreted as a clash between two institutional cultures—military and civilian/academic—each of which has distinct values and features. Institutions create unique or characteristic cultural practices. For instance, military cultural values emphasize the importance of structure, rules, orders, and hierarchical relationships to accomplish a mission, whereas academic culture values individual freedom, critical thinking, and equal relationships to cultivate creative ideas and human development. Service members are trained to survive in dangerous, chaotic, and mistrustful environments; college students live in predominantly safe and orderly environments ideally built on mutual trust. As one student veteran told Chris, ''In the Navy I was told even when to pick up my dry cleaning; here I am only told when to go to class.''

Unlike civilian students, important aspects of student veterans' lives are closely overseen and managed by the institutional practices of the VA

TABLE 12.1. THE LIST OF ACA ADVOCACY COMPETENCIES FOR COMMUNITY COLLABORATION AND SYSTEM ADVOCACY.

Advocacy Domain →	Community Collaboration *Acting with*	Systems Advocacy *Acting on Behalf*
Advocacy Competencies	1. Provide an opportunity for community members to identify environmental factors that impinge on students' development	1. Identify environmental factors impinging on students' development
	2. Alert community or school groups with common concerns related to the issue	2. Provide data to show the urgency for change
	3. Develop alliances with groups working for change	3. Develop a vision to guide change in collaboration with other stakeholders
	4. Use effective listening skills to gain understanding of the group's goals	4. Analyze the sources of political power and social influence within the system
	5. Identify the strengths and resources that the group members bring to the process of systemic change	5. Develop a step-by-step plan for implementing the change process
	6. Communicate recognition of and respect for these strengths and resources	6. Develop a plan for dealing with probable responses to change
	7. Identify and offer the skills that the practitioner can bring to the collaborations	7. Recognize and deal with resistance

Source: Modified from Lewis, Arnold, House, & Toporek, 2002.

as well as the U.S. Armed Forces and Department of Defense, in the case of tuition assistance programs. From the cultural clash perspective, the variety of problems that student veterans experience on this campus stems from cultural oppression as the university asserts its academic cultural worldview without considering the students' military cultural backgrounds. Advocacy can surface and address the cultural oppression that is manifested in institutional practices, policies, social, and academic environments as well as the stereotypes, biases, and attitudes of individuals on campus that hold them. The goal of advocacy is to facilitate the cultural transition of student veterans through recognizing and respecting their cultures and experiences.

Alert community or school groups with common concerns related to the issue. With the recognition of these contextual barriers to student veterans' academic success, Chris began communicating the importance for the university to better support student veterans' transitions from the military culture to an academic culture at her own department meetings as well as divisionwide meetings. These discussions presented Chris with the opportunity to hear other professionals' perspectives, learn about barriers to their own practice in providing services to this population, and discover ideas for directions and resources for improvement. For instance, some professionals in the division were unaware of the unique challenges these students faced in their college experiences. Others recognized the needs, but did not feel that they had adequate resources, training, or time to provide additional services specific to the student veteran population. There were also differences of opinion about who should take a leadership role in creating a veteran-friendly campus. For example, some student affairs colleagues believed that academic affairs—as the overseer of retention efforts—should lead this initiative, but many faculty members with whom Chris spoke felt it should be a student affairs initiative. Sadly, a number of educators and students believed that the university was interested in increasing the enrollment of student veterans for financial reasons only and did not expect to receive much in terms of support or resources.

Develop alliances with groups working for change. With increased knowledge of those perspectives and barriers, Chris began identifying individuals and organizations with whom to form alliances for the purpose of dismantling cultural barriers to student veterans' success. Chris contacted the president of the Sheraton Student Veteran Association (SSVA) and offered to work collaboratively with this student group to identify ways to make the campus more veteran-friendly. In addition, Chris contacted a local Veterans Center as well as the National Guard Family Support Program to develop and provide support programs to student veterans as well as to military families and significant others on campus.

Use effective listening skills to gain understanding of the group's goals. To facilitate the process of change through collaboration, Chris focused on developing strong and cohesive relationships, especially with SSVA members. She knew that it would take time to earn the students' trust because she was a civilian with limited exposure to and knowledge of the military, so she actively participated in the student group meetings, assisted with their projects, and communicated with individual SSVA members. This gave Chris exposure to and appreciation for the strong influence of aspects of military culture on student veterans' lives, and she shared her experience and learning with campus colleagues. Chris conducted a focus group with the goals of understanding student veterans' experiences and soliciting their recommendations for change. The focus group yielded the following recommendations: (a) provide outreach programs to student veterans, (b) provide additional training and resources to key student support services staff members, (c) host events to honor veterans' service, and (d) educate the campus community about transitions from military to civilian life.

Identify the strengths and resources that the group members bring to the process of systemic change. To maximize the effect of collaborative action for change, Chris assessed strengths and resources that student veterans can offer to meet the four goals mentioned above. She was impressed with the students' commitment, work ethic, dedication to service, maturity, and leadership skills. As a group, they were also closely connected to a variety of community organizations related to the military and veterans. Building on these strengths and resources, Chris and the SSVA collaborated with various local and campus organizations to implement the following: (a) the SSVA provided presentations during orientation programs and created and delivered additional presentations for students, faculty, and staff during the academic year; (b) the university, SSVA, and local veterans and military organizations collaborated to host a 9/11 Memorial Event as well as a Veteran Appreciation Day; (c) the community-based veterans center, the counseling center, and SSVA conducted a variety of in-service trainings and workshops for the university community on military culture, the effects of deployment, readjustment issues, and combat-related injuries; (d) the SSU alumni magazine featured interviews with student veterans; (e) the SSVA secured campus office space to facilitate interaction among veterans and service members; and (f) a support group for military families and significant others was offered by the counseling center with the assistance of the National Guard Family Support Program and SSVA.

Communicate recognition of and respect for these strengths and resources. To maintain the momentum for change among the group of collaborators, Chris provided continual encouragement, ongoing recognition, and respect for each ally's contributions and resources. For instance, Chris and other staff and faculty allies hosted events to honor and appreciate SSVA's hard work and contributions toward creating a veteran-friendly campus. She also kept her supervisor and counseling center colleagues updated on her involvement and the momentum for change.

Identify and offer the skills that the practitioner can bring to the collaboration. A significant role that Chris played in collaborating with student veterans was to serve as a translator/interpreter between academic culture and military culture. Student veterans were often frustrated with the slow and inefficient decision-making and change processes of the university, contrasted with the military's hierarchical decision-making process. By adopting a cultural adjustment framework, Chris supported student veterans' transitions to the academic culture by explaining the importance of shared governance at institutions in the context of a complex bureaucratic and political organization (Birnbaum, 1988) that often entailed considerable time for decisions to be made.

Chris also utilized her own professional networks to expand collaboration. For instance, she asked for support from faculty members who were veterans themselves. She also identified a number of faculty members who were interested in veterans' issues. In collaboration with others, she reached out to representatives from the U.S. Department of Defense, Traumatic Brain Injury Association, and Veterans and Military Services offices at peer institutions. She was able to identify local counselors and physicians who specialized in treating PTSD and TBI. Chris joined the SSVA's faculty advisory board, where she assisted with fundraising efforts and securing institutional resources made available to recognized student groups. Chris and other advisory board members encouraged SSVA members to become more active in state and national advocacy work, resulting in the university's hosting the first statewide conference of student veterans.

Assess the effect of the counselor's interaction with the community. By reflecting on her individual-level actions to develop collaborations with student veterans and others, Chris recognized the need to pursue changes in the university's policies and systems that served to create barriers to student veterans' academic adjustment. Thus, she expanded her role to encompass systems advocacy.

Systems Advocacy

Identify environmental factors impinging on students' development. In working closely with student veterans, Chris had become more aware of the institutional systems and policies that posed barriers to students' academic success. These barriers—most of which were actually *omissions*—included: (a) lack of a full-time veteran services staff person to certify veterans' benefits, and coordinate related processes, (b) lack of recruitment efforts related to student veterans, and (c) lack of policies for transfer articulation of military credits and accommodations for students' military training and active duty commitments. The dean of student affairs created a veterans affairs committee that sought representatives from multiple offices including the counseling center, disability services, the Reserve Officer Training Corps (ROTC) program, learning assistance center, career services, academic advising, student health services, SSVA, and the institutional research office. Chris joined the committee with her supervisor's approval, and the committee began to explore and investigate student veterans' concerns in order to formulate recommendations.

Provide and interpret data to show the urgency for change. "A system change must be accompanied by information that supports the need for change and demonstrates the adverse effects of not changing" (Lopez-Baez & Paylo, 2009, p. 280). SSU had no process for monitoring the enrollment, persistence, and graduation rates of student veterans. Thus, the committee initiated the following data collection efforts to explore needs for systemic change: (a) conducted additional student veteran focus groups, (b) estimated the size of the veteran and military population in the surrounding region, and (c) estimated the tuition revenues generated from enrolled student veterans and service members.

In collaboration with other stakeholders, develop a vision to guide change. Based on this investigation, the committee made a variety of final recommendations that included the following: (a) hire a full-time professional to coordinate campus services for veterans and service members; (b) assign a designated admissions counselor to increase veteran recruitment, provide assistance to veterans submitting applications for admission while on deployment, and offer application fee waivers to self-identified veterans; (c) create a faculty task force to study the transfer and application of credits for military service; (d) create withdrawal and reenrollment policies and procedures to accommodate military training and active duty service students; and (e) systematically track veterans and service members to monitor enrollment, retention, persistence, and graduation rates.

However, the recommendations generated little interest among or response from institutional leaders, including the vice president of student affairs and the provost. The weakness of the committee was demonstrated by a lack of political power among its members. Thus, the committee began to actively look for strategies to gain power to attract stakeholders' attention to these issues.

Analyze the sources of political power and social influence within the system. One attempt to increase political influence with the university was to apply for a U.S. Department of Education grant to create a Center of Excellence for Veterans Student Success. This grant offers a significant amount of financial assistance for creation of a comprehensive support services program that addresses student veterans' needs. Because of the potential for securing financial resources as well as the high prestige of this grant, institutional leaders became increasingly interested in the committee's efforts to effect change. As a result, the committee succeeded in obtaining an official letter from the university's president clearly stating an institutional commitment to provide necessary support to the veteran population on campus.

Another strategy of utilizing political power to influence the system on behalf of student veterans was to for the committee to collaborate with student veterans to expand and augment a 9/11 memorial event on campus. A number of influential public officials participated as speakers for the event, which attracted a large audience, including the leaders of the university. This community-wide event provided an opportunity for committee members to connect with powerful state and local political figures. The local media reported on the event and on the challenges faced by student veterans on campus. Thus, the event also served to educate the university and local communities about the increasing need to support student veterans on campus.

Develop a step-by-step plan for implementing the change process. The committee's recommendations included short- and long-term goals for change. Some changes that did not require significant financial resources were established quickly, especially once it was established that over 3 percent of the student population were student veterans or active duty military. A student veteran lounge for fellowship activities was created. In-service training opportunities were offered to key individuals who provide direct services to student veterans, including staff in the learning center, financial aid office, and counseling center. Also, more outreach programs for student veterans were funded by the university. As the university culture began to move toward interest in student veterans and service members, some faculty members began to incorporate veterans' issues in their class materials, expressed interest in research on the student veteran population, and implemented credit-bearing service learning projects involving veterans and military families. These indicators of cultural shift within the campus community were highlighted by the committee in advocating for further changes in the university's policies and practices.

Develop a plan for dealing with probable responses to change. Despite the positive changes in the campus culture, the university's support was manifested principally by providing some funding for outreach programs (discussed earlier) and by supporting the U.S. Department of Education grant application. When the grant application was not funded, no alternative plans for providing and funding a comprehensive support program were discussed.

Recognize and deal with resistance. Committee members were disappointed by the outcome of the grant application and frustrated with the university's resistance. However, they understood that because the purpose of a system is to maintain its current balance (Lopez-Baez & Paylo, 2009), resistance can be interpreted as a system's normal response to attempts at change. The committee reframed resistance as natural; they began to examine the sources of the resistance and formulate strategies to deal with it.

Assess the effect of the advocacy efforts on the system and constituents. In reflecting upon the efforts to prompt systemic change, Chris recognized the need to expand her focus to the public level of advocacy where she could inform the public about the macro-systemic issues regarding student veterans' experience on campus. As one example, she has shifted her focus to conducting a formal research study to investigate barriers and facilitators to promoting systemic changes to support student veterans on campus. She anticipates disseminating her findings, implications, and recommendations in academic as well as policy arenas.

Case Analysis

As a pedagogical tool, case studies allow educators to "examine realistic situations, problem solve, and reflect on their learning" (Hamrick & Benjamin, 2009, p. 17). Important aspects to examine when using cases to improve professional practice include identifying "relevant situational characteristics," exposing what is "troubling" or disconcerting, "consulting ethical principles" and "standards," "recommending actions and strategies," and " appraising" "the decision" (Hamrick & Benjamin, 2009, pp. 19–20).

This case takes place in a comprehensive public four-year institution in a state with sizable population of veterans and active duty military personnel. Consequently, educators would expect the student veteran and active student military populations to be high. As public institutions continue to lose proportional financial support from their state governments, public higher education institutions become increasingly reliant upon tuition revenues. Federal funding of student veteran tuition can be seen as a boon for public institutions. However, as many institutions struggle with resource scarcity, adequately meeting the needs of students, including student veterans, is a financial as well as an ethical issue.

CAS (2010) specified adequate standards for offices of veterans and military programs and services, and strategies for addressing these students' needs has been discussed in the American Council on Education's *From Soldier to Student: Easing the Transition of Service Members on Campus* (Cook & Kim, 2009). Ethical principles dictate that student affairs educators act to benefit others, promote justice, and be faithful (American College Personnel Association [ACPA], 2006). Institutions need to act to benefit active duty students when enrollment, registration, and billing processes do not accommodate their mandatory duty and training requirements. Moreover, institutions need to be faithful in their presentations of being veteran-friendly campuses and "trustworthy in the performance of their duties" (ACPA, 2006, p. 7) by carrying out the processes that create and maintain these environments.

In exploring what is troubling in the case, it is imperative to address the issue of resistance. We stated in the case that no alternative plans for providing a comprehensive support program were discussed, and that many committee members were frustrated with the university's resistance. However, the responsibility of serving these students and educating the campus community should not continue to fall disproportionately on enrolled students and groups such as the SVAA, whose members have played a significant volunteer role on behalf of the institution thus far. Change, even when deemed beneficial, can be fraught with emotional responses: "Fear, anxiety, loss, danger, panic" are associated with change (Fullan, 2001, p. 1). In addition, staff and resources are already stretched thin at many institutions.

In this case scenario, staff members may fear extra workloads, may be anxious about the skills and knowledge they will need to learn to serve veterans and active duty military personnel, and may regret losing the comfort of familiar procedures. Conversely, change can also elicit "exhilaration, risk-taking, excitement, [and] improvements" (Fullan, 2001, p. 1). Positive emotional reactions to change are more likely to occur when community members see the ethical purpose behind the change, witness other peoples' enthusiasm about the change, understand what the change entails, participate in creating the change, and build relationships through the change process (Fullan, 2001). For example, offering training and resources to staff and faculty can ease the fear and anxiety about having adequate skills and knowledge to serve this population.

Lopez-Baez and Paylo (2009) noted that serving as an ally and in a leadership role are both necessary for organizational change. The Veterans Affairs Committee members should take leadership roles in trying to persuade senior campus leaders of the need for organizational change and then constantly advocate for processes that accomplish the change. For example, educators are frequently expected to be knowledgeable about and capably serve diverse student populations, so expectations for serving student veterans could be added as a required or preferred skill in position descriptions and announcements. Also, performance appraisals should be amended to include how procedures are being adopted to better meet the needs of student veterans as well as other student populations.

Kotter (1996) noted the importance of "short-term wins" (p. 117). Short-term wins "build credibility ... to sustain efforts over the long haul" (p. 199). In this case, such short-term wins include the presentations that occurred and were well attended, the 9/11 events that included high-profile regional leaders, and the creation of collaborations with community agencies. Chris, the other Veterans Affairs Committee members, and SSVA members should recognize these outcomes as important gains. To maintain this momentum, Lopez-Baez and Paylo (2009) recognized that having "a critical mass of like-minded sojourners aids in the process of bringing about change" (p. 281). Although the leadership of the institution has not responded, the Veterans Affairs Committee members may continue to meet to offer support for each other as they face this resistance. Lopez-Baez and Paylo (2009) noted that knowledge can be empowering. They also recommended identifying concrete barriers to change and brainstorming strategies to overcome them. Such a brainstorm session might have similar results to those shown in Table 12.2.

TABLE 12.2. CHANGE—BARRIERS AND STRATEGIES.

Barriers	Strategies
No institutional response to Veterans Affairs Committee recommendations and grant funding proposal	Assign members to meet with key administrators to follow up on the committee's recommendations
No full-time paid veterans services coordinator	Assign members to meet with dean of students on process steps for proposing such a position and crafting a description Meet with director of development and president of the Student Government Association about alternative sources of funding
No resources or time to provide additional services to student veterans, active duty students, and their family members and significant others	Have candid conversations about how tasks can be prioritized to make time for these issues
Growing but low awareness among staff and faculty about student veterans' issues	Continue trainings and presentations in collaboration with SSVA members Facilitate outreach trainings across campus at specific sites
Skepticism about the university's meaningful support for the population of student veterans and service members	Identify respected and persuasive individuals with power (such as long-serving faculty and staff members) to articulate these concerns to campus leaders
Confusion about who should take leadership for developing a veteran-friendly campus	Approach leaders individually to advocate that creating a veteran-friendly campus be addressed at cabinet-level meetings

The Veterans Affairs Committee can use their short-term wins as momentum to focus on the identified barriers. However, organizational change takes time. In complex, bureaucratic, political organizations like colleges and universities, change may take years, or if thousands of people are involved, a decade (Kotter, 1996). However, change can only be accomplished if efforts are begun and sustained.

Assessing Change

It is insufficient to speak of change without also addressing how change will be assessed. "Assessing the effect of advocacy on the system and its members reinforces and strengthens change" (Lopez-Baez & Paylo, 2009, p. 282). The authors of this chapter subscribe to Upcraft and Schuh's comprehensive assessment model (1996). In implementing comprehensive assessment, an institution should create a plan of conducting a variety of assessments over the course of a regular cycle (Arminio, 2009). Types of assessments Upcraft and Schuh (1996) described include user, satisfaction, outcomes (gains from attendance), inputs (such as standards and benchmarking), needs, and environment. A comprehensive assessment plan would include these approaches conducted over a regular cycle of, for example, seven to ten years (Arminio, 2009). Some assessment studies should be collaborative or campuswide. "Not all of the approaches within a comprehensive assessment plan need to be the responsibility of an individual campus unit" (Arminio, 2009, p. 14). Below we offer descriptions of these types of assessments and examples that would be valuable in determining whether the goal of creating organizational change to establish a veteran-friendly campus is being met.

User data assessments include knowing the number of student veterans and active duty military students who are enrolled at the institution, the percentage of student veterans and active duty personnel in the student population, the number of veterans using specific services, the graduation rate of student veterans, and how they compare to their peers at the institution. For example, student veterans may or may not use the career center and counseling center at similar rates as the general student population. In addition, student veterans may be more or less satisfied with these services.

In the case study, discovering that 3 percent of SSU's students are student veterans or active duty military is a necessary beginning point in assessing whether the campus is veteran-friendly, and in this case, the focus groups that Chris conducted indicated that student veterans and service members considered SSU quite unfriendly. Once educators know the number of student veterans and that at least some of them are dissatisfied with campus processes, more complex assessments must be conducted that offer more refined information about what student veterans and active duty military students are experiencing. Unfortunately, some campuses continually spend considerable time and energy collecting user and satisfaction data, but focus little effort on studying what students are gaining from their experiences.

Outcomes data—what students gain from educational opportunities—have generated much attention in the K–12 community and now higher education. Most notably, the Spellings Commission criticized higher education for having no "comprehensive strategy" on measuring "how much students learn in colleges or whether they learn more at one college than another" (U.S. Department of Education, 2006, p. 14). Just as educators would be concerned about what any student gains from attending, institutions must also be concerned about what student veterans and active duty military students gain from attending college. Also, what is it they bring to campus with them? Many campuses, including those that are members of the Voluntary System of Accountability, are utilizing learning outcome assessment instruments such as the Collegiate Assessment of Academic Proficiency, Collegiate Learning Assessment, or the Measure of Academic Proficiency and Progress to measure learning gains in critical thinking and subject knowledge (Stephen, Liu, & Sconing, 2009). In addition, in 2011, 537,000 students at 751 institutions completed the National Survey of Student Engagement (NSSE; 2011). It would be fruitful for institutions to add veteran status to the demographic information of such instruments. At the institution in our case study, Sheraton State University, the NSSE is given to first-year students and seniors every other year, but veteran status is not reported. Additionally, institutional NSSE data are not distributed at the department level. Doing both would offer a more complete picture of how and in what ways student veterans and active duty students are or are not engaged at the institution.

Although assessing outcomes has become politically and pedagogically essential, concentrating only on outcomes at the expense of process is short-sighted. Assessment "inputs" (such as standards, ethical codes, benchmarks) assist in ensuring high-quality processes that offer students a model demonstrating ethics, care, and the application of knowledge. Standards such as those created by CAS (2010) clarify educational processes for veterans and military programs and services that include admissions, orientation, applying for financial aid, advising, mentoring, communications, and faculty and staff training. For example, according to CAS (2010), veterans and military programs and services (VMPS) "must be highly visible to student veterans, military service members, and their family members with at least one staff member as an institutional single point of contact to coordinate services, provide advice, and advocate for students with issues related to their military experiences and student status" (p. 7).

Sheraton State University does not currently meet this CAS standard, and the Veterans Affairs Committee could use the CAS standard to advocate for additional staff. CAS (2010) further requires that VMPS "must advocate for clear and facilitative articulation agreements between home institutions and colleges and universities providing education to military members serving on active duty" (p. 13) and that VMPS "must advocate for and work with the bursar to ensure deferment of tuition and fees for students when education benefits are delayed beyond normal payment due dates for military withdrawals due to activation" (p. 13).

Benchmarks are criteria for comparisons across institutions and help educators address the question, "Can information from other organizations help my organization and solve my problem?" (Upcraft & Schuh, 1996, p. 244). The key in assessment using benchmarks is determining appropriate comparison organizations (Upcraft & Schuh, 1996). Institution type, size, location, demographics, and similar mission are important characteristics to consider. ACE's publication *From Soldier to Student* (Cook & Kim, 2009) offers a benchmarking model based on percentage of student veterans and active duty military in the student population. For example, because 3 percent of Sheraton's student population is comprised of student veterans, it would be considered a moderate veteran enrollment (MVE) institution. Cook and Kim (2009) found that 63 percent of MVE institutions reported that increasing services for student veterans is part of their strategic plans, less than 50 percent offer training opportunities on issues related to student veterans, more than 50 percent plan to offer professional development for faculty in the next five years, 46 percent have offices exclusively dedicated to serving student veterans, and MVE institutions are more likely to award college credit for military service than low veteran enrollment (LVE) schools in the next five years. As is evident, Sheraton's practices are somewhat in line with other MVE institutions based on intuitional demographics. It is important to note, however, that benchmarks do not always reflect best practices; rather, they align institutions with common practices—good, poor, or mediocre—based on a selected comparison characteristic.

The focus group conducted by Chris in the case was an example of using a qualitative research method to begin to explore student needs. The challenge in assessing student needs is "that it can be difficult to separate student needs from student wants" (Upcraft & Schuh, 1996, p. 127). Educators should look to identify the problems or harm that would arise if something is not provided (Upcraft & Schuh, 1996). Conducting a needs assessment would allow the counselor at Sheraton to determine, for example, appropriate interventions to prevent active duty military students from withdrawing from class due to duty requirements, since this practice creates problems for students. The student needs assessment could occur through surveys, interviews, and review of documents, such as the student newspaper.

Campus environment assessments identify the ways that the campus environment (defined broadly to include physical facilities, physical geography, curriculum, density) affects students (Upcraft & Schuh, 1996). It is important to understand that "students and their environment have a transactional relationship, that is, one affects the other, and vice versa" (Schuh & Upcraft, 2001, p. 165). A number of environment assessments would be useful in understanding student veterans' perceptions of the campus, such as the ways in which the campus is friendly or unfriendly. The Veterans Affairs Committee at Sheraton might find results from a campus climate survey about student veterans' perceptions of the campus environment useful in advocating for additional funds for services and programs. A frequently referenced campus climate instrument is the University Residence Environment Scale (Upcraft & Schuh, 1996, Schuh & Upcraft, 2001; Strange & Banning, 2001), but if few student veterans live on campus, such an instrument would not be useful. Upcraft and Schuh (1996) and Schuh (2009) list various instruments that could be utilized including the College Students Experiences Questionnaire, the Community Colleges Experiences Questionnaire, Environmental Assessment Inventory, and Involving Colleges Interview Protocol as other possible campus climate instruments. Sedlacek (1989) promoted the use of perceptual mapping as a means of detailing where on campus students feel what. Students are given maps and asked to place dots on the map using a color-coded scheme. The researcher then aggregates the maps and interprets the patterns.

Because Sheraton has no dedicated full-time staff member to serve student veterans, and because all Veterans Affairs Committee members have other full-time positions, how can they be expected to initiate such assessment practices? One possible solution to this dilemma is for Veterans Affairs Committee members to encourage adding the demographic of student veteran or military status to assessment measures already being conducted in campus divisions and departments. Also, once user and satisfaction data have been collected, educators can concentrate on other assessment approaches. Furthermore, the process of collaborating with others in conducting assessments, particularly those resistant to organization change, could convince resisters of the need for change.

In summary, when assessment data indicate that student veterans and active duty personnel use services at similar rates as nonveteran students, graduate at similar rates, and are as engaged at the institution at similar rates, change has begun. When institutions' processes meet CAS standards and the benchmarks provided by the literature and aspiring institutions, organizational change has begun. In addition, when student veterans feel welcomed, and when asked for needs they respond with wants (because the needs are being addressed already), organizational change has begun.

Conclusion

Implementing organizational change to better serve a student population without guidance of a model or structure is to venture on a journey without directions. When that happens, travelers often find they are lost. If institutions are to respond to the needs of student veterans and active duty students, we believe a planned organizational change is imperative. We offered an advocacy model embedded in an institutional context to demonstrate how such a model can inform grassroots, initial efforts toward creating a veteran-friendly campus. We also highlighted the importance of collaborating with other professionals and organizations and provided some strategies for assessing new programs and interventions. Though organizational change can be difficult, time-consuming, and emotionally draining, educators and advocates commence this work on behalf of a student population most worthy of best efforts.

References

Ackerman, R., DiRamio, D., Garza Mitchell, R. L. (2009). Transitions: Combat veterans as college students. In R. Ackerman & D. DiRamio (Eds.), *Creating a veteran-friendly campus: Strategies for transition and success.* (New Directions for Student Services, 126, pp. 5–14). San Francisco: Jossey-Bass.

American College Personnel Association (ACPA). (2006). Statement of ethical principles and standards. Washington, DC: Author. Retrieved from http://www.myacpa .org/au/documents/Ethical_Principles_Standards.pdf

Arminio, J. (2009). Conducting sophisticated assessments. *Programming Magazine, 41*(7), 13–17.

Birnbaum, R. (1988). *How colleges work: The cybernetics of academic organization and leadership.* San Francisco: Jossey-Bass.

Cook, B. J., & Kim, Y. (2009). *From soldier to student: Easing the transition of service members on campus.* Washington DC: American Council on Education. Retrieved from http://www.acenet.edu/AM/Template.cfm?Section=HENA&Template=/CM/ContentDisplay.cfm&ContentID=33233

Council for the Advancement of Standards in Higher Education (CAS). (2010). *Veterans and military programs and services.* Washington, DC: Author.

DiRamio, D., Ackerman, R., & Mitchell, R. L. (2008). From combat to campus: Voices of student-veterans. *NASPA Journal, 45*(1), 73–102.

Fullan, M. (2001). *Leading in a culture of change.* San Francisco: Jossey-Bass.

Hamrick, F. A., & Benjamin, M. (2009). *Maybe I should . . . Case studies on ethics for student affairs professionals.* Lanham, MD: University Press of America.

Kotter, J. P. (1996). *Leading change.* Boston: Harvard Business School Press.

Lewis, J. A., Arnold, M. S., House, R., & Toporek, R. L. (2002). *ACA advocacy competencies.* Retrieved from http://www.counseling.org/publications/

Lewis, J. A., Lewis, M. D., Daniels, J. A., & D'Andrea, M. J. (1998). *Community counseling: Empowerment strategies for a diverse society* (2nd ed.). Pacific Grove, CA: Brooks/Cole.

Lopez-Baez, S. L., & Paylo, M. J. (2009). Social justice advocacy: Community collaboration and systems advocacy. *Journal of Counseling and Development, 87*(3), 276–283.

National Survey of Student Engagement. (2011). *Announcements: NSSE institutional report 2011* [web page]. Retrieved from http://nsse.iub.edu/

Ratts, M. J., & Hutchins, A. M. (2009). ACA Advocacy Competencies: Social justice advocacy at the client/student level. *Journal of Counseling and Development, 87*(3), 269–275.

Rumann, C. B., & Hamrick, F. A. (2009). Supporting student veterans in transition. In R. Ackerman & D. DiRamio (Eds.), *Creating a veteran-friendly campus: Strategies for transition and success.* New Directions for Student Services, 126, pp. 25–34. San Francisco: Jossey-Bass.

Schuh, J. H. (2009). *Assessment methods for student affairs.* San Francisco: Jossey-Bass.

Schuh, J. H., & Upcraft, M. L. (2001). *Assessment practice in student affairs: An applications manual.* San Francisco: Jossey-Bass.

Sedlacek, W. E. (1989). Perceptual mapping: A methodology in the assessment of environmental perceptions. *Journal of College Student Development, 30,* 319–322.

Stephen, K., Liu, O. L., & Sconing, J. (2009). *Test validity study report.* Washington, DC: Volunteer System of Accountability. Retrieved from http://www.voluntarysystem.org/docs/reports/TVSReport_Final.pdf

Strange, C. C., & Banning, J. H. (2001). *Education by design: Creating campus learning environments that work.* San Francisco: Jossey-Bass.

Toporek, R. L., Lewis, J. A., & Crethar, H. C. (2009). Promoting systemic change through the ACA advocacy competencies. *Journal of Counseling and Development, 87*(3), 260–268.

Toporek, R. L., & Liu, W. M. (2001). Advocacy in counseling: Addressing race, class, and gender oppression. In D. B. Pope-Davis & H.L.K. Coleman (Eds.), *The intersection of race, class, and gender in multicultural counseling* (pp. 285–413). Thousand Oaks, CA: Sage.

United States Department of Education. (2006). *A test of leadership: Charting the future of U. S. higher education.* Washington DC: Author.

Upcraft, M. L., & Schuh, J. H. (1996). *Assessment in student affairs.* San Francisco: Jossey-Bass.

Zinger, L. & Cohen, A. (2010). Veterans returning from war into the classroom: How can colleges be better prepared to meet their needs? *Contemporary Issues in Education Research, 3*(1), 39–51.

CONCLUSION: LOOKING BACK, MOVING FORWARD

Corey B. Rumann and Florence A. Hamrick

C orey writes:

On November 11, 2011, I helped coordinate the National Military Honor Roll Call event on the campus at the University of West Georgia. During the event, the names of all the service members who had died since September 11, 2011 while serving in Operation Iraqi Freedom and Operation Enduring Freedom were read in chronological order. The reading of names—totaling 6,313—began at 9:30 a.m. and ended just after 5:00 p.m. and was a chilling reminder of the sacrifice of the United States military service members serving in the armed forces during times of war. On my way to the event, I listened to a radio report about the high unemployment rates of military veterans in the United States and thought about how institutions of higher education could take the lead in helping student veterans find employment through furthering their educations and enhancing their military training by pursuing college degrees. Higher education is in a unique position to have a major influence on the future of service members currently serving in the military and those who are now student veterans. Serving those who have served is the responsibility of everyone who works at U.S. colleges and universities.

Flo writes:

At 11:00 am on November 11, 2011, I attended the Veterans Day commemoration on the Rutgers University campus. Brief remarks were delivered, the wreaths were laid, and a uniformed bugler played "Taps." I thought about my father, who *passed away in 2004. He served in the Navy during World War II. When my brother and I were children, sometimes he would hum "Taps" rather than announce that it was bedtime.*

On the morning of November 10, 2011, I attended a separate Veterans Day program in the campus's beautiful, historic chapel. The program, including remarks by a Medal of Honor recipient, was impressive. But what is most memorable for me happened before the program began.

I had walked to the chapel by myself, and some of the pews were already full. I asked two gentlemen if I could join them, and they agreed. When I asked what brought them to the program, one gentleman told me that he had been a high school senior when Pearl Harbor was attacked. The other gentleman nodded in agreement, and we both listened to the first man's story. The military recruiters made him wait until he graduated before enlisting, and then he was inducted despite health conditions that would have otherwise disqualified him from serving. He smiled, "I didn't lie about it, but I didn't tell them either." I asked what he did after the war ended, and he waved his hand in a broad arc, indicating the chapel. "I came here. I went to college because of the GI Bill. No one in my family had gone to college before. Then I got married, bought a house, and started a family." He told me proudly that all of his children and grandchildren had gone on to graduate from college.

The second gentleman mainly listened and nodded. But just before the program began, he tapped my arm and held out the keys he had taken from his jacket pocket: "I still have my dog tags. I keep them with me." I took the keys and smiled, read his name on the well-worn metal, and handed the keys back. Both gentlemen left shortly before the program ended—to avoid the crowds, one whispered.

In this handbook, chapter authors have examined myriad issues and topics that affect contemporary student veterans and service members enrolling in higher education. They have also offered recommendations and suggestions to help faculty, student affairs professionals, and administrators support these students on campus. The momentum and attention to serving veterans and service members continues to grow, which is an optimistic sign that college and university representatives are more aware of the needs and circumstances of these students and are seeking strategies and services to help them succeed. Popular attitudes and reactions to veterans and service members have changed from those of the Vietnam era of more than thirty years ago. Support for military service members is one indication that the prevailing sentiment is one of recognizing and reaching out to veterans and service members rather than ignoring or excluding them.

Chapter authors have recommended a range of strategies and approaches to help colleges and universities prepare for and foster student veterans' success in college. To be sure, there are multiple ways to provide this support, and no single strategy can be deemed most effective across all sectors of higher education. As noted throughout the handbook, each institution has its own mission and purposes, and institutions must design and implement programs that fit their particular circumstances and—most important—their populations of enrolled veterans and service members. Institutional size, type, geographic location, existing services and expertise, and institutional support are all factors that will inform the development of programs and outreach that make sense at individual campuses.

For institutions that are beginning to create programs and services on their campuses, the guidance provided in the handbook chapters ensures that this process can be systematic, deliberate, and designed at the outset to meet identified needs. For institutions that seek to evaluate the contributions of existing services and programs to identify successes or strengthen the programmatic offerings, the handbook chapters provide strategies to implement that can yield the needed information.

If previous patterns of scholarship on enrolled veterans and service members hold true, it appears that veterans and service members are most visible during times of war or major conflict, with attention waning as the conflicts draw to a close. One challenge for colleges and universities is to sustain momentum and commitment to support veterans and service members irrespective of military engagements. Colleges and universities are in an influential position to make such a case and to develop and retain policies and programs for veterans and service members that will be available to support them. Sustaining a research focus on student veterans and service members will also be necessary because empirical research on student veterans—and the higher education institutions in which they enroll—will provide a foundation for creating or adapting programs and services. High-quality, rigorous studies must be conducted to develop a stronger knowledge base about veterans and service members as well as their experiences, challenges, and successes in higher education. Grant funding to support such research and related programmatic efforts will be key; "Operation Diploma," which is funded primarily by Lilly Endowment Inc. and housed at the Military Family Research Institute at Purdue University, is only one example of targeted efforts.

Creating spaces, if not entire campuses, where veterans and service members are welcomed and supported is a common theme throughout the majority of chapters in this handbook. Categorical descriptions of a veteran-friendly campus are elusive, and relative "friendliness" may depend in large part on institutional contexts and factors. Although critical aspects of friendliness certainly include individual-level relationships and supportive interactions, a generalized wish to be helpful and welcoming to veterans and service members is insufficient. Institutional leaders must provide appropriate infrastructures of resources and personnel that enable high-quality, personalized, and effective services to be delivered.

In addition, creating services, adapting policies, and gaining expertise to better serve veterans and service members can help campuses evolve to better serve all students in the process. For example, military combat veterans are not alone in experiencing posttraumatic stress disorder (PTSD), as combat is not the only "trauma" that can lead to extreme if not disabling physical and emotional manifestations. As student services professional staff members become more familiar with and develop stronger, more nuanced understandings of PTSD, and as counseling professionals become even more skilled at recognizing and treating PTSD, all students who experience this condition will benefit as a result of this growing awareness. As one analogy, "universal design" is a principle used in a number of fields including instructional design and architecture to encompass strategies for creating learning opportunities and physical spaces that are accessible to all learners and all inhabitants. In some ways, adapting services and policies to better serve student veterans can help campuses continue to develop toward a type of "universal design" that is consciously structured to improve the overall campus and ensure accessibility and success for all students.

Another way to frame this perspective is to entertain the possibility that a college or university's normal practices for serving students may not necessarily be the best or the optimal practices for serving all students. The influx of new populations of students enrolling in colleges and universities—such as veterans and service members—provides occasions for institutions to carefully reexamine existing policies, practices, environments, and services. The processes of reexamination and change help to ensure that enrolled students can meet their goals of degree attainment and that the institution can continue to provide educational environments that are conducive to students' success.

As colleges and universities move forward with their efforts to support student veterans, there may be a desire to implement programs and services as quickly as possible. This handbook is a valuable resource to help guide those efforts and to help ensure that this work is proactive and planned rather than reactive and potentially misguided. Some of the models and approaches discussed in various chapters will provide ideas and potential starting points for moving forward.

Generally speaking, building awareness of the entire campus community may be a component in many campus plans. This awareness can foster stronger interpersonal relationships for veterans and service members and further the goal of creating welcoming climates. Many existing programs and services models are geared toward easing veterans' and service members' transitions by reducing or eliminating admissions and enrollment barriers that are created or enforced by strict application of administrative policies and procedures. In addition, the broader social and academic transitions must be considered as well. Programs such as learning communities and orientation sessions can serve many purposes, including providing information specifically relevant to veterans and service members and offering venues for student veterans to meet and interact. However, policies and services must also convey that although student veterans and service members may face unique challenges in the college environment, many also experience the same apprehensions, desires, and goals as their nonmilitary fellow students. To maximize the impact of programs, policies, and services, additional research is needed to identify social and academic engagement factors with particular relevance to enrolled veterans and service members.

Although much of this handbook is focused on meeting the needs of student veterans and service members, readers must also remember that these students have a great deal to offer the campus community. Offering tailored support and services is critical to ensuring the success of these students, but care must be taken so that they are not inadvertently segregated and made to feel even more disconnected or alienated from the rest of the campus. Veterans and service members can enrich the campus through the additional levels and types of diversity represented by their experiences and backgrounds. If individuals are comfortable, they may be willing to share their experiences and perspectives in classes or through campus programming or leadership opportunities.

Corey writes:

As I write this, I am reminded of the Veterans Day event held on my campus that I briefly described at the beginning of this chapter. These types of events are necessary to honor those who have served and are currently serving in the military. But more can and needs to be done on college campuses outside of Veterans Day activities. Concern and attention to student veterans on campus must become a part of the daily dialogue in higher education and be engrained in college and university practices and culture. We currently have a strong foundation from which to build programs, create supportive policies, and raise campus awareness about student veterans' issues, concerns, and successes. The wheels have been put in motion, but intentional efforts must be maintained in order to ensure the sustainability of efforts in higher education. Furthermore, ongoing evaluation and assessment will bring about modifications and adjustments to current policies and practices further addressing the continuing and changing needs of all student veterans on campus. Innovative thinking, deep reflection, and ongoing conversations will create an environment in higher education that recognizes those who have served.

Flo writes:

As I thought about the Veterans Day events I attended, it reaffirmed how many people—including me—are part of the living legacy of the original GI Bill. On the one hand, World War II veterans such as my father earned a set of benefits, including educational benefits, by virtue of their military service. Large numbers of these veterans used these benefits to further their own educations and careers. On the other hand, people who are one, two, or even three generations removed from their World War II forebears are GI Bill beneficiaries as well. The one gentleman with whom I spoke at the program was a first-generation college student who set the example, if not the expectation, that his own children and grandchildren would also attend college. My father, who grew up in rural North Carolina, was also a first-generation college student. Just one generation later, my own aspirations to attend college were normal, expected, and supported. It never occurred to me to question whether I would earn a college degree, as well as graduate degrees if I so chose.

The two gentlemen who attended the chapel program, along with other living World War II veterans, clearly recall the pivotal events of December 1941—seventy years ago. As young men, they may have anticipated that their military service would be life-changing, but I don't know if they realized how other sets of changes would affect, in succession, the quality of life and opportunities available to themselves and their descendants. The current generation of veterans and service members enrolling in higher education has the same opportunities to pursue educational opportunities that may otherwise have been out of reach. In the final chapter of his book Outliers, *Malcolm Gladwell (2008) described the sacrifices his grandmother made to educate her daughters—an outlandish goal, considering their life circumstances. Then he traced the legacy of her sacrifice on his own life and the educational opportunities that his parents provided to him.*

Speaking for myself, I realize that an important basis for my own educational and professional successes was laid, in part, well before my birth. It is important that colleges and universities assist the current generation of veterans and service members to succeed so that future generations will have similar—if not wider—breadths of opportunity to benefit their own families as well as the larger society.

Reference

Gladwell, M. (2008). *Outliers: The story of success.* New York: Little, Brown.

GLOSSARY

Accommodations: Due to a barrier in the campus environment, whether physical, curricular, informational, or instructional, accommodations may be necessary to provide access. Typically, a student will provide documentation of his or her disability and will work with disability services staff to explore reasonable accommodations so that he or she will have equitable access to the full campus experience.

Activation: "An order to active duty" to engage in "full-time duty in the active military service of the United States" (Gortney, 2011, p. 2).

Active duty: "Full-time duty in the active military service of the United States. This includes members of the Reserve Component serving on active duty or full-time training duty, but does not include full-time National Guard duty" (Gortney, 2011, p. 2).

Chain of command: The succession of commanding officers from a superior to a subordinate through which command is exercised (Gortney, 2011).

Demobilization: The transition "to a peacetime configuration while maintaining national security" (McGinn, 2010, p. 103).

Deployment: "The relocation of forces and material to desired operational areas" (McGinn, 2010, p. 105).

Deployment cycle: The typical deployment cycle has four phases: predeployment, deployment, postdeployment, and reintegration (U.S. Department of Defense, 2011).

Deployment phase: The second phase of the deployment cycle. It is during this phase that units and personnel are physically moved to the theater of operation to conduct their missions and associated military duties (U.S. Department of Defense, 2011).

Disability studies: Disability studies is an interdisciplinary academic field that focuses on the diverse history of disabled individuals, and the representation of disability across various areas; it promotes a greater understanding of the experience of disability and advocates for social change (Albrecht, Seelman, & Bury, 2001).

Drill (training period): An authorized and scheduled regular inactive duty training period. It must be at least two hours for retirement point credit and four hours for pay. This term has been used interchangeably with other common terms such as *drill period, assemblies,* and *periods of instruction* (Gortney, 2011).

Individual augmentee: A service member who is called up for active duty as an individual and designated to join a unit; these individuals sometimes have shorter notifications of deployment (U.S. Department of Defense, 2011).

Individual Ready Reserve (IRR): A pool consisting of individuals who have had some training or who have served previously in the Active Component or in the Selected Reserve, and may have some periods of their military service obligations remaining. Members may voluntarily participate in training for retirement points and promotion, with or without pay (Gortney, 2011).

Mobilization: The act of assembling and organizing national resources to support national objectives in time of war or other emergencies (Gortney, 2011).

National Guard (Inactive National Guard; ING): Army National Guard personnel in an inactive status not in the Selected Reserve who are attached to a specific National Guard unit, but do not participate in training activities. Upon mobilization, they will mobilize with their units. In order for these personnel to remain members of the Inactive National Guard, they must muster once a year with their assigned units. Like the Individual Ready Reserve, all members of the Inactive National Guard have legal, contractual obligations. Members of the Inactive National Guard may not train for retirement credit or pay and are not eligible for promotion (Gortney, 2011).

Operation Enduring Freedom (OEF): U.S. military operations in Afghanistan and other nations that began in 2001 as part of the search of Osama bin Laden and al Qaeda leaders in response to the September 11, 2001 terrorist attacks (Torreon, 2011).

Operation Iraqi Freedom (OIF): U.S. military operations in Iraq that began in 2003 to overthrow the regime of Saddam Hussein. In 2010, OIF received a new designation of Operation New Dawn to signify the shift from a military operation to one of support. The war in Iraq ended in 2011 (Torreon, 2011).

Pipeline: In logistics, the channel of support or a specific portion thereof, the means by which material or personnel flow from sources of procurement to their points of use (Gortney, 2011).

Predeployment phase: The first phase in the deployment cycle that focuses on unit readiness. It is during this phase that units are activated and mobilized (U.S. Department of Defense, 2011).

Postdeployment Phase: The third phase in the deployment cycle. During this phase, personnel return home and their units begin to demobilize (U.S Department of Defense, 2011).

Ready Reserve: The Selected Reserve, Individual Ready Reserve, and Inactive National Guard liable for active duty as prescribed by law (Title 10, United States Code, Sections 10142, 12301, and 12302) (Gortney, 2011).

Reintegration phase: The fourth and final phase in the deployment cycle. During this phase, personnel return home and begin the process of reacclimating to and reengaging in civilian life (U.S. Department of Defense, 2011).

Reserve (Reserve Component; RC): The Armed Forces of the United States Reserve Component consists of (a) the Army National Guard of the United States, (b) the Army Reserve, (c) the Navy Reserve, (d) the Marine Corps Reserve, (e) the Air National Guard of the United States, (f) the Air Force Reserve, and (g) the Coast Guard Reserve (Gortney, 2011).

Theater of operation (TO): An operational area defined by the geographic combatant commander for the conduct or support of specific military operations (Gortney, 2011).

Unit: Any military element whose structure is prescribed by competent authority, such as a table of organization and equipment; specifically, part of an organization. An organization title of a subdivision of a group in a task force. With regard to Reserve Components of the Armed Forces, denotes a Selected Reserve unit organized, equipped, and trained for mobilization to serve on active duty as a unit or to augment or be augmented by another unit. Headquarters and support functions without wartime missions are not considered units (Gortney, 2011).

United States Veterans Administration (VA) Disability Rating System: This system refers to the amount of disability compensation for which a veteran is eligible due to injuries acquired or exacerbated while on active duty. The amount of compensation varies depending on disability type, the overall impact of the disability, and family status (VA, 2011a).

United States Veterans Administration (VA) Vocational Rehabilitation: Commonly referred to as Chapter 31, the VA Vocational Rehabilitation and Employment VetSuccess Program assists eligible veterans with service-connected injuries in procuring employment. For injured veterans who are not ready to pursue work, this program offers assistance in living independently (VA, 2011b).

Universal design: Born of the architecture, engineering, and design industries, universal design strives for equitable, inclusive, and sustainable environments for the broadest potential audience. Incorporating principles of universal design may increase the usability of the product and reduce or eliminate the need for individual accommodations (Center for Universal Design, 2011).

Wheelchair athletics: Wheelchair athletics encompass the array of sports that are inclusive of wheelchair or disabled athletes. Recognized by the U.S. Olympic Committee, these sports are competitive and rigorous. Disabled athletes train to be eligible to compete in the Paralympic Games, which follow the schedule of the Olympic Games (Wheelchair & Ambulatory Sports, USA [WASUSA]; n.d.).

References

Albrecht, G. L., Seelman, K. D., & Bury, M. (2001). *Handbook of disability studies.* Thousand Oaks, CA: Sage.

Center for Universal Design. (2011). The principles of universal design. Raleigh: North Carolina State University. Retrieved from http://www.ncsu.edu/project/design-projects/udi/center-for-universal-design/the-principles-of-universal-design/

Gortney, W. E. (2011, May 15). *Department of Defense dictionary of military and associated terms* (joint publication 1–02). Washington, DC: United States Department of Defense. Retrieved from http://www.dtic.mil/doctrine/new_pubs/jp1_02.pdf

McGinn, G. H. (2010, February 4). *Department of Defense instruction number 1235.12.* Washington, DC: United States Department of Defense. Retrieved from http://ra .defense.gov/documents/rtm/123512p.pdf

Torreon, B. S. (2011). *U.S. periods of war and dates of current conflicts.* Washington, DC: Congressional Research Service. Retrieved from http://www.fas.org/sgp/crs/ natsec/RS21405.pdf

United States Department of Defense. (2011). *DOD dictionary of terms* [Searchable database]. Retrieved from http://www.dtic.mil/doctrine/dod_dictionary/?zoom_ query=&zoom_sort=0&zoom_per_page=10&zoom_and=1

United States Department of Veterans Affairs. (2011a). *VA disability compensation* [web page]. Retrieved from http://www.vba.va.gov/bln/21/compensation/

United States Department of Veterans Affairs. (2011b). *Vocational rehabilitation and employment service* [web page]. Retrieved from http://www.vba.va.gov/bln/vre/

Wheelchair and Ambulatory Sports, USA. (n.d.). *About WASUSA* [web page]. Retrieved from http://www.wsusa.org/index.php?option=com_content&task=view&id=1& Itemid=439

APPENDIX: MILITARY RANKS—ENLISTED

	Army	Navy/Coast Guard	Marines	Air Force
E1	Private	Seaman Recruit (SR)	Private	Airman Basic
E2	Private E-2 (PV2)	Seaman Apprentice (SA)	Private First Class (PFC)	Airman (Amn)
E3	Private First Class (PFC)	Seaman (SN)	Lance Corporal (LCpl)	Airman First Class (A1C)
E4	Corporal (CPL) Specialist (SPC)	Petty Officer Third Class (PO3)	Corporal (Cpl)	Senior Airman (SrA)
E5	Sergeant (SGT)	Petty Officer Second Class (PO2)	Sergeant (Sgt)	Staff Sergeant (SSgt)
E6	Staff Sergeant (SSG)	Petty Officer First Class (PO1)	Staff Sergeant (SSgt)	Technical Sergeant (TSgt)
E7	Sergeant First Class (SFC)	Chief Petty Officer (CPO)	Gunnery Sergeant (GySgt)	Master Sergeant (MSgt) First Sergeant
E8	Master Sergeant (MSG) First Sergeant (1SG)	Senior Chief Petty Officer (SCPO)	Master Sergeant (MSgt) First Sergeant	Senior Master Sergeant (SMSgt) First Sergeant
E9	Sergeant Major (SGM) Command Sergeant Major (CSM)	Master Chief Petty Officer (MCPO) Fleet/Command Master Chief Petty Officer	Master Gunnery Sergeant (MGySgt) Sergeant Major (Sgt Maj)	Chief Master Sergeant (CMSgt) First Sergeant Command Chief Master Sergeant
E10	Sergeant Major of the Army (SMA)	Master Chief Petty Officer of the Navy (MCPON) & Coast Guard (MCPOCG)	Sergeant Major of the Marine Corps (SgtMajMC)	Chief Master Sergeant of the Air Force (CMSAF)

Source: United States Department of Defense, *The United States Military Enlisted Rank Insignia*, http://www.defense.gov/about/insignias/enlisted.aspx

APPENDIX: MILITARY RANKS—OFFICER

	Army	Navy/Coast Guard	Marines	Air Force
O1	Second Lieutenant (2LT)	Ensign (ENS)	Second Lieutenant (2ndLt)	Second Lieutenant (2d Lt)
O2	First Lieutenant (1LT)	Lieutenant Junior Grade (LTJG)	First Lieutenant (1stLt)	First Lieutenant (1st Lt)
O3	Captain (CPT)	Lieutenant (LT)	Captain (Capt)	Captain (Capt)
O4	Major (MAJ)	Lieutenant Commander (LCDR)	Major (Maj)	Major (Maj)
O5	Lieutenant Colonel (LTC)	Commander (CDR)	Lieutenant Colonel (LtCol)	Lieutenant Colonel (Lt Col)
O6	Colonel (COL)	Captain (CAPT)	Colonel (Col)	Colonel (Col)
O7	Brigadier General (BG)	Rear Admiral Lower Half (RDML)	Brigadier General (BGen)	Brigadier General (Brig Gen)
O8	Major General (MG)	Rear Admiral Upper Half (RADM)	Major General (MajGen)	Major General (Maj Gen)
O9	Lieutenant General (LTG)	Vice Admiral (VADM)	Lieutenant General (LtGen)	Lieutenant General (Lt Gen)
O10	General (GEN)	Admiral (ADM)	General (Gen)	General (Gen)
	General of the Army (wartime only)	Fleet Admiral (wartime only)		General of the Air Force (wartime only)

Note: The Army, Navy, Coast Guard, and Marine ranks also include Warrant Officers.

Source: United States Department of Defense, *The United States Military Officer Rank Insignia,* http://www.defense.gov/about/insignias/officers.aspx

NAME INDEX

SUBJECT INDEX

A

A&M colleges. *See* Morrill Land-Grant Act of 1862
ACA (American Counseling Association), 279, 280–283
ACA Advocacy Competencies model: based on culture clash model, 280–281; community collaboration and systems advocacy of, 283; illustrated, 281; public arena advocacy, 282–283; school/community advocacy, 282; student advocacy within, 281–282
Accessibility standards, 120–121
ACE (American Council on Education), 78–79, 81, 83, 97–98, 124, 145, 148, 150–154, 185, 224, 291–292
ACPA (American College Personnel Association), 233, 291

Activation: administrators' support during, 27–28; deployment of active duty service members, 44; effect on student service members, 46–48; providing refunds due to, 176; working with students before and after, 75
ADA (Americans with Disabilities Act), 120–121
Administrators: adding OVMS, 182–183; advising student veterans organizations, 232–239; assisting transitional students, 62–66; awareness of student veteran transitions, 56; clarifying support networks for students, 62; easing challenges of returning veterans, 143; establishing veteran-friendly campuses, 64, 154, 258–259, 263–264; identifying and tracking

student service members, 63; investigating sources of student veteran funding, 32–33; learning about VA education benefits, 34; measuring success of initiatives by, 104–105; orientations for service members, 63, 80; providing pre- and postdeployment checklists, 64–65; questions for assessing veteran services, 155–156; reducing enrollment barriers, 148–150; running OVMS, 198–200; sensitivity to deployment cycle phases, 46–47; simplifying credit transfers, 145–146, 150–152; staffing OVMS, 181–185; supporting students through activation, 27–28; taking part in policy development, 257–261;